CRIMINAL JUSTICE **PIONEERS** IN US HISTORY

CRIMINAL JUSTICE PIONEERS IN US HISTORY

SECOND EDITION

MARK JONES
Professor Emeritus, East Carolina University

cognella®
SAN DIEGO

Bassim Hamadeh, CEO and Publisher
Zoe Flores, Project Editor
Jeanine Rees, Production Editor
Emely Villavicencio, Senior Graphic Designer
JoHannah McDonald, Licensing Coordinator
Natalie Piccotti, Director of Marketing
Kassie Graves, Senior Vice President, Editorial
Alia Bales, Director, Project Editorial and Production

This book was previously published by Pearson Education, Inc.

Printed in the United States of America.

cognella® ACADEMIC PUBLISHING
320 South Cedros Ave., Ste. 400, Solana Beach, CA 92075

Brief Contents

SECTION III LAW AND THE COURTS 161

SECTION IV CORRECTIONS 231

Detailed Contents

Preface

The idea for the first edition of this book came from a book I read while I was an undergraduate at the University of Georgia. It contained short biographies of the 100 greatest baseball players of all time. I wondered why a similar book has not been written about people in criminology and criminal justice. As I read the book on great baseball players, I found myself disagreeing with the author about who had been included and who had been omitted. *How*, I thought, *could you possibly include X, and/or exclude Y?* Readers of *Criminal Justice Pioneers in U.S. History* may wonder why I chose to include some of these people, and they will be astounded as to why I left others out. Everyone I spoke with about this project, including some of the subjects themselves, had a suggestion about whom to include. This book is not intended to be a definitive list of criminal justice Hall of Famers; it is simply my partial list of some people who have strongly influenced America's criminal justice system and public perceptions about crime and criminal justice.

Neither the criminal justice system nor the study of criminology exists in a political, social, religious, or economic vacuum. As criminal justice is a social science, it is important to acknowledge the influence of impersonal forces when studying its history. But what is sorely neglected are the individual personalities who have helped shape the modern criminal justice system and the study of crime. It allows students to see how human personalities with all their frailties and strengths impact the criminal justice system.

The people examined in this book are not saints to be idolized or demons to be vilified. No person is perfectly good, and no one is perfectly evil. Everyone profiled in this book had flaws and strengths. Simply because someone makes a significant contribution to the history of criminal justice does not mean that they should be seen as role models or as villains.

Overview of Each Biography

Each biography is arranged roughly as follows:

1. Important Figure Named
    a. Introduction
    b. Primary accomplishment

2. Background
   a. Birth date and location
   b. Schooling
   c. Relevant childhood information
3. Career
   a. Early occupation
   b. Primary employment
   c. Contributions, controversies
4. Conclusion
   a. Death (when applicable)
   b. Legacy
5. Sources and suggestions for further reading

The book is divided into four sections: (a) theorists, (b) law enforcement, (c) courts/law, and (d) corrections. The fine people at Cognella and I had one of those typical debates about the length of the book and the number of chapters. Like most writers who are motivated more by having something to say rather than something to sell, I wanted the book to be longer and include more chapters. But recognizing that students and instructors are turned off by a book with too many chapters, I agreed to shorten some chapters and delete others. We struck a compromise—agreeing to insert an honorable mention section for people that I wanted to include but did not either out of space constraints or because I simply could not find enough information for a chapter. An annotated table of contents chapter presents a little information about the chapter subjects and short bios of the people in the honorable mention category.

Criteria for Inclusion

Everyone discussed in this book is or was American, either born or naturalized. To make the book international in scope would have made the book too broad and too long. In deciding whom to include, I considered several factors. I did not include people whose crimes or victimization have made an impact on the criminal justice system. There are plenty of books about famous criminals and plenty of protesters carrying signs for famous victims. The included personalities are arranged in chapters by date of birth, oldest to most recent.

Those from Underrepresented Populations

White men have dominated criminal justice professions historically, but some people broke gender and racial barriers. Were it not for the efforts of people such as these, criminal justice professions would still be stocked exclusively with white males, and many of the people reading this book would have no chance for a career in criminal justice. Individuals who fall into the category of breaking barriers include Penny Harrington, Alice Stebbins Wells, Lola Baldwin, Samuel Battle, Bass Reeves, Sonia Sotomayor, Thurgood Marshall, and Lee Brown.

Practical Pioneers

Others are pioneers because of the contributions they made to the everyday workings of the criminal justice system. Joseph Ragen and Clinton Duffy were world-renowned wardens in Illinois and California, respectively. Thomas Mott Osborne pioneered inmate self-governance at Sing Sing. August Vollmer shaped 20th century municipal policing. O. W. Wilson literally wrote the book on practical police administration. Sandra Day O'Connor was pragmatic in both her politics and judicial philosophy. In addition, John Haviland, an 19th century architect, had the skills to design modern prisons.

Humanitarians

Those who make it their ambition to help others use many methods and institutions to accomplish their mission. Some use religious institutions; others use businesses or educational institutions. Some pioneers were humanitarians who used the criminal justice system to improve the lives of others. Among those who fall into this category are Dorothea Dix, Jane Addams, and John Augustus.

Trendsetters

Some social and legal trends are forged by collective groups of people at a given time, while others are launched by individuals. Many of the policies and laws observed and enforced today are the culmination of efforts made by some of the people covered in this book. Earl Warren led the due process revolution, which changed the course of procedural due process. Greg MacAleese devised the idea of paying for anonymous tips, which led to solving crimes.

Thinkers

Aristotle once said, "In general it is a sign of the man who knows, he can teach, and therefore we think art more truly knowledge than experience is; for artists can teach and men of mere experience cannot." Many aspects of modern criminal justice are the brainchild of those who taught or acknowledged the importance of learning from great minds. Just as all disciplines have their great thinkers, criminal justice has its geniuses whose work has helped define the field.

To divorce the great thinkers and writers from those who work in the streets, prisons, and courthouses of America would ignore the contributions of many important people. Edwin Sutherland pioneered views on white-collar crime. Robert Merton and Lloyd Ohlin's research provided the ideological framework for federal efforts to combat crime in the 1960s. Herman Goldstein, one of the best blends of academe and policing, is linked with problem-oriented policing. Joseph Wambaugh's writing talents brought the gritty realities of policing to a wide audience.

Radicals

It takes a special personality to be willing to be unpopular for the sake of doing what they think is right. Although no one can accomplish anything if they are not willing to endure some criticism, some of the people profiled here were willing to endure more than their share. James Q. Wilson was vehemently criticized by many of his liberal academic criminologists for his outspoken advocacy of punishment. Frank Serpico was despised by much of the rank-and-file and management at the New York City Police Department for blowing the whistle on corruption. William Kunstler proudly bore the label as the most hated lawyer in America, largely because he was usually successful in putting the justice system on trial. Thomas Mott Osborne's ideas about inmate self-governance were widely criticized during and after his lifetime as being too radical.

Conclusion

One of the most inspirational tidbits I discovered while writing this book was that the path to prominence is neither easy nor direct. Many of these people did not embark on a career in criminal justice and they seemed to have little chance of success in the field either as children or as young adults. Some, like Clinton Duffy, were practically ordained to their career from birth, while Sonia Sotomayor aspired to a judicial job after watching *Perry Mason* on television as a child. Others, like Lee Brown, only took the job because it was the most convenient option at the time. Born into slavery, Bass Reeves could have had no idea that he would one day become a famous federal deputy marshal. Thurgood Marshall was usually the class clown, not the teacher's pet who made the top grades. Kathleen Sawyer grew up in rural West Virginia far from the environs of Washington, D.C., where she would become well known. All the women profiled here battled tremendous odds to enter their professions. I hope readers of this book that are planning a career in criminal justice will be inspired by these biographies, and I am confident that novice and experienced practitioners and academicians will have a better appreciation of America's criminal justice system after reading this book.

Acknowledgments

I would like to thank the following people and/or acknowledge their memory for their contributions and/or personal interviews and correspondence: Harriet Zuckerman, James Q. Wilson, Herman Goldstein, Frank Serpico, the office of former Houston Mayor Lee Brown, Penny Harrington, Greg MacAleese, G. Robert Blakey, Kathleen Hawk Sawyer, and Dan Beto.

SECTION I

THE THEORISTS

Members of any academic discipline often think that professors with a steady publication record in prestigious, but obscure academic journals that are read only by their colleagues and a few reluctant students are "big names" in the field. But when academics step outside their own echo chambers, they usually discover that much of the research they conduct, while worthy of kudos from their colleagues, seldom impacts public policy. For this section, I focused on criminologists, i.e., those who study crime causation and have made an impact outside the halls of academic institutions.

- **Edwin Sutherland** was the originator of the term "differential association," one of the most studied theories of criminal behavior in existence. In addition, the phrase "white collar crime" is part of everyday language today, also traceable to Edwin Sutherland. Sutherland is noted for his work on homelessness and delinquency in the 1930s when the United States was mired in the Great Depression. Sutherland's rocky academic trajectory to the top of the academic ladder is also valuable knowledge.
- **Eleanor Glueck**, teaming with her husband Sheldon, produced a plethora of quality work on juvenile delinquency during her long career at Harvard. She was a female who broke through the

male-dominated field of criminological study, standing in the face of the discrimination she encountered not only because of her gender, but because of her Jewish roots as Harvard was a hotbed of anti-Semitism during much of her career.

- **Robert Merton,** or "Mr. Sociology," left his imprint on the study of crime with strain theory, one of the foundational theories of criminology study. His imprint goes beyond sociology and criminology. Phrases like "role model," "self-fulfilling prophecy," "the Matthew effect" and "focus groups" are traceable to Merton.
- **James Q. Wilson** found that the academic world can be a lonely place for political and social conservatives. James Wilson, a political scientist and criminologist, unflinchingly stated that he believed in punishment and had to have a thick skin to even survive, let alone thrive in the academic world. The man behind the "broken windows" policing idea described himself as more conservative than most academics, but more liberal than the average American. He presents an interesting study. Some of the information for his chapter came from a telephone interview I conducted with him several years prior to his passing.

Criminological Theory Honorable Mentions

IMG I.1

Robert Park (1864–1944), was born in Pennsylvania and became one of the premier criminology researchers at the University of Chicago in the early 20th century, beginning his work there in 1914. He has been called the central figure in the development of Chicago sociology, and by extension, criminology. Chicago, which was rapidly becoming one of the largest urban centers in the United States, was his laboratory. Park, a muckraking journalist before receiving his doctoral degree in Heidelberg, Germany, called cities "organisms" and believed that a "state of mind" was not just a physical mechanism, but could better be described by a term he coined, "human ecology."

Park was not afraid to get his hands dirty, and he argued that the only way to do that was to leave the hallowed halls of the academy and venture into the field, saying, "Go and sit in the lounges of luxury hotels and on the doorsteps of the flophouses; sit on the Gold Coast settees and on the slum shakedowns;

sit in the Orchestra Hall and in the Star and Garter Burlesque. In short, go and get the seat of your pants dirty in real research."

The following sources can help you learn more about Robert Park and his work:

- *New World Encyclopedia*: https://www.newworldencyclopedia.org/entry/Robert_E._Park
- American Sociological Association: https://www.asanet.org/robert-e-park/
- The University of Chicago Centennial Catalogues: https://www.lib.uchicago.edu/collex/exhibits/university-chicago-centennial-catalogues/university-chicago-faculty-centennial-view/robert-e-park-1864-1944-sociology/
- Mutchnik, R. J., R. Martin and W. T. Austin (2009). *Criminological Thought: Pioneers Past and Present.*
- Park, R. E. (1952). *Human Communities: The City and Human Ecology.*
- Shils, E. (1996). "The Sociology of Robert E. Park." *The American Sociologist* 27 (4): 88–106.

IMG I.2

Lloyd Ohlin (1918–2008) was born in Massachusetts and specialized in examining juvenile delinquency. Ohlin was a graduate of the University of Chicago School of Sociology and worked primarily at Columbia and Harvard. Ohlin challenged the idea that juvenile delinquency resulted from irresponsibility, arguing that poverty and obstacles to upward mobility were more important. Ohlin worked on several government-sponsored delinquency prevention measures, including Manhattan's Mobilization for Youth, an antipoverty program that formed the basis of similar programs at the federal level in the 1960s.

From 1961–1962, Ohlin worked under President John F. Kennedy, heading the President's Committee on Juvenile Delinquency and Youth Crime. From 1965 to 1967, during the presidency of Lyndon Johnson, Ohlin served as associate director of the President's Commission on Law Enforcement and Administration of Justice, the most significant federal study conducted on the criminal justice system, crime prevention, and criminal justice education in American history. Ohlin's differential opportunity theory, which he devised with Richard Cloward, was consistent with President Johnson's Great Society domestic agenda, which included a war on poverty. Read more about Ohlin from the *Harvard Law Bulletin* (Summer, 2009) and the other sources listed below:

- https://hls.harvard.edu/today/lloyd-e-ohlin-expert-in-criminal-justice-1918-2008/
- Cloward, R. A. and L. E. Ohlin (1966). *Delinquency and Opportunity: A Theory of Delinquent Gangs.*
- Mutchnik, R. J., R. Martin and W. T. Austin (2009). *Criminological Thought: Pioneers Past and Present.*

IMG I.3

Donald Cressey (1919–1987) was born in Minnesota and impacted the study of organized crime in the 1960s more than any other academic. After obtaining his doctorate degree from Indiana University in 1950, where he was mentored by Edwin Sutherland, Cressey joined the sociology faculty at the University of California at Santa Barbara where he remained until his death. Cressey wrote *Other People's Money*, a study of occupational fraud and embezzlement which stemmed from his doctoral dissertation and was influenced by white collar crime guru Edwin Sutherland.

Cressey served on the President Lyndon Johnson's Commission on Law Enforcement and the Administration of Justice in the mid-1960s. Thanks to an increasing interest in organized crime generated by years of televised congressional hearings featuring mobsters, one wing of the Commission's work was devoted to organized crime. Based on his work with the Commission, Cressey authored *Theft of the Nation*, where he discussed why traditional law enforcement was ineffective in combatting criminal organizations.

Cressey was among the first to provide a scholarly assessment of the structure and nature of organized crime, especially the Italian brand of organized crime replete with terms like "mafia" and "cosa nostra." Although his work was criticized by many, including Italian-American anti-defamation groups, Cressey provided the foundation for the study of organized crime for decades to come. Cressey also wrote *Criminal Organization*, which expanded his discussion of organized crime beyond Italian criminal groups.

The following sources can help you learn more about Donald Cressey and his work:

- Cressey, D. (1953). *Other People's Money: A Study in the Social Psychology of Embezzlement.*

- Cressey, D. (2008). *Theft of the nation: The Structure and operations of organized crime in America.*
- Organized Crime Research: http://www.organized-crime.de/cressey.htm
- Online Archive of California: http://texts.cdlib.org/view?docId=hb967nb5k3;-NAAN=13030&doc.view=frames&chunk.id=div00014&toc.depth=1&toc.id=&brand=oac4
- Akers, R. L., & Matsueda, R. L. (1989). *Sociological Inquiry, 59*(4): https://onlinelibrary.wiley.com/doi/pdf/10.1111/j.1475-682X.1989.tb00118.x

IMG I.4

Travis Hirschi (1935–2017) was born in Utah and obtained his doctorate degree in sociology from the University of California at Berkeley. Hirschi spent most of his career at the University of Arizona. In *Causes of Delinquency*, published in 1969, Hirschi posited that the absence of social bonds is a key factor in delinquency. Hirschi's arguments resonated with the commonsense belief that family upbringing plays a role in delinquency prevention. Almost anyone who holds a doctorate in criminal justice or criminology recalls the AICB of Hirschi's social control theory: (a) *attachments* to parents, teachers, and other positive influencers, (b) *involvement* in constructive activities like school, church, or social clubs, (c) *commitment* to societal norms and goals, such as obtaining a high school diploma and holding legitimate employment, and (d) *belief* in the legitimacy of laws and rules as something that should be obeyed.

In 1990, Hirschi collaborated with Michael Gottfredson on *A General Theory of Crime.* Consistent with social control theory, they argued that delinquency is associated with low self-control and is characterized by impulsivity, insensitivity, physical aggression, and short sightedness. Hirschi's theories were criticized as paternalistic and simplistic, but nonetheless they have been among the most influential in the study of criminology. Hirschi's biography can be read at *Encyclopaedia Britannica*, and other sources are listed below:

- https://www.britannica.com/biography/Travis-Hirschi
- Bernard, T.J., J.B. Snipes and A.L. Gerould (2010). *Vold's Theoretical Criminology.*
- Hirschi, T. (1969). *Causes of Delinquency.*
- Hirschi, T. and Michael Gottfredson (1990). *A General Theory of Crime.*
- Mutchnik, R. J., R. Martin and W. T. Austin (2009). *Criminological Thought: Pioneers Past and Present.*

Credits

IMG I.1: Source: https://commons.wikimedia.org/wiki/File:Robert_E._Park.jpg.

IMG I.2: American Society of Criminology, https://asc41.org/about-asc/officers/#list-of-asc-presidents. Copyright © by American Society of Criminology. Reprinted with permission.

IMG I.3: Associated Students, https://commons.wikimedia.org/wiki/File:Donald_Cressey_-_Southern_Campus_1960.jpg, 1960.

IMG I.4: American Society of Criminology, https://asc41.org/about-asc/officers/#list-of-asc-presidents. Copyright © by American Society of Criminology. Reprinted with permission.

CHAPTER 1

Edwin Sutherland (1883–1950)

IMG 1.1

No academician has made a greater impact on the study of criminology than Edwin Sutherland. Perhaps more than anyone else, he can lay claim to making sociology the dominant discipline in the study of crime causation. Prior to Sutherland, studying and identifying the roots of criminal behavior took place in the fields of law, religion, biology, medicine, and psychology. Criminal behavior, the thinking went, was predetermined or was a moral matter, rather than learned behavior. The term *differential association*, a basic staple of criminology, originated with Sutherland.

Sutherland's influence extends beyond colleges and universities, leaving a lasting impact on criminal justice policy. The term *white collar crime*, now a part of everyday vocabulary, reflects the culmination of 25 years of diligent research by Sutherland. Yet the road to prominence in criminology was not a likely one for Sutherland, and he encountered stumbling blocks along the way.

Early Life and Education

Edwin Hardin Sutherland was born on August 13, 1883, in Gibbon, Nebraska. He was the third of seven children born to Lizzie Pickett Sutherland and her husband George, a descendant of Scottish immigrants, a Baptist minister, and a history professor at Ottawa College. The Sutherlands moved to Grand Island, Nebraska, in 1893, where George Sutherland assumed the presidency of Nebraska Baptist Seminary. The school's name was soon changed to Grand Island Baptist College.

George Sutherland's strict religious ideals along with the modest lifestyle lived by the Sutherlands made Edwin loathsome of the white-collar criminals that he would later disparage as an academic. Edwin Sutherland made his initial forays into education not at an Ivy League school or large Midwestern university, but living and working in America's heartland. Inheriting his father's interest in religion—at least for a time—Edwin attended Grand Island Baptist College, played football there, and graduated with a bachelor's degree in 1904. After being rejected for a Rhodes scholarship, Sutherland taught Greek and Latin at Sioux Falls College, a Baptist College in South Dakota.

Although his interests in graduate education were geared toward history and religion, Sutherland took his first sociology class while teaching at Sioux Falls—a correspondence course offered by the University of Chicago. He left South Dakota to study at the University of Chicago in 1906, and while there he developed an interest in criminal studies. But he still did not dive headlong into the discipline that would make him famous. The University of Chicago was renowned for its divinity school—an attraction for Sutherland—but it also housed the country's premier and emerging sociology department. At the time, Chicago housed some of the greatest minds in the country in sociology and the behavioral sciences, including George Herbert Mead, Robert Park, and Ernest Burgess.

In 1909, Sutherland returned to Grand Island without completing his doctoral degree and taught sociology and psychology, only to return to the University of Chicago in 1911 to focus on sociology. Rather than focus exclusively on sociology, Sutherland obtained a doctorate degree in sociology and political economy in 1913; the latter discipline would prove useful in his subsequent inquiries into white collar crime. His doctoral dissertation was titled "Unemployment and Public Employment Agencies," with no direct connection to the field of criminology.

William Jewel College and Marriage

Sutherland's first position after getting his doctorate was with William Jewel College, a Baptist school in Liberty, Missouri, cofounded by Robert James, a Baptist minister and the father of infamous outlaws Jesse and Frank James. Sutherland stayed from 1913–1919, teaching geometry, Greek, shorthand, sociology, and political science, but not criminology. While there he authored only one article, a paper on rural health.

While in Missouri, he married Myrtle Crews, his landlady's daughter, in 1918. The couple had one daughter. However, Sutherland was unsatisfied with the intellectual environment at such a small school, and he moved to Big Ten schools where he began to make his mark on criminology.

University of Illinois and Criminology

Sutherland started working at the University of Illinois in 1919. Although his primary interests were labor and employment, his department chair, Edward Hays, required all faculty members to take on a major research project, and he suggested Sutherland write a criminology textbook. *Criminology* was released in 1924, when Edwin Sutherland was 41 years old. Prior to Sutherland's book, the literature on crime causation was dominated by psychology and medicine. With the publication of *Criminology*, Sutherland began capturing the study of crime causation for the field of sociology.

Sutherland suggested that crime was not solely the result of internal factors. This flew in the face of those who advocated sterilization and other medical procedures—an idea in vogue in the United States and Europe at the time—to address the problem of "born criminals" or inherited criminality. Sutherland held that while individual personal traits are important, how those traits relate to the culture in which a person lives is more important. The culture includes groups large and small, ranging from an entire nation, a particular city, a local neighborhood, to a person's peer and family groups. In short, Sutherland believed that criminal behavior is not inherited but is learned and based on a rational decision, rather than being the product of a diseased mind.

University of Minnesota

Encountering problems at Illinois, especially with Edward Hays, Sutherland left for the University of Minnesota in 1926. But Minnesota's sociology department, though highly regarded, was beset with infighting to the point where Sutherland was not productive. The fact that he served as interim department chair did not help Sutherland and may have even made his stay there even more unpleasant. He left Minnesota after 3 years.

Social Hygiene, New York, and England

Sutherland's next appointment came in New York City, working for the Bureau of Social Hygiene, a philanthropic organization established by John D. Rockefeller and others to study adverse social conditions. He lived in England from 1929–1930 to study prisons there and to discover a blueprint for establishing a criminology institute in the United States. It was the only period of his life where he lived outside the American Midwest.

Return to Chicago

After 2 years working for the Bureau, Sutherland returned to the University of Chicago and its highly ranked sociology department to assume a research position.

In a textbook example of the best institutions making the worst decisions, Sutherland's contract with the University of Chicago was terminated in 1935. But he managed to publish the second edition of his *Criminology* textbook before he left.

Home at Last: Indiana University

Sutherland took a position with Indiana University in 1935 and was there for the remainder of his career. During this time, he established Indiana University's sociology program and served as its first chair.

Twenty Thousand Homeless Men

In 1936, shortly after arriving at Indiana, Edwin Sutherland and Harvey Locke published *Twenty Thousand Homeless Men*, an account of work they had done in Chicago. As the United States was in the throes of the Great Depression, the study was especially relevant, not just to academics, but to the entire population. Sutherland and Locke were credited with producing the best work on homelessness of the era because the book was rich in both quantitative and qualitative information.

The Professional Thief

One of Sutherland's strengths was that he was not an adherent to only one method of inquiry. Unlike many researchers today who spend more time defending their favorite chosen method than producing valid results, Sutherland saw both qualitative and quantitative methods as means to an end rather than ends in themselves. He made great use of the qualitative method in his research for *The Professional Thief,* which was published in 1937.

The Professional Thief was the result of detailed questionnaires and more than 80 hours of personal interviews between Sutherland and Chic Conwell, a thief who had been in the business of stealing for more than 20 years, most of his adolescent and adult life. The book's original table of contents attributes authorship of the book to Chic Conwell, with Sutherland providing annotation.

Sutherland opens the book by stating that the professional thief devotes his entire time and energy to larceny, that all thefts are carefully planned, and that the thief has the technical skills necessary to perform his job, just as any other professional does. Thievery is its own profession with a code of ethics (a questionable conclusion) and a professional subculture. Sutherland provided a glimpse into the mind of a person that thought of himself as a professional criminal, an unusual research venture for its time, and more importantly, one of several groundbreaking qualitative studies conducted through the University of Chicago's sociology department. *The Professional Thief* paved the way for Sutherland's differential association theory, which would be disseminated 2 years later.

Differential Association

In 1939, Edwin Sutherland published his third edition of *Criminology*. Building on his work in *The Professional Thief*, Sutherland's 1939 edition laid out his general theory of criminal behavior. He called it "differential association," a theory that is still one of the basic staples of criminology textbooks today. Sutherland's differential association theory originally contained seven propositions, with two more added to the fourth edition of *Criminology*, which was published in 1947:

1. Criminal behavior is learned.
2. Criminal behavior is learned in interaction with other persons in a process of communication.
3. The principle part of the learning of criminal behavior occurs within intimate personal groups.
4. When criminal behavior is learned, the learning includes techniques of committing the crime, some complicated and some simple, and the specific direction of motives and attitudes.
5. The specific direction of motives and drives is learned from definitions of the legal codes as favorable or unfavorable.
6. A person becomes delinquent because of an excess of definitions favorable to violation of the law over definitions unfavorable to violation of the law.
7. Differential associations may vary in frequency, duration, priority, and intensity.
8. The process of learning criminal behavior by association with criminal and anticriminal patterns involves all the mechanisms that are involved in any other learning.
9. Criminal behavior is an expression of needs and values, but it is not explained by those general needs and values since noncriminal behavior is an expression of the same needs and values.

White Collar Crime

The most significant work of Sutherland's career was *White Collar Crime*, released in 1949. The book introduced the term into the English vocabulary, but Sutherland had been using it in writings and speeches 10 years before the book's publication. He had been refining the concept for more than 25 years prior to the book's publication.

The stock market crash in October 1929 signaled the beginning of the Great Depression, a time when millions of Americans were stricken by bankruptcy, unemployment, poverty, and even starvation. As the number of poor people skyrocketed during the 1930s, so did the study of crime. Prior to the 1930s, practically all crime studies had focused on the lower class and the poor, to the neglect of crime among the upper class.

The stock market crash and its aftermath brought into focus several unsavory shenanigans committed by big business during the 1920s. In 1932, a public utility tycoon from Chicago named Samuel Insull was charged with mail fraud and embezzlement. Insull's 1934 trial resulted in acquittal. The public outrage over Insull's behavior and his acquittal prompted Congress and President Franklin Roosevelt to authorize creation of the Securities and Exchange Commission, still the primary agency charged with investigating financial crime. Sutherland, also outraged over Insull's acquittal, began studying white collar crime.

Although Sutherland had broken formal ties with his Baptist church roots years earlier, even indulging in some of the vices his father abhorred such as drinking and smoking, his religious background was still very much in focus in his attitudes about white collar crime. According to Sutherland, legal statutes alone should not determine whether something is a crime, in the moral sense. There must be a higher concept than the law to judge the morality of human actions. He believed that crime was spread among all economic classes and not confined to the poor and that corrupt businessmen were the archenemies of American capitalism.

Sutherland put political economy expertise to work with his white-collar crime studies. He researched crimes committed by 70 large business firms during the late 1920s and early 1930s. He found almost 1,000 convictions spread among the 70 firms. The offenses included embezzlement, misappropriation of funds, violation of antitrust laws, patent infringement, and other unfair trade practices. He defined white collar crime as "a violation of criminal law by a person of the upper socioeconomic class in the course of his occupational activity."

Sutherland's first public revelation of his white-collar crime concept came in a 1939 speech, titled "The White Collar Criminal," (Sutherland, 1940) before the American Sociological Society (ASS), an organization he would head several years later. He published two journal articles on the subject, one in the *American Sociological Review* in 1940 and the other in *The Annals of the American Academy of Political and Social Science* in 1941, both prior to the publication of *White Collar Crime* in 1949. Under pressure from publishers and Indiana University administrators, Sutherland deleted most of the names and identifying information before the book was published. A subsequent edition, released in 1983, was uncut and included the names Sutherland originally deleted. The list of accused offenders included General Motors, Ford, Montgomery Ward, Alcoa, and DuPont.

Death and Legacy

If numbers alone determined success as it does in today's academic environment, Sutherland would not stand out in the field of sociology or criminology. However, if actual impact on criminological thought is important, Sutherland is without peer. His work was noticed inside and outside academic circles. FBI director J. Edgar Hoover had the Bureau keep secret files on Sutherland, monitoring his writings and public appearances. No one knows just how much Sutherland had stored in his mind that was never disseminated. Many of his writings were simply passed out to a class for discussion and critique and were never published. Sutherland authored four books, three of which stand as classic works in the field of criminology and criminal justice, even more than 70 years after his death.

Failing health led to Sutherland's resignation as department chair in 1949, but he remained on the faculty. Sutherland died of a stroke on October 11, 1950, while walking to work in Bloomington, Indiana. He was 67 years old.

During his checkered but monumental career, Edwin Sutherland mentored some of the nation's top future criminologists, including Donald Cressey and Lloyd Ohlin. Donald Cressey described Sutherland as a terrible teacher, a dry, monotone class presenter. But Cressey's remarks were no doubt tongue in cheek, at least as far as Sutherland's ability to mentor students one-on-one or in small groups, for Cressey took the mantle of Sutherland's work and revised *Criminology* in 1982, and he always spoke glowingly of Sutherland as a man and as a mentor. Sutherland was described as gentle, simple, and modest, not possessing the arrogance that is common among successful academicians, but seemingly oblivious to his colossal reputation in his field.

Sources and Suggested Readings

Cressey, D. R. (1983). Interview with Donald Cressey. In J. H. Laub (Ed.), *Criminology in the making: An oral history.* Northeastern University Press.

Friedman, L. M. (1992). *Crime and punishment in American history.* Basic Books.

Friedrichs, D., Schoultz, I., & Jordanoska, A. (2018). *Edwin H. Sutherland.* Routledge.

Galliher, J. F. (2002, August 19). Edwin Hardin Sutherland. *American national biography online.* www.anb.org.

Galliher, J. F., & Guess, T. J. (2009). Two generations of Sutherland's white-collar war crime data & beyond. *Crime, Law & Social Change, 51,* 163–174.

Gaylord, M. S., & Galliher, J. F. (1988). *The criminology of Edwin Sutherland.* Transaction Publishers.

Goff, C. H. (1982). *Edwin H. Sutherland & white-collar crime.* University Microfilms International.

Keen, M. F. (1999). *Stalking the sociological imagination: J. Edgar Hoover's FBI surveillance of American sociology.* Greenwood.

Mutchnick, R. J., Martin, R., & Austin, W. T. (2008). *Criminological thought: Pioneers past and present.* Macmillan.

Snodgrass, J. (1973). The criminologist & his criminal: The case of Edwin H. Sutherland & Broadway Jones. *Issues in Criminology, 8*(1), 1–17.

Sutherland, E. H. (1937). *The professional thief. By a professional thief.* University of Chicago Press.

Sutherland, E. H. (1940). White collar criminality. *American Sociological Review, 5*(1), 1–12.

Sutherland, E. H. (1947). *Principles of criminology* (4th ed.). J. B. Lippincott.

Sutherland, E. H. (1983). *White collar crime: The uncut version.* Yale University Press.

Sutherland, E. H., & Locke, H. J. (1936). *Twenty thousand homeless men: A study of unemployed men in the Chicago shelters.* J. B. Lippincott.

Vold, G. B., & Bernard, T. J. (1985). *Theoretical criminology* (3rd ed.). Oxford University Press.

Discussion Questions

1. In what ways has Edwin Sutherland impacted criminal justice policy?
2. What does Sutherland's career teach criminal justice students about the importance of understanding other academic disciplines?
3. Where would the study of white collar crime be without Sutherland's contributions?

Credit

IMG 1.1: "Edwin Sutherland," https://webapp1.dlib.indiana.edu/archivesphotos/results/item.do?itemId=P0021850&searchId=0&searchResultIndex=1. Copyright © by Indiana University. Reprinted with permission.

CHAPTER 2

Eleanor Glueck (1898–1972)

IMG 2.1

The fields of law enforcement, law, and corrections in the United States have historically been dominated by men. The same is true for higher education, especially the study of criminology and criminal justice. One female pioneer in criminology scholarship study was Eleanor Glueck, whose work at Harvard University made her one of the most important figures in the history of criminological inquiry. Modern criminology scholars and students probably have no appreciation for the obstacles Eleanor Glueck faced in her academic career, one checkered by gender discrimination and anti-Semitism not only at one of America's most prestigious universities, but by the academic community as a whole.

Early Life and Career

Leonia "Eleanor" Touroff was born April 12, 1898, in Brooklyn, New York. Her immigrant father Bernard was from a prosperous Russian family of architects who had worked for the Czar. In the United States, Bernard obtained wealth as a factory owner and in the real estate business. Her mother Anna, also an immigrant, was given jewels by her parents to emigrate from Warsaw, Poland. Anna was an avowed socialist who was involved in women's rights, which at the time centered on several issues long since settled, including birth control and the right to vote. Raised in a Jewish household, Eleanor Touroff described her family atmosphere as warm and supportive; she had good relationships with both parents.

Raised with her younger brother in a life of privilege in New York City, Eleanor Touroff graduated from Hunter College High School in 1916. Eleanor was not acquainted firsthand with the harsh lives of the city's underclass, but her socialist mother endowed her with a sense of *nobles oblige*; her mission in life should be to help those less well off than herself. After graduating from high school, Eleanor Touroff attended Barnard College, an elite, recently chartered women's college in New York City that was spun off from the all-male Columbia University. She majored in English and journalism, graduating in 1920.

Social Work and Sheldon Glueck

Eleanor's brother became a physician, and Eleanor considered a medical career as well, but career opportunities for women were few in the 1910s, especially in traditionally male-dominated fields. Since these barriers existed even for many women of privilege like Eleanor Touroff, she explored a career in one of the few areas being pioneered by women, the recently created and developing field of social work. Thinking it would be a segue into a journalism career, Eleanor Touroff continued her education at the New York School of Social Work, which was eventually affiliated with Columbia University. There Eleanor encountered the lives of the poor and disenfranchised in New York City and developed an interest in social work, which lead to her abandoning her journalism ambitions.

One of her instructors at the New York School of Social Work was Bernard Glueck, who had worked as a psychiatrist at the Ossining Correctional Facility (Sing Sing Prison) in New York. Bernard Glueck introduced Eleanor to his brother Sheldon, a Polish immigrant and Georgetown-educated lawyer who was interested in the buddling fields of psychiatry and criminology.

Eleanor Glueck left New York City without obtaining her master's degree, taking a job in Boston as director of the Dorchester Welfare Center, a settlement house for runaway and at-risk females. Sheldon Glueck followed her to Boston, and they married on April 16, 1922. The marriage would produce one daughter, Anitra. Sheldon and Eleanor continued their academic studies at Harvard University, where Sheldon earned his master and doctoral degrees. The only school offering graduate studies for women at Harvard was the College of Education.

During Eleanor's time at Harvard, a key event sparked her later work—a seminar led by physician Richard Cabot. In a presentation on social ethics, Cabot stressed the importance of long-term follow-up in medical social work. In Eleanor's mind, this underscored the need for follow-up of inmates released from reformatories and for long-term studies of delinquency, two phenomena barely touched upon at the time.

Eleanor Glueck earned her master of education degree in 1923 and a doctorate in education degree in educational sociology in 1925. One of her earliest publications was an article titled "Training for Parenthood." Published in 1924, long before parenting self-help books were as common as rain, she argued that women should not represent the sole domain of parenthood; men should do more than just work to pay the bills. Such thinking was not as commonplace in the 1920s as it is today. Men were to be the breadwinners; it was the wife's job to raise and nurture the children.

Eleanor's doctoral dissertation, *The Community Use of Schools*, was published as a book in 1927. While her dissertation was not directly related to criminology, her idea that schools were a strong factor in the building of a sense of community was a theme that would run through her work on delinquency prevention.

Criminology Careers and Obstacles

After receiving their doctoral degrees, Eleanor and Sheldon Glueck started a career that would make them the most famous husband–wife team in the history of academic criminology. Fortuitously, their partnership was also interdisciplinary. Both came from multidisciplinary backgrounds that included social work, law, mental health, education, English, journalism and sociology. Throughout their career, they emphasized a multidisciplinary approach to criminology and had little patience for criminologists who were wedded to just one academic area. The Gluecks could not be pigeonholed into one discipline.

But the path to prominence for Eleanor was hampered by two factors. First, she and her husband were Jewish. Anti-Semitism was overt at Harvard University in the 1920s. In 1881, only 1% of the undergraduate student body at Harvard was Jewish. By 1922, that percentage had increased to 22%. The increased presence of Jews at Harvard, a school steeped in Protestantism, generated resentment in the 1910s and early 1920s. In 1922, Harvard President Lawrence Lowell said that Harvard had a "Jewish problem" (Feldberg, n.d., para. 6) as the increasing number of Jewish students highlighted the anti-Semitism at the school. Lowell's solution was not to change the hearts and minds of anti-Semites, but to impose a quota on Jewish admissions. After his first attempt to use geographic location as a proxy for placing quotas on Jewish admissions failed, in 1926, Harvard flatly established a 15% cap on Jewish enrollment. Jewish graduate students like Eleanor Glueck were told that the only way they could secure a paid position was to find a Jewish donor to pay their salary. Repression of Jewish identity was encouraged.

Eleanor's second obstacle was her gender. In the year she received her doctorate in education, only 24 such degrees were awarded to women in the United States. Academe was the domain of men. Among the few females that were in academe, most worked in disciplines that were traditionally female dominated, such as nursing, education, home economics and in recent years, social work. Put simply, women did not teach men and were usually below men on the hierarchy.

Eleanor Glueck knew what awaited her in her academic career the day she graduated with her EdD from Harvard—thanks to her experiences as a student and the actions of Lawrence Lowell at her commencement ceremony. As she and another female graduate approached the podium to receive their degrees, President Lowell instructed them to stop and stand by a tree to allow male graduates to proceed ahead of them. Glueck always remembered the exact location of that tree and thought about that moment every time she walked by it.

Eleanor and Sheldon Glueck wanted to stay at Harvard and embark on their research career. Sheldon was granted a tenure-track professor's position, but tenure track jobs were not offered to females. Any female wishing to get paid for conducting research at Harvard had to be under the sponsorship of a male faculty member. The years 1920–1965 have been called the dark era of patriarchal ascendancy, when women needed a powerful male sponsor or they suffered professionally. Eleanor Glueck was hired as a research assistant for her husband.

The anti-Semitism directed at both Gluecks and the sexism directed at Eleanor made them outcasts among much of the Harvard faculty and within academic circles. Their response was a stronger bond with each other and a fierce streak of independence. The Gluecks adopted a bunker mentality. Said one woman who knew them, "They lived within a circle, but nobody entered that circle except their daughter and Eleanor's father. Next came their staff, and all others were outside the circle" (Laub & Smith, 2008, p. 3).

Criminology Research

The Gluecks were also set apart by their research interests. In a law school, where the Gluecks were assigned, research on the causes of crime was an anomaly. But stand-alone criminal justice and criminology programs were practically nonexistent, so most criminology and criminal justice research, what little there was in the 1920s, was conducted by sociologists, psychologists, social workers, legal scholars. Meanwhile, Eleanor and Sheldon Glueck researched with a combination of several disciplines in their backgrounds.

The Gluecks made a good team at the Department of Social Ethics at Harvard. Sheldon's legal background and interest in psychiatry and his penchant for flowery prose paired well with Eleanor's social work/health focus background, her gift for attending to detail, and her mastery of research methods, statistics and keeping meticulous notes. Sheldon was more interested in theory and more likely to engage in academic debates with other scholars than was Eleanor. He called Eleanor "the scientist" (Laub & Smith, 1995, p. 16) as she was more attracted to the details of their work and collecting data. Unlike Sheldon, as a research assistant, Eleanor did not teach at Harvard; research was her sole focus.

One major contribution made by the Gluecks was the longitudinal or long-term study. In most criminal justice and criminology departments at most universities, faculty are assessed every year during their tenure track period, which is typically 5 to 6 years. Every year they must demonstrate that they are engaged in research that leads to publication in academic journals. Longitudinal or long-term studies take years to produce results and are costly in terms of personnel and financial resources, resources that most academic institutions do not have. As a result, long-term studies are rare. A typical faculty member cannot afford to wait 5 years for the outcome of a study before publishing their findings, and few have the resources to conduct long-range studies.

500 Criminal Careers

The Glueck's first major joint project was a study of 500 male offenders at the Massachusetts Reformatory. They followed the offenders for 5 years after their release. The result was *Five Hundred Criminal Careers*, published in 1930. Keeping extremely meticulous records on all the research subjects, the Gluecks concluded that reformatories did a poor job at reforming. The structure of the reformatory, according to the Gluecks, hampered its ability to rehabilitate.

They proposed building "cottages" (Mastorilli, Norton-Hawk, & Rousseau, 2014, p. 46), reminiscent of homes, to replace the impersonal environment of reformatories. Most of the sample was followed up 15 years later, with similarly dismal recidivism results.

Five Hundred Delinquent Women

A few years later, the Gluecks embarked on a similar study, this one involving females who completed their sentences at the Massachusetts Reformatory for Women. The results were published in 1934 under the title *Five Hundred Delinquent Women*. That same year, they published *One Thousand Juvenile Delinquents*, a study of young offenders referred to the Boston Juvenile Court. The 1934 studies included two controversial Glueck trademarks, attempting to predict delinquency among young people and predicting the likelihood of rehabilitation.

Unraveling Juvenile Delinquency

In 1940, one year before the United States entered World War II, the Gluecks set about working on what would become their defining and most ambitious work. They paired 500 adjudicated delinquent boys with 500 other boys, being as careful as possible to match them equally in every other possible respect, with the idea of tracking them for 10 years. Over a 10-year period, the Gluecks studied the boys' intelligence, body type, peer associations, and residences—even taking note of how well their residences were maintained by their parents.

The result was the 1950 publication of *Unraveling Juvenile Delinquency*. The most controversial aspect of the book was the Social Prediction Table. Using their table, the Gluecks argued that delinquency could be predicted as early as age 6. They even marketed a do-it-yourself prediction table for parents to ascertain whether their 6- or 7-year-old was likely to engage in delinquency. Among the most consistently found factors associated with delinquency were an absence of family cohesion, an absence of maternal supervision, and an absence of maternal affection.

Critics

Not everyone was a fan of Eleanor and Sheldon Glueck or their work. Although their prediction table was replicated and lauded by many, others thought the idea of predicting whether a 6-year-old would become delinquent was fanciful at best and dangerous at worse. Even the Gluecks acknowledged the potential negative misuse of an instrument that might generate a self-fulfilling prophecy.

Edwin Sutherland criticized their work as well, and some accused them of chicanery in their manipulation of data, although it should be noted that such accusations are common in social science research when the consumer does not like the research findings. Jon Snodgrass charged that they were image conscious, that Sheldon cultivated the public spotlight, and that the Gluecks shamelessly promoted some materials, especially the prediction tables. Snodgrass also claimed that although the Gluecks had over 300 publications, much of it was repetitious and was merely refreshed and reformatted to reprove or reiterate their arguments. Snodgrass also claimed that the Gluecks never actually knew a delinquent, a questionable claim as Eleanor conducted some of her own fieldwork—although she also maintained that fieldwork was best left to men and she continued to engage in social work activities with young women while conducting her research at Harvard.

Later Years

Even though Eleanor Glueck had gained fame as one of the world's most prominent criminology researchers, incredibly, she was never given a tenure track position at Harvard. In 1953, she was promoted to the position of research associate and eventually was appointed Director of the Harvard Law School Research Project into the Causes, Treatment, and Prevention of Juvenile Delinquency. She would hold the title of research associate until her "retirement" in the 1960s, after which she continued her work.

Even though Harvard never granted Eleanor tenure, in 1958, she and Sheldon became the first husband and wife team to be awarded an Honorary ScD (doctor of science) degree at Harvard, and Eleanor received the Distinguished Alumna Award from Barnard College in 1969. During her career, Eleanor

Glueck studied approximately 5,000 research subjects, mostly delinquents, an astounding number when one realizes the depth of qualitative information that she collected.

For much of her career, Eleanor was an outcast at Harvard and lived in a small inner circle. She was not even mentioned in the Harvard catalogue until her 1953 promotion to research associate. But this situation abated at Harvard with the changing attitudes toward Jews and toward the roles of women. Eleanor Glueck was remembered fondly by many students who worked under her. One of her favorite activities was the Sunday teas she hosted at her apartment in the Continental Hotel in Cambridge where she invited law school students and students from other nearby women's colleges.

The Gluecks suffered a devastating tragedy when their only daughter, Anitra, an accomplished poet, passed away in 1956 at age 32. Eleanor and Sheldon Glueck were married for more than 50 years and took 37 trips abroad for work and pleasure.

Eleanor Glueck passed away unexpectedly on September 25, 1972, the victim of an accidental drowning in her bathtub at home. She was 74 years old. In 1977, Sheldon published a tribute to his wife and their work together called *Lives of Labor, Lives of Love: Fragments of Friendly Autobiographies*. Eleanor was characterized as a "born social worker," although she was engaged in the most intricate scientific research and was a scientist and humanitarian extraordinaire.

Sources and Suggested Readings

Axelrod, A., Phillips, C., & Kemper, K. (1996). *Cops, crooks & criminologists: An international biography dictionary of law enforcement*. Facts on File.

Barnard College. (2024). *A fearless history*. Columbia University. https://barnard.edu/boldly-barnard/fearless-history, date of retrieval February 10, 2024.

Berlin, Miriam H. (2024). *The Shalvi/Hyman encyclopedia of Jewish women*, Jewish Women's Archive. https://jwa.org/encyclopedia/article/glueck-eleanor.

"Eleanor Glueck, expert on crime." (1972, September 26). *New York Times*. https://www.nytimes.com/1972/09/26/archives/eleanor-glueck-expert-olq-grime-writer-on-delinquency-with-her.html.

Feldberg, M. (n.d.). Anti-Semitism in the U.S.: Harvard's Jewish problem, *Jewish Virtual Library*, a Project of AICE. https://www.jewishvirtuallibrary.org/harvard-s-jewish-problem.

Glueck, S. (1977). *Lives of labor, lives of love: Fragments of friendly autobiographies*. Exposition Press of Florida.

Glueck, S., & Glueck, E. (1930). *500 criminal careers*. Alfred A. Knopf.

Glueck, S., & Glueck, E. (1934). *Five hundred delinquent women*. Alfred A. Knopf.

Glueck, S., & Glueck, E. (1950). *Unraveling juvenile delinquency.* Harvard University Press.

Justice Department. (2012). *John H. Laub and Rob Samson—The Stockholm Prize in criminology* [Video]. YouTube. https://www.youtube.com/watch?v=oqmUa9PLw8U, date of retrieval February 11, 2024.

Laub, J. H., & Smith, J. S. (1995). Eleanor Touroff Glueck: An unsung pioneer in criminology. *Women & Criminal Justice*, *6*(2), 1–22.

Levine, R. L. (1963, May 20). Gluecks pioneer in delinquent study. *The Harvard Crimson.* https://www.thecrimson.com/article/1963/5/20/gluecks-pioneer-in-delinquency-study-pin/

Mastorilli, M. E., Norton-Hawk, M. & Rousseau, D. (2014). How far have we come? The Gluecks' recommendations from 500 delinquent women. *Federal Probation*, *78*(1), 44–47.

Snodgrass, J. (1972). *The American criminological tradition: Portraits of the men & ideology in a discipline.* University Microfilms.

Vaillant, George E. (1980). Glueck, Eleanor Touroff. In B. Sicherman, C. Hurd Green, H. Kantov, & H. Walker (Eds), *Notable American women the modern period: A biographical dictionary*, pp. 278–280. Belknap Press.

Discussion Questions

1. What are your thoughts after reading of the obstacles Dr. Glueck encountered because of her religion and gender?
2. Dr. Glueck specialized in longitudinal research, something that many criminology scholars cannot focus on given the logistical realities of academe. Should universities be more encouraging of her brand of research? Do you have any other thoughts on her research?

Credit

IMG 2.1: Copyright © 1964 Alamy/Keystone Press.

CHAPTER 3

Robert Merton (1910-2003)

IMG 3.1

Some people believe that a professor's duty is to make the world a better place through their teaching, research, and public service. Others believe that if they cannot make the world better, perhaps they can at least explain in understandable terms how the world works. This is true in both the physical and the social sciences. And no professor did a better job of explaining crime and other social phenomena than Robert Merton. No criminologist has had a greater impact on crime-related policy or the way the public perceives the causes of crime than Merton. Like Edwin Sutherland, Merton introduced scientific terms into everyday vocabulary, even outside the realm of criminology, which this chapter will illustrate.

Early Life and Education

Meyer Schkolnick, the son of Jewish immigrants from Eastern Europe, referred to himself as a "Yankee Doodle baby" (Gieryn, 2004, p. 91) because he was born on July 4 (or 5), 1910, in a lower-class neighborhood in South Philadelphia, Pennsylvania. His father scraped out a living by working at several jobs, including carpentry, truck driving, and selling dairy products. Growing up in what he called his "urban village" (Gieryn, 2003, p.91) where he had little money but access to all the cultural activities that Philadelphia had to offer, Meyer Schkolnick developed a love of books early in life, but he was also streetwise. Robert Merton, as he later became known, once stated that growing up in Philadelphia provided him "with every sort of capital—social capital, cultural capital, human capital, and above all, what we may call public capital" (Calhoun, 2003, para. 2).

The young Meyer Schkolnick developed an aptitude for sleight of hand and began performing magic shows in public around age 12. He decided to take the stage name Robert Merlin as homage to the mythical medieval magician. Although he never forsook his Jewish roots, Schkolnick changed his name to something more "American" to assimilate more easily. Schkolnick/Merlin's aspiring career in prestidigitation was derailed in part thanks to a trick that got him into a bit of hot water. In front of several hundred Sunday school children, he performed his "Houdini needle trick," where he "swallowed" several needles and a length of black thread, washing it down with water and pulling the thread from his throat. The problem came when some of the children in the audience attempted to replicate the trick, prompting complaints from parents.

Schkolnick graduated from South Philadelphia High School for Boys in 1927. Then he entered Temple College and officially changed his name to Robert King Merton, being told that "Merlin" was too cliche. His initial interest was in philosophy, but he soon became enamored with the fledgling field of sociology, which even in its early years was sharply divided into two camps, the theorists, and the empiricists. As his career began, Merton aspired to belong to the empirical camp, but in time he became known more for his theoretical contributions than for empirical research.

During his time at Temple, Merton met Suzanne Carhart, a social worker. He graduated in 1931 and entered Harvard University to pursue a graduate degree in sociology. They married while he was a student at Harvard and ultimately would have three children. He was part of the first cohort of graduate students to enter Harvard's sociology department, completing the program in 1936. His doctoral dissertation—*Science, Technology and Society in 17th-Century England*—was published as his first book in 1938.

Merton stayed at Harvard as an instructor after graduation, but he soon realized that he would not be able to attain a position as a tenured professor. In fact, no new positions were created during Merton's time there because of the impact of the Great Depression. As anti-Semitism was rife at Harvard in the 1930s, Merton's Jewish ancestry may have also been an impeding factor.

Tulane and Columbia

Merton had always been fascinated with New Orleans, and when he realized Harvard was a dead end, he decided he wanted to live somewhere besides the Northeast. He accepted a position at Tulane University in 1939, and within 2 years, Merton had achieved the rank of full professor and department chair. In 1941, Merton left Tulane for an assistant professor position at Columbia University, where he would spend the remainder of his career. While at Columbia, Merton would make the contributions to crime, American culture, and sociology as a discipline that made him famous.

The Great Depression profoundly affected Merton's intellectual development and worldview. Like other sociologists of his time, Merton observed "the collapsing and deregulation of social traditions and the effect that it had on both individuals and the institutions of society." He was strongly influenced by President Franklin Roosevelt's attempt to rebuild societal structures through his New Deal programs, and like many who spent their formative years under Roosevelt's New Deal administration, Merton gravitated toward socialism.

Merton and Criminology

The four concepts that defined Merton's contributions to criminological thought are basic to all students of criminology today. His conceptions on the causes of crime did not come about at one time but were decades in development and were disseminated in stages. To some degree, they reflected Merton's socialist ideals, but they also reflected the realities of a capitalist society. Four of his key concepts were: (a) *social structure and anomie,* (SS&A); (b) *strain*; (c) *self-fulfilling prophecy*; and (d) *role model.*

Anomie was a term Merton borrowed from the French sociologist Emile Durkheim. It refers to a state of normlessness, usually caused by a sudden social upheaval. An individual cannot cope with the new rules or the lack of rules, which leads to strain or a sense that nothing matters. Merton adopted the term for criminology and made it part of the emerging study of criminology as a social science in 1938, with his publication "Social Structure and Anomie" (Merton, 1938).

Strain has been one of the most dominant criminological theories of the part 60 years and was derived and developed by Merton's students, Richard Cloward and Lloyd Ohlin, from Merton's work. It guided policy decisions for decades, especially during the 1960s as it meshed with the ideology of the Kennedy and Johnson presidential administrations. More specifically, it spun off opportunity theory, which laid the theoretical groundwork for the Mobilization for Youth program of the 1960s.

While Merton's name is attached to strain theory, he only used the term when discussing the conflicting demands that several roles can produce without anyone intending that such strains exist. He employed the term "disjunction" to imply inconsistency in the demands associated with normatively approved means and goals and the opportunities to comply with them, and the extent of incompatibility between norms, goals and opportunities.

The theory suggests that most if not all individuals in American society strive for the common goal of material success. The American dream contains a recipe for success but also recipes for failure for those who want the dream but cannot attain it. The drive to get ahead may generate deviance. Stumbling blocks such as poverty, racism, or class bias stand in the way of some people attaining those goals, and those individuals choose one of five mindsets to guide their behavior:

- conformity—accept both the goals and the legitimate (legal) means of achieving them
- innovation—accept the goals, but reject the legal means of achieving them
- ritualism—do not accept the goals but go through the motions of achieving them
- retreatism—reject both the goals and the means of achieving success
- rebellion—individual goes outside the social structure to change it

The concept of the self-fulfilling prophecy is another contribution from Merton that is important to criminology and has made its way into everyday American vocabulary. The self-fulfilling prophecy provides an example of Merton blending creativity with simplicity in a way that makes people wonder why they didn't think of it themselves. The term first surfaced in 1948, in an *Antioch Review* article penned by Merton. The self-fulfilling prophecy is a false definition of a situation, that is, it is a prediction that is false, but then becomes the basis for "a new behavior which makes the originally false conception come true" (Merton, 1948, p. 195). In other words, it is the belief that bad or good will happen.

The self-fulfilling prophecy has found applications in all spheres of life, including criminology. It laid the groundwork for labeling theory, in which a person, usually a child, is labeled delinquent from an early age and treated as a delinquent, with the result that the child actively fulfills the role imposed by that label.

In addition, Merton introduced the concept of a *role model*, which is today used in everyday language throughout the English-speaking world. The idea emerged in research he did on the education of medical students in which he found that they often sought role models to emulate while learning how to become physicians. He said that one answer to delinquency is the presence of individuals that can make a positive difference in the life of a child. By the same token, negative role models can lead a child to delinquency.

Merton and Racial Integration

Merton played a part in a landmark decision handed down by the United States Supreme Court. In 1954, under the leadership of newly confirmed Chief Justice Earl Warren, the Court ruled unconstitutional the "separate but equal" doctrine that had perpetuated racial segregation for several decades. The ruling was handed down in *Brown v. Board of Education of Topeka*, 347 U.S. 483, which declared school segregation unconstitutional and paved the way for gradual school desegregation throughout the country. Merton had written about the benefits of racially integrated communities. Kenneth Clark, one of the social scientists preparing a brief for the Supreme Court and a friend of Merton's, worked with him on the arguments presented to the Court. Clark was a psychologist who did research on the effects of school desegregation on children's views of race. His findings were central to the brief presented to the Supreme Court in *Brown v. Board of Education of Topeka*. Merton helped him prepare the argument that resulted in the Court's decision to outlaw school segregation.

The Focus Group

Merton was one of the founders of the "focus group," an achievement that will solidify his place in American history (Kaufman, 2003, p. 1). Now a staple of commercial marketing and political campaigns, Merton devised the concept somewhat by accident in the mid-1950s. At the request of colleague Paul Lazarsfeld, Merton went to a radio studio where Lazarsfeld wanted his assistance in observing a small audience's reactions to a radio program. Merton and Lazarsfeld became fascinated with what was occurring and brainstormed ways to improve the research process. Lazarsfeld, the founder of the Bureau of Applied Social Research at Columbia, did much to further studies of political and consumption influences. These drew on interviews more broadly. Merton's own research, also done under the aegis of the Bureau, aimed to explain how mass persuasion worked. It too drew, in part, on group interviews along with other research procedures and aimed to show how and why Kate Smith, a popular singer at the time, sold War Bonds so successfully. The focus group idea was eventually refined and used in a more sophisticated fashion. Later, the focus group was so frequently used and abused in politics and marketing that it irritated Merton, who nonetheless wished he had gotten a royalty from the concept.

On the Shoulders of Giants

Merton demonstrated to modern professors the value of reading the original works of great authors and thinkers, rather than merely reading from modern text writers and article authors that discuss the great thinkers. His reasons for doing so mirror the rationale of those who advocate the study of history. Merton believed that students should study the classics because

- it avoids reinventing the wheel;
- it aids in the clear formulation of ideas;
- it ensures that ideas will stand up to previously issued challenges;
- it provides a model for theory development; and
- the reader gleans something different each time a classic work is read.

Merton's 1965 book *On the Shoulders of Giants* expands on that idea and on the complex connections between accumulated past knowledge and new contributions. The title of his book was taken from a phrase often attributed to Isaac Newton, "If I have seen farther, it is by standing on the shoulders of giants." Merton's book explores the history of the phrase and traces it back to Bernard of Chartres, a 12th-century French philosopher. By standing on a giant's shoulders, we get a better view of the future—that is, the past provides the basis for new contributions to knowledge but is not their only source.

The Matthew Effect

Matthew's Gospel, chapter 25 verse 29, states:

> For unto every one that hath shall be given, and he shall have abundance: but from him that hath not shall be taken away even that which he hath (KJV).

Similarly worded verses are found elsewhere in the New Testament Gospels. The text mirrors Merton's advocacy for socialist ideals, while recognizing the reality of capitalism, not just in the economy and business but in academe and scientific inquiry. In 1968, Robert Merton and his Columbia colleague (and future wife) Harriet Zuckerman postulated that the Matthew Effect holds sway in scientific discovery. Credit for scientific discoveries tends to go to already established scientists, not to lesser-known scientists who may have been the real innovators, as was the case with the "shoulders of giants" idea. In other words, with scientific inquiry and credit for discovery, the rich may, intentionally or otherwise, get richer, while the poor get poorer.

Oral Publication

As a classroom professor, Merton adopted a habit of formulating ideas and presenting them before a class, or as he called it, a "microenvironment." He considered himself as engaged in an "oral publication" or thinking it aloud in the presence of an audience, in preparation for a written publication. While typically described as a generous and kind person and never cruel or needlessly rude or arrogant, Merton could be moody and intimidating. One of his assistants stated that whenever he saw Merton smoking a pipe, he knew he could approach him, but if Merton were smoking a cigar, he knew it was best to stay away. As Merton's reputation grew, he seemed larger than life to his students, or at least larger than he was. The above-referenced assistant, who went on to become provost at Columbia, conducted an informal survey of students in one of Merton's classics, asking students "how tall is Robert Merton?" With scant variation, students responded that Merton was at least 6′3″ In fact, he was 6′1″.

Retirement, Death, and Legacy

Robert Merton retired from Columbia in 1979, assuming the title of university professor emeritus, but he stayed active, usually arising at 4:30 a.m. In 1994, Merton received a National Medal of Science from President Bill Clinton, becoming the first sociologist to receive the honor. Merton was cited for "founding the sociology of science and pioneering contributions to the study of social life, especially the self-fulfilling prophecy and the unintended consequences of social action." One magazine interviewer described Merton as possessing "a surprising catholicity of interests and a talent for good conversation, alarmingly well informed about everything from baseball to Kant and ready to tell anybody about it."

The Travels and Adventures of Serendipity tackled the topic of the future of anomie theory and serendipitous scientific discovery, an interest area of his since he published "The Unanticipated Consequences of Purposive Social Action" in *American Sociological Review* in 1936. Merton's "last" publication, *The Travels and Adventures of Serendipity*, tackled the topic of the future of anomie theory and serendipitous scientific discovery, and appeared in 2002. Already ill with five forms of cancer, Merton's interest in unanticipated consequences had remained with him. As early as the 1950s, he had collaborated on a book on serendipity, a kind of unplanned discovery, but he was unsatisfied with the manuscript and decided not to publish it. It was only the efforts of Italian publisher friends that persuaded him to allow an augmented version of the manuscript to be published in Italian in 2002. It appeared to enthusiastic reviews which then led him to agree to publish an edition in English which appeared in 2004, after his death.

Robert King Merton, nicknamed Mr. Sociology, died on February 23rd in New York City at the age of 92. At his death, his obituary appeared in the mainstream media, including ABC, the Cable News Network, the *New York Times,* and all the major British and Italian newspapers. Such was his recognition outside his academic discipline. His son Robert C. Merton, a Nobel laureate in economics, said of his father, "If there were a Nobel Prize in sociology, there would be no question he would have gotten it" (Kaufman, 2003).

Sources and Suggested Readings

American Society of Criminology. (2013). *Robert K. Merton* [Video]. YouTube. https://www.youtube.com/watch?v=Wdgfg485ekU

American Sociological Association. (2024). Robert K. Merton. https://www.asanet.org/robert-k-merton/

Archival Collections. (2021). *Robert K. Merton Papers, 1928–2003, Bulk 1943–2001.* https://findingaids.library.columbia.edu/ead/nnc-rb/ldpd_6911309/dsc/8

Axelrod, A., Phillips, C., & Kemper, K. (1996). *Cops, crooks & criminologists: An international biographical dictionary of law enforcement.* Facts on File.

Calhoun, C. (2003). *Remembering Robert K. Merton.* chrome-extension://efaidnbmnnnibpcajpcglclefindmkaj/https://www.asanet.org/wp-content/uploads/savvy/images/asa/docs/pdf/Merton,%20Robert%20SSRC%20Remembering.pdf

Columbia College. (2003). *In memoriam: Robert K. Merton, influential sociologist.* https://www.college.columbia.edu/cct_archive/may03/quads11.html

Columbia University. (2010). *Robert K. Merton at 100: Reflections & recollections* [Video]. YouTube. https://www.youtube.com/watch?v=XBpI_xrWsTQ

Crothers, C. (2021). *Reintroducing Robert K. Merton*. Routledge.
Gieryn, Thomas F. (2004). Eloge: Robert K. Merton, 1910–2003. *Isis*, 95(1), 91–94.
Holton, G. (2004). Robert K. Merton. *Proceedings of the American Philosophical Society*, *148*(4), 506–517.
Kallenberg, R. (2007). Robert K. Merton: A modern sociological classic. *Journal of Classical Sociology*, *7*(2), 131–136.
Kaufman, Michael T. (2003, February 24). Robert K. Merton, versatile sociologist and father of the focus group, dies at 92. *New York Times*.
Merton, R. K. (1936). The unanticipated consequences of purposive social action. *American Sociological Review*, *1*(6), 894–904.
Merton, R. K. (1938). Social structure and anomie. *American Sociological Review*, *3*(5), 672–682.
Merton, R. K. (1948). The self-fulfilling prophecy. *The Antioch Review*, *8*(2), 193–210.
Merton, R. K. (1968). The Matthew Effect in science. *Science*, *159*(3810), 56–63.
Merton, R. K. (1968). *Social theory & social structure*. The Free Press.
Mutchnick, R. J., Martin, R., & Austin, W. T. (2009). *Criminological thought pioneers past & present*. Pearson.
Sztompka, P. (1986). *Robert K. Merton, An intellectual profile*. St. Martin's Press.
Sztompka, P. (1998). Robert K. Merton: Recipient of the 1997 Cooley-Mead Award. *Social Psychology Quarterly*, *61*(2), 97–100.
Vold, G. B., & Bernard, T. J. (1985). *Theoretical criminology* (3rd ed.). Oxford University Press.

My thanks to Dr. Harriet Zuckerman and Dr. Robert C. Merton for their assistance with this chapter.

Discussion Questions

1. How has Merton impacted the field of criminology? How has he impacted issues outside the criminology arena?
2. In what ways might it be beneficial for criminal justice students to emulate Robert Merton?

Credit

IMG 3.1: Eric Koch, https://commons.wikimedia.org/wiki/File:Robert_K._Merton_(1965).jpg, 1965.

CHAPTER 4

James Q. Wilson (1931–2012)

IMG 4.1

An unfortunate aspect of academic life is the tendency of professors and researchers to cluster in the academy with their colleagues to the exclusion of unpopular viewpoints and viewpoints outside the academic arena. Like any other professional subculture, academics often find it very difficult to go against the prevailing norms and opinions of their colleagues and academic superiors. Such reticence is understandable as promotion and tenure decisions may hang in the balance, and advancing in the academic profession requires conforming.

From the 1960s until shortly before his death, James Q. Wilson was a scholar that rose above such academic isolationism and was never afraid to be unpopular. He was one of the most prolific and influential public policy scholars of the late 20th and early 21st centuries. Wilson had considerable impact on several areas of public policy and social thought, his most significant in theories of crime causation and approaches to policing. Jennifer Jenkins wrote that Wilson set the tone for criminal justice policy for several decades with his statement that "wicked people need to be separated from the rest of us" (Jenkins, 2011, para. 1).

Although Wilson rejected the idea that any one person, including himself, could produce that sort of impact, his impact on crime and public policy was significant.

Early Life and Education

James Quinn Wilson was born in Denver, Colorado, on May 27, 1931, and he grew up in Long Beach, California, the state where, as Wilson said, America was headed in the 1930s and 1940s. He received a bachelor's degree in political science from the University of the Redlands in 1952. Soon after graduating, he entered the Navy and rose to the rank of Lieutenant Junior Grade. After being discharged in 1955, Wilson entered graduate school at the University of Chicago and graduated with a doctorate in political science in 1959. Wilson married Roberta, his childhood sweetheart from California.

Looking back at Wilson's early life, his successful career as an academician was predictable. However, like many academic pioneers in criminal justice, he had to make his own way in a new academic discipline that did not enjoy the benefit of decades of precedent as guidance. His first job after obtaining his doctorate was as instructor in the University of Chicago's Political Science Department. While he was in graduate school at Chicago, he never took a course in criminology or criminal justice, and he showed no interest in the field that would garner him fame in later years. With few exceptions, universities in the 1950s did not even recognize the study of criminal justice as an academic endeavor.

One fortuitous factor that steered Wilson toward criminal justice was attending the University of Chicago—one of the few universities that had already established a national reputation for the study of crime causation. That reputation had been established by sociologists, not by political scientists. However, University of Chicago political scientists, who were situated in one of America's largest cities, devoted considerable efforts to the study of urban politics. Wilson's first two books, *Negro Politics*, published in 1960 (when Wilson was only 29 years old), and *The Amateur Democrat*, published in 1961, reflected this interest. Wilson moved from Chicago to Harvard University in 1961 as a lecturer in government, where he was promoted to the rank of associate professor in 1963.

An Accidental Criminologist

Wilson claimed that he became a criminologist by accident. He wanted to study cities and African American politics, not crime, but history would intervene to change the direction of Wilson's academic career. In the early 1960s, the academic community exhibited an increasing curiosity about how America's criminal justice system functioned. A historically significant event would steer Wilson to the study of crime—the 1964 presidential election that pitted incumbent Democrat Lyndon Johnson against an abrasive Republican challenger from Arizona, Senator Barry Goldwater. Goldwater's campaign included blunt, acid rhetoric, accusing Johnson and the Democrats of being soft on defense, communism, and crime.

Johnson won the 1964 election in a landslide, but Goldwater's accusation of his being soft on crime stung Johnson, leading to his resolve to address crime and criminal justice in the United States. He established a blue-ribbon commission to conduct a multi-year, comprehensive study of the state of crime and criminal justice in the United States. Johnson's commission included experts from all areas of America that were touched by crime. In addition, the commission formed a scientific advisory committee, which included Harvard University's James Vorenberg. Vorenberg was a friend and colleague of Wilson's and advised him to assume an active role in the work of the presidential commission. Wilson replied that he was unqualified and knew nothing about crime. Vorenberg told Wilson not to worry as no one else did either. So Wilson started reading up on crime.

Wilson was later appointed to serve on the Science Advisory Committee of President Johnson's Commission on Law Enforcement and the Administration of Justice from 1966–1967. Despite working for President Johnson, a Democrat, Wilson was critical of many of the Johnson Administration's Great Society measures, which expanded the role of the federal government in hopes of solving social problems. He was also critical of what he called "new politics" among African Americans and civil rights activists who "marched on city halls" when their time would have been better spent completing school, learning a skill, and getting a job. He chaired the White House Task Force on Crime in 1967 and co-chaired Vice President Hubert Humphrey's Task Force on Order and Justice in 1968.

In a 1968 publication titled *Varieties of Police Behavior*, Wilson differentiated the following three styles of police behavior:

1. The watchman, with an order maintenance function, who uses the law as a means of maintaining order rather than regulating conduct.
2. The legalistic officer, who sets a single standard for the community and enforces the law even if public order is not breached; and
3. The service officer, or the officer who responds as the community desires but is less likely to make an arrest.

While at Harvard, Wilson met Daniel Patrick Moynihan, an astute, outspoken political liberal and renowned author with immense political and intellectual talent, and a man who had political ambitions and connections to match his talent. Moynihan would go on to serve as United States ambassador to the United Nations and as a United States senator. Although Moynihan, a liberal Democrat, and Wilson, who would eventually join the Republican Party, were often on opposite ends of the political spectrum, they remained fast friends and colleagues from the time they met until Moynihan's death in 2003. In my telephone interview with Dr. Wilson, I asked how such a friendship can endure so many political differences. Wilson replied that such is the stuff that makes America great and unique.

Thinking About Crime

During Republican Richard Nixon's presidency (1969–1974), Daniel Moynihan told Nixon that he simply had to meet James Wilson because Wilson was the "smartest man in America." Nixon asked Wilson to head the National Advisory Commission on Drug Abuse Prevention, which he did from 1972–1973. Wilson concluded that the Commission was doing nothing that had a positive impact. He suggested to President Nixon that the Commission be abolished. Nixon agreed, but he asked that Wilson appear before Congress and advocate the creation of the Drug Enforcement Administration. Wilson and Nixon's efforts were successful, and the DEA was created in 1973.

Wilson's writings on crime began receiving more prominent notice during the 1970s. President Gerald Ford, who succeeded Nixon in 1974, was so impressed with Wilson's *Thinking About Crime* that he invited him to the White House in December of 1974 to discuss his views. Ford subscribed to Wilson's analysis of core crime issues, namely that most crime is committed by repeat offenders, that the certainty of imprisonment deters crime, and that crime victims deserved more attention than they were getting from the criminal justice system. Ford also agreed with Wilson's belief that local governments could combat crime more effectively than the federal government, and that correctional rehabilitation efforts were much like social welfare policies that not only failed to deliver but made bad situations worse. According to Wilson, "Our goal is not to enlarge the welfare system but to change it. All about us lies the wreckage of the therapeutic state" (Wilson, 1997, para. 41).

More important than his specific proposals on crime control was his basic moral stance in *Thinking About Crime*—that wicked people exist and that they had to be set apart from innocent people. Moral terms such as "wicked" had been absent from academic discussions about crime for several decades, during which societal conditions or medical problems were viewed as the prime factors in crime causation. While Wilson continued writing about crime and serving on the Harvard faculty, he served President Ronald Reagan as an adviser on foreign intelligence, overlooking international activities of the Central Intelligence Agency, which had fallen into disrepute with many Americans by the 1970s.

Broken Windows

One of the most significant writings of Wilson's career was an article he coauthored with George Kelling for *The Atlantic* in 1982. In that article, he and Kelling lay out a prescription for addressing crime in neighborhoods called the "fixing broken windows" approach, which became a staple of criminal justice study and police work around the country. The basic premise of broken windows crime prevention is that public order is as important a goal for the police as catching criminals.

A subordinate but unverifiable argument is that crime flourishes in neighborhoods that fall into disrepair, where panhandling and drug dealing occur in the open, dilapidated houses serve as meeting places for criminals, and where it appears that neither the police nor the neighborhood residents care about the quality of life in the neighborhood, and that little crimes lead to bigger crimes. The solution is to clean up the neighborhoods, tear down abandoned buildings, harass petty street criminals, and try to improve the overall quality of life in neighborhoods, all of which involve aggressive policing.

No proposal from an academic made a greater impact on criminal justice policy than the fixing broken windows idea. Police departments large and small implemented the broken windows approach. Some credit the broken windows approach with the precipitous decline in crime in New York City during the 1990s, though that point is debatable as increases or decreases in crime are seldom attributable to one factor alone.

During a telephone interview with Wilson for the first edition of this book, I informed him that his broken windows idea was being applied outside the context of policing. In fact, a book on housekeeping advocated the broken windows idea in house cleaning. Keep a house clean by performing small maintenance chores regularly, and those who live in the house will take greater pride in keeping the house clean rather than using it as a dumping ground.

Wilson laughed at the idea at first, but then stated that he applied the broken windows idea to his neighborhood. His house was the only one on his street, where trucks frequently came by and their drivers often deposited their trash on the street. Even though most of the street was not part of his property, Wilson cleaned the trash from the street regularly, realizing that a dirty street invited more dirt and trash. According to Wilson, "Arresting a single drunk or a single vagrant who has harmed no identifiable person seems unjust, and in a sense it is. But failing to do anything about a score of drunks or a hundred vagrants may destroy an entire community" (Weber, 2012, para. 11).

Wilson's Critics

Wilson was the target of criticism, especially from the political left. He never shied away from mentioning race as a factor in crime, noting that African Americans are involved in violent crime in higher numbers than other ethnic groups, and he did not attribute factors outside the person as the prime cause of crime. Wilson was even accused of promoting "scientific racism," or using scientific methods to suggest that African Americans are more prone to commit crime than other racial groups. When I mentioned the term "scientific racism" to Wilson, he immediately bristled and became defensive, asking me to explain what I meant. While our interview was mostly pleasant and I expressed my gratitude for him being so generous with his time, the phrase angered him. He stated that it is a fact that African Americans are involved in a disproportionate amount of violent crime, that no one explanation can be offered for this involvement, and that social scientists should be seriously engaged in discovering why this phenomenon occurs. Wilson maintained that most of his academic colleagues were wrong about crime causation and proper responses, and that the average man on the street was right.

Although he proudly proclaimed that he was a social scientist, James Wilson was a strong critic of most of what passed as social science, claiming that most social scientists—be they in anthropology, political science, sociology, sexual behavior, or criminal justice—usually find what they set out to find when embarking on a social scientific "experiments," and that they come up with findings to make a name for themselves or to impress the cultural elite with findings that affirm the prevailing sentiment in academe. Most academics, said Wilson, are tucked away in libraries and offices studying narrow topics, manipulating data for articles that are published in journals that no one reads, and presenting information that does not add to the sum of human knowledge. According to Wilson, liberal and conservative scholars are equally guilty.

Wilson believed that his unpopularity with the political left also stemmed from his steadfast and unchanging belief in punishment, and his belief that general deterrence is effective and that most attempts at rehabilitation fall short. Wilson also echoed the phrase that social science is the "god that failed" (American Enterprise Institute, 2021) that while good social science has advanced the study of criminology, "reformists" social science has been abused by political activists on the political left and right to the point where much of it is worthless. According to Wilson, mainstream Americans believe that moral concepts such as punishment have a place in the criminal justice system, but social leftists that dominate colleges and universities do not share that belief. As for his own political beliefs, Wilson stated that he was more liberal than the average person on the street, but more conservative than most of his academic colleagues.

The Moral Sense

The book that Wilson was most proud of was *The Moral Sense.* In that book he laid out his ideas for the underlying factors that caused crime and much dysfunction in society. According to Wilson, the moral sense consists of four virtues: (a) sympathy, (b) fairness, (c) self-control, and (d) duty. Wilson was a strong believer in the traditional two-parent family, sex within the context of marriage, and the value of religious influence on young people. He saw the dissolution of the traditional American family with one-parent families becoming the norm as prime factors in crime causation. He saw modern culture and the proliferation of the welfare state as prime factors in that dissolution.

Wilson claimed that Americans are materially better off than their parents but spiritually worse off. In a 2002 lecture televised on C-Span, Wilson delivered an address on his book *The Marriage Problem.* A female audience member asked at what point in history marriage became the norm for human relationships. He simply replied, "With Eve." Despite his advocacy of traditional Judeo-Christian principles and behaviors, Wilson was not devoutly religious. He simply saw traditional conservative values as the bulwark of a civilized society. He argued that the impact of religious beliefs is scientifically testable, and that it correlates with avoiding crime.

Retirement, Legacy, and Death

Wilson retired from Harvard in 1987 and moved to California. He served as professor of management and public policy at the University of California at Los Angeles until his retirement, whereupon he served as professor emeritus of management at UCLA and then at Pepperdine University. He remained active with the American Enterprise Institute for Public Policy, a conservative think tank. In 2003, Dr. Wilson was awarded the Presidential Medal of Freedom by President George W. Bush. He and his wife eventually returned to Boston to be near family.

Wilson never wavered from the beliefs about crime, social mores, and ethics that he had espoused since the 1960s. Of all Wilson's writings and quotes, perhaps one more than any other captures both his wry wit and his philosophy about dealing with crime: "There are no more liberals; they have all been mugged" (25 Great Quotes by James Q. Wilson, n.d., para. 2). James Q. Wilson died at age 80 on March 2, 2012, in Boston, due to complications from leukemia.

Sources and Suggested Readings

25 Great Quotes by James Q. Wilson. (n.d.). Wisdomly. https://www.wisdomly.net/james-q-wilson-1746.php, accessed August 2, 2024.

American Enterprise Institute. (2020). *An interview with James Q. Wilson.* (1995, January 27). Think Tank. [Video]. YouTube. https://www.youtube.com/watch?v=I1qDTHLVLDE

American Enterprise Institute. (2021). *Is social science the god that failed? (1998)—with James Q. Wilson.* Think Tank. [Video]. YouTube. https://www.youtube.com/watch?v=Asm-wLigSmo

Jenkins, J. (2011, August 2). *Jennifer Bishop Jenkins on punishment and teen killers.* Juvenile Justice Information Exchange. https://jjie.org/2011/08/02/jennifer-bishop-jenkins-on-punishment-teen-killers/, accessed August 2, 2024.

Kelling, G. L., Coles, C. M., & Wilson. J. Q. (1998). *Fixing broken windows: Restoring order and reducing crime in our communities.* Touchstone Books.

Pierson, J. (2012). Reflections James Q. Wilson, 1931–2012. *The New Criterion, 30*(8), 1–4.

Weber, B. (2012, March 2). James Q. Wilson dies at 80: Originated 'Broken Windows' policing strategy. *New York Times.* https://www.nytimes.com/2012/03/03/nyregion/james-q-wilson-dies-at-80-originated-broken-windows-policing-strategy.html#:~:text=Kelling%20wrote.,may%20destroy%20an%20entire%20community.%E2%80%9D

Wilson, J. Q. (1960). *Negro politics: The search for leadership.* Free Press.

Wilson, J. Q. (1966). *The amateur democrat.* University of Chicago Press.

Wilson, J. Q. (1968). *Varieties of police behavior.* Harvard University Press.

Wilson, J. Q. (1983). *Thinking about crime.* Basic Books.

Wilson, J. Q. (1997, December 4). Two nations [Speech]. American Enterprise Institute. https://www.aei.org/research-products/speech/two-nations/

Wilson, James Q. (2001, November 20). Telephone interview.

Wilson, J. Q. (2002). *The marriage problem: How our culture has weakened families.* Harper Collins.

Wilson, J. Q., & Hernstein, R. (1985). *Crime and human nature.* Simon & Schuster.

Wilson, J. Q., & Kelling, G. L. (1982). Broken Windows. *The Atlantic Monthly, 249*(3), 29–38.

Discussion Questions

1. How did James Wilson impact policing during his career?
2. Do you think that contemporary academic criminologists should be open to conservative voices like Wilson's?

Credit

IMG 4.1: Screenshot from "Understanding America," https://www.c-span.org/video/?204860-1/understanding-america. Copyright © by National Cable Satellite Corporation.

SECTION II

LAW ENFORCEMENT

While it seems to be generally accepted that a police officer has always been a phone call away, policing as currently known in the United States did not always exist. Municipal policing did not come about until the 1830s, and then in only a few American cities. This chapter examines a few of the people who helped make modern policing what it is. Some of these names are known to even the most casual observer of police history; others will be somewhat familiar to criminal justice scholars; still others may be new to even the most ardent students of law enforcement. Some of these people are included because of their leadership accomplishments, others for their innovations, and others because they broke barriers, usually sexual and racial. Although the categories are not hard and fast, I group them as barrier breakers, innovators, leaders, and honorable mentions.

Barrier Breakers

- **Bass Reeves**, born into slavery, became a legendary deputy marshal in the 19th century American West.
- **Joseph Petrosino** was a pioneer among Italian immigrant police officers in New York City whose leadership and innovative approach to battling the fledgling criminal syndicates made him a hero and cost him his life.

- **Lola Baldwin**, a pioneer for women in law enforcement and a disciple of the social hygiene movement at the turn of the 20th century, paved the way for female police officers while working in Portland, Oregon.
- **Alice Stebbins Wells** helped create the police profession for women while working in Los Angeles, and she spread the word about the need for women in policing to other cities in the United States and Canada.
- **Samuel Battle**, the first African American police officer for the New York City Police Department, withstood discrimination to make himself one of the most famous police officers in New York history.
- **Lee Brown**, a police officer and doctorate scholar, was among the earliest African American leaders of large, urban police departments.
- **Penny Harrington**, the first female chief of a large American police department, whose tenure in Portland, Oregon, while brief and controversial, paved the way for other women leaders in law enforcement.

The Innovators

- **Herman Goldstein** is the only person named in this section who never served as a police officer. He was a gentlemen scholar whose research has been recognized in law enforcement and academe.
- **Frank Serpico**, whose name is synonymous with exposing police corruption, is one of the few chapter subjects easily recognized by people outside the field. His controversial career with the New York Police Department has been the subject of study among scholars, writers, and filmmakers.
- **Joseph Wambaugh** is the most famous police officer turned novelist in history. His books on the gritty aspects of law enforcement and true crime have taught the public—not only academics and criminology majors—more about policing than can be learned from many textbooks.
- **Greg MacAleese**, a former municipal police officer and journalist, was the founder of Crime Stoppers, which now extends to countries around the world.

The Leaders

- **August Vollmer** was among the first to integrate higher education with policing, an idea scorned at the time but accepted today. If any one person invented modern municipal policing, it would be Vollmer.
- **J. Edgar Hoover** is among the most famous and infamous of the people profiled in this book. Hoover almost single-handedly created the world's most renowned investigative agency. His directorship of the FBI from 1924–1972 made him a cultural icon, in ways good and bad, depending on

one's point of view. He was one of the most consequential public figures of the 20th century.

- **O. W. Wilson**, Vollmer's protégé, pioneered the integration of academe, modern management techniques and modern law enforcement through his work in several American cities, especially Wichita and Chicago.

Honorable Mentions

IMG II.1

Allan Pinkerton (1819–1884) was born in Scotland and became the first famous private eye in the United States. Pinkerton settled in Chicago, working first as a Cook County deputy sheriff and then as the first detective in the history of the Chicago Police Department. Then he worked as a postal agent and eventually opened his own detective agency.

In the 19th century, local law enforcement agencies were not as well funded, equipped, or trained to handle many of the investigative tasks they perform today. Businesses turned to private detectives like Pinkerton to provide protection or investigate crimes. The Pinkerton Agency established a reputation as a crack detective firm, but also went down in history as hired henchmen who worked for big business to suppress the burgeoning organized labor movement in the United States. His agency helped thwart a reported attempt on the life of President Abraham Lincoln and sided with the Union during the Civil War. The Pinkerton Agency still exists today.

For more information about Allan Pinkerton, see the sources below:

- Jeffreys-Jones, R. (2025). *Allan Pinkerton: America's Legendary Detective and the Birth of Private Security.*
- Mackay, J. (1997). *Allan Pinkerton: The First Private Eye.*
- O'Hara, S. P. (2016). *Inventing the Pinkertons; or Spies, Sleuths, Mercenaries and Thugs: Being a Story of the Nation's Most Famous (and Infamous) Detective Agency.*

Wyatt Outlaw (c. 1820–1870) was born into slavery in Virginia. His career in law enforcement was brief, tragic, and symptomatic of the time in which he lived, the Reconstruction era of the post-Civil War South. Outlaw escaped slavery around 1864 and joined the Union Army, with the 2nd United States Colored Infantry Regiment. He was discharged in 1866 and settled in Alamance County (Graham), North Carolina, to work as a carpenter.

As happened in many cities throughout the South after the Civil War, Outlaw, now a free Black man and affiliate of the new Republican Party, assumed a measure of political prominence. His efforts to bring churches and schools to the Black community in Alamance County caught the attention of North Carolina Governor William Holden. Holden appointed Outlaw to the Graham Town Council and later to constable.

Graham's White citizenry, especially those associated with one of the recently formed branches of the loosely confederated Ku Klux Klan, could not stand the thought of being policed by an armed Black man. One night, when a group of suspected "Ku Kluxers" were riding through Graham terrorizing the African American community, Outlaw and a group of other African American men confronted them. No one was killed or injured, but the Ku Kluxers vowed to kill Outlaw. On the night of February 26, 1870, dozens of Ku Kluxers raided Outlaw's home, dragged him down the street to the town square, lynched him, and left his hanging body for the townspeople to see the next day. It was a typical Ku Klux operation; operate in the dark but leave a warning for all to see in the daylight. No one was convicted of Outlaw's murder. His death was indicative of the terror inflicted on many African American communities in the post-Civil War era.

Little is known about the life of Wyatt Outlaw, but for more information, see the following:

- Carolina Public Humanities (2021). 'A Reign of Terror' in North Carolina: Wyatt Outlaw, the Kirk-Holden War, & the KKK Hearings." https://youtu.be/JZnCufHth4E.
- Jones, M. (2025). *A History of the United States through High-Profile Assassinations.*
- Keoni Productions (2024). "Crime Chronicles with Mark Jones: Wyatt Outlaw." https://www.youtube.com/watch?v=g7l_c0XuW-Q&list=PLAtLcyBx8fGTPcSV_W4JiD2uwc8AJDQnQ&index=22&t=343s

Alexander Williams (1839–1917) was born in Nova Scotia. Alexander "Clubber" Williams was one of the most famous and controversial police officers of the 19th century. He joined the New York City Police Department in 1866, and within 6 years he was promoted to captain. He first gained notice for breaking up a group of criminals known as the "Gashouse Gang" who ruthlessly ran the Gashouse District of Manhattan. Williams's methods were simple and unsophisticated; he formed a squad that beat criminals unmercifully, sometimes without provocation.

Williams wrote an account of his exploits for the New York *Evening World* that attracted wide readership. Williams was said to have gotten in at least one fight a day. While much of New York City feared and loathed Williams, the media of the day was not sympathetic to the criminals, the homeless and the labor

IMG II.2

agitators of the 19th century—in contrast to the modern media.

In 1876, Williams was transferred to the 29th precinct, an area near Broadway full of gambling houses, saloons, and brothels. Asked his impression of the district, Williams spoke of his intentions to reap the financial benefits of working that area: "I have had chuck for a long time, and now I'm going to eat tenderloin." This resulted in the area being known as the Tenderloin District.

Williams's brutal attacks and corrupt activities, which made him a wealthy man, occasionally precipitated legal action, but he usually had enough political allies to shield him from serious criminal prosecution. One of the most famous quotes in the history of policing came from Williams when he said, "There is more law in the end of a policeman's nightstick than in a decision of the Supreme Court." He was finally forced out of the NYPD in 1895 by newly appointed police commissioner and future US President Theodore Roosevelt. But he left with a healthy pension and considerable wealth.

You can learn more about Alexander Williams here:

- https://policingnewyork.wordpress.com/2015/07/10/alexander-clubber-williams/
- Axelrod, A., C. Phillips & K. Kemper (1996). *Cops, Crooks and Criminologists: An International Biographical Dictionary of Law Enforcement.*
- Oiler, J. (2021). *Rogue's Gallery: The Birth of Modern Policing and Organized Crime in Gilded Age New York.*
- Richardson, J.F. (1970). *The New York Police: Colonial Times to 1900.*

Thomas Byrnes (1842–1910) was born in Ireland and joined the New York City Police Department, which was heavily populated with Irish immigrants, in 1863. He first gained notice for saving the life of a fellow officer in the infamous 1863 New York City draft riots. For Byrnes, who did much to build the Department's detective bureaus, his big break came when he was assigned to protect the Wall Street area of lower Manhattan. Byrnes was effective at catching criminals who victimized wealthy Wall Street regulars, and he had an incentive to do so. Wealthy investors rewarded him with stock tips or cash; Thomas Byrnes became very wealthy.

Byrnes is remembered for creating the "rogue's gallery" in a book called *Professional Criminals in America*, with pictures and crude descriptions of known criminals in New York City. He coined the term "the third degree" as a description for physically coercing confessions from suspects. In the 1890s, a commission chaired by New York State Senator Clarence Lexow issued a report showing that the NYPD was rife with corruption, bribery, kickbacks, and promotions based on favoritism. The Lexow Committee singled out Byrnes and the detective bureau for criticism. NYPD Commissioner and future President Theodore Roosevelt, who had no use for Byrnes, forced him out. Byrnes never worked in law enforcement again, but he lived well from his Wall Street earnings.

IMG II.3

For more about Thomas Byrnes, see below.

- Byrnes, T. (2000). *1886 Professional Criminals of America: Thomas Byrnes Police Inspector and Chief of Detectives 1880–1895.*
- Byrnes, T. (1974, original publication date, 1886). *Rascals and Rogues of Long Ago.*
- Conway, J.N. (2011). *Big Policeman: The Rise and Fall of Thomas Byrnes, America's First, Most Ruthless, and Greatest Detective.*
- Richardson, J.F. (1970). *The New York Police: Colonial Times to 1900.*

Wyatt Earp (1848–1929) embodies the blurred lines of myth and reality in the American West. Born in Illinois, he was a small-town frontier marshal who helped shape popular perceptions of western law enforcement. Contrary to some popular presentations, Wyatt Earp was hardly a saint. He operated on the fringes of the law and outwardly broke the law as often as he enforced it.

IMG II.4

The fourth of six sons, Wyatt Earp began his law enforcement in the 1870s, working in Missouri, Wichita and Dodge City, Kansas, and Texas before heading to Tombstone, Arizona, to join his brothers in silver mining ventures. The brothers also worked in the gambling, saloon, and brothel businesses. While in Tombstone, he and his brothers Virgil, and Morgan, who all worked as marshals for the town, along with a friend of Wyatt's named John Henry "Doc" Holliday, became embroiled in a feud with a group of "cowboys," a euphemism for cattle thieves. Ike Clanton led the cowboys. The feud was partly personal, partly political, and partly legal. It culminated in the most well-known gunfight in American history. The gunfight at the O.K. Corral took place on October 26, 1881, and resulted in the deaths of three cowboys. Far from settling the feud, the gunfight only inflamed it, and other murders on both sides occurred later.

Wyatt Earp spent the next several decades dabbling in business ventures in several states and the Alaska territory before settling in Southern California as the film industry was in its genesis. Then he often served as a technical advisor for western films, counting among his friends early silent picture cowboy stars such as William S. Hart and Tom Mix. John Wayne, the most famous cowboy actor in the film industry, was acquainted with Earp and based his cowboy persona on Earp. Wyatt Earp has been the subject of countless films and books, most almost totally fictional. The most realistic western films in recent decades were *Tombstone* with Kurt Russell and *Wyatt Earp* with Kevin Costner.

For more on Wyatt Earp, see below:

- Barra, A. (1998). "Who Was Wyatt Earp?" *American Heritage* 49 (6): 76–85.
- Boessenecker, J. (2023). *Ride the Devil's Herd: Wyatt Earp's Epic Battle Against the West's Biggest Outlaw Gang.*
- Isenberg, A.C. (2024). *Wyatt Earp: A Vigilante Life.*
- Lake, S.N. (1994, original publication date 1927). *Wyatt Earp: Frontier Marshal.*
- Tefertiller, C. (1997). *Wyatt Earp: The Life Behind the Legend.*

Charles Bonaparte (1851–1921), born in Baltimore, was the grandnephew of French Emperor Napoleon Bonaparte. Charles was a Harvard-educated lawyer with a keen interest in civil service reform. One of his Harvard friends was future President Theodore Roosevelt. After Roosevelt assumed the presidency, Bonaparte worked under his old friend in several positions before being confirmed by the Senate as Attorney General in 1906.

IMG II.5

At the turn of the 20th century, the thought of a national police force conjured images of a secret police, an idea abhorrent to America's founders during the 1780s and still held in disfavor in the early 20th century. Consequently, President Roosevelt's attempt to create a national police investigative force, the Bureau of Investigation, was denied by Congress. On July 1, 1908, while Congress was in recess, Bonaparte secretly established the Bureau with the approval of President Roosevelt and without Congress's knowledge. Congress was outraged and many pointed out the irony of Bonaparte's relationship to Napoleon, whose national police in France was the reason there was so much opposition to a similar agency in the United States. Nevertheless, the Roosevelt Administration and Attorney General Bonaparte forged ahead with the Bureau that would later be known as the Federal Bureau of Investigation.

Bonaparte, a fervent advocate of civil service reform, had become associated with the very sort of back-door dealing he claimed to despise. Most of the first Bureau agents were the sort of political hacks that Bonaparte said should not be a part of the federal government. Bonaparte returned to his law practice in March 1909 when President Roosevelt left office.

For more on Charles Bonaparte, see below.

- Axelrod, A., C. Phillips & K. Kemper (1996). *Cops, Crooks and Criminologists: An International Biographical Dictionary of Law Enforcement.*
- Bishop, J.B. (1922). *Charles Joseph Bonaparte: His Life and Public Services.*
- Civil Service Auxiliary of Maryland (1921). *Charles Joseph Bonaparte, 1851–1921: An Appreciation.*
- Lowenthal, M. (1950). *The Federal Bureau of Investigation.*
- Shafer, R.G. (2022). "The Architect of the FBI was Napoleon's Great-Nephew, Charles Bonaparte." *Washington Post* August 16.

IMG 11.6

William Burns (1858–1932) was one of the most famous private detectives of his era. Born in Baltimore and raised in Ohio, Burns was a theater devotee in school and employed his acting skills to work cases, often posing as someone else doing undercover work. Once he took a job as an insurance agent to investigate a fraud case. Burns worked for the Secret Service in the 1880s, primarily investigating counterfeiting cases, but also working cases where local law enforcement could not be trusted or lacked adequate resources.

Burns enjoyed going after the wealthy and well connected, working for the Department of the Interior and investigating the Mayor of San Francisco. The most important case in Burns's career was the 1910 bombing of the *Los Angeles Times*, which killed 21 people. Burns succeeded in finding the culprits, radical labor agitators. Burns served as director of the Bureau of Investigation in the 1920s and was involved in investigating the crimes dramatized in the film *Killers of the Flower Moon* before he was forced out for corrupt activities committed under his watch.

For more about William Burns, see below:

- Caesar, G. (1968). *Incredible Detective: The Biography of William J. Burns.*
- Hunt, W.R. (1990). *Front-Page Detective: William J. Burns and the Detective Profession.*

IMG II.7

Georgia Ann Robinson (1879–1961) was born in Louisiana and raised by her sister and by nuns in a convent. Georgia Ann Hill lived in Kansas and married Morgan Robinson before moving to Colorado and finally to Los Angeles, where she started performing volunteer work for the Los Angeles Police Department in 1916, a move prompted by her concern for the plight of women and children in the rapidly growing city. In 1919, Georgia Robinson began her job as a jail matron, becoming the first African American female police officer in LAPD history. Some claim that she was the first African American female officer in the United States, but that is uncertain.

Like most female policing pioneers, Robinson did not perform the same tasks as her male counterparts, but she moved from working strictly as a jail matron to assisting with cases involving women and juveniles. In some cases, she referred females accused of minor crimes to social service agencies or brought them to her home, rather than making an arrest. Recognizing the need for safe housing for women who were either victims of domestic violence or released prisoners that had nowhere to go, Georgia Robinson oversaw the establishment of a home for homeless women, the Sojourner Truth home, named after the African American abolitionist preacher of the 19th century.

Robinson's law enforcement career ended in 1928 when she was trying to break up a fight between two drunken female inmates. One of the inmates repeatedly bashed Robinson's head against the cell bars, rendering Georgia Robinson completely blind. She retired on disability. Though she could no longer actively serve as an officer, Georgia Robinson continued to work on behalf of the African American community in Los Angeles, being active in desegregation efforts in schools and other public facilities and working with the local NAACP branch. In a 1954 *Ebony* magazine interview, "Robbie" as she was called, said, "I have no regrets. I didn't need my eyes any longer. I had seen all there was to see." (Bryan, E. [2016, March 19]). Georgia Ann Hill Robinson (1879–1961). *Black Past*, https://www.blackpast.org/african-american-history/robinson-georgia-ann-hill-1879-1961/).

For more on Georgia Ann Robinson, see below:

- African-American History is American History, "Georgia Ann Robinson: The First Black Female Police Officer in America." https://www.youtube.com/watch?v=_4o_nZJODsY, retrieved January 29, 2025.
- Halverstadt, A. (2022). "The First African-American Woman Police Officer." https://www.barclaycollege.edu/news/first-african-american-woman-police-officer/, retrieved January 29, 2025.
- National Law Enforcement Officers Memorial Fund, https://nleomf.org/georgia-ann-robinson/, retrieved January 29, 2025.

IMG II.8

Harry Anslinger (1892–1975) was born in Pennsylvania and served as director of the Federal Bureau of Narcotics from 1930–1962. He was the first federal law enforcer to make social pariahs of narcotics users, and one of the first to paint drugs as a threat to America's existence. Anslinger's draconian attitude toward drug use, especially marijuana, and his successful misinformation campaigns about the effects of drugs reflected the uninformed sentiments of the American public and set the pace for American drug policy for his lifetime and beyond. He overtly believed that drug use was a factor in miscegenation, i.e., interracial sexual relationships, and vehemently asserted that drug use, especially marijuana, was the province of African American men who wanted to seduce White women.

While Anslinger was not the only American whose perceptions of marijuana were based largely on ignorance, he was instrumental in creating the phobias about marijuana that existed for many decades. He claimed that his directorship of the FBN caused a decline in addiction but offered no supporting evidence. He never expressed sympathy for addicts and believed that punishment—not medical treatment—was the answer to addiction. Anslinger's attitudes toward marijuana gradually fell from favor, and his place in history is largely viewed negatively even by proponents of punitive drug laws.

For more on Harry Anslinger, see below.

- Adams, C. (2016). "The Man Behind the Marijuana Ban for All the Wrong Reasons." https://www.cbsnews.com/news/harry-anslinger-the-man-behind-the-marijuana-ban/, retrieved January 28, 2025.
- DEA Museum (n.d.). "A Life of Service: Harry Jacob Anslinger." https://museum.dea.gov/exhibits/online-exhibits/anslinger, retrieved January 29, 2025.
- McWilliams, J. C. (1990). *The Protectors: Harry J. Anslinger and the Federal Bureau of Narcotics, 1930–1962.*

IMG II.9

Eliot Ness (1903–1957), born in Chicago, is remembered for his work with the U.S. Treasury Department against gangsters during Prohibition, especially Al Capone. In film and on television in *The Untouchables*, the fictional Eliot Ness has been portrayed as an almost mythical figure, but the story of Eliot Ness is one of two lives: an idealistic, crime fighting crusader and a middle-aged playboy and problem drinker whose lifestyle brought an early death.

Ness started working as a "T-man" in 1926. Although he was ambivalent about the wisdom of Prohibition, he believed in the rule of law and thought it was the enforcers' job to enforce it. Ness relentlessly pursued Al Capone and his criminal empire, but Capone was ultimately done in by the Internal Revenue Service because of a Supreme Court decision that allowed prosecution for failure to declare income generated from illegal activities. Ness's exploits have been exaggerated and fabricated. Capone was not nearly as obsessed with Ness as Ness was with Capone. Contrary to what is portrayed in the film *The Untouchables*, Ness never shot anyone, did not push Frank Nitti from a rooftop, never had a daughter, and only fired his weapon once—at a lock.

After Prohibition, Ness assumed the duty of public safety director in Cleveland. Ness weeded out some corruption in the Cleveland Police Department, but a series of events led to his downfall. Ness became a fixture at Cleveland nightclubs and bars with a proclivity for chasing women. He resigned in 1942 after being involved in a hit-and-run accident.

Ness never rebounded, and his financial fortunes nosedived. In desperation, he collaborated in 1957 with Oscar Fraley on a book titled *The Untouchables*, which embellished and fabricated his Prohibition exploits and was adapted for a television series with Robert Stack portraying a fictional Eliot Ness. Ness received payment for his participation in the book, but he died before his name became famous in television and film folklore.

For more on Eliot Ness, see below.

- Bureau of Alcohol, Tobacco, Firearms and Explosives (2024). "Eliot Ness." https://www.atf.gov/our-history/eliot-ness, retrieved January 18, 2025.
- Heimel, P. (2000). *Eliot Ness: The Real Story*, 2nd ed.
- McFarland, R. (2012). "Eliot Ness and His Role in Cleveland History." https://www.clevelandpolicemuseum.org/collections/eliot-ness/, retrieved January 13, 2025.
- Ness, E. and O. Fraley (1957). *The Untouchables*.

Josephine Serrano Collier (1922–2014), a Los Angeles native, was the first female Mexican American officer in the Los Angeles Police Department. Josephine Serrano grew up in Los Angeles during a time when some stores and restaurants would hang a sign on the door saying "sorry, no Mexicans." Josephine Serrano lived in the Hispanic enclave of East Los Angeles and witnessed the bad interactions between residents and city police officers.

IMG 11.10

Like millions of American women who had not worked outside the home prior to World War II, Josephine Serrano did her part to aid the war effort by working for the Lockheed Corporation to produce P-38 Lightning fighter aircrafts. The factory jobs were returned to men after the war ended in 1945, and she had to give up her job.

As the LAPD force was still decimated by the departures and deaths of so many young men, it put out ads recruiting female officers. Of the 200 applicants, Josephine Serrano was one of nine women who were hired, and the only Hispanic woman. She joined the force on October 1, 1946, at the age of 24. The department did not award her a graduation ceremony, a uniform, or a gun. Policing was a male-dominated profession, and many Angelenos were not welcoming toward Mexican Americans, including many officers in the police department. Her traditionalist family opposed her employment; she came from a culture where women were expected to be subservient, and where police were not trusted. Nevertheless, she worked several assignments, including foot patrol, vice, and the Lincoln Height Jail. Josephine's daughter Suzanne Collier says that her mother had a knack of rooting for the underdog and that she was interested in improving the lives of the Mexican American community in Los Angeles.

While working with the LAPD, she married Darwin Collier, a fellow officer. Josephine Serrano Collier retired on October 24, 1960, after suffering a back injury. She and her husband moved to Idaho and then to Arizona. Josephine Serrano Collier passed away in Tucson at age 91.

The following sources provide more information about Josephine Serrano Collier and her work:

- Meraji, M. S. (2014, March 19). *LAPD pays tribute to Josephine Serrano Collier, a Latina pioneer* [Podcast]. NPR. https://www.npr.org/2014/03/19/291475068/lapd-pays-tribute-to-josephine-serrano-a-police-pioneer-for-latinas
- KCAL News. (2014, March 18). *First Latina woman to join LAPD dies at 91.* CBS. https://www.cbsnews.com/losangeles/news/first-hispanic-woman-to-join-lapd-died-at-91/

IMG II.11

Daryl Gates (1926–2010) was born and raised in California and served on the Los Angeles police force from 1949–1992 and as chief from 1979–1992. Gates was toasted by American presidents, lauded by many of his colleagues throughout the United States and around the world, but berated by many politicians and civil rights leaders. He developed programs and law enforcement innovations that are common to many police departments today. He developed SWAT and believed in a strict no-nonsense approach to police work and crime control. Gates should also be remembered for developing DARE (Drug Abuse Resistance Education), partly in reaction to his son Scott having been severely drug addicted.

Before the early 1990s, Gates had been criticized by civil rights activists and ethnic minorities in Los Angeles. The event that sealed his departure occurred on March 4, 1991, when a bystander with a camcorder captured the beating of Rodney King at the hands of LAPD officers. A series of savage deadly riots ensued after the officers were acquitted of most of the charges, but they would be convicted in federal court of violating King's civil rights. A commission chaired by future Secretary of State Warren Christopher laid the blame for the LAPD's problems squarely at Gates's feet. Gates resigned in 1992, never to work in law enforcement again.

For more on Daryl Gates, see below:

- Gates, D.F and D.K. Shah (1993). *Chief: My Life in the LAPD.*
- Woo, E. and E. Malnic (2014). "Daryl F. Gates Dies at 83; Innovative But Controversial Chief of the LAPD". https://www.latimes.com/local/obituaries/la-me-daryl-gates17-2010apr17-story.html, retrieved January 30, 2025.

Credits

IMG II.1: Source: https://commons.wikimedia.org/wiki/File:Allan_Pinkerton-retouch.jpg.

IMG II.2: The New York Times, https://commons.wikimedia.org/wiki/File:Alexander_S._Williams_-_NYT.png, 1895.

IMG II.3: Thomas F. Byrnes, https://commons.wikimedia.org/wiki/File:Thomas_F._Byrnes.jpg, 1886.

IMG II.4: Source: https://commons.wikimedia.org/wiki/File:Wyatt_Earp_portrait.png.

IMG II.5: J.E. Purdy, https://commons.wikimedia.org/wiki/File:CJBonaparte.jpg, 1903.

IMG II.6: Source: https://commons.wikimedia.org/wiki/File:William_J._Burns.jpg.

IMG II.7: Source: https://commons.wikimedia.org/wiki/File:Georgia_Ann_Robinson.jpg.

IMG II.8: Source: https://commons.wikimedia.org/wiki/File:Harry_Jacob_Anslinger_portrait_1930.tif.

IMG II.9: US Department of the Treasury, https://commons.wikimedia.org/wiki/File:Eliotness.jpg, 1933.

IMG II.10: Los Angeles Police Department, https://hapcoa.org/advisory-death-of-lapds-first-latina-policewoman/.

IMG II.11: Los Angeles Police Department, https://commons.wikimedia.org/wiki/File:DarylGatescolorportrait.jpg.

CHAPTER 5

Bass Reeves (1838–1910)

IMG 5.1

The western law officer is part of American folklore, the stuff of myth and legend. Some fictional law officers are so symbolic of American culture that the public practically sees them as real people. Examples include Matt Dillon of television's *Gunsmoke*, Gary Cooper's Will Kane character in the 1952 film *High Noon*, and one of many characters portrayed by John Wayne, a theatrical symbol of what many believe to be the ideal American man. Some of the real-life law officers from the Wild West have become part of American folklore as well, often blurring the lines between myth and fact. Some have become bigger in death than they were in life. Examples include the Earp brothers, especially Wyatt.

In movies, TV shows, and books about law enforcement in the early American West, the characters are almost exclusively White. As with much of American history, African Americans, with a few exceptions, have been omitted or marginalized from such examination, at least until recently. Bass Reeves was an African American Deputy U.S. Marshal whose life and career have received significant recognition in popular culture in the form of a 2023 Paramount television series and a 2010 motion picture, along with some books and many articles. While some of what is written about Reeves may be exaggerated or fictional, if only half of what has been written about him is true, he provides an interesting case study and a window into the challenges of law enforcement on the American western frontier. He also serves as an example of the blurring of lines between law officers and lawbreakers. During his lifetime, he was alternately praised as a hero and vilified as a thief and a murderer.

Early Life

As with many African Americans of the 19th century, especially those born into slavery, little is known about Bass Reeves's early life. He is believed to have been born in 1838 in Van Buren, Arkansas, to owner Army colonel William Reeves, who was probably stationed at nearby Fort Smith. Like many slaves, Bass Reeves assumed his owner's last name. Bass Reeves was raised primarily in Grayson County, Texas, which adjoins the Oklahoma state line.

The American Civil War began in 1861, when Bass Reeves was 23 years old and still living in slavery. Bass Reeves's part in the Civil War remains in dispute. By one account he served with the Union Army with the Indian Home Guard Regiments. Another claim, reportedly from Bass Reeves himself, was that he served in the Confederate Army under the command of William Reeves's son, Colonel George Reeves, and that he fought in several major battles. Other sources state that Bass Reeves escaped slavery after a dispute in a card game and fled to Oklahoma, a U.S. territory where he could be safe from recapture, and lived in Native American territories, especially Cherokee, Creek, Choctaw, Chickasaw and Seminole areas, learning the languages and culture during this time.

In 1864, Bass Reeves married his first wife, Nellie. Bass Reeves would father 11 children. After the Civil War ended in 1865, Bass, by this time about 27 years old, returned to Van Buren, Arkansas, and began farming. Owing to his experience in the Indian Territories, Reeves, who said he knew the Indian Territories "like a cook knows her kitchen" (Burton, n.d., para. 1) was sometimes hired as a scout and tracker for U.S. Marshals based in Arkansas, jobs which brought substantial monetary rewards.

Deputy U.S. Marshal

Bass's skill as a tracker and scout, essential ingredients for a law enforcer in the West at that time, earned him notice. Like many enslaved people, Bass never learned to read or write, but despite being illiterate, Reeves managed to navigate the considerable paperwork that came with his job. Sometimes he would ask someone he trusted to read a document for him, and he always found a way to interpret a written document accurately. One judge said, "He had a faculty of telling what warrants to serve on any one and never made a mistake. When his superior officers asked him to produce (a warrant or writ) the old man would run through them and never fail to pick out the one desired" (Burton, 2006, p. 297).

Reeves's other attributes, his intelligence, poise, imposing physical presence—standing 6′2″ and weighing 180–200 pounds—and ability as a crack shot, brought him to the attention of Marshal James Fagan and Federal District Judge Isaac Parker in Western Arkansas. Despite his imposing presence, Reeves was described as nonconfrontational in his manner, whether he was dealing with the poorest of the poor or the richest of the rich—unless a situation demanded the opposite. It was said of Reeves that he "never quailed in facing any man" (Burton, 2006, p. 297).

In 1875, Isaac Parker, nicknamed the "hanging judge," (National Park Service, n.d., para. 40) appointed Bass Reeves Deputy U.S. Marshal for the Western District of Arkansas. It was a jurisdiction that encompassed 75,000 miles, mostly in the Oklahoma Territory, and which sometimes required journeys up to 800 miles. Since Oklahoma was not a state at the time, there was no state law enforcement or judicial apparatus, and since Native American tribal courts had limited jurisdictional authority, most matters of justice were left to the federal government. The wide open, almost lawless Oklahoma Territory invited the worst of the worst of all racial groups to exploit conditions there.

Usually when a deputy journeyed to track an outlaw, he took a wagon, a cook, and a posse man. But Bass often worked alone. Unlike law enforcement officers today who work strictly on salary, Bass was paid fees for his work. He was handsomely rewarded for long journeys that sometimes lasted several months, but the fee was forfeited if the tracker or deputy killed the suspect. The accused had to be returned alive, and the deputy was responsible for burying the deceased if no family could be located. Judge Isaac Parker demanded that any deputy who killed a suspect be tried for murder, the 19th century version of an internal affairs investigation. But Reeves, who reportedly killed 14 men, always successfully claimed self-defense.

Bass enforced many laws, bootlegging among the most common. He arrested suspects of all races—White, Native American, African American, and multiracial (as interracial marriages were common in Indian Territories)—something that African American law enforcers in America's eastern and southern cities dared not do. Bass was probably not the first African American to serve as deputy marshal west of the Mississippi, but he is the best remembered due to his longevity and performance. Over the next 32 years, Reeves made more than 3,000 arrests and killed 14 men. One of Reeves's most famous arrestees was legendary female outlaw Belle Starr, who turned herself in before Reeves had to track her down. Reeves was the only deputy appointed by Judge Parker who would remain with the marshals until Oklahoma achieved statehood in 1907.

Bass Reeves was remembered as much for his cunning as for his skills with his fists and guns. Disguise and role-playing were Reeves's trademarks. In one case, Bass walked nearly 30 miles disguised as an outlaw beggar on the run. When he came to the home of the two brothers he was seeking, the men and their mother invited Bass to stay the night. Bass stayed overnight and handcuffed the two brothers while they were sleeping. He then escorted them on foot for the 30-mile journey to his camp and on to jail.

Bass Reeves: Murder Suspect

Although Bass Reeves lived long enough to see himself become a legend in his own time, he was not universally admired. Some accounts paint a negative picture of him. This did not distinguish him from most lawmen on the frontier, many of whom, like the Earp Brothers, were on the opposite side of the law as often as they enforced it. Bass was rumored at one point to be involved with a Texas cattle rustling ring, but he was never formally accused. He did not engage in some of the borderline illegal activities such as brothel ownership and gambling that some of his law enforcement counterparts did. However, Bass Reeves faced the greatest challenge of his career with a murder charge in the 1880s.

In April 1884, in the Chickasaw area of Oklahoma, Bass Reeves shot and killed his African American posse man and cook, William Leech. That much is clear, but other details about the incident were disputed. Most of the people in Reeves's company said or thought little of the event, believing it to be an accident, and Reeves continued working as a deputy for several months. He was involved in three more shooting deaths before the Leech case came under formal investigation in 1886.

Reeves's good reputation in some quarters notwithstanding, he received hostile treatment in specific press releases. To some, Reeves was a cold-blooded killer who mistreated his charges and simply worked as a mercenary. In addition to being implicated in cattle rustling, it was said that he would allow a prisoner to escape if more money could be made that way than by holding him. An 1886 New Orleans newspaper article, which contained some inaccuracies, read:

> Bass Reeves, a former Deputy United States Marshal (he was suspended pending outcome of his case), was arrested last night for murder, and put in the United States jail here, where he has been instrumental in placing so many men. In April 1884, while out on a trip through the Indian territory arresting criminals, Reeves, who is a Negro, had another Negro, a man named Wm. Leech, cooking for him and his prisoners. One night, Leech's dog put his nose into a skillet, and was cruelly beaten by Reeves. Leech remonstrated with him when Reeves drew his pistol and shot him dead. He then reported the killing to the marshal's office as having been done in self-defense while attempting Leech's arrest for some crime with which he was charged. The only eyewitness to this killing was sent to the Detroit House of Correction for assault with intent to kill, and Reeves felt safe. But others had heard of the case, and as Reeves was hated bitterly wherever he had been, the case was brought up for investigation, with the above result. Steps are now being taken to secure the pardon of the prisoner who saw the murder committed,

> in order that he can testify against Reeves, who will get but little sympathy, for he has been a cruel and brutal man to his prisoners, and was put off the marshal's force several times, but always managed to get back. (Bass Reeves Arrested for Murder, 1886)

Contrary to the account given in this article, Leech was not an accused criminal and Reeves never suggested that he killed Leech in self-defense or while trying to make an arrest.

Bass Reeves was indicted for his murder in 1886, 2 years after Leech's death. He was tried in October 1887. Reeves maintained that Leech's killing was accidental, due to a malfunction with his weapon, and that he tried to no avail to render first aid to Leech. Reeves employed two of the best attorneys in the area, who noted among other factors that given Reeves's expertise with firearms, had Reeves intended to kill Leech, he would have shot him so that he died instantly, rather than inflict a wound that would not kill him until the next day. Reeves claimed that the argument over the dog was in jest, and that Reeves intended to kill the stray dog but accidentally shot Leech instead. Most of the witnesses against Reeves were people he had arrested and may have had an ax to grind. In the end, Bass Reeves was acquitted and returned to duty.

The Arrest of Benjamin Reeves

One of the most difficult tasks of Bass Reeves's career came in 1902 and concerned his son, Benjamin, or Bennie, who was well known in his community and had a good reputation as a hard-working porter. He was not a habitual lawbreaker nor a violent man, with one press account condescendingly referring to him as "a quiet, orderly negro" (Burton, 2006, p. 146). One day, Bennie came home to find his wife with another man. According to one account, Bennie reacted by trying harder to reclaim his wife's affections, only to catch his wife with another man sometime later. Bennie Reeves shot his wife to death.

Press accounts of the shooting were varied, with some sympathizing with a loyal husband who had caught his wife in adultery, and others, invoking racial overtones by referring to Benny as a "jealous Moor" (Burton, 2006, p. 146) ala William Shakespeare's *Othello*, claimed that Benny killed his wife in a calm, cool manner. According to Bennie, he once asked his wife if she were engaged in an improper relationship with a man named John Wadly, to which she responded that she "thought more of his little finger than she did of (Bennie's) whole body" (Burton, 2006, p. 146).

Bennie Reeves fled Muscogee, leaving the Marshal's service the chore of tracking him down. Bass Reeves's colleagues offered to assign the chore to someone else, but Bass claimed that duty trumped familial loyalty and insisted that he be the one to arrest his son and bring him to stand trial in Muscogee. On January 22, 1903, 21-year-old Bennie Reeves was convicted, found guilty, and sentenced to life in prison at Fort Leavenworth, Kansas. After serving 11 years at Leavenworth, Bennie Reeves's sentence was commuted by the Department of Justice, and he was released.

Retirement and Death

Bass's first wife Nellie died in 1896. He remarried in 1900 to Winnie Sumter. They remained married until Bass's death. As his career continued, Reeves was written about extensively in the press, especially in Oklahoma. At a time when many African Americans were demonized in popular culture and the news media, and when lynchings were at their height, Bass Reeves became a legend in the western territories, thanks in part to the fact that he lived long enough to have a long career as a marshal, a profession that many did not survive. Outlaws thought little about killing a deputy marshal. More than 120 of his fellow deputies were killed in the Oklahoma territory during Reeves's tenure. He escaped several assassination attempts and dozens of gunfights.

Bass Reeves resigned as deputy marshal in 1907 when Oklahoma attained statehood. Oklahoma's statehood status negated the need for federal law enforcement; law enforcement duties were assigned to local police and sheriff's departments rather than federal agents in neighboring states. But Reeves continued working in law enforcement, taking a job as police officer in Muskogee, Oklahoma. He worked until 1909, when failing health forced his retirement. Bass Reeves died from complications from Bright's Disease on January 10, 1910, at the age of 72.

Bass Reeves's Legacy

Upon Reeves's death, the *Muskogee Phoenix* wrote, "In the history of the early days of Eastern Oklahoma the name of Bass Reeves has a place in the front rank among those who cleansed out the old Indian Territory of outlaws and desperadoes" (Burton, n.d., para. 5). A 1990 article captured the mixed legacy of Bass Reeves, saying, "Was Reeves a cold-blooded killer who took advantage of his badge or was he a gifted frontiersman whose natural instincts enabled him to survive many daring challenges?" (Williams, 1990, p. 155). During his lifetime and ever since his death, Bass Reeves has been praised as one of the greatest heroes in the history of law enforcement and criticized as just another corrupt western law enforcer who abused his authority. Was some of the criticism directed at Reeves, especially in southern newspapers, based on race, resentment against a Black man who was empowered to arrest Whites? Such an assertion is not outrageous given the exceptional status occupied by Reeves at a time when Black Americans were relegated to second-class citizenship.

In recent decades, a claim has emerged that Reeves was the inspiration for a famous fictional law enforcer, the Lone Ranger. The impetus behind the Lone Ranger idea came in 2006, when Arthur Burton published a definitive biography of Reeves titled *Black Gun, Silver Star: The Life and Legend of Frontier Marshal Bass Reeves.* According to Burton, since many of the men that Reeves arrested were imprisoned at the Detroit House of Correction, and since the Lone Ranger made its radio debut on Detroit's WXYZ in January 1933, Burton reached the tenuous conclusion that the tales told by Detroit inmates about Reeves inspired the Lone Ranger idea. The results of a Google search indicate that the Lone Ranger–Reeves connection is not just a possibility but an incontrovertible fact. But in *Bass Reeves and The Lone Ranger: Debunking the Myth*, Martin Grams, Jr. emphatically asserts that the Bass Reeves–Lone Ranger tie makes a good story but is purely myth.

Like many real-life western figures, Bass Reeves's legacy is mixed. Like every other chapter subject in this book, Bass Reeves was human, not superhuman, no doubt with many flaws and strengths. At a minimum, his career is worth examination as a true pioneer in law enforcement, especially among African Americans in the 19th century.

Sources and Suggested Readings

Bass Reeves arrested for murder. (1886, January 22). Newspapers.com. *The Times-Democrat.* https://www.newspapers.com/article/the-times-democrat-bass-reeves-arrested/9798444/.

Brady, Paul L. (2005). *The black badge: Deputy United States Marshal Bass Reeves from slave to heroic lawman.* Milligan Books.

Burton, Art T. (n.d.). Reeves, Bass (1838–1910). *The encyclopedia of Oklahoma history and culture.* https://www.okhistory.org/publications/enc/entry?entry=RE020.

Burton, Arthur T. (2006). *Black gun, silver star: The life and legend of frontier marshal Bass Reeves.* University of Nebraska Press.

Encyclopaedia Britannica Editors. (June 25, 2024). Bass Reeves. *Encyclopaedia Britannica.* https://www.britannica.com/biography/Bass-Reeves.

Grams, Martin, Jr. (2018). *Bass Reeves and the lone ranger: Debunking the myth.* Create Space Independent Publishing.

Morgan, T. (2018, February 1). Was the real lone ranger a Black man? *History.* A & E Television Networks. https://www.history.com/news/bass-reeves-real-lone-ranger-a-black-man, accessed June 27, 2024.

National Park Service. (n.d.) *Judge Isaac C. Parker.* NPS.gov. https://www.nps.gov/fosm/learn/historyculture/judge-parker.htm, accessed August 2, 2024.

Paulsen, G. (2008). *The legend of Bass Reeves: Being the true and fictional account of the most valiant marshal in the West.* Laurel-Leaf Books.

Williams, Nudie E. (1990, Summer). *United States vs. Bass Reeves: Black lawman on trial.* The Gateway to Oklahoma History, Oklahoma Historical Society. https://gateway.okhistory.org/ark:/67531/metadc2031632/: accessed June 27, 2024.

Discussion Questions

1. What lessons can be learned from the personal life and professional career of Bass Reeves?
2. Is Bass Reeves's exalted place in American folklore justified or exaggerated? Explain.

Credit

IMG 5.1: Source: https://commons.wikimedia.org/wiki/File:BassReeves.jpg.

CHAPTER 6

Joseph Petrosino (1860–1909)

As legions of Southern Italian and Sicilian immigrants came to the United States in the late 19th and early 20th centuries, they faced many challenges, including poverty, urban squalor, and overt discrimination. The following was a popular quote among Italian immigrants circa 1900:

IMG 6.1

> Before I came to America, I thought the streets were paved in gold. When I came here, I learned three things: The streets were not paved in gold, the streets weren't paved, and that I was expected to pave them. (Roberts, 2007, para. 1)

Italians, most of whom were Roman Catholics, were despised by much of mainstream Protestant America, considered a criminal underclass, a dirty, alien race. They were equally disliked by the Irish who dominated New York City politics, or Tammany Hall, and its police department.

Italian immigrants also faced an internal menace: *La Mano Nera*, the Italian Black Hand, later associated with terms like "mafia" and "la cosa nostra," terrorized Italian Americans in American cities, including New York City. One New York City police detective dared to take on *La Mano Nera*—Joseph Petrosino, himself an Italian immigrant, battled this menace more effectively than anyone before him. He paid with his life, becoming the first New York City police officer to lose his life in the line of duty outside the United States.

Early Life

Giuseppe Michael Pasquale "Joseph" Petrosino was born in Padula, in the Salerno Province of Southern Italy, on August 30, 1860, the son of Prospero and Maria

Petrosino. Maria died during Giuseppe's childhood, which was marred by a bout with smallpox that scarred his face for life. Southern Italians and Sicilians, long looked down upon by their northern neighbors, immigrated to the United States in modest numbers in the 1870s, a decade before a tsunami of Italian immigrants came to American shores in the 1880s and 1890s. In the 1850s, New York City was home to just under 1,000 Italian immigrants. By 1910, the number had swelled to over 500,000.

Joseph Petrosino immigrated to New York City at age 13. Most southern Italian immigrants to New York City were tucked away in squalor in Manhattan's Lower East Side, isolated from other New Yorkers, with "Little Italy" residents unable to speak English and lacking formal education. Conditions were filthy; disease and crime were rife and struggling to survive was a full-time occupation. Italian schoolchildren were often picked on by their Irish counterparts, but one Italian boy fought back—Joseph Petrosino. If Irish children threw rocks at him, he would chase them down and pound their heads into the pavement. Always a strong, brawny lad, even with a 5′3″ frame, Joe Petrosino never hesitated to use his fists to settle differences, a proclivity that followed him into adulthood.

Joe Petrosino's first job was as a shoeshine boy. One day, in a fit of anger, he slammed his shoeshine equipment on the ground and vowed that he would never shine shoes again and that he was going to make something of himself. Petrosino got a job working for the city as a street sweeper. Even though the job consisted primarily of sweeping refuse left by thousands of horses that trod Manhattan streets, it was a lofty position with steady pay compared to those of many others in Little Italy.

Police Career

Joe Petrosino was a tireless worker, and he became a familiar face on the streets of Little Italy. One man who noticed him was Alexander Williams, the infamously corrupt inspector on the Irish-dominated New York City Police Department (NYPD). "Clubber" Williams, so nicknamed because of his propensity to use his nightstick, was not modest about his notoriety, saying that even the horses nodded to him when he passed. Williams thought Petrosino was excellent police material. There were two obstacles: First, due to the prejudice that "Tammany Hall" (NYPD) officers felt toward Little Italy, there were very few Italian police officers. Second, Petrosino stood 5′3″ and the minimum height requirement was 5′7″. Williams got him hired anyway. Joe Petrosino assumed his duties as a police officer in 1883, at age 23.

NYPD leadership thought Little Italy could best be policed by fellow Italians, as few other officers could speak or understand any of the Italian dialects, and many Little Italy residents spoke little or no English. Fiercely patriotic to his adopted homeland despite the discrimination he faced, Petrosino dove headlong into police work. Although lacking little formal education, especially in English, he had a photographic memory and was able to memorize the names and faces of practically anyone he met. He rose to the rank of lieutenant, the first Italian American to do so, but his deficiency with written English cost him an advancement to captain.

Petrosino had the advantage of being conversant in several Italian dialects. But he faced the daunting challenges of being snubbed by his fellow officers and hostility from fellow Italians. Manhattan's Mezzogiorno (southern Italian) population distrusted outsiders, an attitude they brought from Italy along with "omerta," a code of silence in the presence of outside authority. A person's loyalty was to family, kinsmen, and neighbors. Police represented the government that oppressed them. To many in Little Italy, Petrosino was a traitor and was not to be trusted, a perception that changed over time.

La Mano Nera

While most of the Italian immigrants to New York City simply wanted to make a better life for themselves, the boatloads of immigrants included a cadre of hardened criminals, many of whom were escaping criminal charges in Italy. The term "black hand" originated with European anarchists, but "*La Mano Nera*" became associated with a gang of loosely confederated or autonomous Italian immigrant criminals who preyed on other Italians by running protection rackets, extortion schemes, organized kidnapping rings, terrorists bombing operations, and brutal murders to control Little Italy and other Italian communities throughout the United States.

Joseph Petrosino despised *La Mano Nera* because it perpetuated the stereotype that southern Italians were a dirty, crude criminal class, and he despised them even more for preying on people who were afraid to report crimes to the police and had no one to turn to. *La Mano Nera* was more a method of operation than a formal organization. A typical Black Hand operation involved sending a threatening letter containing a skull and dagger to an Italian-run business, demanding "protection" money, and retaliating if they failed to pay by either vandalizing, burning, or blowing up their business or home. In some cases, a child of the business owner was kidnapped and held for ransom, with the child sometimes returned and in other cases murdered. In many such cases, if the perpetrators were prosecuted, the parents of the child would testify in court that the accused were innocent due to the fear that the *La Mano Nera* instilled in Little Italy and other American cities.

The story of John Bozzuffi illustrates several elements of a typical *La Mano Nera* operation. An Italian immigrant and self-made successful banker on Manhattan's Upper East Side, Bozzuffi was visited by two nearby business owners, fellow Italians, who, like Bozzuffi, had received threatening letters from *La Mano Nera*. The threats included having their dead bodies stuffed in a barrel, having their homes and businesses bombed, or having their children kidnapped. When approached by his fellow businessmen to withdraw their money from his bank, Bozzuffi urged them not to give in.

One day, Bozzuffi's 14-year-old son Antonio was kidnapped by *La Mano Nera* and was forced to handwrite a letter demanding $20,000 ($700,000 today) ransom. The extortionists realized that Bozzuffi had (illegal) access to other people's money stored in his bank. Rather than give in, Bozzuffi contacted Petrosino, even though he knew it might cost his son's life, and stated that he would not pay a cent for tribute. Word of the kidnapping quickly spread throughout the tight-knit Italian community, and a run on the bank ensued as depositors feared Bozzufi would pay the ransom with their money. Even though Bozzuffi placed a note on his bank door saying, "THE MONEY IN THIS BANK BELONG TO THE DEPOSITORS AND IT WILL BE PAID TO THEM IF I NEVER SEE MY SON AGAIN," (Mele, 2020, p. 49) his business was nearly ruined within days. Fortunately, Antonio Bozzuffi escaped his captors, and father and son were reunited. Word of Bozzuffi's stance against the Black Hand spread, and his business boomed as a result.

As is the case with "mafia" figures today, many Americans were simultaneously intrigued and repulsed by the Black Hand, even though there was nothing about them to admire. Black Hand memorabilia was a hot item. Those on the receiving end of Black Hand crimes were not amused.

One of the most notorious *La Mano Nera* extortion plots involved the most famous Italian entertainer of his day, opera singer Enrico Caruso. Caruso was a serial philanderer and had been accused of sexually assaulting women. In the early 20th century, such public allegations could be devastating. Caruso received a letter containing the signature dagger and skull in a black hand, demanding he pay $2,000 ($69,000 today). Whether the extortion was related to the sexual assault allegations is uncertain, but Caruso paid the $2,000 and shortly after received another demand for a much greater amount. While Caruso publicly called the extortionists "a set of cowards" and claimed all they would get from him was "cold steel and bullets" (Talty, 2017, p. 98), he was frightened and contacted Lt. Petrosino.

Petrosino laid a trap for the extortionists, setting up a meeting and posing as Caruso. Instead of receiving the hoped-for payment, the extortionists Antonio Misiano and Antonio Cincotto received a beating from Petrosino and were arrested.

The Mysterious Six

Most of the rank-and-file NYPD officers cared little about Little Italy, and even fewer of its officers, most of whom were Irish or German, were able to deal with crime there. Joe Petrosino knew that traditional reactive policing from officers who were disconnected from the community they served was not the answer. He knew that policing Little Italy required officers who cared about the community. With that in mind, Joe Petrosino approached Chief William McAdoo with the idea of creating an "Italian squad" of specialized officers to deal with Little Italy, especially the despised *La Mano Nera*. Although reluctant at first, McAdoo approved Petrosino's request, and a six-officer Italian squad was created.

The Italian squad, or the Mysterious Six, was not supported by much of the NYPD leadership or its rank-and-file officers, not even being given an office at first. But Petrosino forged ahead and trained his officers in the techniques needed to combat the Black Hand, namely, vigorous undercover work, constant harassment of Black Hand criminals, and an unflinching willingness to employ brute force, in a day when police use of force was not broadcast to the public. The *Washington Post* called them a "band of zealots" (Talty, 2017, p. 62).

Although his notoriety spread inside and outside police circles, even being interviewed by journalists was a rarity for police officers, Petrosino was also distrusted by many of his fellow Italians in Little Italy. Although many of them despised *La Mano Nera*, they hated the NYPD more. *La Mano Nera* operatives or sympathizers who recognized Petrosino on their street, which was sometimes difficult to do because Petrosino often disguised himself, would yell "fresh parsley for sale" (Talty, 2017, p. 11) parsley being the rough translation for "Petrosino" in some Italian dialects. But Petrosino was undaunted and effective. Arrests of Black Hand members skyrocketed, and crime in Little Italy plummeted under his watch. He set records for solving homicides, with 17 convictions in 1 year. But Petrosino was frustrated by the leniency shown in the courts.

As long as Black Hand crimes were confined to other Italians, many Americans were unconcerned. But when their reach extended beyond Italian communities, attitudes changed. When the daughter of a non-Italian family was kidnapped in New Jersey, the Secret Service assisted in the investigation, something rare at the time. President Theodore Roosevelt sent a personal letter to the family. When Charles Wesson, cofounder of the Smith & Wesson weapons empire, received a threatening letter at his Springfield, Massachusetts, home, the Secret Service investigated with Petrosino's assistance. Members of Congress also received threatening letters from the Black Hand.

In 1900, King Umberto I of Italy was murdered by Gaetano Bresci, an Italian immigrant anarchist from New Jersey who returned to Italy to carry out the assassination. Petrosino went to Bresci's hometown of Paterson, New Jersey to work as an undercover operative. There he discovered anarchist plots to assassinate President William McKinley. But American authorities were dismissive. McKinley was assassinated in 1901 in Buffalo, New York, but not by the Italian Black Hand or Italian anarchists, but instead by a lone wolf anarchist of eastern European ancestry from the Midwest named Leon Czolgosz.

The End of the Chase

In 1908, 1 year before his trip to Italy, Petrosino married a widow named Adelina Saulino. He did not wed her as early as he wished because, in keeping with Italian tradition, he requested her hand in marriage from her father, who refused to give his blessing. Adelina's father did not dislike Petrosino, but because of his dangerous line of work, he feared his daughter would be made a widow again, which was an unfortunate but accurate prediction. After her father died, the two wed and had a daughter, Adelina.

As fiercely as he tried to protect his family and himself from the Black Hand, Adelina's father's worries were justified. Although Petrosino would not publicly acknowledge them for fear that they might become Black Hand targets, Petrosino was fatalistic. He said publicly, "Someday, they will get me" (Talty, 2017, p. 144).

For years, Joe Petrosino did not believe that *La Mano Nera* was multinational in scope or had ties to southern Italy. Petrosino was eventually convinced otherwise. To attack the Black Hand, one needed to go to its source, Sicily. He departed the United States in February 1909. Petrosino's journey to Italy was endorsed by the NYPD and President Theodore Roosevelt, a New York City native and former NYPD Police Commissioner. King Victor Emmanuel III of Italy welcomed Petrosino and promised full cooperation. Petrosino wanted to gather information about alleged Black Hand associates in the United States and on Italian criminals to thwart any attempted entry into the United States

Thanks to assistance from Italian authorities, Petrosino's visit was a success. He gathered the names of hundreds of suspected mafiosi in Sicily, planning to provide their names to immigration authorities in the United States in case any tried to immigrate. He discovered that hundreds of Black Hand associates in the United States, including New York and New Jersey, were wanted for crimes in Italy. His plan was to return to New York, turn the names over to immigration authorities, and have them deported to Italy to face prosecution.

Petrosino's trip to Italy was supposed to be secret, but word reached the *New York Herald* that he was going. Foolishly, the *Herald* published the story, and Black Handers in the United States alerted their compatriots in Italy to Petrosino's arrival. While the Italian mafioso knew Petrosino was in the country, they did not know what he looked like. They were told that Petrosino often worked in disguise. In small Sicilian towns where strangers stood out, the mafiosi would yell Petrosino's name at people they did not recognize.

On March 12, 1909, at around 8:45 p.m. in the Piazza Marina in the Sicilian capital of Palermo, a group of mafiosi saw a stout, short Italian woman and yelled "Petrosino" (NoirCity, 2010, 3:01), prompting the woman who was Joe Petrosino in disguise, to momentarily forget himself and acknowledge their call. He was shot several times and died that night at age 49. Although several local mafiosi were suspected in the killing, as were *La Mano Nera* affiliates in New York, no one was convicted. In 2014, Palermo police arrested 95 suspected mafiosi. One of those arrested, Domenico Palazzoto, was heard on a wiretap saying, "My father's uncle, Paolo Palazzotto, killed Joe Petrosino" (Talty, 2017, p. 219). Palermo police and Petrosino's grandnephew Joseph believed Palazzoto was telling the truth.

Funeral and Aftermath

Joseph Petrosino's body was transported back to his beloved adopted home country. By the time of his death, Petrosino had become a hero not just among Italian Americans in New York City, but across the entire United States. An estimated 250,000 people attended his funeral.

Petrosino's legacy lived on in the NYPD. His undercover techniques were passed on to subsequent generations of police departments. He established a bomb squad, a first in the entire country for a municipal police department. Although often accused of brutality against suspects, he never took a bribe.

Petrosino's legacy lived on in pop culture. In 1912, the earliest days of cinema, Italian filmmakers released a three-part series, *The Adventures of Lieutenant Petrosino*. In 1960, Oscar-winning actor Ernest Borgnine, the son of Italian immigrants who knew firsthand about *La Mano Nera*, portrayed Petrosino in a film heralded for its artistry and historical accuracy, *Pay or Die*. Petrosino was the subject of a 2006 made-for-television movie. He has also been the subject of comic books and several books. In 2023, Leonardo DiCaprio announced plans to make a film based on Petrosino.

Despite his toughness and brilliance as a police officer, perhaps Petrosino should be remembered as a man simply devoted to doing what he thought right. Perhaps even more he should be thought of as a family man, for when his body was discovered, authorities found his badge, #285, and a written note to his daughter whom he had not seen in months: "a kiss for you" (Talty, 2017, p. 199).

Sources and Suggested Readings

Bankoff, C. (2014, June 23). NYPD detective's murder solved after just 105 years. *New York Intelligencer*. https://nymag.com/intelligencer/2014/06/nypd-detectives-murder-solved-after-105-years.html, date of retrieval December 8, 2023.

Corradini, Anna Maria. (2009). *Joe Petrosino, a 20th century hero*. Provincia Regionale di Palermo.

Films by the Year. (2020). *The adventurers of Lieutenant Petrosino (1912)*[Video]. YouTube. https://www.youtube.com/watch?v=u8E8Xrsu1l0&t=45s, date of retrieval December 7, 2023.

The History Guy: History Deserves to Be Remembered. (2018). *Joseph Petrosino versus the Black Hand* [Video]. YouTube. https://www.youtube.com/watch?v=57X_g0PNoeM, date of retrieval December 8, 2023.

Lt. Det. Joseph Petrosino Association in America. (2019). *Joe Peterosino* [Video]. YouTube. https://www.youtube.com/watch?v=L-9etL4Vw7s, date of retrieval December 5, 2023.

Lt. Det. Joseph Petrosino Association in America. (2023). DiCaprio to Star in Movie About Mafia-Fighting NYPD Detective. https://www.petrosinousa.org/media/article/dicaprio-to-star-in-movie-about-mafia-fighting-nypd-detective-3570#:~:text=The%20movie%2C%20called%20%E2%80%9CThe%20Black,and%20expected%20out%20-next%20year, date of retrieval December 9, 2023.

Mele, Andrew Paul. (2020). *The Italian squad: How the NYPD took down the Black Hand extortion ring*. McFarland.

NoirCity. (2010). *Ernest Borgnine Pt 1—Pay or die, the Black Hand* [Video]. YouTube. https://www.youtube.com/watch?v=MWoLaYBfMCc&t=19s, date of retrieval December 8, 2023.

Petacco, Arrigo. (1974). *Joe Petrosino*. McMillian.

Roberts, Sam. (2007, October 31). Streets aren't paved with gold, but there's plenty below. *New York Times*. https://www.nytimes.com/2007/10/31/nyregion/31gold.html, accessed August 2, 2024.

Sauchelli, D., & Rosenbaum, S. (2014, June 23). Italian police solve 105-year-old NYPD mob detective's murder. *New York Post*. https://nypost.com/2014/06/23/italian-police-solve-105-year-old-nypd-mob-detectives-murder/, date of retrieval December 8, 2023.

Talty, Stephan. (2017). *The Black Hand: The epic war between a brilliant detective & the deadliest secret society in American history*. Houghton-Mifflin.

Whitlowe, S. (2023, March 13). *The Black Hand* [Audio podcast]. Tales of History and Imagination. https://historyandimagination.com/2023/03/13/the-black-hand/, date of retrieval December 1, 2023.

Discussion Questions

1. The problem of crime-ridden communities who are terrorized by criminals but distrustful of police has not gone away. Are there any lessons to be learned in this regard from the life of Joe Petrosino?
2. Joe Petrosino was a great leader in police circles, but he faced obstacles to advancement because of his lack of English proficiency. What are your thoughts about that? Should those deficiencies be examined on a case-by-case basis?

Credit

IMG 6.1: New York City Police Department, https://commons.wikimedia.org/wiki/File:Joe_petrosino.jpg, 1909.

CHAPTER 7

Lola G. Baldwin (1860–1957)

IMG 7J

Lola Greene Baldwin paved the way for women who work in municipal policing. Although she was a maverick for her time and very strong willed, she differed from many modern feminists, both in terms of personal mores and her functions as a police officer. She was a mix, a woman who saw her job as a police officer as an extension of motherhood, yet someone not shy about advancing her ideas of what was right and imposing those ideas on others. Baldwin's work and life reflected the mood of American feminists during the Progressive Era of the early 20th century, most notably the social hygiene strain of thought that dominated some efforts to improve life in large cities.

Early Life and Career

Lola Greene was born in 1860 in Elmira, New York, and the Greene family moved to Rochester when Lola was a child. The death of her father in 1877, while Lola was still in high school, altered the course of her professional and personal life. As the oldest of three daughters, Lola assumed childcare duties. She was forced to drop out of high school to support herself and her two sisters. Lola secured a teaching license in New York; her first teaching job, at age 20, was in Monroe County, New York.

Lola Greene moved to Lincoln, Nebraska, in 1880, where she taught high school. There she met and married LeGrand M. Baldwin, a Vermont native and dry goods merchant. Instead of teaching, Lola Baldwin worked as a clerk for the Nebraska Public Lands Commissioner. While living in Nebraska, the Baldwins had two sons, Myron and Pierre. The Baldwins left Lincoln in 1893. LeGrand Baldwin plied his dry goods trade in several cities, all located on the East Coast. LeGrand Baldwin landed a position with a Massachusetts-based company in 1904. The company transferred him to Portland, Oregon.

It was clear even from her early life that Lola had no intention of being a stay-at-home mother and housewife. Baldwin was feisty, vocal, opinionated, and loved a good fight. She stood only 5′3″ and wore steel-rimmed glasses, the visual stereotype of a Victorian-era matron.

The Social Hygiene Movement in Portland, Oregon

Lola Baldwin was a product of the Progressive Era of 1890–1920. A hallmark of the Progressive Era was the social hygiene movement, which maintained that life in America's big cities could be improved by addressing moral issues that related to public health. Prostitution, seduction at the hands of unscrupulous men, alcohol use, and other vices bred disease and other health maladies, both physical and moral. Wrapped in this school of thought was the idea that teenage girls needed protection from the evils of big city life that bred such ills. Social hygienists saw it as their duty to protect young women from these misfortunes.

Upon moving to Portland, Baldwin immersed herself into social hygiene activities. With the support of several charitable organizations, most notably the YWCA Traveler's Aid, she sought homeless and delinquent girls, trying to shepherd them either into group homes or other protective environments, and sometimes taking young women into her home. She would locate families for some runaways, and she tried to rescue and protect young female immigrants from dishonest immigration brokers.

A prime catalyst for advancing the social hygiene mentality and Lola Baldwin's career came in 1905, with Portland's Lewis and Clark Exposition, the first World's Fair on the American West Coast. Americans had been migrating westward for several decades prior to the turn of the 20th century, and Portland, like other large western cities, had become a magnet for runaways and get-rich-quick schemers and scam artists. Portland government officials anticipated that the World's Fair would exacerbate such problems, as previous World's Fairs had been beset with women being trafficked or engaging in prostitution.

Baldwin had already played an important role in establishing a juvenile court in Portland; the number of juvenile courts had gradually increased since the pioneering efforts of Ben Lindsey in Colorado and Jane Addams in Illinois several years prior. Baldwin, already a vocal force in Portland's government, was appointed by a local judge as an unpaid probation officer and as vice prevention agent. Her task was protecting Portland's young women from those who would try to lure them into prostitution, sexual assault, or other unsavory behaviors.

Portland officials thought that the need for Baldwin's work would be eliminated after the World's Fair. But because of her good work, Baldwin was kept in her position. She worked well with Portland police officers, judicial officials, and local government leaders. She handled hundreds of cases referred by police officers over a 3-year period. Unlike many other women reformers of that era, she thought it best that girls be helped by women, as opposed to merely advocating that men in positions of authority pay more attention to the plight of young women with crime-related problems.

When her term as an unpaid probation officer was nearing its end, Baldwin petitioned local government officials to make her position a paid one, with her becoming a fully sworn police officer with the Portland Police Department. The primary task of this female police officer would be to aid young women and address the root causes of female delinquency. Baldwin pointed out that the city of Portland had spent more money on dog pounds than on the type of work she wanted to do. Her lobbying paid off, and on April 1, 1908, at the age of 48, Baldwin was sworn in as a detective with the Portland Police Department, in a newly created branch called the Women's Auxiliary Police Department for the Protection of Girls, later renamed the Women's Protective Division.

Although she was a fully sworn officer, she did not work alongside male officers daily. Her office was not located in police department headquarters, but in the local YWCA, with the idea that a YWCA was a less intimidating environment than a police department full of uniformed men. Baldwin had no desire to do the same type of police work as most of her male colleagues. She did not show her badge or wear a uniform. She was not viewed as a woman trying to do a man's job, and therefore she was not viewed as a threat by the overwhelmingly male police department.

But Baldwin was paradoxical. While she had no desire to do the work normally assigned to men, she was a far cry from the typical married woman of her era. She loved the outdoors and traditionally male-oriented activities. She wore pants—though not while on the job—at a time when doing so was taboo. Baldwin specialized in dealing with wayward girls, but she pursued what she believed to be the causes of delinquency as vigorously as she did the protection of those who came to her attention.

Like many people of her era, Baldwin believed that men committed crime by choice, but that women lacked the capacity to make such decisions on their own. She and others of that time period believed that most, if not all, women who were in trouble with the law, especially women under 16, were led astray by men. She identified several causes (such as low wages for women) and venues for promulgating sexual and economic exploitation. Some venues were obvious targets, such as houses of prostitution. Lola Baldwin waged war against brothels that functioned as an open secret throughout Portland at the turn of the century, especially those that employed underage girls.

Another target was saloons, a place where it was unseemly for a woman to enter at all, especially alone. She visited some of Portland's saloons and politely but firmly asked owners to report any unaccompanied female who looked underage and entered their saloon. She vigorously pursued cross-dressers. Cross-dressing, considered indicative of homosexuality, was a moral offense in Portland at the time, and offenders were charged with disorderly conduct.

Baldwin viewed dance halls as a prime area to lure girls into sexually compromising situations. She did not seek their outright ban, although that was her desire, but she succeeded in having many of them licensed and regulated. Officials could order dance hall operators to close on Sundays, increase lighting, and stop couples from touching while dancing. The situation became especially dicey when Portland residents noted that Baldwin and her colleagues only targeted dance halls populated by the lower classes, while the dance halls frequented by upper-class residents were left alone. Some dance hall operators responded by opening halls just outside the city limits or on ships accessible to Portland residents but beyond the jurisdiction of Baldwin and the police department.

In 1909, a new group of politicians sweeping into Portland threatened to abolish the women's division of the Portland Police Department, a division that by then included several women officers. Baldwin gathered support from the YWCA, the mayor, the local Woman's Club, and the Social Hygiene Society to have an amendment to the city charter placed on the June election ballot. The amendment passed, and the Women's Protective Division became a permanent part of the Portland Police Department.

Baldwin's ability to lobby successfully for resources was uncanny, especially given the fact that most government leaders of the day paid little attention to the demands of women. At a time when many of America's police departments owned automobiles (the automobile being a recent invention) and very few women knew how to drive, Baldwin convinced the city of Portland to purchase a new 1914 Ford Model T for the exclusive use of the Women's Protective Division.

Lola Baldwin went even further in addressing the roots of female delinquency. She sought out pornography at every turn. Once, she confiscated some objectionable viewing material from a young boy on a train, tracked down the seller, and had him prosecuted in a neighboring county.

But what to do with females who ran afoul of the law and needed institutional structure, i.e., a reformatory? Baldwin noticed that while there were reform schools for boys, there were none for girls, and she succeeded in getting the State Industrial School for Girls opened in 1913. Leaders in other cities and states sought help from Baldwin to create similar agencies.

Battle with Sophie Tucker

One of Baldwin's most public moral battles was with Sophie Tucker, a blond, buxom, early 20th-century dance hall and nightclub performer whose sexually suggestive shows delighted male audiences, much to the consternation of an increasingly powerful and prudish female population in Portland. After viewing Tucker's performance in November 1910, Baldwin swore out a warrant for Tucker, charging her with public indecency. Baldwin biographer Gloria Myers quotes Baldwin as saying of Tucker, "Many are wondering why we have so much trouble with the young people. What can you expect when such performances as this one have only one effect on the public mind—that of debauchery and indecency" (Myers, 1995, p. 58). Tucker, feeling the glare of Baldwin and the city of Portland, glared right back, threatening Baldwin and the city with legal action. After a series of nasty public exchanges and a one-on-one meeting between Tucker and Baldwin, the case against Tucker was dismissed.

Social Hygiene Wars

Movie theaters, a new phenomenon during the 1910s, also received Baldwin's scrutiny. It was not the movies Baldwin objected to, but as with dance halls, she fretted that they were places where girls would go to meet men. Still, she would use movie theaters, asking theater owners to plaster the pictures and names of missing women on the screen with a plea for the audience to contact police if they could assist in locating them.

Baldwin also enforced laws prohibiting interracial sexual relations, especially when it involved Black men (a very small portion of Portland's population) and White women, feeling little need to enforce such laws when the situation was reversed or when it involved other ethnic groups. Although Baldwin was progressive and a maverick in many respects, her beliefs about race reflected that of many White Americans just after the turn of the century.

World War I

Her objectionable views on race relations notwithstanding, Baldwin became known throughout the United States for her work with transient girls and other female offenders. Her reputation came into play around 1917, when America prepared to enter World War I. New York police czar Raymond Fosdick was appointed by President Woodrow Wilson to head a nationwide "moral martial law" around military facilities. Baldwin was appointed to head efforts to keep military facilities free from prostitutes and other women who might lead servicemen astray. With this assignment, Baldwin sought to protect decent men from unsavory women, a reversal from her past efforts. Baldwin was placed in charge of efforts in four states: Washington, Oregon, California, and Arizona. The new job necessitated her move to San Francisco, where she remained for the duration of World War I.

Rather than simply hauling prostitutes and other wayward women off to jail only to see them back on the streets (or near military bases) plying their trade, Lola Baldwin established four houses that took in prostitutes. She and her colleagues were empowered by wartime emergency laws to hold these female offenders for indeterminate lengths of time. The houses, located in San Diego, Tacoma, Portland, and Los Angeles, targeted prostitutes with venereal disease. Officials in other cities followed Baldwin's lead, and 13 similar facilities were established around the country.

Return to Portland

Baldwin's job with the federal government ended in December 1920, 2 years after the end of World War I. She returned to her position in Portland and to a warm reception from the citizenry. However, the police department, under the direction of a different police chief, had downsized the women's division that Baldwin had fought so hard to build. She traveled the country and to other countries espousing the benefits of women performing police work. Baldwin still advocated that women officers work exclusively with women and girls, rather than performing all the duties of male officers, and that female officers never display a badge or wear a uniform. Baldwin's legacy lived on in this respect for decades to come. No female police officer in Portland wore a uniform for the next several decades.

Retirement, Death, and Legacy

Baldwin retired from the Portland Police Department on May 1, 1922. She remained active with the parole board and with her sons and husband in the commercial bakery business. She was appalled by the changes in American culture, i.e., the decadence of the Roaring Twenties, and its effect on social hygiene in the cities. She did not like some of the behaviors (e.g., smoking, provocative clothing) of newly liberated women, all of whom were empowered by receiving the right to vote in 1920. She watched with dismay what she viewed as the dissolution of the American family. Her Victorian-era morality still intact, she continued to lecture on venereal disease prevention, and she remained active in many of the organizations that she had been involved with during her tenure with the Portland Police Department. Baldwin continued balancing customary male and female roles, which was a difficult job for professional women during the Progressive Era.

Lola Baldwin died on June 22, 1957 at the age of 97. Gloria Myers called Baldwin Portland's "municipal mother." She viewed the city of Portland and other West Coast cities as an extension of her own household. Lola Baldwin thought she was a mother charged with protecting her children, and any female was her child, subject to her rules, her mores, and her uncompromising dictates. Although many of her moral beliefs seem quaint at best and objectionable at worst, she helped lay the foundation for other women to enter police work, especially in Portland—the city that would later be the first major metropolitan area to hire the first female police chief in 1985. Baldwin's stubbornness and myopic view of morality, often a detriment, was also her greatest asset. One of her admirers, Elizabeth Moorad, said of Baldwin: "She couldn't be bought; she couldn't be influenced, and she couldn't be intimidated" (Myers, 1995, p. 162).

Sources and Suggested Readings

HerStory. (2023). *Lola Baldwin 00113 Lola Baldwin* [Video]. YouTube. https://www.youtube.com/watch?v=XHQEZZpLuZ0

McMenamins. (2013). *History Pub with Lola Baldwin's grandchildren* [Video]. YouTube. https://www.youtube.com/watch?v=Us-QxyaTMXY, date of retrieval February 2, 2024.

Myers, Gloria E. (1995). *A municipal mother: Portland's Lola Greene Baldwin, America's first policewoman.* Oregon State University Press.

Myers, Gloria E. (2022). *Lola Greene Baldwin (1860–1957)*, Oregon Encyclopedia, A Project of the Oregon Historical Society. https://www.oregonencyclopedia.org/articles/baldwin_lola_1860_1957_/, date of retrieval February 1, 2024.

Oregon Experience. (2008, May 15). Lola G. Baldwin. *OPB.* https://www.opb.org/television/programs/oregonexperience/article/lola-g-baldwin-/, date of retrieval February 2, 2024.

Schulz, Dorothy. (1995). *From social worker to crime fighter: Women in the United States.* Praeger Press.

Viki History. (2018). *Lola Baldwin* [Video]. YouTube. https://www.youtube.com/watch?v=KA0YIjRsqQY&t=185s, date of retrieval February 2, 2024.

Discussion Questions

1. How does police work performed by contemporary women differ from that done by Lola Baldwin?
2. If Lola Baldwin were alive today, what type of role would she play in policing?

Credit

IMG 7.1: Source: https://commons.wikimedia.org/wiki/File:Lola_Greene_Baldwin.jpg.

CHAPTER 8

Alice Stebbins Wells (1873–1957)

IMG 8.1

Who was the first female police officer in the United States? The answer depends on how one defines "police officer." Prior to Alice Stebbins Wells's work in Los Angeles, many law enforcement agencies employed females in quasi-law enforcement capacities such as jail matrons, court bailiffs, or workers interacting with children or women suspects and victims. Marie Owens joined the Chicago Police Department in 1891; she had arrest powers but only over child labor law violations. Lola Baldwin of Portland, Oregon, had arrest powers, but she worked from the local YWCA, rather than the police station. And although there is no way of knowing whether one of the thousands of small law enforcement agencies in the United States employed female officers prior to Baldwin and Wells, Alice Stebbins Wells of Los Angeles is considered by some to be the first full-fledged female police officer. More than any before her, she was a tireless and effective advocate for hiring female officers throughout the United States and in other countries.

Early Life

Not much is known about Alice Stebbins's early life. She was born June 13, 1873, in Manhattan, Kansas. Both of her parents were graduates of Oberlin College in Ohio at a time when few women attended college. Perhaps Alice Stebbins inherited her pathbreaking personality from her mother. The family moved to Hiawatha, a small town in northeast Kansas, where her father operated a newspaper. Alice Stebbins attended high school in Atchison, Kansas, about 40 miles from Hiawatha. It is unknown whether the family moved to that location or if she lived with others during her high school years.

Alice Stebbins spent her adult life breaking traditional gender roles, both in policing and other disciplines. At a time when Christian ministers were mostly male (which is still true in some denominations), she embarked on a career as a minister. At some point in her early adulthood, Alice Stebbins moved east and worked as a pastor's assistant under Dr. Newell Dwight Hillis, a famous Congregationalist minister, at the historic Plymouth Church of the Pilgrims in Brooklyn, New York. Plymouth Church was renowned for its slavery abolition efforts in the 1850s, having served as an arrival point for people escaping slavery through the famous Underground Railroad (Plymouth Church, n.d., para. 1).

Alice Stebbins went on to study theology at Hartford Seminary (now the Hartford International University for Religion and Peace) in Connecticut, the first seminary in the United States to admit women. While there, she focused on Old Testament history. Stebbins traveled New England while in seminary, substituting for absent or vacationing pastors, a rare role for women at the time. She is believed to be the first female to deliver a sermon in a Maine church. A budding social advocate and social worker before the profession officially came into existence, Alice Stebbins worked as a student pastor and social welfare worker as well, gradually becoming concerned about the plight of women and children in urban areas.

During a visit to Perry, Oklahoma, Stebbins was offered a position as pastor of a church there, an offer she accepted. While in Perry, she met and married Frank Wells, a farmer and Wisconsin native who had migrated to Oklahoma. They would have three children. The Wells family lived in Perry from 1903 to 1906 before moving to Los Angeles, where Alice abandoned professional ministry and began her campaign for including women on the police force. Guided more by her social work orientation and her religious sense of love for neighbor than a desire to fight crime, Wells believed that communities would be safer for women and children if women were allowed to serve as police officers.

Policewoman

In May 1910, Alice Wells submitted a petition signed by 100 Los Angeles citizens to request that city officials appoint her as a police officer. She was appointed to the Los Angeles Police Department in August (or September) of that year. She was assigned to work with Leo Marsden as a juvenile probation officer, at a time when separate systems for juveniles were in their infancy and before there was a clear distinction between policing and juvenile probation work.

According to Wells, a female police officer's greatest task was preventing crime rather than reacting to it. Unlike women police officers today, she did not do the same work as male police officers; she never used force and or carried a weapon. According to Wells, women police officers did the work that male officers could not do or had failed to do, namely preventing crimes against women and children by offering a woman's touch in a way men could not.

Alice Stebbins Wells was far from intimidating. She was petite, probably under 5′4″, and she weighed only about 120 pounds. Her voice was described as thin, birdlike, and far from serious or threatening; she was prone to laughter at a moment's notice. At first, Wells did not wear a uniform because the department had never had to design a uniform for a female and had no intention of making her as visible as her male counterparts. Wells designed her own uniform to wear on special occasions, a khaki-colored jacket and long skirt.

Intimidation played no part in Wells's approach to policing. She bore the title of policewoman and was issued the same badge as the other officers—along with a first aid kit and a key to the call boxes posted around Los Angeles to notify headquarters of an incident. But Wells did not perform the same duties as her male colleagues. Consistent with the social hygiene movement that was prevalent at the time and her membership in the Society of Hygiene, her primary duties pertained to preventing women, especially young women, girls, and other children, from getting lured into situations or settings where they were apt to commit crime or become victims of crime. Wells conducted sex education courses at a time when public discussion of sex—even for educational purposes—was taboo in American society. Searching for runaways also fell under Wells's purview. She was instrumental in forming a missing person's bureau in the department, which primarily focused on women and children.

Wells's duties expanded a few months after assuming her job. The LAPD adopted a policy banning male officers from questioning young females, so the task was assigned to female officers, namely Wells and the few female officers that followed her. Within 2 years of Wells's appointment, six more female officers were hired.

Wells supervised public areas often frequented by teenaged girls and children, such as skating rinks, dance halls, and picture houses (movie theaters). The film industry was in its infancy at the time, and Los Angeles was gradually becoming its capital. To Wells, owners of these establishments were akin to vice operators today. Wells was also active in the "purity squad" (Kelly, n.d., para. 19). She would roam her beat looking for theater shows, films, or billboards that she deemed unsavory, and then she would report her sightings to her superiors.

Alice Wells advocated for the rights of women living in abusive relationships. It was widely, though not universally, accepted that a husband had the right to deal with his wife as he deemed fit, even physically. Although by law a man was usually not allowed to assault his wife, commonly accepted police and judicial practice allowed a husband to physically assault his wife without fear of legal reprisal in many American cities.

Wells and her coworker Minnie Barton, the second policewoman hired by the LAPD, worked to secure a safe place for women released from custody to reside. They opened the Minnie Barton Home, at first using Barton's residence as a halfway house for these women, some of whom were pregnant. In time, the Minnie Barton Home became an incarceration alternative for some female offenders. Eventually, the Minnie Barton home was absorbed and merged with the Children's Institute of Los Angeles, which still exists.

Wells's efforts included educating citizens, especially women, in crime prevention and self-defense. Following a perceived rash of robberies and burglaries, a women's group in Los Angeles invited Wells to address its membership on safety and self-defense. Her first tip was to scream. Wells said, "The weapon nature gave a woman was a scream" (Kelly, n.d., para. 24), but she noted that in rural communities or in some settings a scream might not be heard, in which case, "It would not be bad to know a few bone-breaking tricks" (Kelly, n.d., para. 24). She then urged them to grab the first available weapon, often a hairpin, and use ju-jitsu. She reminded women that in the case of a house burglary, the burglar was usually just as nervous as the homeowner, who should capitalize on that nervousness.

Not surprisingly, traditionalists maintained that police work should be the sole domain of men, and others simply saw the idea of a female police officer as an impossibility, as unlikely as a woman playing professional baseball; it simply could not exist. This attitude presented itself in some strange ways to Wells, who no doubt had to deal with naysayers both in the LAPD and the community. In one example, Wells was refused the privilege given to Los Angeles's police officers to ride streetcars free of charge if they were in uniform or presented their badge. A conductor refused to allow her on the car, accusing her of using her husband's badge. She told her supervisors of the incident and was given a badge clearly identifying her as a policewoman, with the number 1.

To the news media, Wells was a curiosity that made for good stories. Some media outlets struggled with what to call her, referring to her alternately as "officeress" and "Officerette Wells" (Kelly, n.d., para. 16) before settling on the title Wells preferred, policewoman. According to the *Los Angeles Herald*, Wells's salary was $75 per month, 25% less than that of her male counterparts.

Spreading the Message

Not content merely to advance her own career, Alice Wells founded the International Association of Women Police in 1915. Higher education and training were part of her agenda as well, decades before August Vollmer and others integrated police training into higher education. Partnering with the University of California Southern Division (now UCLA) Criminology Department, Wells created the first academic course dealing specifically with women and policing. The course was offered for the first time in 1918.

Throughout her career, Alice Wells traveled throughout the United States and to other countries advocating hiring of female police officers. A 1915 St. Louis newspaper article ballyhooed Alice Wells's visit, stating that never had a real-life policewoman visited the city. A Toronto political official said of Wells's appearance there, "Not in many years of social work and interest in social problems have I heard an address so comprehensive, so intelligent and so full of 1913 common sense as that to which we listened last night" (Kelly, n.d., para. 29). An Albany, New York, paper, ever conscience of gender roles, wrote, "She wore a khaki uniform and a large shield. Her brown hat, with an attractive plume, was distinctly feminine" (Kelly, n.d., para. 31).

In her public appearances, Wells described policing as the most misunderstood area of city government. She believed that while breaking up riots and making arrests garnered headlines, real police work was done seven days a week, in time between such calamitous events. The police were, in her view, a "peace army" (Martyn, 1915).

In 1928, Alice Wells cofounded the Women Peace Officers Association of California and served as its first president. Realizing her own contributions to the history of Los Angeles as well as those of her fellow officers, she opened and curated the Los Angeles Women's Police Museum, which is still in operation.*

Retirement and Death

Alice Stebbins Wells retired from policing in 1940. Little is recorded or known about her retirement life. She passed away on August 17, 1957, in Los Angeles at age 84. Her casket was handled by an all-female police honor guard.

Had Alice Stebbins Wells not joined the ranks of the Los Angeles Police Department, a woman somewhere would have eventually became a police officer. But as is the case with several other chapter subjects in this book, someone had to be first, and having the gumption and determination to be first requires a bold personality, the sort of personality possessed by Alice Stebbins Wells.

---

* I question the quality of that operation because multiple attempts over a period of several months to obtain information or even speak to the museum operators were unsuccessful. The same can be said about the Los Angeles Police Museum.

Sources and Suggested Readings

Hartford International University for Religion and Peace. (2024). History. https://www.hartfordinternational.edu/about/history, retrieved June 24, 2024.

Kelly, K. (n.d.). *Alice S. Wells: Among first policewomen*. America Comes Alive. https://americacomesalive.com/alice-s-wells-among-first-policewomen/, retrieved June 20, 2024.

Los Angeles Women Police Officers and Associates. (2024). *Women in the LAPD*. https://www.lawpoa.org/about-us/our-history/, retrieved June 20, 2024.

Martyn, M. (1915, May 13). First policewoman in America tells just why women are needed to help men keep the peace: Experience of Mrs. Alice S. Wells in Los Angeles. *St. Louis Post-Dispatch*, p. 15. https://www.proquest.com/criminaljusticeperiodicals/docview/579378321/pageviewPDF/55DF5B6076504963PQ/1?accountid=10639&-sourcetype=Historical%20Newspapers

Plymouth Church. (n.d.) Social justice: The underground railroad. https://www.plymouthchurch.org/underground-railroad, accessed August 3, 2024.

Sedey, C. J. (2024, June 9). Alice Stebbins Wells: American minister and welfare worker. *Encyclopaedia Britannica online*. https://www.britannica.com/biography/Alice-Stebbins-Wells, retrieved June 23, 2024.

Women Police Officers Association of California. (2007). *The first woman police officer in the U.S.* https://archive.ph/20120919192115/http://www.wpoaca.com/archives/wells.htm, retrieved June 22, 2024.

Discussion Questions

1. Was Alice Wells too bold in her efforts to become a police officer, or not bold enough, or about right? If she had tried to perform the same work as her male colleagues, what do you think would have been the result?
2. What is your opinion of Alice Wells's involvement in activities that today would not be seen as directly related to police work, such as teaching sex education and trying to steer women and girls away from what she thought were hazardous environments?

Credit

IMG 8.1: J.R. Finnell & Sons Publishing Co., https://commons.wikimedia.org/wiki/File:Alice_Stebbins_Wells_in_a_1936_book.png, 1936.

CHAPTER 9

August Vollmer (1876–1955)

IMG 9.1

August Vollmer was the most important pioneer in municipal policing in the United States. Vollmer is owed a debt for his work not only by modern police officers, but by everyone that has studied criminal justice in an academic setting. It was Vollmer who first blended the worlds of academe and police work.

Early Life

August Vollmer was born on March 7, 1876, in New Orleans, the oldest of two sons born to German immigrants. His father, John, and his mother, Philopine, ran a grocery business. John Vollmer died in 1884, and 2 years later, owing to Philopine's bad health, the Vollmers moved to Germany to live with her parents for 2 years. When August was 12, the family returned to New Orleans, but moved to San Francisco while Vollmer was still a teenager, again due to Philopine's health issues. In 1891, the Vollmer family moved to Berkeley, California, the city where Vollmer would eventually make a name for himself. Raised in a lower-class household, Vollmer worked odd jobs while attending public schools. O. W. Wilson wrote that Vollmer enjoyed a happy childhood in Berkeley, with pleasant memories of rabbit hunting, fishing, swimming, boating, and hiking.

In 1895, at the age of 19, Vollmer started a successful coal and feed business with a man named Ted Patterson. Vollmer also helped organize the North Berkeley Volunteer Fire Department. His successful business venture was interrupted by the outbreak of the Spanish-American War in 1898. Vollmer sold his half of the business and enlisted in the Army. He spent the war in the Pacific Theater, participating in the capture of Manila from the Spanish and later battling Philippine independence insurgents. The fighting left Vollmer with a punctured eardrum and accolades for his bravery. He returned to California in August 1899. But Vollmer's army experience rendered him ill-suited for life behind a desk; he needed a more stimulating career.

Law Enforcement Career

Upon his return, Vollmer worked several odd jobs before landing a position as a mail carrier, a job he held for 4 years. Prior to the age of radio, television, the internet, and sophisticated package delivery systems, the U.S. Post Office was the primary means of communication and dissemination of information, and postal employees were held in high regard. Such steady paying civil servant jobs were highly sought after at the time, and the job allowed Vollmer to become acquainted with the people of Berkeley.

An unplanned incident during Vollmer's postal career propelled him into the public spotlight in Berkeley. He stopped a runaway rail cart from hitting a passenger train, an act which garnered public kudos. In January 1905, a friend who worked with the *Berkeley Daily Gazette* encouraged Vollmer to run for town marshal. He knew that Vollmer had good rapport with the public, that he was being hailed as a hero in the press, and that he could truthfully be called a war hero, all of which he thought would serve Vollmer well in attacking the drug dens, gambling parlors and prostitution houses that had become a problem in Berkeley. Although reluctant at first, Vollmer ran after receiving further encouragement from the local Republican Party, the mayor, and the fire chief. The 29-year-old Vollmer defeated the incumbent by a three-to-one margin.

Vollmer's law enforcement career began on April 15, 1905. Always believing that there is no such thing as luck in police work, his first action was requesting that the city council increase the size of his force from three to 12 officers and that they be given uniforms. Arming each deputy with a revolver and a short-handled 16-pound sledgehammer, Vollmer began raiding Chinese opium dens only to be frustrated when the arrestees were immediately bailed out by the Caucasian families they served as cooks and housekeepers.

Vollmer realized early on that the support for cleaning up Berkeley would not be unanimous. He also realized that temptation would come his way. He was offered money and real estate in exchange for not raiding lotteries and other gambling operations. Once Vollmer repaid the man who offered him a bribe by immediately raiding his gambling operation.

Vollmer demonstrated his knack for innovation early in his career. He purchased bicycles for his deputies, which provoked laughter from the San Francisco newspapers but attention from news outlets around the country, as Vollmer was among the first to implement bike patrol. Since bicycles were three times faster than foot patrol, Vollmer viewed it as not as a way to get in touch with the community (as with community policing later) but to catch criminals more efficiently.

In 1905, Vollmer visited Los Angeles and went on patrol with a private detective named Jim Foster. Foster, in the employ of private citizens in Los Angeles, patrolled on bicycle in the hope of preventing burglaries. Foster placed call boxes on telephone poles that were wired to his residence. He would dismount from his bicycle and phone his wife, who would tell him of any reported crimes. Foster later attached a red light to each phone that would light up all phones if it were pressed on any one phone. Although it seems primitive by today's standards, it was innovative for its time.

Eager to implement a similar system across Berkeley, Vollmer persuaded the city council to place a $25,000 bond referendum on the next election ballot to pay for such a program. The referendum was approved, and Vollmer contracted with Gamewell Signal and Alarm Company to install the system.

On April 18, 1906, an earthquake devastated the American West Coast, one of the most devastating earthquakes in recorded history. The devastation was greatest in San Francisco, one of the largest population centers in the earthquake's sphere, where more than 700 people died. It brought 50,000 refugees into Berkeley. About half that number remained in Berkeley after the earthquake's immediate aftermath, and the size of Vollmer's marshal force doubled.

The 1907 death of a milkman—deemed a suicide, but which Vollmer believed was a murder—convinced him that police officers needed to know more than just how to catch and fight criminals. That same year, Vollmer began having "crab sessions," where he would hold weekly meetings with his officers to educate them on any topic. In an unusual move for a police officer, Vollmer, who was not college educated but a voracious reader and learner, began studying criminal psychology. He immediately employed his new knowledge to catch a psychologically maladjusted arsonist—a young man from out of state visiting relatives—after reading that homesick people are inclined to commit arson. The use of psychology, a new field of study at the time, became a hallmark of Vollmer's work. After being reelected by a huge margin, Vollmer devised the idea of a police school to train officers, realizing that very little had been written about police work and criminal investigation.

In 1908, with the assistance of the Oakland Police Department, Vollmer created a police academy, the first in the California Bay Area. Vollmer's police school was at first met with resistance by line officers who had to attend classes during their spare time. Resistance from line officers never mattered much to Vollmer; he had little faith in the rank-and-file, assuming that most people were basically lazy and needed strong leadership.

The school included four teachers. Vollmer taught first aid, police methods, public health and sanitation, photography, and basic law. Walter Peterson, an Oakland police captain, taught detective work. Most significantly, Vollmer blended the world of academe and policing by employing William Herms from the University of California Parasitology Department to lecture on sanitation. In addition, A. M. Kidd from the University of California Law School taught about courtroom evidence.

Police Chief

Vollmer was appointed chief of the Berkeley Police Department on August 13, 1909. He gladly accepted the move, motivated in large part by not having to run any more political campaigns. Vollmer's personal life changed soon after becoming police chief. He married Lydia Sturtevant in 1911, but the marriage ended in divorce in 1920.

As chief, Vollmer made two innovative changes. First, he put his officers on motorcycles, and then in 1913, gained nationwide publicity by putting his officers in automobiles, though it had first been done in Akron, Ohio, several years earlier. Second, in 1916, Vollmer convinced the city to lure Dr. Albert Schneider, an expert in pharmacology and bacteriology, away from the University of California Medical School to become a full-time criminologist for the police department.

Meanwhile, the University of California added a bachelor's degree in criminology in 1916. Willard Oliver (2016) points to 1916 as a seminal year in criminology/criminal justice education. Oliver points out the difference between training, which Vollmer fervently advocated as well, versus education. The training courses were devoted to the everyday aspects of police work and organizational issues, whereas the higher education courses delivered at Berkeley included psychology and the natural sciences, especially those tied to the forensic aspects of police investigation. In a 1917 article published in the *Journal of the American Institute of Criminal Law and Criminology* (based at Northwestern University in Illinois), for which Vollmer served as associate editor, Vollmer and Schneider laid out their rational for a degree program for police officers, along with a detailed listing of course offerings. The suggested degree program differed considerably from that of most modern criminal justice/criminology programs, which emphasize social science more than natural sciences. Vollmer's program more closely resembled modern forensic science programs. It included courses in physics, chemistry, anatomy, anthropology, toxicology, psychology, administration, police procedure, public health, first aid, and criminal law. The first degree in the criminology program was awarded in 1923.

Vollmer had four unusual demands of his police officers: His men would accept no gifts, do no special favors, put no juveniles in jail, and use no excessive force or torture, all four of which were common in the 1910s. Violators were fired instantly. One of the most innovative moves of his career was his decision to hire police officers attending college. Vollmer purchased an advertisement in the *Daily Californian,* the University of California student newspaper. The ad read:

> College men wanted for police force. Interesting experience. Learn a new profession. Serve on the Berkeley police force while you go to college. Contact August Vollmer, Chief of Police. (Oliver, 2017, p. 305)

Psychiatry, a new medical endeavor, was frowned upon by much of the public and the medical profession in the 1910s. Vollmer, however, saw the need for psychiatric assistance in hiring. He employed Dr. Don Ball of the University of California to screen applicants and give intelligence tests to ensure that applicants had high intelligence, sound nerves, "a fast reaction time, a good memory, and the ability to make accurate observations" (Oliver, 2017, p. 305).

Some newspapers lampooned the hiring of college graduates by featuring cartoons of boys in caps and gowns wearing pistols, but the move was widely popular. One of Vollmer's first college cops was O. W. Wilson, a man who would be mentored by Vollmer and succeed him as one of the greatest innovators in police work of the 20th century. Another college recruit, John Larson, helped him develop a method of fingerprinting and also developed a lie detector in 1921. Vollmer kept a modus operandi file as well. He developed the first police radio car in 1921.

That same year he was unanimously elected to serve as president of the International Association of Chiefs of Police (IACP). At the IACP meeting in 1922, Vollmer called for the creation of a national bureau of criminal records and statistics. His efforts culminated in a congressional bill changing the name of the Bureau of Investigation to the Federal Bureau of Investigation, which was charged with maintaining criminal records and statistics.

Los Angeles and Return to Berkeley

In 1923, Vollmer agreed to serve 1 year as police chief in Los Angeles. He brought some of his methods to Los Angeles, hiring UCLA professors to conduct some of the work done by UC professors in Berkeley. He tried to ferret out corrupt police officers through undercover stings. He used the Army Alpha test of intelligence as a tool in making promotion and assignment decisions. He oversaw the construction of a new jail in Los Angeles. Along with bringing professors into the police department, Vollmer conducted guest lectures on police work at the University of Southern California.

Vollmer was not pleased with his stay in Los Angeles, thinking he had not been able to do enough and believing that corruption and cronyism were well engrained in the Los Angeles Police Department. He returned to Berkeley in 1924, the same year that he married Millicent "Pat" Fell. At that time, he began sharing his police innovations with police chiefs around the world, including chiefs in Detroit, Chicago, and Havana.

In 1929, he accepted President Herbert Hoover's offer to serve on the Wickersham Commission, which was formed to conduct the first national study of criminal justice administration in American history. He accepted a part-time teaching position at the University of Chicago, given by personal invitation of university president Robert Maynard Hutchins, and later at the University of California at Berkeley. Oliver calls Vollmer the first professor of police administration in history. Vollmer was also instrumental in creating a 2-year program at San Jose State College (University).

Another Vollmer innovation occurred in concert with some of his collaborators and mentees, including O. W. Wilson. On December 30, 1941, three weeks after the United States entered World War II, seven men met in Vollmer's home at Euclid Avenue in Berkeley "for the purpose of furthering college police training and standardizing police training curricula" (Morris, 1975, p. 123). The meeting lasted 15 hours. Vollmer and his "V Men" (Morris, 1975, p. 125) agreed to create the National Association of College Police Training Officials, which was renamed The Society for the Advancement of Criminology. While others in the group, especially O. W. Wilson and V. A. Leonard from Washington State College took the lead in getting the organization up and running, Vollmer's ideas were the foundation for the Society. Vollmer was elected to the honorary position of president emeritus.

In the late 1950s, the Society changed its name to the American Society of Criminology (ASC). It is one of two national criminal justice/criminology organizations still in existence today, the other being the Academy of Criminal Justice Sciences (ACJS), an offshoot of the ASC. The 1941 founding of the ASC is noted in its website, www.asc41.com.

Post-Berkeley

Vollmer resigned from the Berkeley Police Department on June 30, 1932, after serving 26 years in law enforcement. He became an international consultant, traveling throughout Asia and Europe advising police departments, while retaining his teaching position at the University of California. His life slowed down in the 1940s, especially after the death of his wife, Pat, though he continued to write and consult on occasion. In failing health, suffering from depression, and with deteriorating eyesight, Vollmer committed suicide on November 4, 1955, at the age of 79.

In an address before the IACP in 1919, Vollmer said that making arrests was not enough to prevent crime. He believed that police officers should "go up the stream a little" by working with families and schools. Consistent with his idea that criminality cannot be eliminated by legislation, Vollmer believed that a sentiment favoring law observance must be nurtured in all people, including children, hence his creation of a junior police league and School Boy Patrol, along with a Community Council for the Prevention of Delinquency in 1919. O. W. Wilson said of Vollmer, "He possesses the qualities which he listed, many years ago, as desirable for a policeman: The wisdom of Solomon, the courage of David, the strength of Sampson, the patience of Job, the leadership of Moses, the kindness of the Good Samaritan, the faith of Mary, the diplomacy of Lincoln, and the tolerance of Confucius" (Wilson, 1953, p. 91). Such praise may be a bit over the top, but August Vollmer did more to bring police studies into the educational arena than any person in the first half of the 20th century.

Sources and Suggested Readings

Carte, G. E., & Carte, E. H. (1975). *Police reform in the United States: The era of August Vollmer.* University of California Press.

Morris, A. (1975). The American society of criminology: A history, 1941–1974. *Criminology, 13*, 123–167.

Oliver, W. (2016). Celebrating 100 years of criminal justice education, 1916–2016. *Journal of Criminal Justice Education, 27*(4), 455–472.

Oliver, W. (2017). *August Vollmer: The father of American policing.* Carolina Academic Press.

Parker, A. E. (1961). *Crime fighter, August Vollmer.* Macmillan.

USGS. (n.d.). *The great 1906 San Francisco earthquake.* https://earthquake.usgs.gov/earthquakes/events/1906calif/18april/

Vollmer, A., & Schneider, A. (1917). The school for police as planned at Berkeley. *Journal of the American Institute of Criminal Law and Criminology, 7*, 877–898.

Walker, S. (1980). *Popular justice: A history of American criminal justice.* Oxford University Press.

Wilson, O. W. (1953). August Vollmer. *Journal of Criminal Law and Criminology, 44*(1), 91–103.

Discussion Questions

1. How did August Vollmer forge a link between police work and the academic environment?
2. What lessons can be learned from Vollmer in terms of crime prevention?

3. Despite his insistence on high educational standards and a rigorous screening process, August Vollmer had little faith in his rank-and-file employees. What are your thoughts on this aspect of his management style?

Credit

IMG 9.1: Underwood & Underwood, https://commons.wikimedia.org/wiki/File:August_Vollmer_cph.3b17374.jpg, 1929.

CHAPTER 10

Samuel Battle (1883–1966)

IMG 10.1

For more than two centuries after the United States came into existence, examples of African Americans being employed in the criminal justice system at all were rare, let alone in great numbers or in leadership positions. However, several individuals have had a tremendous impact by working through the system, former lawyer and Supreme Court Justice Thurgood Marshall among them. Some African Americans, such as Martin Luther King, Jr., have effected change in the administration of criminal justice by working outside the system. Many criminal justice pioneers from under represented populations have have remarkable biographies, but only those within specific locales or small towns might know them. Samuel Battle—the first African American police officer for the New York City Police Department—had an important story.

Early Life

Samuel Jesse Battle was born January 16, 1883, in New Bern, one of North Carolina's oldest cities. He was the son of Thomas and Annie Battle, both former slaves. By at least one account, "Big Sam" (a nickname he considered demeaning compared to his real name, Samuel) held the record for being the largest baby born in North Carolina. He weighed 16 pounds at birth, and he was big his entire life, growing to 6′3″ and weighing around 280 pounds. Years later, Battle said, "I guess I've always wanted to be large, and I have been large" ("Harlem's Legendary Samuel Jesse Battle," 2022, para. 3). Battle attended segregated schools in New Bern.

The son of a Methodist minister, Battle aspired to a career in law enforcement—in part because of a minor crime he committed as a teenager. He was caught stealing cash from his wealthy employer, R. H. Smith. Smith, a friend of Battle's father, did not press charges, but he predicted that the young Sam Battle would wind up in jail within a year. As a teen, Battle was called a bully for his propensity to fight, and he was known to steal from other New Bern residents as well. Determined not to endure the fate of so many other young Black men, and in defiance of Smith's prediction, Battle decided to turn in a positive direction by becoming a police officer. Battle said, "That was the turning point of my life. I said, 'From this day on, I shall always be honest and honorable, and I'm going to make Mr. Smith out a liar'" (Roberts, 2011, para. 4).

Battle had known a few people who migrated to the North. Hearing tales from New Bern natives about New York City created a determination on Battle's part to leave his life in the rural, impoverished South to experience the excitement of the nation's biggest city. Like many other African Americans of his era, Battle moved north to seek a better life than he could find in the Jim Crow South. He moved to New Haven, Connecticut, to attend a manual training school as a young man. In 1901, Battle moved to New York City where he held several jobs, including working as an attendant at the Sagamore Hotel, and as a train porter and baggage handler, or "Red Cap" at Grand Central Station (Washington, 2019). As a Red Cap, he carried bags for heavyweight boxing champion and civil rights icon Jack Johnson, conversed with President Theodore Roosevelt, a New York City native and a man Battle admired immensely, received opera tickets from famed Italian tenor Enrico Caruso, and even made a small appearance in a Broadway musical.

While it is true that Samuel Battle was the first Black officer with the NYPD, there were those who preceded him in Brooklyn, which had been a city of its own but is now officially a borough of New York City. Wiley Overton is believed to be the first African American police officer in Brooklyn, having been hired in 1881. Another Brooklyn officer was Moses Cobb, Samuel Battle's brother-in-law. After talking the matter over with Cobb and while still working 12-hour shifts at Grand Central, Samuel Battle took the radical and unusual step of studying for the civil service exam to become a police officer. Moses Cobb continued to serve as mentor to Sam Battle.

Badge Number 782

Battle passed the exam in 1910, ranking 119th (or 199th) out of 638 candidates, but city officials, uneasy with the prospect of hiring a Black officer, delayed his appointment under the pretext that Battle had a heart condition that might affect his suitability for police work. Battle, a very large, strong man who had spent the past several years carrying heavy baggage as a Red Cap at Grand Central

Station, argued that the heart condition diagnosis was intentionally falsified by the department's official physician. So he hired his own doctor, a prominent White physician, to successfully debunk the false diagnosis. A Black-owned newspaper, the *New York Age*, joined the controversy and applied pressure on Mayor William Gaynor and the NYPD to hire Battle.

Samuel Battle was hired as a police officer for the city of New York in June 1911 at the age of 28, badge number 782. He was the only African American police officer on the NYPD's force of 10,000 men (no women). Police Commissioner Rhinelander Waldo told Battle, "You will have some difficulties, but I know you will overcome them." (McKnight, 2015, para 3.) Soon after he was sworn in, he returned to Grand Central Station to submit his resignation as porter. All the Black porters at the station stopped in their tracks and put down their bags to stare in disbelief at Battle, a Black man in a police uniform.

In 1911, African Americans comprised only 2% of New York City's population, many of whom lived in an area known as San Juan Hill, now the site of the Lincoln Center for Performing Arts. Battle was assigned to the San Juan Hill area, the 28th Precinct at the West 68th Street station. On his first day on the job, a group of White spectators gathered outside, also staring in disbelief at the sight of a Black man in a police uniform.

While undergoing the 30-day training program for the NYPD, Battle was treated respectfully, but things were different once he graduated and officially became a uniformed police officer. Upon his arrival to the New York City Police Department, Battle was greeted mostly with stony silence. Unwelcome by most of his peers, Battle was subjected to the silent treatment by other police officers that refused to even acknowledge his existence, let alone accept him as a colleague. Battle received no guidance or mentorship, nor did he enjoy any camaraderie with his fellow officers. He once found a note with racially derogatory language and a hole the size of a bullet. Rather than being allowed admission to the NYPD dormitory when officers needed to sleep, Battle was given a cot in the precinct's flag storage loft. The irony of being relegated to sleep in a room used for storing the American flag, a symbol of liberty, was not lost on Battle. He described the scene:

> Sometimes, lying on my cot on the top floor in the silence, I would wonder how it was that many of the patrolmen in my precinct who did not yet speak English well, had no such difficulties in getting on the police force as I, a Negro American, had experienced ... My name had been passed over repeatedly. And now, after a long wait and a lot of stalling, I had finally been given a trial appointment to their ranks and these men would not speak to me. Native-born and foreign-born whites on the police force all united in looking past me as though I were not a human being. In the loft in the dark, with the Stars and Stripes, I wondered! Why? (Browne, 2015, p. 85)

Battle continued to be the target of gawkers during his first 2 years with the department. Tour buses were brought to look at him, with the tour guide saying, "Look, there's the colored cop." Streetcar conductors would ring their bells and also point Battle out to the passengers.

Harlem

By one account, 2 years went by before any of the White officers spoke to him, but Battle never complained in public, knowing that doing so would probably just make matters worse. Although he was never accepted by many of his colleagues, Battle's perseverance, easygoing demeanor (rebellion would have been the death knell for Battle's career), and courage to withstand the hostility of those around him began to pay dividends. In 1913, New York City police officials recognized that African Americans were populating the city's Harlem area in growing numbers and sought to use Battle's race to their advantage. Thinking that Black residents in Harlem would have better rapport with a Black officer than with White officers, they assigned Battle to the West 135th Street station in Harlem. The movement of Black residents to Harlem proliferated after World War I ended in 1918.

Battle's transfer to Harlem was well received by the area's Black residents. It worked well for Battle too—so well that he was encouraged to apply for a promotion to sergeant in 1919. The year 1919 was one of the worst in American history in terms of urban riots, some of which were race related. The most infamous was in Chicago, but a riot broke out that year in Harlem as well. Fitting an all-too-familiar pattern in U.S. history, Harlem's Straw Hat Riot erupted over the shooting of a young Black man by a White police officer. A White officer, when cornered and in danger of being murdered by a rioting Black mob, was saved by Battle. In return, the New York Police Department, which had been holding up Battle's admission to sergeant's school because he lacked the requisite approval from his colleagues, promptly admitted him to sergeant's school. Battle had gained the blessing of his colleagues and the respect of many.

One challenge facing many American communities in the Prohibition era of the 1920s was speakeasies, established to sell alcohol illegally and so named because patrons would knock and "speakeasy" to be allowed entry. Harlem had its share of speakeasies, some of which were operated by major organized crime bosses, most notably the infamous Charles "Lucky" Luciano. Others operated under the protection of New York politicians and police officers. Battle attacked Harlem speakeasies, making powerful enemies in the process. Barron Wilkins, a prominent Black businessman and baseball entrepreneur, operated a speakeasy under the protection of the city's Democratic Party bosses. After Battle led a raid on Wilkins's illegal establishment, he was transferred to an unpleasant area of Brooklyn, an assignment that did not last.

Battle made high marks on the sergeant's exam, but he had to wait 7 years for his promotion. In 1926, Battle, already the first African American police officer in the New York Police Department history, became its first African American sergeant. Battle became the department's first African American lieutenant in 1935. He also headed one of the NYPD's first SWAT teams.

Parole Commissioner

After Lou Gehrig retired from baseball in 1939, he was appointed to a New York City parole commissioner's position by Mayor Fiorello La Guardia, a position he held until 1 month before his death on June 2, 1941, from the disease that would bear his name. Upon Gehrig's death, LaGuardia appointed Samuel Battle to fill the position formerly occupied by Lou Gehrig. La Guardia insisted that Battle's race was not a factor in his decision; he simply believed Battle was the best person for the job.

Battle assumed the role of parole commissioner in 1941, another first for an African American. However, rather than deciding whether a person should be released early from incarceration, Battle's primary task was working with delinquent and at-risk Black youths in Harlem. Part of the reason for this move was Battle's history of reaching out to the Harlem community and his crime prevention measures. In addition to the commonsense crime prevention practices he used on his patrol beat, he raised money to buy Thanksgiving dinners and trips to movie theaters for poor Harlem residents.

In 1943, while the United States was in the throes of World War II, there was another outbreak of urban riots, one of which occurred in Harlem. It was the result of the shooting of a Black soldier (and a false rumor that he had died) by a White police officer. At the request of New York Mayor Fiorello La Guardia, Battle took charge of the city's response to the Harlem riots. One of his first orders was that all-White civilians, including Mayor La Guardia, vacate Harlem's streets. Then he ordered officers to be placed in strategic rooftop locations and on mounted patrol. Battle personally patrolled the Harlem area, making sure he was visible to the Harlem residents who knew and trusted him.

After the 1943 riots, Battle resumed his work as parole commissioner. Not only did he monitor his charges' whereabouts, he devised methods he saw as conducive to rehabilitation of inner-city youths. He organized and administered summer camps, sports leagues, and other community activities. Battle solicited the involvement of Black and White police officers in hopes of bringing Harlem residents and the police closer together. One of the youths that Battle referred to as a protégé was Walker Smith, a Georgia native who moved to Harlem and who went on to become one of the greatest middleweight boxers in history under the name "Sugar Ray Robinson."

As Battle was a celebrity of sorts in New York City's Black community, he befriended many other famous African Americans of the period. Track and field star Jesse Owens lived in Battle's townhouse after winning four gold medals at the 1936 Olympics in Berlin, a feat that shot holes in the Aryan supremacy ideals of the Olympic games host, German Chancellor Adolph Hitler. In June 1941, when world heavyweight boxing champion Joe Louis narrowly defeated challenger Billy Conn, Samuel Battle sat in Louis's corner.

Retirement, Death, and Legacy

Battle kept his position as parole commissioner until his retirement in 1951, having served the city of New York for 40 years. He continued working with Harlem's youth in crime prevention and other community activities, but finally found time to travel to Europe with his wife Florence. In 1964, the New York City Police Department held a special ceremony with the 81-year-old Battle as special guest.

Battle believed that his story was worth being told, and he collaborated with Langston Hughes, one of the most famous poets of the 20th century, often called the poet genius of the Harlem Renaissance, to write his biography. Hughes and Battle compiled an 80,000-word manuscript, which included a foreword written by fellow New Yorker and former First Lady Eleanor Roosevelt, who wrote, "This is a record of a man's life and as he tells it you not only see one life, but you see the struggles and the victories and the defeats of a whole group of U.S. citizens" (Browne, 2015, p. 289). Hughes's manuscript was never published.

As the civil rights struggle reached its zenith in the 1950s and 1960s, many African American civil rights activists became household names. Thurgood Marshall, Jackie Robinson, Rosa Parks, and Martin Luther King, Jr. would eventually become well-known to all Americans, Black and White. Unfortunately, Samuel Battle did not join the pantheon of famous African American pioneers during his lifetime. But his story has gotten some long overdue recognition in recent years. In 2018, Arthur Browne released a biography of Battle titled *One Righteous Man: Samuel Battle and the Shattering of the Color Line in New York* in which he borrowed substantially from Hughes's manuscript.

It is worth noting that Battle, unlike many other civil rights pioneers, was not part of any movement, nor did he have the sponsorship of any organization, such as the fledgling National Association for the Advancement of Colored People; Battle did what he did largely on his own. When Battle joined the NYPD in 1911, Blacks comprised 2% of New York City's population and Battle was its first Black officer. Much had changed in a century. By 2011, 100 years later, the Black population of the city stood at 23%, and 18% of the NYPD officers were African American. In 2009, the NYPD named the intersection of 135th Street and Lenox Avenue (Harlem) the "Samuel J. Battle Plaza." It was the spot where Battle had saved the life of a White officer in Harlem's 1919 riots.

Battle died from leukemia on August 7, 1966, at the age of 83, leaving behind his wife Florence, a son, a daughter, and a legacy as one of America's bravest criminal justice pioneers. His final words to several of his younger relatives were, "The torch has passed" (Browne, 2015, p. 290). According to Battle biographer Arthur Browne, Battle's final words in his memoir were, "Not just for the Negro's sake, but for the sake of my country I look forward to the day when all of us will do unto others as we would have others do unto us" (Browne, 2015, p. 290).

Sources and Suggested Readings

AAHIAH Video Series. (2016). *AAHIAH episode #2: "The Samuel J. Battle story"* [Video]. YouTube. https://www.youtube.com/watch?v=bmdPdH1cpb4, date of retrieval February 5, 2024.

Alexander, James I. (1978). *Blue coats: Black skin.* Exposition Press.

Axelrod, A., Phillips, C., & Kemper, K. (1996). *Cops, crooks and criminologists.* Facts on File.

Browne, A. (2015). *One righteous man: Samuel Battle & the shattering of the color line in New York.* Beacon Press.

Fratus, M. (2021, February 24). Samuel J. Battle: The forgotten hero of the NYPD who broke the city's color barrier. *Coffee or Die Magazine.* https://coffeeordie.com/samuel-battle-nypd, date of retrieval February 2, 2024.

Harlem's legendary Samuel Jesse Battle, the first African-American New York City Police Department officer, 1883–1966. (2022, March 11). *Harlem World Magazine.* https://www.harlemworldmagazine.com/harlems-samuel-jesse-battle-a-career-of-firsts/, accessed August 4, 2024.

Hooton, L. (2013, October 6). *Samuel James Battle: 1883–1966.* BlackPast.org. https://www.blackpast.org/african-american-history/battle-samuel-james-1883-1966/, date of retrieval February 3, 2024.

McKnight, Matthew (2015). "Darker Than Blue: Policing While Black in N.Y.C." The New Yorker https://www.newyorker.com/news/news-desk/darker-than-blue-policing-while-black-in-n-y-c, date of retrieval January 13, 2025.

National Law Enforcement Museum. (2018, February 5). *Book details the life of Samuel Battle, the first Black police officer in NYC.* https://www.police1.com/national-law-enforcement-museum/articles/book-details-the-life-of-samuel-battle-the-first-black-police-officer-in-nyc-LvJuB2PJTW06jUUx/, date of retrieval February 6, 2024.

National Law Enforcement Officer Memorial Fund. (2024). Samuel J. Battle: A Black officer of NYPD with many firsts. *Black Trailblazers in Blue.* https://nleomf.org/lieutenant-samuel-j-battle/, date of retrieval February 7, 2024.

New York Daily News Video. (2016). *Samuel Battle: First African-American to join NYPD.* YouTube. https://www.youtube.com/watch?v=6nmDMeSYr4g, date of retrieval February 7, 2024.

NYPD. (2018). *Sam Battle: The right man at the right time* [Video]. YouTube. https://www.youtube.com/watch?v=b46n3F9piH4, date of retrieval February 7, 2024.

Roberts, Sam. (2011, June 26). Recalling first Black appointed to New York Police Dept. *New York Times.* https://www.nytimes.com/2011/06/27/nyregion/recalling-samuel-battle-who-became-first-black-on-nypd.html, accessed February 5, 2024.

Washington, Eric K. (2019). *Boss of the grips: The life of James H. Williams and the red caps of Grand Central Terminal.* Liveright.

Discussion Questions

1. If you were faced with the same obstacles as Samuel Battle, could you persevere as he did?
2. In what ways did Samuel Battle go beyond conventional police work to fight and prevent crime? What can be learned from his efforts?

Credit

IMG 10.1: Source: https://www.columbia.edu/cu/iraas/harlem/neighborhood/battle.html.

CHAPTER 11

J. Edgar Hoover (1895–1972)

IMG 11.1

Some subjects of this book made so great an impact that not even an entire book, let alone one short chapter, can capture that impact. J. Edgar Hoover, the man who directed the Federal Bureau of Investigation from 1924 to 1972, is one such person. His presence still looms larger than life, not only within the Federal Bureau of Investigation (FBI), but over American law enforcement, politics, and culture. No one was as lionized in life and as vilified after death as Hoover. Since his death, history has not been kind to him. Much has been written and said about J. Edgar Hoover, some true and some myth. His personal strengths, accomplishments, and contributions to law enforcement, often overlooked by modern historians, are exceeded only by his personal quirks, his fascinating frailties, and his glaring faults.

Early Life and Career

Hoover seemed destined from birth to become a spectacularly successful Washington bureaucrat. John Edgar Hoover was born on January 1, 1895, in Washington, D.C., not far from the Capitol building that his great-granduncle helped construct. Of all the subjects of this book, Hoover was probably the least traveled. He knew or cared little about other places or other cultures. He was a product of the small-town provincial and bureaucratic atmosphere that was Washington at the turn of the 20th century. He was the youngest of four children born to Dickerson and Anna Marie Scheitlin Hoover. Dickerson Hoover, who worked for the U.S. Coast and Geodetic Survey, was not a strong influence on him; in fact, Dickerson Hoover's institutionalization for mental health problems was a family embarrassment. J. Edgar Hoover's strongest influence was his mother, with whom he lived until her death in 1938.

A devoutly religious child, Hoover at one point aspired to be a Presbyterian minister. Hoover was short and slight of build and stuttered as a child. He overcame his stuttering by speaking in a rapid-fire, staccato fashion, and he sharpened his speaking skills through participation on high school debate teams. He was always short of stature, something of which he was very conscious. He avoided social gatherings where tall people were present, and while many FBI field agents were tall, few tall agents worked in FBI headquarters in physical proximity to the diminutive Hoover. Hoover always kept a dais under his desk that he could stand on when anyone entered his office.

J. Edgar Hoover was the valedictorian of his high school graduating class in 1913. Rather than accept a scholarship from the University of Virginia, Hoover lived at home and attended night school at George Washington University. During the day, Hoover worked at the Library of Congress, which was located four blocks from his home. There Hoover learned two things that would serve him well throughout his career: First, he honed his ability to research and keep meticulous records, which would lead to his FBI director trademark of keeping thousands of secret files on public figures. Second, Hoover discovered that even the most powerful politicians come and go in Washington; bureaucrats are there to stay, and they are the real power brokers.

Hoover received a bachelor of law degree in 1916, his master of law degree a year later, and passed the District of Columbia bar exam that same year. On July 26, 1917, Hoover took a job as a clerk with the United States Department of Justice (DOJ), a job that exempted Hoover from the draft. Only 3 months earlier, America had entered World War I.

Throughout his life, Hoover viewed people and issues in absolute terms; someone or something was either good or evil, with no in-between. What he perceived as un-American was bad, and anyone that did not conform to his idea of a patriotic American was not only wrong, but evil. Hoover, already a skilled, humorless, patriotic, no-nonsense bureaucrat while still in his early 20s, rose rapidly through Justice Department ranks, heading the DOJ's Alien Enemy Bureau by 1917.

In 1919, Hoover was placed in charge of the DOJ's radical division. The first public display of using criminal law to advance his idea of patriotism came with his role in the deportations of Emma Goldman, Alexander Berkman, and more than 200 other political radicals in 1919. Hoover took an active part in the prosecution of the radicals, who had been suspected of, among other things, sabotaging America's war effort and trying to assassinate Attorney General A. Mitchell Palmer. Hoover used the news media to proclaim his actions, something he grew increasingly adept at doing as the years progressed. When the raids fell into public disfavor, Hoover just as effectively distanced himself.

The Bureau of Investigation

Hoover was appointed assistant director of the Bureau of Investigation (BI) in 1921, 14 years before it would be renamed the FBI. During the early 1920s, the Bureau was filled with corrupt, feckless agents with shady backgrounds and little in the way of qualifications. Presidents, cabinet officials, and members of Congress had used it as a political football. The Teapot Dome scandal, in which numerous Interior Department officials accepted bribes and kickbacks in exchange for leasing oil rights on government property, led to President Calvin Coolidge's call for the Bureau and the entire Justice Department to be cleaned up.

BI/FBI Director

Upon the departure of William Burns in 1924, Attorney General Harlan Fisk Stone offered the job of Bureau director to Hoover. Hoover accepted but with conditions. Hoover demanded that the Bureau be divorced from politics and not a "catch-all for political hacks" (Mansky and Boissoneault, 2017, para. 4), that appointments and promotions be based on merit, and that Hoover be answerable to the attorney general and the president, not to any member of Congress or other cabinet officials. Stone gladly agreed, effectively giving the 29-year-old Hoover a blank check to establish the department in his own image and render him virtually unaccountable. Hoover assumed his duties as director on May 10, 1924; he would serve for more than 48 years.

Hoover was determined to make the Bureau the world's premier law enforcement agency. He imposed qualifications for his agents far and above those required by even the most progressive police agencies. Bureau agents were required to have backgrounds in either law or accounting. Bureau agents would be called on to investigate complex financial crimes. Hoover did not want agents that would lose cases in court due to ignorance of the law. Procedural guarantees such as the exclusionary rule, which would not apply to the states until the 1960s, already were required at the federal level.

Calling the Bureau an investigative agency—not a law enforcement agency—Hoover took advantage of every available investigation tool he could find. The FBI boasted the world's most highly trained agents and one of the world's top training programs and regimens. Agents were required to be always dressed neatly in coat and tie. Utter patriotism and loyalty to the Bureau and to Hoover were agent trademarks.

Hoover, the consummate Washington insider, knew how to get things done and how to get what he wanted, both for himself and his agency. He obtained a fingerprint identification unit that was accessed by law enforcement agencies from around the country, and he developed a crime laboratory unmatched by any that had ever existed. Not long after Hoover assumed directorship, the FBI became the envy of law enforcers around the world. The FBI represented the unquestioned elite in American law enforcement.

Prior to the 1930s, the United States had no empirical measure of how much crime occurred or how many crimes were reported to police. Hoover oversaw administration of the Uniform Crime Report (UCR), which was started in 1933. Crude and imperfect, especially in its founding stage, the UCR consisted of crimes reported to police agencies, or at least the local agencies that chose to participate by sending their reports to the Bureau. It was the United States' first systematic method for gathering and analyzing crime statistics, and it is still in use today.

Although Hoover was effective at improving the qualifications of his agents and the facilities and technologies at their disposal, his real strength was in selling his agency and himself to the public. Even though he possessed a dour and colorless personality, Hoover became the object of public fascination and downright adoration. Hoover developed a following like no other American law enforcer before or since his time, even though he made very few arrests, all of which, though genuine, were carefully staged to bolster Hoover's image as a top-notch cop. He portrayed crime as a public menace, and he offered his own guidance in crime prevention to whoever would listen, even though he seldom encountered criminals personally. His beliefs on the causes of crime reflected simple homespun conservatism that resonated with the American heartland:

> The cure for crime is not the electric chair, but the high chair. (BrainyQuote.com, n.d., para. 1)

Public Enemies

One of Hoover's greatest strengths was his ability to personalize America's crime problem, to put a face on crime, to create in the public mindset the idea that there were good guys and bad guys. Take the bad guys off the street, courtesy of the FBI, and feel a sense of closure and relief. Hoover created this image by making America's first public enemies list. The public enemies list would consist of America's most-wanted criminals, with their names and faces plastered on federal office buildings around the country.

The 1930s was the decade of G-men (FBI agents) hunting down notorious bank robbers and murderers. Hoover inadvertently created folk hero images as well. Lester Gillis, a.k.a. Baby Face Nelson, Alvin "Creepy" Karpis, Charles "Pretty Boy" Floyd, George "Machine Gun" Kelly, Kate "Ma" Barker, and "Handsome" John Dillinger became household names. By tracking down and capturing or killing such criminals, most of who operated in the Midwest, Hoover was able to portray the FBI as the agency that "always got its man [or woman]" ("They Always Get Their Man," 1981, para 1).

John Dillinger's case provides some insight into Hoover's thinking. Dillinger was one of the most notorious armed robbers of the decade, and he had gained folk hero status for robbing banks, an institution hated by Americans that had lost their uninsured savings during the Great Depression. After months of fruitless searches, embarrassing escapes, and shoot-outs, including one notorious jail escape courtesy of a wooden gun (after Dillinger posed for a photo with the local sheriff, draping his arm across the local prosecutor's shoulder), Hoover made it his passion to get Dillinger, partly because he was a genuine threat to public safety but mostly because he had embarrassed Hoover and the Bureau. Bureau agents killed Dillinger in 1934 outside a Chicago theater.

The long-awaited killing of Dillinger should have made Hoover ecstatic, but instead it sent him into a jealous frenzy because one of his agents, Melvin Purvis, who directly supervised the Dillinger killing, was hailed as a hero. Hoover could not stand to see one of his own agents grab the limelight. The public adulation heaped on Purvis spelled the end of Purvis's career with the Bureau.

World War II

World War II brought new challenges to Hoover and the FBI. Investigating espionage and industrial sabotage became the top priorities. The FBI investigated many such cases, including the case of the bungling German saboteurs that landed ashore in Florida and New York via German submarine, but were easily caught and prosecuted with some being executed.

A sad footnote to America's World War II victory was the forced relocation and internment of Japanese Americans on the Pacific Coast and German Americans in Texas. Many Americans, including prominent names associated with 20th-century liberalism, such as Earl Warren (Attorney General of California at the time) and President Franklin Roosevelt, ordered the internment of the Japanese and German Americans. Most of Hoover's critics fail to mention that he opposed the forced relocation, believing that most Japanese Americans posed no threat to American security and that those who did could be effectively monitored, as was being done on the East Coast and in the Midwest with people of German ancestry.

Communism and the Cold War

After World War II, American anger and suspicion was directed at a new enemy—Communism, which had also been viewed as a threat immediately after the end of World War I. Hoover hated Communism with every fiber of his being, saying,

> The individual is handicapped by coming face to face with a conspiracy so monstrous they cannot believe it exists. The American mind simply has not come to the realization of the evil which has been introduced into our midst. (Good Reads, n.d., *J. Edgar Hoover quotes*)

The concern over Communism brought Hoover into contact with two people, both of whom enjoyed a symbiotic relationship with Hoover, one for a short time and the other for many years to come. They were Joseph McCarthy, a United States senator from Wisconsin that whipped America into a paranoid frenzy over Communism, and Richard Nixon, a young California congressman that joined the fray. Hoover and the FBI, with the aid of Nixon, succeeded in prosecuting a high-level State Department official named Alger Hiss on charges of perjury, related to supplying intelligence information to the Soviet Union.

President Harry Truman, who disliked both Hoover and McCarthy, grudgingly allowed the FBI to conduct background checks on all prospective and current federal employees. Hoover, who had already accumulated hundreds of secret files, delighted in his new duty. He had a virtual blank check to investigate almost anyone.

McCarthy fell from grace, but Hoover and Nixon thrived in the Cold War era. The FBI even led the prosecution of the only Americans of the 20th century to be executed for espionage during peacetime. Julius and Ethel Rosenberg were executed in 1953 for selling nuclear secrets to the Soviet Union.

Enemies List

The 1960s, the age of civil rights and anti-Vietnam war protests, brought out even more paranoia in Hoover. He had directed the FBI for more than 40 years and was in his 70s when critics and even some agents quietly charged that he was losing touch with reality. The list of people he tracked and secretly investigated grew astronomically. It included Malcolm X, Elvis Presley, Edwin Sutherland, John Lennon, journalist Daniel Schorr, the Kennedy family, and hundreds of other academics, entertainers, political figures, and public figures, most on the political left. Hoover also kept tabs on right-wing extremists like George Lincoln Rockwell, the head of the American Nazi Party and Ku Klux Klansmen in the South.

Martin Luther King, Jr.

Of all the people on Hoover's enemies list, none rankled him more than Martin Luther King, Jr., the leader of the Southern Christian Leadership Conference and the most famous Civil Rights Movement leader of the 20th century. Hoover's agents conducted surveillance on Dr. King with the approval of Attorney General Robert Kennedy, secretly bugging his phone calls and other conversations. J. Edgar Hoover became aware of King's marital infidelities. Hoover viewed King, an ordained Baptist minister, as a degenerate and a hypocrite, and was especially angered at King's accusations that the FBI was remiss in their investigation of violent right-wing groups in the south. Hoover called King "the most notorious liar in the country" (Pruitt, 2024, para. 12).

When it was announced in 1964 that King was to receive the Nobel Prize, Hoover was determined to prevent him from accepting the award. William Sullivan, one of Hoover's top men, penned an "anonymous" letter to King in November 1964. The letter, intended to read as if it had been written by a disenchanted Black man, accused King of "immoral conduct lower than that of a beast," and of being "a giant liability to all of us Negroes" (Prokop, 2018, para. 7). It contained cassette tape recordings of King's private moments and said, "It is all there on the record, your sexual orgies. Listen to yourself you filthy, abnormal animal." Sullivan threatened to expose King and urged him to commit suicide. He wrote, "There is only one thing left for you to do. You know what it is" (Pruitt, 2024, para. 14). Undeterred, King went to Norway in December and accepted the Nobel Peace Prize.

Hoover and the Presidents

J. Edgar Hoover had working relationships with presidents from both major political parties. Some like Richard Nixon liked him. Some like Harry Truman disliked him but could not get rid of him because of the feared political fallout. Others such as John Kennedy and Franklin Roosevelt were afraid he would release damaging information about their personal or political lives. Eleanor Roosevelt, the activist wife of Franklin Roosevelt and a person that Hoover detested, called the FBI an American gestapo. Neither Dwight Eisenhower nor Lyndon Johnson particularly liked Hoover, but they knew he was useful. When asked by an aide why he kept Hoover around, President Johnson replied, "I'd rather have him inside the tent pissing out than outside the tent pissing in" (Good Reads, n.d., Jeffrey Archer quotes).

Death and Legacy

J. Edgar Hoover died on May 2, 1972, at the age of 77. Hoover never married and was never known to have seriously dated a woman. Many believe that Hoover had a long-term gay relationship with Clyde Tolson. Tolson served several decades as assistant director to the FBI and was one of the few people with whom Hoover was ever seen in a casual setting, such as lounging around the home or visiting the race tracks, something any other FBI agent would have been forbidden to do. Hoover and Tolson were the only FBI employees exempt from mandatory retirement regulations,

Evaluating J. Edgar Hoover's place in American history is not easy. He was in many ways a true giant in the field of law enforcement and criminal investigation. The FBI, even with its many faults and political manipulations, still stands as one of the world's elite law enforcement agencies, thanks in large measure to Hoover, for whom FBI headquarters are named. As large as Hoover was in many ways, he was equally small in other respects. He was petty, paranoid, and bigoted. The question is whether Hoover merely reflected the attitude of most Americans of his era, or whether he was responsible for shaping mainstream America's attitudes toward crime, civil rights, and left-wing politics. He was smart enough to take on battles he could win, such as nabbing gangsters and spies, but he was also smart enough to avoid battles he knew he could not win, such as stopping prohibition and organized crime. However one chooses to view Hoover, his impact on American law enforcement is significant.

Sources and Suggested Readings

BrainyQuote.com. (n.d.). J. *Edgar Hoover quotes.* https://www.brainyquote.com/quotes/j_edgar_hoover_391970, accessed August 4, 2024.

Dallek, R. (1998). *Flawed giant: Lyndon Johnson and his times, 1961-1973.* Oxford University Press.

EJI.org. (2023). *52 individuals, including Dr. Martin Luther King Jr., arrested in Atlanta sit-in protest.* A History of Racial Injustice. https://calendar.eji.org/racial-injustice/oct/19, date of retrieval March 1, 2023.

Gentry, C. (1991). *J. Edgar Hoover: The man and his secrets.* Norton.

Good Reads. (n.d.). *J. Edgar Hoover quotes.* https://www.goodreads.com/author/quotes/204006.J_Edgar_Hoover, accessed August 4, 2024.

Good Reads. (n.d.). *Jeffrey Archer quotes.* https://www.goodreads.com/quotes/7261748-remember-what-lyndon-johnson-said-about-j-edgar-hoover-i-d, accessed August 4, 2024.

Keen, Mike F. (1999). *Stalking the sociological imagination: J. Edgar Hoover's FBI surveillance of American sociology.* Greenwood Press.

Lowenthal, M. (1950). *The Federal Bureau of Investigation.* William Sloan.

Mansky, J., & Boissoneault, L. (2017, May 11). Has the FBI ever been divorced from politics? *Smithsonian Magazine.* https://www.smithsonianmag.com/history/has-fbi-ever-been-divorced-politics-180963257/, accessed August 4, 2024.

The Nobel Prize. (2023). Martin Luther King Jr. facts. https://www.nobelprize.org/prizes/peace/1964/king/facts/, date of retrieval March 8, 2023.

Powers, R. G. (1987). *Secrecy and power: The life of J. Edgar Hoover.* Free Press.

Prokop, A. (2018, January 15). Read the letter the FBI sent MLK to try to convince him to kill himself. *Vox*. https://www.vox.com/xpress/2014/11/12/7204453/martin-luther-king-fbi-letter, accessed August 4, 2024.

Pruitt, S. (2024, January 3). Why the FBI saw Martin Luther King, Jr. as a communist threat. *History*. https://www.history.com/news/martin-luther-king-jr-fbi-j-edgar-hoover-communism, accessed August 4, 2024.

Stanford University. (1968, April 4). *Assassination of Martin Luther King, Jr.* The Martin Luther King, Jr. Research and Education Institute. https://kinginstitute.stanford.edu/encyclopedia/assassination-martin-luther-king-jr, date of retrieval March 7, 2023.

They always get their man. (1981, November 9). *Time* [online]. https://time.com/archive/6856517/they-always-get-their-man/, accessed August 4, 2024.

Discussion Questions

1. Was J. Edgar Hoover a case in point of one man being granted too much power? Why or why not?
2. In what respects did J. Edgar Hoover create American perceptions that matched his own, and in what respects did he simply mirror popular perceptions of his time?

Credit

IMG 11.1: Marion S. Trikosko, "J. Edgar Hoover," https://commons.wikimedia.org/wiki/File:Hoover-JEdgar-LOC.jpg, 1961.

CHAPTER 12

O. W. Wilson (1900–1972)

If August Vollmer deserves the title of America's premier police pioneer of the 20th century, O. W. Wilson was the chief protégé of that pioneer. Vollmer's and Wilson's lives and careers were inextricably linked, with Wilson owing his career to Vollmer while carving his own distinctive niche in the history of American policing. Several labels are appropriate for O. W. Wilson, including police scholar, police reformer, and consummate police professional.

IMG 12.1

Early Life and Career

Orlando Winfield Wilson was born in 1900 in Veblen, South Dakota. His father, Ole Vraalson, was a Norwegian immigrant who changed his last name to Wilson because he thought it would be easier for business purposes. Both he and his wife, Olava, were schoolteachers, while Ole also worked the family farm and served as county treasurer and state legislator. The Wilsons moved to Saskatchewan in 1905, then to Anderson, California, in 1911, then to Orland, California, in 1913, and finally to Pacific Beach near San Diego. O. W. Wilson graduated from San Diego High School in 1918. Motivated by his interest in a gold mine his father had purchased years earlier, O. W. left San Diego to attend the University of California at Berkeley and pursue a degree in mining engineering.

August Vollmer and the Berkeley Police Department

Shortly after World War I ended in 1918, the United States entered a severe recession. Ole Wilson fell on bad times and was unable to provide his son's college expenses. O. W. Wilson needed a job to put himself through college and noticed an advertisement in the student newspaper placed by August Vollmer, the city's police chief. Vollmer was recruiting college students to work as municipal police officers, something unheard of in American policing at that time. Desperate for funds, Wilson applied for one of Vollmer's "college cop" positions, considering it merely a college meal ticket.

The standards set by Vollmer were much higher than Wilson expected. Wilson scored higher than any of the other applicants on the Army Alpha test and performed well on the physical and psychological examinations. The last step was a personal interview with Chief August Vollmer. Vollmer hired him and informed Wilson that he would have to furnish his own personal vehicle and .38 caliber Smith & Wesson revolver. Wilson started working for the Berkeley Police Department in 1921 at a monthly salary of $140 ($2,400 today), plus $30 ($450 today) monthly car allowance (Bopp, 1977, p. 23).

Most police departments in the 1920s were riddled with inefficiency, corruption, political meddling, and uneducated, untrained feckless officers. Not so in Berkeley; Wilson and his young colleagues worked and learned under the most progressive police chief in the country. Wilson learned to work with polygraphs, and he learned to use call boxes on streets to contact police, which although crude by today's standards, were innovative for their day. Vollmer's recordkeeping was also ahead of its time. Wilson learned to keep a modus operandi file that catalogued robbery and burglary techniques.

Some veteran officers resented Vollmer's college cops. Wilson overcame this resistance by working hard, not flaunting his education, maintaining a serious, mature demeanor, and doing good work. Early in his tenure, Wilson captured a notorious escaped prison inmate named Kid Benet by himself, solidifying his reputation as an effective officer (Bopp, 1977, p. 24).

Like most Berkeley police officers, Wilson spent much of his time responding to calls from the University of California campus. He did not make many friends at the school, mostly because he cited fraternity members for city health code violations and minor thefts discovered during house inspections. His serious demeanor and the fact that he was the same age as the people he policed did not win him friends either.

However, Wilson met people who would play important roles in his personal life and his career while at Berkeley. In addition to August Vollmer, one such person was Earl Warren, an assistant prosecutor in the Alameda County district attorney's office who worked closely with Wilson. Warren and Wilson became friends in the 1920s, bonded over their shared philosophy in strict law and order and vigorous prosecution of criminal defendants. Forty years later, when Warren, as chief justice of the United States, led the due process revolution despised by many police officers, Wilson called Warren "treacherous" (Bopp, 1977, p. 25) for turning his back on law enforcement.

While at Berkeley, Wilson met university student Vernis Haddon, whom he stopped for speeding in 1921. Haddon was one of the few people Wilson released from an infraction. Wilson and Haddon eloped 6 weeks later and were married in Sacramento, a rare act of impulsivity that he later regretted.

While working as an officer, Wilson's studies suffered, and he even flunked out of Berkeley for one semester. He returned and changed his major to economics, thinking a career in business would be his future. He graduated in 1925. Chief Vollmer had other plans for Wilson. Realizing that Wilson would prove an asset to the professionalization of law enforcement, Vollmer recommended that Wilson accept the job of police chief in Fullerton, California.

Fullerton and Los Angeles

Wilson accepted the Fullerton police chief job in 1925. His experience in Fullerton proved disappointing. The liberal atmosphere of Berkeley that permitted Vollmer to innovate was not present at Fullerton. Some citizens were puzzled and alarmed at his call for birth control as a crime prevention measure. Wilson was criticized for being overzealous when he strictly enforced a dog leash law. He was criticized for curtailing the use of motorcycle patrol, which he thought inefficient, but which locals liked because the motorcycles made impressive funeral processions.

Although he was lauded for many of his efforts, Fullerton civic leaders tired of hearing citizen complaints about Wilson. He resigned on December 1, 1925, and moved to Los Angeles to work as an investigator for the Pacific Finance Corporation while his wife embarked on an acting career. He worked there for 2 years.

Wichita

Relying again on Vollmer's recommendation, Wilson reluctantly accepted the position of chief of police in Wichita, Kansas, in March 1928. There he would make his historic mark on American law enforcement and academe. Wichita was ripe for reform and posed an enormous challenge for Wilson. In many ways, it was still tied to the frontier law enforcement mentality of Wyatt Earp, who had worked in Wichita law enforcement half a century prior. Bootleggers and vice purveyors were entrenched in Wichita, and many police officers had been co-opted by that criminal element.

Corruption and inefficiency were hallmarks of Wichita policing, but during his 11-year tenure, Wilson turned the area police department into one of the most progressive police departments in the nation. Wilson hit the ground running. In his first year as chief, he fired more than 20% of the force, including anyone even suspected of being corrupt. He required weekly written quizzes in the squad room. Wilson began in-service training, adding a small library and a gymnasium.

He established a 6-week training program for police cadets, the first of its kind in the United States. When he discovered that the best criminology and police science texts were written in French and German, he had them translated into English. Wilson implemented a sophisticated (for its day) record and reporting system. Each officer was provided a worksheet on which they were required to log all their shift activities.

One of Wilson's most innovative ideas was in patrol. After careful study, Wilson concluded that two-officer patrol cars were wasteful, and that officers spent too much time lollygagging when they were paired together. He implemented one-officer patrols. Wilson introduced crime labs, lie detector equipment, and clearly marked police vehicles, all considered cutting edge changes at the time.

Just as Vollmer did in Berkeley, Wilson created a relationship between law enforcement and academe that would handsomely benefit both entities. Not only did Wilson hire students to serve as part-time "liquor lords" in the struggle against bootlegging, but Wilson and Wichita State University created a program that is still heralded as one of the top academic police programs in the United States.

Not wishing to repeat the mistakes he had made in Fullerton, Wilson engaged and educated the community on the work of the police and sought their input. He did not do so with his subordinates because, like his mentor, August Vollmer, he distrusted his rank-and-file officers, paying little attention to their concerns or input.

Wilson and Academe

Taking a cue from Vollmer's experience with the University of California, Wilson established a good working relationship with the Municipal University of Wichita, later renamed Wichita State University. He enlisted sociologists to work with his officers in assisting wayward youth. He never hesitated to contact university professors when starting a new project they might be able to improve. Wilson never doubted the value of a college education for a police officer—the question was what the police officer should study. Should the police officer specialize in police courses, or would the officer be better off with a degree in liberal arts? Wilson was not even sure that police science merited university study on its own.

In preparing an academic curriculum for police officers, Wilson began by listing the tasks performed by a police officer. First, he eliminated tasks best taught at a police academy and subjects that would not be worth the time of a university professor. He decided that political science would be the best vehicle for offering a police studies program and that the following seven courses should be taught:

- criminal law
- personal identification
- police patrol practices

- criminal evidence
- traffic control
- criminal investigation
- police administration

Curriculum Implemented

Wilson's star shone from Wichita throughout the 1930s, in large measure due to his own brilliance and because of support from Wichita city officials. He received praise and support from law enforcement officials across the United States and in other countries. Not surprisingly, Wilson eventually became the enemy of FBI director J. Edgar Hoover, for reasons unknown to Wilson. Hoover's negative attitude toward Wilson probably stemmed from the same reason he had negative attitudes toward other prominent law enforcers; J. Edgar Hoover simply could not stand being upstaged.

Professor/Lieutenant Colonel Wilson

During the 1930s, Wilson had the luxury of selecting the best candidates for police work. The Great Depression left many people out of work and desperate, which made the steady pay that police jobs offered highly attractive. Wilson's training was so effective that many of his officers relocated to other jurisdictions to assume jobs as managers and chiefs. Wilson's department acquired the nickname "West Point of Law Enforcement" because of the highly qualified police leaders that passed through its ranks.

As the 1930s ended, the situation in Wichita changed. Wilson was no longer able to have his pick of police candidates as Kansans returned to work. City officials grew increasingly uncooperative. Wilson finally wore out his welcome in Wichita. Despite widespread recognition for his work, vice operators eventually flexed the political muscle needed to rid Wichita of Wilson. He took a leave of absence in 1936 to teach at Harvard University's Bureau for Street Traffic Research before officially resigning the Wichita police force.

Wilson soon went to work as a consultant with the Chicago Police Department, but soon after he arrived in Chicago, August Vollmer enticed Wilson to accept a tenured professorship at the University of California at Berkeley. He began his professorship in July of 1939.

The United States entered World War II just after the Japanese attack on Pearl Harbor on December 7, 1941. On December 30, during a meeting at the home of August Vollmer, Wilson was tagged as the first president of the National Association of College Police Training Officials, which eventually changed its name to the American Society of Criminology, the largest organization in the United States devoted to the study of criminology. Separated from his wife (they divorced in 1943) and in his 40s, Wilson enlisted in the Army and was commissioned at the rank of lieutenant colonel. When it became clear that the tide was turning toward American victory over Germany and Italy, the United States organized a School of Military Government in Charlottesville, Virginia. Its charge was to rebuild civilian police services in postwar Germany in accordance with a democratic system of government.

After the war ended in 1945, Wilson went to Germany, which was by then divided into two countries, East Germany under the domination of the Soviet Union and West Germany a U.S. ally. One of the most controversial aspects of the rebuilding program was installing former Nazi Party members in positions of police responsibility. Nevertheless, Wilson and those around saw it as the only practical move, agreeing with the highly questionable assessment of General George Patton that many Nazis were just party members in the same sense that Americans were either Democrats or Republicans. Wilson received the Bronze Star Medal for writing a public safety manual and helping establish a civilian police force in West Germany.

In 1947, Wilson returned to Berkeley, this time assuming the role of Dean of the School of Criminology, an unpopular move with some academics because he lacked an advanced degree. Nonetheless, Wilson succeeded in raising the profile of the school, making it one of the few prestigious criminological study centers in the United States.

Police Administration and Chicago

O. W. Wilson continued to write and teach with great success. He authored *Police Administration,* the seminal work in that field that stands even today. but his work in municipal government was not done. In 1960, at the age of 60, Wilson was asked to serve on a selection committee to hire a new Chicago Police Chief. Members of the committee tagged Wilson for the job, and he accepted. He took over a department with a long history of corruption, the most recent embarrassment being the conviction of eight officers for running a burglary ring. Though he did not totally rid Chicago policing of corruption, his tenure was marked with great successes.

Working for the city of Chicago was not easy for many reasons, including dealing with the city's mercurial and powerful Mayor, Richard Daley, but Wilson thrived. He tried to modernize the operation and the culture of the department so that it would be professional and not perceived as the public's enemy. He reduced the number of police stations to remove the power of community fiefdoms operated by neighborhood officers. He emphasized motorized patrol over foot patrol, which increased efficiency and inadvertently made officers more detached from the citizenry.

Wilson also fought to make the promotion process based more on merit than personal favoritism, implementing promotion exams. He hired women as crossing guards and hired African American police officers. He changed the look of the department, replacing black and white squad cars with blue and white cars, introducing checkered hatbands and brass name tags, and allowing officers to wear short-sleeved uniform shirts. Although Wilson was never known to trust his rank and file, he took measures to gain their confidence, including striving for higher pay, allowing side jobs, improving training and education opportunities, buying better equipment and cars, and discontinuing the use of three-wheeled motorcycles. Wilson also introduced the official motto, "We Serve and Protect."

The 1960s was the most turbulent decade of the 20th century. It was marked by riots and protests for many causes, civil rights and anti-Vietnam War protests topping the list. Police officers around the country found themselves the unwitting frontline soldiers in many of these protests. Unlike many police officials who chose a strictly defensive and hostile posture toward protesters, Wilson did just the opposite, hoping Chicago would avoid the black eye given to police departments in Birmingham and other cities for their actions against demonstrators.

In 1966, Martin Luther King, Jr. decided to stage a protest march in Chicago, a town often referred to as the most segregated city outside the south. Wilson invited King to Chicago to meet with him in advance of the protest. Rather than vowing to fight King as many other police officials had done before, Wilson treated King as an honored guest. He worked patiently with Dr. King, giving him a tour of Chicago police facilities, arranging for King's and other marchers' protection, and doing his best to ensure that the protest avoided violence. Wilson's treatment of King should have served as a model for handling similar events in the turbulent 1960s, but unfortunately, few police chiefs, including his successor in Chicago, heeded his model. But Wilson had restored some measure of self-respect to the police department, even if it only lasted for his tenure.

Retirement, Death, and Legacy

O. W. Wilson resigned in 1967 and returned to California, settling in Poway and living with Ruth Wilson, whom he had married in 1950. He reworked *Police Administration* but stayed out of the public eye. O. W. Wilson died of a stroke on October 18, 1972, at the age of 72.

If Vollmer was the Socrates of modern policing, Wilson was his Plato, and Herman Goldstein—Wilson's top assistant and the subject of another chapter in this book—was Wilson's Aristotle. After Vollmer, Wilson ranks as the most significant figure in American municipal policing.

Sources and Suggested Readings

American Society of Criminology. (2023). *A brief history of ASC & the society publications.* https://asc41.org/wp-content/uploads/History_of_ASC_and_Society_Publications.pdf, date of retrieval January 31, 2024.

Axelrod, A., Phillips, C., & Kemper, K. (1996). *Cops, crooks & criminologists: An international biographical dictionary of law enforcement.* Facts on File.

Benzkofer, S. (2018, June 18). Legendary lawmen, no. 8: O. W. Wilson. *Chicago Tribune.* https://www.chicagotribune.com/news/ct-per-flash-owwilson-0707-20130707-story.html, date of retrieval January 31, 2024.

Bopp, William J. (1977). *O. W. Wilson and the search for a police profession.* Kennikat Press.

Chicago Police Department. (2024). https://home.chicagopolice.org/about/history/, date of retrieval January 31, 2024.

Wilson, O. W. (1972). *Police administration* (3rd ed.). McGraw-Hill.

Discussion Questions

1. If you were a police manager with a subordinate who was dating a person they met through a traffic stop, and that subordinate had read the story of how O. W. Wilson met his wife, what would you say to the subordinate?
2. What was the most significant act of O. W. Wilson's career?

Credit

CHAPTER 13

Herman Goldstein (1931–2020)

IMG 13.1

Herman Goldstein is the third in the line of 20th century American police patriarchs, behind August Vollmer and O. W. Wilson. Goldstein is the patriarch of problem-oriented policing, which subsequently spawned neighborhood and community-oriented policing, among the most significant law enforcement philosophies of the past 50 years. Marie Rosen provided the best description of Herman Goldstein when she wrote, "Goldstein is a fascinating study in contrasts: a police expert who never wore a uniform; a law professor who was never a lawyer; a giant in his field who prefers to mingle with those in the trenches" (Dodenhoff, 1987, p. 10). Goldstein, a gentle, self-effacing scholar, ranks as one of policing's greatest minds, in part because of his willingness to admit that many ideas, including his own, can run their course.

Early Life and Career

Herman Goldstein was born on December 8, 1931, in New London, Connecticut, the youngest of three children. Goldstein's parents, Max and Bella, were poor, though not poverty-stricken, Jewish immigrants. His father immigrated from Poland, his mother from Lithuania. Both of Goldstein's parents came to America to escape the rising persecution of Jews that swept Europe throughout the first 4 decades of the 20th century.

Goldstein grew up in a lower-middle-class home in Connecticut and attended public schools. Although Goldstein, an observant Jew his entire life, was cognizant of anti-Semitism and knew that some doors to success were closed to him because of his ethnicity, being Jewish in Connecticut did not present the barriers that it did for his extended family in Europe. The abuses of government power throughout Europe left an indelible mark on him. Goldstein was acutely aware that a great number of unspeakable atrocities perpetrated against the citizens of Europe came not only at the hands of an invading German military but through the actions of local police, like the Lithuanian police officers who murdered his maternal grandparents. As a result, Goldstein worked to ensure that government, especially the police, remained responsive to the needs of its citizens. Police officers, as representatives of the government in the streets, should partner with the public, not oppress them. According to Goldstein, government officials should be ever aware of (a) their ability to oppress citizens, (b) the anomalousness of police officers in a free society, and (c) the need for government to constrain its own authority.

After graduating from high school, Goldstein enrolled at the University of Connecticut. He earned a bachelor of arts degree in 1953 and then enrolled in the University of Pennsylvania's Wharton School. Goldstein earned a master's degree in governmental administration in 1955. At the time that Goldstein embarked on his career, very few government officials focused on systematic methods of improving police services. Goldstein did not take courses in criminal justice as that academic discipline was practically nonexistent. When he took his first job as administrative assistant to the city manager in Portland, Maine, his primary interest was in municipal government and public administration, not policing.

Portland, Maine

Goldstein's entrée into police scholarship was serendipitous. One of the first problems he noticed in Portland was that the study of police management was practically nonexistent. The field was ripe for a young government administrator to carve out an area of expertise, and Goldstein proceeded to do just that. It was during this time that Goldstein first met O. W. Wilson. Wilson's *Police Administration* had been released 5 years earlier, and the two men collaborated on police research. The Portland collaboration was the beginning of a lifelong friendship and partnership between them.

Goldstein's work in Portland did not go unnoticed. From 1956-1957, he worked as a research associate for the American Bar Association's Survey of the Administration of Criminal Justice, focusing on municipal and state police in Michigan and Wisconsin. The ABA study was the first body of empirical data on the daily work of street-level police officers. This marked Goldstein's transition from working strictly for local government to bridging the gap between local governments and research agencies. For the remainder of his career, Goldstein would have feet in both the academic/research arena and the everyday operations of government and criminal justice. Goldstein realized that two things are true about criminal justice research: (a) research findings are useless unless they are shared with criminal justice policymakers and practitioners, and (b) researchers can learn much from criminal justice professionals in the field, a lesson still not learned by most academics who communicate almost exclusively with each other.

Chicago and O. W. Wilson

From 1957-1958, Goldstein worked as assistant director of the Governmental Research Institute in Hartford, Connecticut. From 1958-1960 he worked as a staff member with the Public Administration Service, a nonprofit organization that provided consulting services to local and state governments. Goldstein made one of the most important moves of his career in 1960 when he moved to Chicago to take a position as executive assistant to Police Chief O. W. Wilson. Goldstein would stay in this position until 1964.

Even though Goldstein had no experience as a police officer, Wilson was confident that the 28-year-old "boy wonder genius" would make a great impact on policing in Chicago and around the country. Wilson and Goldstein enjoyed some success in Chicago, but they were not successful in creating the mental revolution required to effect significant and long-lasting change in the historically corrupt Chicago Police Department.

Goldstein learned about policing by getting on the street with line officers. While many police managers viewed line level police officers almost as natural enemies, Goldstein discovered that rank-and-file police officers have much to offer, calling them an area of untapped expertise. Goldstein's greatest talents were his ability to listen and his ability to persuade people to change their way of thinking in a gentle, nonthreatening manner. Both traits came in handy when he was observing police officers and explaining his findings.

Herman Goldstein wrote one of the most significant articles on policing in the 1960s while he worked for Wilson in Chicago. Goldstein discovered something that most police officers on the street already knew—and that few police managers would admit. He found that policing is more than just running from one call to another. He found that officer discretion is a vital part of police work. In 1963, he published his views on the importance of individual discretion in *The Public Administration Review.* His article, "Police Discretion: The Ideal Versus the Real," was one of the most important contributions to police literature in the 1960s.

Goldstein's reputation flourished in Chicago. He worked as a police consultant and expert for the Ford Foundation. In addition to his landmark article on discretion, he published an article in *Public Management* titled "Guidelines for Effective Use of Police Manpower." His tireless efforts in the street, behind the desk, as a writer, and as a consultant prompted a deputy chief to say, "I hope this guy gets married so he won't be around so much" (Dodenhoff, 1987, p. 10).

University of Wisconsin

Goldstein got married in May 1964 and had three children, but that did not slow him down. He left Chicago in 1964, making the final job change of his career when he took a position as assistant professor at the University of Wisconsin Law School in Madison. On paper, Goldstein seemed an odd choice for a law school professor. He never attended law school, and he didn't have a doctoral degree. He was hired because the school needed someone who knew police operations, not law books. Goldstein attributed his long tenure at the University of Wisconsin to the school's tradition of studying law in action.

By the time he became a professor, Goldstein had earned a reputation as one of the best police minds in the country. The University of Wisconsin provided fertile ground for furthering his career. This might be surprising at one of the most politically and socially liberal universities in the United States where one might assume that academic inquiry into policing would not flourish. On the contrary, said Goldstein, the University of Wisconsin, even with its liberal tradition, prided itself on practical innovation, be it in policing, political science, or agriculture.

Goldstein developed a policy-making process aimed at systematically controlling police discretion. He was promoted to associate professor in 1967 and to the rank of professor in 1968 at the age of 36, a notable accomplishment at one of the nation's most prestigious law schools. Although some of his Wisconsin colleagues had issues with his lack of a law or doctoral degree, the university president was more concerned with accomplishments than credentials.

During the 1960s and early 1970s, Goldstein worked on the three most significant criminal justice task forces of the era. He gained inroads into elite policing circles, in part thanks to O. W. Wilson. The presidential election of 1964 was the first in which crime was a major issue. In keeping with the fervor of the 1964 campaign, Wilson consulted with Goldstein, wanting to know what universities were doing in response to the public concern over crime. Goldstein served on President Lyndon Johnson's Commission on Law Enforcement and the Administration of Justice from 1964-1967, the task force that practically invented the study of criminal justice in higher education. It made *criminal justice system* an everyday term and called for better educated criminal justice practitioners.

Goldstein worked for the National Advisory Commission on Civil Disorders, commonly referred to as the Kerner Commission, from 1967-1968. The Kerner Commission was a blue-ribbon panel of experts assembled to study urban riots, which had been erupting with increasing regularity in the 1960s. Goldstein served on New York City's Knapp Commission from 1971-1973, which had investigated corruption in the New York City Police Department and featured Frank Serpico as the star witness. The late 1970s witnessed the publication of two seminal police works by Goldstein. *Policing a Free Society*, released in 1977, is the work that Goldstein pointed to as his most significant.

In the book, he discusses the difficulties and complications inherent with police work in a democratic society.

Problem-Oriented Policing

In 1979, Goldstein published an article in the journal *Crime and Delinquency* titled "Improving Policing: A Problem-Oriented Approach." The article signaled the beginning of an entirely new direction in police philosophy. Goldstein also believed that giving police a longer leash is a key to problem-solving in policing. Bragging about response times and focusing on how quickly officers dispose of cases was a disastrous mentality. Goldstein believed that police managers too often sacrifice effectiveness for the sake of efficiency. Problem-oriented policing involves police officers handling cases as a group to discover underlying causes of crime, or at least the underlying reasons for frequent calls for service. According to Goldstein, street officers have an innate sense of what will work and the problems on their beats.

Problem-oriented policing was the result of an evolution on Goldstein's part, dating back to his 1963 article on police discretion. The idea of police officers as problem-solvers evolved from the realization that officers employ a great amount of discretion while doing their work and that beat officers have a good idea of how to solve the problems on their beat, if they are provided the opportunity. Goldstein's embrace of the problem model of policing also signaled his movement away from the "professional" model of policing that was touted for years by his mentor, O. W. Wilson. Although Goldstein and Wilson remained close friends until Wilson's death, they disagreed over the best approach to policing. In Goldstein's opinion, efficiency and professionalism, the hallmarks of Wilson's approach, are good but are not enough, and have the downside of breeding detachment between police officers and the citizenry.

One Philadelphia story told by Goldstein demonstrates the basic premise of how problem-oriented policing works. A Philadelphia police officer noticed that he answered several calls for service to one neighborhood bar. He was never told the source of the complaint—only that the bar was making too much noise and should quiet down. The officer discovered that other officers had also been called to the bar repeatedly, and he decided to get to the bottom of the matter. He also discovered that all the complaints came from one person, a woman whose residence adjoined the bar. When he visited the bar owners, they told him that they would be happy to find some solution to the problem. The officer visited the complainant, and she told the officer that the music from the bar came right into her wall, which was the sole basis for her complaints. The officer returned to the bar and noticed that the bar's stereo speakers were placed directly beside the wall that adjoined the woman's wall. The proposed solution was to ask the bar owners to move the speakers to another part of the bar. They complied, the problem was solved, and no more police time was expended answering complaints at the bar. The problem was resolved by giving one officer a longer leash and allowing the officer to get to the root of the problem, instead of just answering the call.

In 1990, Goldstein released *Problem-Oriented Policing,* which captured his thoughts about police officers working as problem-solvers. Problem-oriented policing and its "cousin," community policing, have some similarities. They developed along parallel lines for two decades, with some elements of problem-oriented policing being incorporated in what became a larger, more umbrella-like concept of community policing. But the two ideas have differences. The main difference is that community policing means involving the community, while problem-oriented policing places its major emphasis on a general reconceptualization of what police do. The problem approach focuses on a wide set of problems and encourages an analytical approach to solving problems. In a perfect world, police would only need to be reactive, but there will always be problems to solve, so police officers should be proactive. Says Goldstein, "We are constantly in a state of reform because we are constantly trying to catch up" (John Jay College of Criminal Justice, 1997, p. 10).

Goldstein became dismayed by what happened to his concept. The problem-oriented label became so popular that it was trivialized, the label superficial, and many who claimed to employ his concept lacked an understanding of the concept. Although he was pleased with its implementation in some departments, its application was patchy. The idea was as popular in some other countries as it was in the United States, with some police agencies in the United Kingdom especially employing his concepts and consulting him. According to Goldstein, the professional model can be just as useful as the problem-oriented approach. Neither should be adopted blindly; the needs of the agency and the community are paramount. Goldstein believed the wrong question is whether the police can handle crime, while the more important question is whether society can handle it.

"Retirement"

Herman Goldstein retired from the University of Wisconsin in 1994, but he remained as professor emeritus and hardly slowed down. He witnessed the creation of the Problem-Oriented Policing (POP) Center at Arizona State University. Goldstein remained active, always in awe of the complexity of policing and of the role that police should play in a free democratic society.

I had the pleasure of interacting with professor Goldstein on three occasions. In 1989, I attended his presentation as a Beto Chair Professor while a student at Sam Houston State University, where, as was almost always the case, he favorably impressed his audience with both his personality and his intellect. In 2001, professor Goldstein very graciously granted more than an hour of his time for a telephone interview, providing information for the first edition of this book. In 2018, I again met professor Goldstein, this time in Stockholm, Sweden, when he was awarded the Stockholm Prize in Criminology, often called the Nobel Prize of criminology. Although unsurprisingly he did not remember me, he very graciously accepted my congratulations for his award. His acceptance speech was excerpted in the journal *Policing and Society.*

Death and Legacy

Herman Goldstein was aptly described, consistent with his Jewish heritage, as a true mensch (Tilley et al., 2020, p. 1582), a man of decency and honor. Goldstein remained cautiously optimistic about the future of policing, saying, "We've suffered greatly in this field from an expectation that you introduce something this month and you reap the harvest the next month. You have to plant seeds and hope that they develop over a period of time" (Goldstein, 2001).

Herman Goldstein passed away on January 24, 2020, in Madison, Wisconsin, at age 88. While he will be remembered by the academic and law enforcement communities for his scholarly work on policing, his priorities in life are best summed up in his obituary, which suggested donations be made to the Beth Israel Center in Madison, the National Alliance on Mental Illness for Dane County (Madison), and the Porchlight of Madison (solutions to homelessness). David Couper, a retired Madison Police Chief who entered the Catholic priesthood, said Goldstein, a devout Jew, helped him become a better Christian. In our 2001 interview, when I asked about his legacy, Goldstein said he had a wish for what would be placed on his tombstone: "A free society is what is most important" (Goldstein, 2001, Interview).

Sources and Suggested Readings

Cambridge Centre for Evidence-Based Policing. (2018). *A conversation with Herman Goldstein* [Video]. YouTube. https://www.youtube.com/watch?v=XNS9d7Vqhno, date of retrieval January 21, 2024.

Chronicle Staff. (2020, February 26). Herman Goldstein, father of problem-oriented policing, dies at 88. *The Wisconsin Jewish Chronicle.* https://www.jewishchronicle.org/2020/02/26/herman-goldstein-father-of-problem-oriented-policing-dies-at-88/, date of retrieval January 30, 2024.

Cress Funeral & Cremation Service. (2020). *Herman Goldstein.* https://www.cressfuneralservice.com/obituaries/herman-goldstein, date of retrieval January 20, 2024.

Dodenhoff, P. (1987). LEN's 1986 man of the year. *Law Enforcement News, 13*(241), 10-12.

Goldstein, H. (1963). Police discretion: The ideal vs the real. *Public Administration Review, 23*(3), 140–148.

Goldstein, H. (1988). *Policing a free society.* Harper & Row.

Goldstein, H. (1990). *Problem-oriented policing.* McGraw Hill.

Goldstein, Herman. (2001, December 1). Curriculum vitae.

Goldstein, H. (2001, November 17). Telephone interview.

Goldstein, H. (2018). On problem-oriented policing: The Stockholm lecture. *Crime Science*, 7–13.

John Jay College of Criminal Justice. (1997, February 14). LEN interview: Herman Goldstein: Father of problem-oriented policing. (1997). *Law Enforcement News, 23*(461), 8–11.

Law School News. (2020, January 27). *Herman Goldstein, author of* "Problem-Oriented Policing," *dies at 88.* University of Wisconsin—Madison. https://law.wisc.edu/newsletter/Faculty/Herman_Goldstein_author_of_Probl_2020-01-24, date of retrieval January 29, 2024.

Mazerolle, L. (2020). Herman Goldstein (1931–2020): A tribute. *Policing & Society, 30*(3), 349–354.

POP Center Library. (2015). *Interview with Herman Goldstein* [Video]. YouTube. https://www.youtube.com/watch?v=d33MoqolDwU, date of retrieval January 22, 2024.

Tilley, N., Laycock, G., Scott, M. S., Barton, M., Eck, J., & Couper, D. (2020). Remembering Herman Goldstein, 1931–2020. *Policing, 15*(2), 1574–1583.

Turner, K. (2015). *Herman Goldstein interviewed by Samuel Walker* [Video]. YouTube. https://www.youtube.com/watch?v=LyfqZEYK_y4, date of retrieval January 18, 2024.

Walker, S. (2005). *Interview with Herman Goldstein.* ASU Center for Problem-Oriented Policing. https://popcenter.asu.edu/content/herman-goldstein-interview, date of retrieval January 28, 2024.

Discussion Questions

1. What role did Herman Goldstein's heritage play in his view of the role of police in American society?
2. How has Goldstein integrated the worlds of law enforcement and academe?

Credit

IMG 13.1: Cambridge Centre for Evidence-Based Policing, Screenshot from "A Conversation with Herman Goldstein (Full Interview)," https://www.youtube.com/watch?v=XNS9d7Vqhno. Copyright © 2017 by Cambridge Centre for Evidence-Based Policing LTD.

CHAPTER 14

Frank Serpico (1936-)

IMG 14.1

As a child, Frank Serpico was convinced that being a police officer in his boyhood home of New York City was the greatest thing he could do. As a young man who joined the New York Police Department, he wanted nothing more than to earn a gold detective shield. Serpico realized his childhood dream of becoming a New York police officer, and he eventually earned his gold shield—but only after his idealism about the nobility of police work had been shattered beyond repair, just as a bullet that entered his head in a 1971 drug raid shattered and left fragments.

Serpico's battle against corruption in the New York City Police Department throughout the 1960s made him a living legend, and he still fascinates the American public. His frustration with bureaucratic inertia and timid government leadership resonates with anyone who has ever faced similar problems, except that Serpico's story is much more extreme. It cost Serpico his career as a police officer, and it nearly cost him his life.

Early Life

Francesco Vincent Serpico was born on April 14, 1936, in New York City, the youngest of four children. Both of his grandfathers worked in the coal mines. His father, Vincenzo, was an Italian immigrant. His mother. Maria Giovanna, was born in Ohio. As a child growing up in lower-middle-class Brooklyn, Serpico idealized police work. His favorite radio program was *Gangbusters.* He viewed the police officer as the ultimate good guy, a dedicated public servant that protected the weak from the bully. Serpico also viewed the world in black-and-white terms, just as he did as a police officer; what is right is right, and what is wrong is wrong, and one should never run when they are in the right.

Although Serpico saw the best of police work as a Brooklyn youth, he also encountered situations that negatively affected his perception of policemen, and which made him vow to be different when his time came. Once, a New York police officer, a "burly cop" as Frank called him, came into his father's store, received a shoeshine from young Serpico, and left without paying. When the officer returned for another shine, he encountered Serpico's father, who greeted him and demanded that he pay in advance. The officer left, never to return. Frank observed officers helping themselves to free fruit from markets. Things would be different when he became a police officer, he thought.

Serpico graduated from high school in 1954 and enlisted in the Army. Already fluent in Italian, Serpico learned to speak French, Spanish, Japanese, and eventually Dutch. After his discharge from the Army, Serpico returned to New York to study police science at Brooklyn College and work as a private investigator and later as a social worker for the New York Youth Authority. Later, as a police officer he told a colleague that he once worked as a social worker, and the officer tapped his nightstick and said, "This is the only rehabilitation they understand."

Police Career: The Early Years

Serpico joined the New York City Police Department in 1959. He quickly realized that straight, hard, honest police work was not always rewarded, especially when it created work for others or if a little petty corruption did not accompany it. Once, while still an academy cadet, he was assigned to guard a synagogue that had been the frequent target of vandals. He arrested two suspects that were wanted for a string of taxicab robberies, an arrest that should have gotten him the mayor's trophy for the best arrest among academy cadets. Instead, the trophy went to an inspector's son for a minor arrest.

Serpico's first brush with corruption occurred when he was set to arrest a suspect who offered him a $35 bribe ($340 today). Serpico told his senior partner about the bribery offer, to which the officer replied, "Wait here; I'll take care of it." The officer returned with $35 and offered Serpico half. Serpico refused the money.

After donning the uniform as a full-fledged police officer, Serpico encountered the oddities of bureaucratic thinking that were a part of the NYPD and the still-existing prejudice against Italian American police officers. He thought that hard work and frequent arrests would earn rewards. Instead, his supervisor became annoyed with the arrests made by Serpico because they interfered with study for his promotion exam. Unlike other officers, Serpico did not take the remainder of the day off after making an arrest. He became known as a "rate-buster," making other officers look bad because he worked more hours and made more arrests than them. He was reprimanded for making an arrest during his off hours in another precinct. He discovered that many officers participated in "cooping" or sleeping on duty, a practice dating back to the 19th century. What surprised Serpico about cooping was that officers did it en masse, finding an empty building and napping as a group without fear of being reported.

Serpico acquired a distaste for the acceptance of gratuities. Although he had always known of police officers helping themselves to free or discounted services, he never liked it but at first went along with it. Once he entered a restaurant and was told by the owner to try a certain entree at a discount. Serpico insisted on ordering something else and was given an inferior cut of meat. He realized then that, contrary to the perception of officers that accepted such favors, restaurateurs had little respect for officers that accepted their favors and only used them to get rid of excess inventory. On one occasion when he laid down the full amount of the restaurant tab and walked out, a restaurant employee chased Serpico down the street and offered to give part of his money back. Serpico refused. From then onward, Serpico received much better treatment at the restaurant.

Plain Dirty Clothes

In 1966, Serpico transferred to the plainclothes division after he heard that it was the best route to becoming a detective and that officers typically needed to spend 4 years in plain clothes to become a detective. He disliked some aspects of plainclothes work, such as arresting prostitutes, but admitted that he enjoyed dressing up in disguises, using different voices, putting his language skills to work, and acting. Fellow officer Eddie Mamet said Serpico was the most innovative cop to ever wear a uniform.

It was as a plainclothes officer that Serpico fully realized the depths of corruption within the NYPD. Rather than finding that acts of corruption were isolated incidents confined to a few officers, Serpico found that almost all the apples were rotten. He would request a transfer to another precinct in the hopes of getting away from corrupt officers, only to find corruption at the new precinct, with plainclothes officers usually the worst offenders. The corruption took numerous forms. Some officers would shake down suspects or accept bribes; others worked with protection rackets, protecting gambling or drug operations by accepting regular payoffs. Far from operating discreetly, officers openly informed Serpico of how the rackets worked. Each precinct had a "pad" kept by one officer, which provided a detailed accounting of how the rackets worked and how much each officer was paid. Serpico's failure to participate resulted in his being ostracized by his colleagues and arousing their suspicion.

Part of Serpico's problem with his colleagues stemmed from his unorthodox appearance and lifestyle. During the 1960s and early 1970s, the height of the hippie era, many police officers detested anyone that wore long hair, a beard, or hippie clothing such as bell-bottom pants and sandals. Serpico did all those things, thinking it necessary to blend in with the community, especially when conducting undercover work. He also felt a closer identity with much of New York's counterculture element than with most of his fellow police officers. Some officers falsely accused Serpico of being gay, especially when a supervisor "caught" him in a dark bathroom with another officer present.

While most police officers lived in working-class neighborhoods, spent off hours with other cops, and disdained intellectual and cultural pursuits, Serpico did just the opposite. He lived in New York City's Greenwich Village, long associated with a bohemian lifestyle. In the 1960s, it was the hangout for avant-garde poets, artists, and hippies. When Serpico went to parties he would not tell anyone he was a police officer unless asked. "Paco," as he was called by his friends (Gleiberman, 2017, para. 3), went to the theater, literary gatherings, and the ballet, and he loved to associate with New York's intellectual circle, finding police shop talk boring after a full day's work.

Every time Serpico informed his superiors of corruption, he was told that the matter was being addressed and that someone would contact him. Since talking with his superiors proved fruitless, he arranged to meet with a member of Mayor John Lindsay's staff, courtesy of a politically connected police colleague named David Durk. Mayor Lindsay would not heed Serpico's call for a thorough top-to-bottom investigation of corruption in the NYPD because he anticipated a disorderly summer of riots and did not want to alienate the police management or rank-and-file officers. Word leaked out that Serpico could not be trusted to keep corrupt activities within the department, and he began to fear for his career and his personal safety. Once, on arrival to a new precinct, he was met by a fellow officer who pulled a knife on him and told Serpico, "We know how to handle guys like you." Serpico disarmed the officer, nearly breaking the officer's wrist and pointing his gun in the officer's face.

Serpico's frustration grew to a point where he did the unthinkable—he aired the NYPD's dirty laundry to the world. He arranged for a meeting with David Burnham, a *New York Times* journalist, and on April 25, 1970, Serpico's account of corruption within the NYPD exploded with the front-page headline "Graft Paid to Police Here Said to Run into Millions." The story was picked up by other New York papers and was disseminated to media outlets across the country. Serpico had also testified before a grand jury, resulting in the indictment of several officers who were prosecuted for various crimes, usually with Serpico serving as chief witness against them. But Serpico was not satisfied. He believed the prosecutors only went after the small fish while letting the systematic and high-level corruption continue to exist. He would not wear a wire, as conversations caught by a wire only involved low-level officers.

Serpico Is Shot

On February 3, 1971, Serpico, acting on an informant tip, went with other plainclothes officers to make a narcotics bust in the Williamsburgh section of Brooklyn. When they arrived at the apartment to make the bust, Serpico, who spoke fluent Spanish, was sent to the door to gain access from the Hispanic drug dealers inside the apartment. Serpico knocked and said in Spanish, "I need something. Joe sent me." The door opened slightly, and Serpico tried to push the door in. Instead, he found himself wedged between the door and the hallway, with a .22 caliber pistol pointed 18 inches from his face. He yelled for help from the two officers behind him. Serpico was shot in the face from almost point-blank range. He managed to return fire, wounding the drug dealer before collapsing into the hallway.

The actions of his two partners are sharply in dispute. Serpico claimed that they never called for backup and left him to bleed to death. Serpico's version of these events is supported by the fact that the call about his being shot was a 10–10 call made by a civilian, while no 10–13 call (made by an officer, officer down), was ever made. Serpico recalls lying in the hallway believing he was dying, his head cradled by an elderly Hispanic man that lived in the building and heard the shot from his apartment.

But in a 2017 documentary, Serpico spoke one-on-one with one of the officers who was there. Arthur Cesare admitted that no 10–13 call was made, but staunchly claimed that Serpico was not set up—as Serpico has implied publicly and as was implied in the feature film starring Al Pacino—and that he and the other officer did not leave him on the floor to bleed to death. Serpico's shooting was a tragic coincidence, not a setup. Not all police officers viewed the shooting as a tragedy. One of the first two officers who took Serpico from the scene stated he would not have assisted had he known the wounded officer was Frank Serpico.

Serpico was rushed to Brooklyn Jewish Hospital, where he spent the next 6 weeks fighting for his life. At the hospital he was given the last rites of the Roman Catholic Church. He was under constant guard by NYPD officers and received frequent mail, but most of the attention he received was not warm. He once overheard an officer guarding his door tell the officer that came to relieve him, "Don't go in there. He's no good" (Poppa, 2017, para. 11). Serpico received a sympathy card that read, "With sincere sympathy that you didn't get your brains blown out, you rat bastard. Happy Relapse." (Cords, 2020, para. 23).

Serpico went home and spent the next several months recovering from his wound. In May he was awarded the gold detective shield that he had sought since becoming a police officer 12 years earlier. By then he did not care; he told the NYPD representative that informed him of the honor to shove it. He would never return to work as a police officer again, and bullet fragments remained lodged in his head.

Post-NYPD Career

Between the time of the *New York Times* headline and the time Serpico was shot, Mayor John Lindsay appointed a special independent commission to investigate corruption within the NYPD, chaired by Whitman Knapp, a Wall Street lawyer. Knapp fought several obstacles while trying to set up the commission's work, most of it from the rank and file of the NYPD. Before he was shot, Serpico had already begun working with the Knapp Commission. After months of secret deliberations, Knapp scheduled public hearings for October 1971. Serpico, assisted by former Attorney General Ramsey Clark, was the star witness before the Knapp Commission. He uttered simple yet profound words, some of which have become indelibly linked with his efforts to fight police corruption:

> The problem is that the atmosphere does not yet exist in which an honest police officer can act without fear of ridicule or reprisal from fellow officers. We create an atmosphere in which the honest officer fears the dishonest officer and not the other way around. (Cooper, 2020, para. 10)

Peter Maas chronicled Frank's story in a 1973 bestseller *Serpico.* A movie based on the book with Al Pacino in the title role was released a short time later. Frank Serpico became a pop culture icon, thanks largely to being portrayed on film by one of the greatest actors of his generation—Al Pacino. A Serpico movie poster adorns the wall of John Travolta's bedroom in the 1977 blockbuster film *Saturday Night Fever.* Serpico was pleased with the overall tenor and message of the movie and with Pacino's portrayal; Pacino received an Oscar nomination for his portrayal of Serpico. But in a behavior that exemplifies both the irascible personality and unbending honesty of Frank Serpico, he stated that during the making of the movie, for which he served as consultant, he quickly wore out his welcome on the set with a visible reaction whenever something was portrayed in a manner that was the least bit fictional. One example was the scene in which Pacino does not shoot the man that shot him. Another fictionalized scene showed Serpico's partner shoving a man's head into a toilet—and resulted in Serpico being ordered off set permanently for yelling "cut."

Serpico spent the 1970s living in various locations in Europe (mostly in The Netherlands) and the United States before returning to the United States permanently. He surfaces in public occasionally, often as a critic of corruption in law enforcement and government.

Serpico granted a telephone interview with this author in the spring of 2002. I asked Serpico if he thought conditions regarding police corruption had changed since the early 1970s. He replied by telling the following story, one he repeated in his 2017 documentary. Serpico was a guest speaker at an awards banquet honoring outstanding American police officers. In addition to being the guest speaker, Serpico handed the recipients their awards and shook their hands. After his speech, when the officers were called forward to receive their awards, several of them leaned over and whispered the same words in his ear. In an action that typified his ability to dominate an interviewer, Serpico repeatedly requested that I try and guess the words they whispered. When I finally gave up, he said he would whisper it to me. I found myself leaning forward in my chair, even though I was on the telephone rather than talking to him from across the desk. He whispered the words "I have to talk to you," to which Serpico replied, "I know."

Serpico was saying that nothing has changed in American police work. Good police officers still fear dishonest officers and feckless managers. Many individual officers still work hard at their jobs and do their best to perform as true public servants, but policing is still rife with corruption, callous indifference to the plight of the poor, and selfish ambition of the political officials that administer police departments.

Serpico describes himself as very spiritual, but very irreligious, considering religion another corrupted institution in American society. He is a vegetarian, believing that people must connect on a respectful level with all animals, both human and nonhuman. In 2017, living in Hudson, New York, Frank Serpico reemerged into the public spotlight in a 98-minute documentary titled *Frank Serpico.* He never married, though he has had some long-term live-in relationships. His only child, Alexander Serpico, a film editor, died of a suspected drug overdose in 2021. He is an occasional contributor to several left-leaning publications and has had several interviews published on YouTube. In 1997, he was the subject of the A&E Network's *Biography* series. He harbors no bitterness toward the NYPD.

Frank Serpico represents what many believe is the ideal in policing. To some of his former police colleagues he will always be remembered as a self-righteous "rat" that, as Arthur Cesare said, only hurt other cops and did no real good. But many officers, including Cesare, admit that they knew of corruption but simply did not want to be the one to do something about it. Unfortunately, the name Frank Serpico also presents a reminder that idealist aspirations often run afoul of some of the bitter realities of police work and public service in general. In a televised shouting match with former Los Angeles Police Chief Daryl Gates, Gates told Serpico that he had a loud mouth. Serpico replied, "At least it's an honest one" (Hi-DoG, 2018, 1:01).

Sources and Suggested Readings

Cooper, R. (2020, September 18). The police protection racket. *The Week.* https://theweek.com/articles/938068/police-protection-racket, accessed August 5, 2024.

Cords, S. (2020, October 29). The cop who told the truth. *Medium.* https://sarahcords.medium.com/the-cop-who-told-the-truth-5d41ea078083, accessed August 5, 2024.

D'Ambrosio, A. (2017). *Frank Serpico* [Documentary]. A Gigantic Pictures Production in Association with La Lutta NMC.

Farberov, S. (2021, May 12). Son, 41, of hero detective Frank Serpico whose life was portrayed by Al Pacino, dies of apparent drug overdose in Manhattan apartment. *Daily Mail.* https://www.dailymail.co.uk/news/article-9571337/Hero-detective-Frank-Serpicos-son-41-dies-apparent-drug-overdose-Manhattan-apartment.html, date of retrieval December 5, 2023.

Gleiberman, O. (2017, October 28). Film review: 'Frank Serpico.' *Variety.* https://variety.com/2017/film/reviews/frank-serpico-review-1202393980/, accessed August 5, 2024.

Hi-DoG (2018). *Frank Serpico original crusader* [Video]. YouTube. https://www.youtube.com/watch?v=MusBpqCnmUE, accessed August 5, 2024.

Maas, P. (1973). *Serpico.* Harper Collins.

Petit, F. (2011). What executives can learn from Frank Serpico. *Journal of Business Case Studies, 7*(5), 29–33.

Poppa, D. (2017, August 3). Serpico sets the record straight, part 8. *Baltimore Post Examiner.* https://baltimorepostexaminer.com/serpico-sets-the-record-straight-part-8/2017/08/03, accessed August 5, 2024.

Serpico, Frank. (2002, May 1). Telephone interview.

Discussion Questions

1. Had you been in Frank Serpico's position, could you have done what he did? Why or why not?
2. What lessons can be learned from Serpico's life about the difficulty of doing what one thinks is right?

Credit

CHAPTER 15

Joseph Wambaugh (1937–2025)

IMG 15.1

No one has done more to merge the fields of literature and police work than Joseph Wambaugh, the "poet laureate of police" (Penfield, 1996, p. 1) and "grandmaster of police stories" (Joseph Wambaugh website, 2024, para. 1). He is the most successful police-officer-turned-novelist in American history. Many crime novelists like Mickey Spillane and Arthur Conan Doyle have glamorized crime detection and investigation, but none has ever shown the gritty, darkly comic, human side of day-to-day police work with greater power than Joseph Wambaugh. Some of Wambaugh's books, like *Echoes in the Darkness* and *The Blooding*, depict his narrative of true crimes. Others are novels in which Wambaugh provides insight into the mind of a police officer on the beat.

Wambaugh presents a view of police officers unlike that which had often previously been depicted in television and movies. Wambaugh's police officers exhibit the signs of stress in police work; they have the same human frailties and flaws as the population they serve, a population that is not always appreciative of the work police officers do. He presents this view as one who has done police work and understands what officers experience. Many of his novels have been required reading in college criminal justice courses.

Throughout the 1950s and 1960s, the image presented to the American public of Los Angeles police officers came from *Dragnet*, a radio and (later) television series that portrayed the LAPD as a force of idealistic, incorruptible, dedicated, almost saintly group of men (and practically no women). Wambaugh's portrayal of Southern California police officers was quite different from what was seen on *Dragnet*. Police officers in Wambaugh's books experienced cynicism, emotional distress, and marital and other personal problems; they lied in court and used excessive force, sometimes unnecessarily. They expected free meals and other gratuities. Wambaugh's police officer was, to say the least, far from saintly. But Wambaugh cannot be accused of being a stereotypical left-wing police basher. Although his characters are flawed, they are presented in a sympathetic manner. Despite the officers' imperfections, they are portrayed as fallible heroes with whom the reader identifies and sympathizes.

Early Life and Career

Joseph Aloysius Wambaugh, Jr., was born in East Pittsburgh, Pennsylvania, on January 22, 1937, the only child in a working-class Roman Catholic family that included his mother, Anne Malloy Wambaugh, a homemaker, and his father, Joseph Wambaugh, Sr., a police officer, and steelworker. Wambaugh was 14 when his family moved to Ontario, California, where his father worked as a washing machine repairman.

Wambaugh was a poor student, but he managed to graduate from high school in 1954. Wambaugh loved to read, calling it his escape. Jack London's *Call of the Wild* was a favorite, which he read 12 times. Wambaugh enlisted in the Marines after graduation, where he remained until 1957. While in the Marines, Wambaugh married his high school sweetheart, Dee Allsup.

After leaving the Marines, Wambaugh took a job at a steel mill and began attending night classes at Chaffey College in Alta Loma, California. He graduated with an associate's degree in 1958 and enrolled at California State College in Los Angeles. Wambaugh's childhood fascination with reading carried over to his collegiate career. Hoping to have a career as a teacher, he majored in English and graduated with his bachelor's degree in 1960.

Los Angeles Police

Instead of becoming a teacher, Wambaugh began working with the Los Angeles Police Department in 1960 while still a student at California State. He took the path of law enforcement over education primarily because the police job came available first, but also in a subconscious desire to follow in his father's footsteps. Although Wambaugh would perform well as a police officer—he began as a patrol officer and eventually rose to the rank of detective sergeant—writing was Wambaugh's passion long before he was published, and police work served as a springboard for his literary career. Says Wambaugh, "I was born to be a writer and trained to be a cop. One can learn to be a cop. I don't think one can learn to be a writer. At least a good writer" (Gregory, 1996).

Wambaugh's career with the LAPD was far from dull. He worked the crime-ridden Hollenbeck Division in East Los Angeles, a predominantly Chicano and Hispanic area of the city. He was close at hand in Watts—a predominantly African American area of Los Angeles—when riots erupted in August 1965. Saying he was always a writer but didn't know it, Wambaugh would scribble notes of his observations as a police officer and put them in a box. Wambaugh's observations of the Watts riots would be depicted in his first novel. According to Wambaugh, then a 28-year-old 5-year police veteran, "People were dropping dead all over the place. I have no idea who was shooting. I had no idea what to do about it. All we did was sort of back up and protect our ass" (Dunn, 2000).

Police Officer-Author

While on the force, Wambaugh returned to California State, this time to earn a master's degree in English, which he obtained in 1968. Wambaugh's first attempt at publishing was with a short story. He wrote several in the late 1960s—and publishers rejected all of them. Wambaugh's break came when he submitted a short story to *The Atlantic*. Editors of the prestigious monthly magazine sent it to Edward Weeks, a former *Atlantic* editor who had recently become a consultant with *The Atlantic*'s book publication division. Weeks suggested Wambaugh develop the story into a novel.

Wambaugh followed the advice, and *The New Centurions* was published in 1971, an event that Wambaugh called the greatest thrill of his life. *The New Centurions* examines the first 5 years of service for three fictional Los Angeles police officers. The officers begin as idealistic public servants, but their attitudes changed; they become cynical, suspicious, and willing to break rules even to the point of falsifying arrest reports. The gritty, gut-wrenching story of the three officers met with enormous critical and commercial success.

Like several of his subsequent books, *The New Centurions* was made into a movie. *The New Centurions* featured fine actors, including Stacy Keach and George C. Scott. However, Wambaugh, who has never hesitated to express criticism in honest, blunt terms, called the screenplay and the film a "comic book" version of his novel. Wambaugh's caustic criticism of this film was only the beginning of his battles with filmmakers eager to capitalize on the popularity of his books.

Wambaugh's second book was another novel, *The Blue Knight*. The novel chronicles the days of soon-to-retire officer Bumper Morgan. Wambaugh covers Morgan's every thought and action in cynical, humorous, gritty detail. Officer Morgan is portrayed favorably, but with serious shortcomings. Morgan overlooks "minor" illegalities and works with corrupt informants. Morgan's cynical attitude toward defendants, attorneys, and judges culminates in the fictional officer getting caught committing perjury on the witness stand.

The Blue Knight spawned several film projects. First came a 1973 NBC miniseries starring William Holden as Morgan, an effort that received favorable comments from Wambaugh, but only after he fought successfully for a second script to be written. In 1975, CBS made a weekly series based on *The Blue Knight* starring George Kennedy, the actor that Wambaugh thought perfect for the role of Morgan. Wambaugh lambasted the initial episodes of the show as just another shoot 'em up cop show, and he was successful in obtaining control over the show's content.

Wambaugh was hired as a consultant for an NBC weekly series called *Police Story*, which ran from 1973-1977. Wambaugh had a running battle with *Police Story* executives and with other filmmakers over the stereotyping of police officers. Contrary to the perception presented by most filmmakers, Wambaugh claims that police work contains some physical risk, but these risks are far outweighed by emotional dangers.

Wambaugh's third book may rank as his best in nonfiction. Wambaugh took a 6-month leave of absence and invested much of his own money in researching *The Onion Field*. He patterned the book on Truman Capote's *In Cold Blood*, a nonfiction novel. Released in 1973, *The Onion Field* chronicles the lives of four men, two police officers and two murderers. It is an account of the 1963 murder of police officer Ian Campbell, who, along with his partner, Karl Hettinger, was kidnapped and taken to an onion field near Bakersfield. California. The kidnappers, two career criminals named Gregory Powell and Jimmy Smith, cold bloodedly shot and murdered Ian Campbell. The book provides powerful insight into the thinking of Jimmy Smith (who consented to the project); it presents a stinging indictment of the justice system that turned the trials of the two killers into a farce. Most significantly, and the aspect that most interested Wambaugh, it follows the tragic life of Karl Hettinger (who also consented to the project), so racked with survivor's guilt over his inability to prevent Campbell's murder that he suffers a psychological meltdown. His guilt was compounded by the treatment he received at the hands of the LAPD, which effectively branded him a coward for surrendering his weapon to the murderers when they were pointing guns at Campbell.

The Onion Field brought Wambaugh the Edgar Allan Poe Award in 1974 and a special award for nonfiction from the Mystery Writers of America. *The Onion Field* also spawned the best movie based on a Wambaugh book. Released in 1979 and starring James Woods, Jon Savage and Ted Danson, the movie was a critical and commercial success.

Post-LAPD

Wambaugh's celebrity status began to interfere with his police work. Citizens would phone in tips, some fraudulent, in hopes of getting Wambaugh to come out and solve the crime. During questioning, suspects would ask him for acting roles. Fellow police officers became overly deferential, the final straw being when a partner held a car door open for him. At that moment, Wambaugh knew it was time to leave, which he did in 1973.

Wambaugh's first work published after his departure from the LAPD, *The Choirboys*, was one of his best novels. Wambaugh's publisher initially frowned on the project. The book was too dark, too cynical, too depressing, one the public would not like. Wambaugh, true to form, stubbornly insisted that the book be published as he wrote it, not with a happy ending rewrite as suggested by the publisher. Wambaugh said, "You can paper your walls with it; I am not rewriting it and I'm not giving you another one" (Dunn, 2000).

Fortunately, Wambaugh prevailed. *The Choirboys* was a huge success. It examines the tumultuous personal and professional lives of 10 fictitious Southern California police officers that meet regularly in Los Angeles's MacArthur Park for "choir practice," which consists of drunken debauchery. As preparation for *The Choirboys*, Wambaugh reread Joseph Heller's *Catch-22* and Kurt Vonnegut's *Slaughterhouse-Five*. Wambaugh said he used a satiric voice, "I'd like to do in a police novel what they did in war novels. I want to make people laugh, but I want them to be embarrassed for laughing at what they're laughing at. I want to really try gallows humor … dark, dark, dark satire" (Penfield, 1996).

The Choirboys blends dark humor and personal tragedy in spectacular fashion. One portion depicts a police officer working an auto accident where an accident victim was decapitated. A group of onlookers stop to ask the officer if anyone had been hurt in the accident. The officer presents the severed head of the accident victim, smiles, and tells the onlookers that "this guy" did not come through so well.

The Choirboys was made into a motion picture that included an outstanding cast, including James Woods (again), Charles Durning, and Louis Gossett, Jr. But no one could save *The Choirboys* from being labeled a "star studded flop." In a *Tonight Show* interview with Johnny Carson, Wambaugh blasted the movie, calling it "filthy," and vented his rage at filmmakers for turning his poignant and tragic novel into a film farce with an upbeat ending. Wambaugh sued Lorimar Productions for "mutilating" *The Choirboys* and was awarded $1,000,000 and the removal of his name from the script.

The Black Marble, released in 1978, was the first book written by Wambaugh that critics did not receive well. As a movie it enjoyed a much better reception, garnering the Edgar Allan Poe Award for best motion picture.

Another significant nonfiction work was *The Blooding*, which took Wambaugh to England. In *The Blooding*, Wambaugh relates the true story of English serial killer Colin Pitchfork. The book is billed as the story of the first criminal case solved by DNA profiling, which is somewhat misleading. Actually, the killer pays someone to provide his DNA sample to police to avoid detection, and when caught, the killer confesses to the killings before his DNA matches that found on the victims.

Wambaugh abandoned nonfiction because he was tired of being sued. In Wambaugh's words, the prevailing mentality in the 1980s was, "Hey, let's sue Wambaugh, what have we got to lose?" He explains, "I have to be ready to defend in court everything I write when I do nonfiction because we live in a nation of lawyers, and the second someone sees their name in one of my nonfiction books and realizes that I'm a deep-pockets writer, off they go to some ambulance chaser, and I'm sued and I have to defend" (Gregory, 1996). He was sued for *Echoes in the Darkness,* a 1987 book-turned-miniseries, which tells the story of a schoolteacher's murder in Pennsylvania at the hands of two other teachers.

Wambaugh has a greater love for fiction than nonfiction, saying, "The nonfiction books are my stepchildren. And the fiction books, the novels, are my blood children. They have my DNA" (Gregory, 1996). Nonfiction is just as challenging however, primarily because one must interact with real people that have been involved in traumatic situations. Says Wambaugh, "Now even though there's not as much imaginative work, it's very, very hard because I've got to interview people. A lot of times they're crime victims; they're people who've been terribly, terribly hurt and wounded, and I've got to portray them in a book. And sometimes I need to portray them warts and all, when they've already suffered a lot."

Wambaugh has a love–hate relationship with writing and with the criminal justice system, and his cynical wit comes through in his interviews just as it does in his writings. He calls police patrol working in "the big sewer." Wambaugh claims that he enjoys researching his books, but he has called writing as much fun as a "hemorrhoidectomy." According to Wambaugh, he writes not because he enjoys it, but to get rid of "the thing that's roiling inside." Writing requires a different persona than policing, says Wambaugh. While the police officer must be distant, the writer must be intimate.

Wambaugh is the stereotypical eccentric writer, saying, "I tend to withdraw from society of various kinds. I don't have a sense of community. I walk into this room and there's my community on those shelves. I probably take too many drinks every day. I work seven days a week doing a novel or a nonfiction book. There are no days off until the first draft is finished. I'm absolutely disciplined. All of these writing clichés apply to me."

Wambaugh hosted dinner parties to gather information and insight from police officers. According to Wambaugh, the optimum number at such an event is three to four. Any more than that and subgroups form, carrying on private conversations. He learned that gender mixing was not good. Men tended to act overly macho to impress the women, and women shut down. Wambaugh did not probe or interrogate at such gatherings, thinking it better to just let people talk while he took mental notes.

In a 1996 documentary titled *We, the Writer*, Wambaugh claimed that he knew how to use computers, which terrify him. He bought one and then sent it back when he realized it would not write the stories for him. He did not use agents, saying that he used one for one book but could not figure out what he couldn't do himself that warranted paying the agent 10%.

Other books by Joseph Wambaugh include *Fugitive Nights* (1992), *The Golden Orange* (1990), *The Secrets of Harry Bright* (1985), *The Delta Star* (1983), and *The Glitter Dome* (1981). Wambaugh's Hollywood Station series, comprised of five books, were published from 2006 to 2012, when his last book, *Harbor Nocturne*, was published. Wambaugh retired to Southern California, where he made occasional media appearances on law enforcement matters, usually defending police officers or at least making sure the police officer viewpoint is disseminated publicly. Finally, Wambaugh offeredthis advice, "Don't join a political party, and get a dog for affection." Joseph Wambaugh passed away on February 28, 2025, from esophageal cancer at age 88.

Sources and Suggested Readings

Bobbie Wygant Archive. (2021). *Joseph Wambaugh "Police Story" 1972* [Video]. YouTube. https://www.youtube.com/watch?v=06l2005oM10

Dunn, A. (2000, October 13). Joseph Wambaugh sounds off. *CNN.com.*

Gregory, Michael S. (1996). *We, the writer: A nonfiction portrait of writers and the creative writing process.*

Jacqueline Bachar Show. (2023). *Joseph Wambaugh interview, Hollywood Moon* [Video]. YouTube. https://youtu.be/OGSqtSMw8Dc?si=wDaZgBTOzbCZ7r-y, date of retrieval January 25, 2024.

Joseph Wambaugh website. (2024). Bestselling author Joseph Wambaugh, Grand Master of Crime and Police. http://www.josephwambaugh.net/, date of retrieval January 24, 2024.

Los Angeles Times. (2013). *Joseph Wambaugh on 'Onion Field' killer* [Video]. YouTube. https://www.youtube.com/watch?v=_BG95fIBNwk, date of retrieval January 25, 2024.

MysteriousPressCom. (2013). *Profile: Joseph Wambaugh* [Video]. YouTube. https://youtu.be/xmYSiODXF8I?si=FEsQRhJCRZdyeQbu, date of retrieval January 25, 2024.

Open Road Media. (2013). *Author and mystery writer Joseph Wambaugh* [Video]. YouTube. https://www.youtube.com/watch?v=9EHtzRAOZOs

Penfield, W. (1996, June 16). Laughing matters. *Toronto Sun.* https://infoweb-newsbank-com.eu1.proxy.openathens.net/apps/news/document-view?p=WORLDNEWS&val-base-0=%20&fld-base-0=Author&val-base-1=Toronto%20sun&fld-base-1=source&val-base-2=&fld-base-2=YMD_date&val-base-3=laughing%20matters&fld-base-3=Title&f=advanced&docref=news/14EA79A0CD558B30

SDSU Global Campus. (2014). *SDSU writers' conference 2014* [Video]. YouTube. https://www.youtube.com/watch?v=jDGncjti2JA

Wilson Biographies. (1980). H. W. Wilson Company.

Discussion Questions

1. How has Joseph Wambaugh increased the public's knowledge of American policing?
2. In what ways does the career of Joseph Wambaugh highlight the importance of criminal justice professionals having a worthy appreciation of fictional literature?

Credit

IMG 15.1: Copyright © by Mark Coggins (CC BY 2.0) at https://commons.wikimedia.org/wiki/File:Wambaugh_(1).jpg.

CHAPTER 16

Lee P. Brown (1937-)

IMG 16.1

In Lee Brown, one finds a blend of several pioneering traits and accomplishments. He is a pioneering minority, among the first African Americans to serve in big city police leadership roles. Brown has been a tireless and high-profile advocate of community and neighborhood policing and has found himself in the middle of some of American law enforcement's most controversial cases.

Brown was also among the most highly educated members of the law enforcement profession at the time he began his career, and he was as dedicated to academe as to law enforcement. Brown has also moved among the highest echelons of American politics, using his law enforcement background to ascend to higher office in a way done by few in the criminal justice or academic professions.

Early Life and Career

Lee Patrick Brown was born on October 4, 1937, in Wewoka, Oklahoma, into a poor farming family at the height of the Great Depression. Like all but one of his siblings, Brown was born at home and delivered by a midwife, his aunt. Like many escaping the Dust Bowl conditions of Oklahoma, Brown's family moved to California when he was 5, where his father, Andrew, a part Choctaw, took a job as a grape picker, and his mother, Zelma, worked as a cook.

Brown's autobiography *Outhouse to the White House* is an homage to his childhood environment in Fowler, California. Although his family was poor, Brown had a happy childhood. He knew that others around him had more, but the small African American community in Fowler was tight-knit and reinforced the idea that it takes a village to raise a child. While he seldom owned more than one pair of pants and had to wear shoes with patches on the soles, he never went hungry, thanks, in Brown's words, to his mother's ability to stretch a dollar. Christianity was a key element of Brown's childhood. The Brown family was seldom absent when the church doors were open.

After graduating from high school in Fowler, Brown attended Fresno State University on a football scholarship. He planned to major in physical education and devote his life to athletics. Although he was an outstanding student in high school, Brown initially struggled at Fresno State, almost flunking out. But Brown developed an interest in criminology, which was still a new discipline at Fresno and most other colleges.

San Jose Police

Brown was not focused on a career in law enforcement, aspiring to a career as a juvenile probation officer instead. As he approached graduation, he applied for a juvenile probation officer job but was rejected because the position required a 4-year degree in hand, rather than in progress. Needing a job, Brown applied for a police officer's position in San Jose, which did not require a 4-year degree.

In retrospect, Brown wondered why he had chosen law enforcement as a career, given his father's violent bouts with the police after a night of heavy drinking. He also saw examples of minor corruption among police officers. Brown's father and other residents of California's lush agricultural landscape would often give free food to police officers. Once, when Andrew Brown was driving while intoxicated, he was stopped by a state trooper, but allowed to proceed after Mr. Brown gave the trooper and other officers free food.

Brown worked as a police officer in San Jose for 8 years, both as a patrol officer and as an undercover vice and narcotics officer, which, according to Brown, was a much safer job then than now. While working as a police officer, Brown continued his education, a rare endeavor for municipal police officers in the early 1960s. Few police officers had 4-year degrees at the time, and obtaining a graduate degree was even more unusual, especially for African Americans. Brown obtained a master's degree in sociology from San Jose State University in 1964 and a master's degree in criminology in 1968 from the University of California at Berkeley.

Portland, Washington D.C., and Return to Portland

Brown left California and municipal law enforcement for a professorial position at Portland State University, where he established Portland State's Department of Administration of Justice. In 1969, Brown contemplated a run for San Jose's city council, but he was denied a spot on the ballot when it was discovered that his voter registration for California was expired. While he was at Portland, Brown capped his educational career in 1970 when he obtained a doctor of criminology degree from the University of California at Berkeley, a rarity, perhaps even a first for an African American in the 1960s. Brown continued his academic career, moving to Washington, D.C. in 1972 to assume the position of associate director of the Institute for Urban Affairs and Research at Howard University while also holding the rank of professor of public administration and director of criminal justice programs.

Brown returned to law enforcement in 1975, serving as sheriff of Multnomah County in Portland, Oregon, an appointed position. A year later Brown was appointed director of justice services, charged with overseeing all criminal justice agencies in the county. Unlike many law enforcement leaders whose sole focus was on their agency, Brown understood the importance of viewing the entire criminal justice process and its agencies as one system. Rather than viewing services like probation, juvenile justice, and policing as autonomous agencies divorced from each other, Brown was an early advocate of a holistic view of the criminal justice process, all involved agencies partnering with each other.

The Atlanta Child Murders

Brown's next move brought him national notoriety, both positive and negative. In 1978, Maynard Jackson, Atlanta's first African American mayor, appointed Brown commissioner of public safety. Brown's hiring was popular with many who knew his reputation, and the educated, erudite members of Atlanta's black community. Atlanta's poorer blacks were disappointed with the hiring of Brown, whose perceived aloofness and polished manners stood in contrast to Brown's populist (and corrupt) predecessor, Reginald Eaves.

Brown owes his notoriety to a series of horrible crimes perpetrated on Atlanta's youth in the late 1970s and early 1980s. Between 1979 and 1981, 27 children and young men were murdered, apparently by the same person. Atlanta was in a state of panic. Since all the victims were Black, conspiracy theories abounded; were the murders a racist plot? Did the Atlanta Police Bureau act quickly enough since most of the victims were poor? Were Atlanta police competent? Any neighborhood stranger came under suspicion. Police officers were bombarded with calls from parents whenever a child disappeared for even the shortest length of time. Nightly newscasts in Atlanta and around the country frequently began their programs with stories about the murders. The airwaves were flooded with public service announcements featuring sports and entertainment celebrities warning parents to always know their children's whereabouts. News outlets and tabloids from around the world descended on Atlanta.

At the center of this firestorm was Lee Brown. He became a fixture on local and national television newscasts. As time went on and the murders remained unsolved, Brown and his department came under increasing criticism, not only for failing to solve the crimes but for having a sloppy and disorganized investigation and for embarrassing moves like hiring a feckless New Jersey-based psychic to visit with the victims' families and the murder scenes, accompanied by Atlanta police officers.

A saturation of patrol resulted in the arrest of Wayne Williams, who was formally charged with two of the murders, but only after a few weeks of embarrassingly public surveillances of Williams's home. Williams was linked to 25 other murders and was convicted and sentenced to life in prison in 1982.

Move to Houston

Brown gained considerable notoriety because of the Atlanta murders. This recognition and Brown's history of not staying in one place too long led to his accepting the job of police chief in Houston in 1982, a job he would keep until 1990. Houston was beset by allegations of corruption, racism, and brutality at the time of Brown's appointment, and not all Houston officers welcomed Brown, believing that the Atlanta Police Bureau was beset with low morale and bad working conditions under his leadership. One senior officer in Atlanta won a lawsuit against Brown, claiming Brown did not follow proper procedure when firing him after he disagreed with Brown's policies. A court ordered Brown to pay damages from his own pocket and froze his assets. Nevertheless, Brown, the most well-known African American police official in America, was brought to Houston to increase minority hiring and improve relations between the police and the minority community.

At the time, community policing ideals were seeping out of colleges and universities and into police departments. Brown, an academic in his own right and a staunch advocate of the concept of community cooperation, was determined to implement community policing in Houston. Brown's preference was for neighborhood policing, with officers ordered to become personally acquainted with citizens in their assigned area. Emphasis was placed on foot patrol, town meetings, problem-solving, crime prevention, and assessment of specific neighborhood needs. Officers were not rewarded simply for the number of arrests made or the number of citations issued.

Brown viewed violent crime as more than a criminal justice problem, but also as a public health issue. In collaboration with the University of Texas Health Science Center, Brown helped create the Center for the Study of Interpersonal Violence. The hoped-for decrease in reported crime did not come about in Houston, but Brown's effort to implement an increasingly popular concept like community policing increased his profile around the country.

New York City

The defeat of Kathy Whitmire, the mayor that appointed Brown, and the election of David Dinkins to the mayor's position in New York City in late 1989 led to Brown's next position, chief of police in New York City, the most prestigious municipal law enforcement position in the United States. Dinkins admired Brown's work in Houston and wanted him to implement similar programs in New York City.

After a comprehensive review of the NYPD administrative structure, Brown implemented a plan called Safe Streets, Safe City, which called for an increase in the number of uniformed police officers in New York. Despite the budget problems faced by the city, Mayor Dinkins approved Brown's proposal. Brown also launched Operation All Out, which, in accordance with the community policing ideal, required a greater emphasis on foot patrol, a throwback to the days of "walking the beat," and required all officers, regardless of rank, to spend some time each week on the street. Town meetings were held with community leaders to assess crime-related needs. The number of minority and female officers increased under Brown's administration.

Consistent with his beliefs about the causes of crime, Dr. Brown knew that police alone could not tackle New York's crime problem. He compared crime in New York City to a national health emergency. Police alone could not solve the problem of crime because, with few exceptions, they do not create crime. Crime stemmed from social and economic problems. Said Brown,

> Any logical, thinking person would tell you that traditional approaches are not solving the problem. Our legacy should not be more prisons. We must look at the underlying factors that produce crime. Education is critical, and yet a large number of our young people are estranged and alienated from the school system. What the mosquito was to malaria, the gun and the young black man's environment are to homicide. Now, you don't just keep swatting the mosquito, you drain the swamp. We need to drain the swamp of guns. (Webber, 1991, para. 10)

Drug Czar

On August 3, 1992, Brown resigned as chief of the NYPD to spend more time with his wife, Yvonne, who was in declining health. Brown returned to Houston, where Yvonne Brown died from cancer at age 55 a few months later. Lee Brown took a professor's job at Texas Southern University, an historically Black college/university (HBCU) in Houston. He did not stay long in that position either. In 1993, Brown was nominated by President Bill Clinton to head the Office of National Drug Control Policy, a cabinet-level post. After confirmation by the United States Senate, Brown assumed his duties as America's "drug czar" on June 21, 1993. Lee Brown was the first law enforcement officer to occupy a presidential cabinet position.

At his confirmation hearings, Brown pledged to curb drug use by coming down hard on dealers and offering treatment for users, toning down the "war on drugs" rhetoric of the Reagan–Bush administrations. Brown claimed that American society had failed to curb drug use by relying too much on the criminal justice system. As with violent crime, Brown argued that drug use is not only a justice system problem, but a public health and medical problem.

Mayor of Houston

Dr. Brown returned to Houston in 1997, this time taking a teaching job at Rice University. He also sought elective office for the first time and was elected mayor of Houston on December 6, 1997, assuming office on January 2, 1998. In addition to overseeing the development of the METRO light rail system and attracting a new NFL franchise to replace the departed Houston Oilers, Brown translated his community policing ideals into municipal government. Working off a principle he called neighborhood-oriented government, Brown encouraged his staff to hold meetings with community leaders to assess neighborhood needs, just as he did when he served as police chief.

Brown was reelected in 1999 and again in 2001 when he began his third and final term as mayor. Brown's tenure as Houston's mayor ended in 2003. Brown, the father of four children, married Frances Young, a Houston schoolteacher.

Post-Houston, Brown Group

After leaving politics and law enforcement, Brown continued to be involved in law enforcement, government, and academic activities. He was a cofounder of the National Organization of Black Law Enforcement Executives, served as president of the International Association of Chiefs of Police, and chair and CEO of Brown Group International, a government consulting business.

In 2023, Brown, though long disassociated from Houston politics, was involved in a political dustup. Two Democrats, Texas State Senator John Whitmire and Shelia Jackson Lee, a bellicose congresswoman, were involved in a runoff for the Houston mayoral seat. Shelia Jackson Lee publicly claimed that Dr. Brown endorsed her, prompting Lee Brown to respond that he had publicly endorsed Senator Whitmire. Whitmire won the mayoral race.

The Lee Brown Legacy

Lee Brown and those who have written about him note that he is a man of many "firsts." He was the first African American big city police chief, the first Black police chief in Houston and New York City, the first African American drug czar, the first law enforcement officer to serve in a presidential cabinet, the first Black mayor in Houston, the first Black sheriff in Portland, Oregon, and among the first, if not *the first*, African Americans to hold a doctorate in criminology from the University of California. Although Dr. Brown acknowledges that he was either a "first" or among the firsts in several positions, his ideas on policing, criminal justice, and governance in general are what he most wants to be remembered for. With Brown, the concept of "community" is essential to good relations between the citizenry and the government, whether the government is represented by police officers or any other government entity.

In 2012, Brown wrote that his beloved community policing ideals, while espoused by many departments, were only given lip service and not really implemented. He predicted that community police is still the wave of the future, but that it might be a full generation before the idea is fully implemented. In an age where more and more people do not know their neighbors by name, Brown's optimism might be tied more to his own childhood memories than reality. Prosecutors and other criminal justice professionals should also be closer to their communities. But given political realities and the fact that the criminal justice system is more a historical accident than a carefully devised plan, such a possibility is probably not a reality. Rather than dwelling on his accomplishments, Brown's ideology is best summed up in this statement:

> The challenge for all of us is to keep focused on the role of the police in a free society and determine how all segments of society can play a role in keeping our neighborhoods safe and, in doing so, improve the quality of life for ourselves and our families. That is a responsibility that we all have. (Good Reads, n.d., para. 23)

Sources and Suggested Readings

Axelrod, A., Phillips C., & Kemper, K. (1996). *Cops, crooks & criminologists.* Facts on File.

Brown, Lee P. (2012). *Policing in the 21st century: Community policing.* Author House.

Brown, Lee P., & Joseph Green-Bishop. (2022). *Outhouse to the White House.* Author House.

Foggy Melson. (2023). *Atlanta police chief Lee P. Brown has wages garnished & lien put on house due to lawsuit (3/18/82)* [Video]. YouTube. https://www.youtube.com/watch?v=XWiExs6V0yU, date of retrieval February 14, 2024.

Foggy Melson. (2023). *Houston police union doesn't want Lee P. Brown as police chief (March 17, 1982)* [Video]. YouTube. https://www.youtube.com/watch?v=pRs34fcJNNs

Foggy Melson. (2023). *Lee P. Brown creates homicide task force to investigate 7 unsolved Atlanta child murder cases 3/382* [Video]. YouTube. https://www.youtube.com/watch?v=N7hDKD8SGd8, date of retrieval February 16, 2024.

Foggy Melson. (2023). *Lee P. Brown on use of psychic Dorothy Allison in Atlanta child murder investigation (Oct 23, 1980)* [Video]. YouTube. https://www.youtube.com/watch?v=2pVeHF6ffMc, date of retrieval February 10, 2024.

Good Reads. (n.d.). *Lee P. Brown quotes.* goodreads.com. https://www.goodreads.com/author/quotes/6491183.Lee_P_Brown, accessed August 5, 2024.

The History Makers. (2024). *The Honorable Lee P. Brown.* https://www.thehistorymakers.org/biography/honorable-lee-p-brown, date of retrieval February 15, 2024.

Institute of Politics Harvard Kennedy School. (2015). *3 with IOP: Lee P. Brown* [Video]. YouTube. https://www.youtube.com/watch?v=waTzGy_oUOk, date of retrieval February 12, 204.

National Policing Institute. (2023, September 12). *National Policing Institute honors legendary law enforcement leaders Charles H. Ramsey, Lee P. Brown.* https://www.policinginstitute.org/press-releases/national-policing-institute-honors-legendary-law-enforcement-leaders-charles-h-ramsey-lee-p-brown/

Sessions, K. (2023, October 25). Shelia Jackson Lee announces endorsement from former mayor. He denies it. *Chron.* https://www.chron.com/news/houston-texas/article/houston-mayor-endorse-jackson-lee-18446940.php, date of retrieval February 16, 2024.

Stoil, Michael J. (1992). A view from President Clinton's drug czar: Dr. Lee Brown. *Behavioral Health Management, 14*, 6–7.

Webber, Alan M. (1991). Crime and management: An interview with New York City Police Commissioner Lee P. Brown. *Harvard Business Review, 3*, 111.

Discussion Questions

1. What personal characteristics and historical events and forces have contributed to Lee Brown's success?
2. If Lee Brown had been born 20 years earlier, would he have become as prominent as he did? Why or why not?

Credit

CHAPTER 17

Penny Harrington (1942–2021)

IMG 17.1

When Lola Baldwin worked as a Portland, Oregon, police officer during the 1910s, she was content to focus on protecting women. She had no desire to perform all the duties of male officers. Likewise, the thought of serving as chief of the department probably did not enter her mind—which was the mindset of even the boldest maverick females during Baldwin's era. However, between the 1920s and the 1980s, the role of women in the American workforce experienced a gradual but radical shift. Women entered the workforce in great numbers during World War II, doing jobs traditionally performed by men and filling in for men who were serving in the military. After the war, women were emboldened by "women's liberation" and continued to make strides in the workforce.

Penny Harrington was the first woman in the United States to serve as chief of a police department in a large city. Like Lola Baldwin, she made her name in Portland, Oregon. Although her tenure as chief was brief and she had many critics, Harrington paved the way for hiring other women police chiefs. Her stormy tenure as chief notwithstanding, her career presents in microcosm the lot of women police officers since the 1960s.

Early Life and Career

Penny Ledyard was born in Lansing, Michigan, on March 2, 1942, the oldest of four children born to Edward and Mary Louise Ledyard. Penny grew up in a lower-middle-class household; her father was a superintendent of steel processing at a plant that manufactured wheels for automobiles. Mary Louise

Ledyard worked as a secretary for a utility company in Lansing—until she was fired when she became pregnant with Penny. During Penny's childhood, she had no memory of her parents assigning gender roles in the family; there was no such thing as girls' work or boys' work.

Penny attributes her decision to enter police work to meeting a Lansing woman police officer on a high school career day. After high school, she took a job as a legal secretary and enrolled at Michigan State University (MSU), one of the few universities in the country that offered a degree in police administration, a forerunner of its criminal justice program. During the early 1960s, most MSU men who were interested in criminal justice studied criminal investigation; their female colleagues studied juvenile justice and child psychology. Men prepared for police work, and women prepared for working with children.

Penny married a fellow police administration major while she was a junior at MSU. Soon after graduating from MSU, a former MSU professor offered her husband a job with the Multnomah County (Portland), Oregon, sheriff's department. So, Penny Orazetti, as she was now known, moved with her husband to Portland. Multnomah County prohibited hiring married couples, so while her husband worked for the sheriff's department, Penny worked as a legal secretary.

The Portland Police Bureau

Penny sat for the Portland Police Bureau entrance exam in 1964 and passed with high marks. She was hired and went to work in a department that had 700 officers, including five African Americans and 18 women. Penny was the first person ever hired by the Portland Police Bureau who had a 4-year degree in police administration. Penny Orazetti's basic training experience illustrates what women police officers had to endure and how much has changed since the 1960s. The term *sexual harassment* was not in vogue in 1964 like it is today. Many of the men with whom she trained thought nothing of making sexual advances toward the female officers, even if both were married. Once, during self-defense training, a male training partner pulled her sweatshirt over her head, leaving her exposed with only a bra on to the whoops and laughter of the other trainees.

For the most part, though, the women in Penny's group were treated relatively well. One of the reasons they received good treatment was that the male officers knew—or thought they knew—that the female officers would never be transferred from the Women's Protective Division. Therefore, the women were not viewed as a threat to the men. Like other female officers, Penny wore a police uniform, but it consisted of white gloves, a hat, a tailored suit, silk blouse, and a pair of slingback pumps. Women were not allowed to carry firearms. The policewoman's primary function was to assist male officers and work with cases involving child abuse and runaways. Since Portland became a frequent destination for runaways in the 1960s, her plate was often full.

Penny learned from an African American officer the importance of connecting with the community. Community engagement, said the officer, was the best way of preventing riots. In a time long before the term *community policing* came into everyday usage, Penny Orazetti understood the importance of making sure that police officers tried to stay engaged with the community they served.

One of her first blatant encounters with discrimination in promotion came in 1968 when Penny tried to sit for the detective exam. She was denied admission to the exam because she lacked the necessary experience as a patrol officer, experience she could not obtain because of her gender. Penny also complained because she and the other women in the bureau received less pay than male officers. She took the sergeant's exam but was passed over in favor of another woman who scored lower.

Although she inherited anti-labor sentiments from her father, Penny Orazetti joined the police officers' union, frustrated by what she perceived as unfair treatment. She became active in the union, recruiting members and volunteering in her off hours. She lobbied for better pay and better work hours, and she advocated for the creation of a research and planning division within the bureau.

Her reputation spread, making her popular with many rank-and-file officers, although some officers were not fans because they thought she had done very little actual policing on the streets. Also, union activism made her unpopular with management. When told by the bureau chief that she would leave the Women's Division only "over his dead body," Penny went to Mayor Terry Schrunk, who would not intervene. Penny angrily left his office—but not before threatening to sue him. Back at her office, she found a message from the mayor stating that she had been transferred to the bureau's planning unit, effective January 29, 1970.

Not long after her transfer to the planning unit, her marriage, which had produced one son, ended. Penny had had an intimate relationship with her captain, Leo Miller, who was also married and serving in the planning unit. Penny's extramarital relations in the Portland Police Bureau led some to refer to her as a "fender lizard" or "badge bunny" (DuPay, 2021, para. 2).

In 1970, Penny became an officer in the International Association of Women Police. She also banded with other women in the Portland Bureau and filed a civil rights complaint over job requirements that discriminated against women, such as height requirements (which also affected Asians) and the title "policewoman." As a result, all police officers in Portland were simply referred to as officers.

Every time Penny was interviewed for a promotion, she encountered questions that would not have been asked of men. One was whether she could juggle her family and childcare responsibilities and still devote enough time to her career. Penny had scored ahead of all others on the detective exam, but the Bureau left five detective positions vacant rather than give one to her. Penny persevered, however, and was promoted to detective in February 1972, another in a long line of firsts for her. Although some of her male colleagues received her warmly, others did not. Penny received more help from secretaries than from other detectives. She received this anonymously authored note from a fellow detective:

> I don't know how a fat homley [sic] double chin humpback cow with two legs that resamble [sic] two fresh butchered hogs hanging sid [sic] by side and naked to within one inch of her crotch can expect to not be conspicuous. One look at a freak like you is enough shock to give a baboon the big jitters. (Roman, 2018, para. 18)

Over the next several years, Penny filed 42 complaints against the Portland Police Bureau, constantly butting heads with officials within the bureau and in city hall. Her critics charged that she was much more competent at complaining than at police work. She was transferred to other divisions within the bureau several times.

By 1974, the stress had become too much. Her situation was exacerbated by her newest job assignment, which required her to work on the Bureau's new computer system in a slightly renovated bomb shelter, where she seldom saw the light of day. In November 1974, Penny suffered an acute anxiety attack and passed out. She became very depressed and suffered mood swings. In January 1975, a time when visiting a psychiatrist still carried a heavy stigma, especially for a police officer, Penny Orazetti started seeing one. Her immune system was depleted, and she was advised by her doctor to quit her job. Instead, she took antidepressant medication and signed a suicide pact with her psychiatrist.

Penny returned to work in July 1975 as a uniformed patrol sergeant, becoming Portland's first female officer to supervise male officers. A uniform had to be specially designed for her, and she had to receive instruction on how to wear her ammunition pouch. She was assigned to Portland's highest crime area, an opportunity she relished because it gave her a chance to do real police work. She liked her fellow officers and enjoyed working with the community and using innovative methods of dealing with crime, such as citing administrative codes to close bars that sold to minors.

Penny's reputation grew in Portland, in part due to favorable media coverage, and she was promoted to lieutenant in 1977. On one occasion, she was reprimanded for insubordination after she struck her captain. She claimed the captain had grabbed her hand and placed it on his genitals.

In July 1980, Penny Orazetti became the youngest and the first female captain in the history of the Portland Police Bureau. One of her priorities was to increase the hiring of minority officers, a move that did not sit well with many of her colleagues. She emphasized the importance of understanding different cultures in Portland. For example, many officers were perplexed at the lack of cooperation from recent Asian immigrants. Penny learned that the officers often made a fundamental mistake when dealing with them. When responding to a call, officers would quickly ascertain that the adults on the scene did not understand or speak English well and would speak to the children in the house, an insulting gesture to the adults. Penny suggested cultural diversity training to remedy such problems.

Chief Harrington

Penny married Gary Harrington, a fellow officer, in February 1982. Penny Harrington made history on January 24, 1985, when Mayor Bud Clark appointed her to head the Portland Police Bureau. Penny Harrington became a national celebrity. She was profiled in magazines and on television shows. A Penny Harrington action figure was also released.

Her tenure as chief would be short and tumultuous. She made several moves that upset rank-and-file officers and union representatives. She placed her sister Roberta in charge of internal affairs and personnel. She dismantled the narcotics unit and created a general vice unit. She reinstituted the juvenile division to attack truancy. Once a staunch union member, she clashed with union leaders over budget cuts.

Harrington banned the use of the carotid hold after a Portland officer killed an African American security guard with the hold. The ban on the carotid hold was popular with the city's Black leadership, but in response, some officers viewed Harrington as disloyal to her officers and wore T-shirts inscribed, "Don't choke 'em, smoke 'em" (Seelye, 2021, para. 24). Some of the officers who wore the shirts were fired, which prompted lawsuits from the fired officers and a no-confidence resolution from the union leadership.

Not all her moves were unpopular. She was the first to ban smoking in police buildings; she implemented greater physical fitness regimens, and she increased diversity training for officers. However, Harrington never gained the confidence of union leadership, who blamed her for bad morale within the department, the drug trafficking problem in Portland, and for fostering an us-against-them mentality by favoring community leaders over police officers.

The final blow involved her husband, Gary. In March 1986, the Harringtons went to a party at a restaurant that had a reputation as a drug-dealing location. Gary saw a known drug dealer there and informed the manager that he should not let the drug dealer hang out at the restaurant. Unknown to Gary and Penny, police officers were conducting surveillance on the dealer. This thwarted a planned drug bust of the restaurant, and police officers accused Gary Harrington of intentionally thwarting the investigation and the bust. Neither the district attorney nor the United States attorney found basis for criminal prosecution of either of the Harringtons, but the political damage had been done. Although

Gary Harrington's actions did not rise to the level of a crime, it constituted misconduct. A mayoral commission recommended that Penny Harrington be replaced and that Gary Harrington receive a 25-day suspension. The commission also cited problems with departmental morale and with her leadership. Penny Harrington resigned as Portland's police chief on September 1, 1986, 19 months after she assumed her duties. She and Gary Harrington eventually divorced.

Post-Portland

Penny Harrington left Portland, Oregon, and began working for the California State Bar Association in 1988. She remained there for 7 years, developing expertise in gender and racial discrimination law. She later worked as a private consultant and public speaker and remained active in women's police organizations such as the National Council for Women and Policing.

In a telephone interview for the first edition of this book, I asked Harrington, who was kind, gracious and forthcoming, if she would have done things differently if she had the chance to do it again. She admitted that her problem was not being a good enough politician, not building adequate bases of support for her decisions, and in general not playing the political game well enough. She liked moves toward community policing, calling it "women's policing," but she also thought the term was frequently misused. Although she acknowledged that women have made great strides in policing, she thought only when women achieve critical mass in a department, i.e., at least 33% of a police force, will women truly impact policing. (Most estimates place the percentage of sworn female law enforcement officers around 20.) Harrington said,

> You don't have to be rabid, screaming in the streets, tearing off your bra feminists. You just have to be smart and figure out what's holding you back. It's usually a stupid rule. (Seelye, 2021, para. 15)

In 1999, she published her autobiography, titled *Triumph of Spirit.* She settled in Morro Bay, California, and went in the opposition direction of law enforcement. She got involved with holistic healing, became a Reiki master teacher and a crystal healer, and opened a shop selling rocks. Penny Harrington passed away on September 15, 2021, at age 79, in Morro Bay.

Penny Harrington was not short on critics, including former Portland police officer Don DuPay who referred to her as a "disgraced former chief" (DuPay, 2021, para. 1) and wrote that policing was always about feminism for her. Perhaps Penny Harrington can best be described as a warrior whose maverick fortitude made her great at fighting battles but did not prepare her for what to do after the battle was won. Nevertheless, she has rightly been hailed as a woman who made great strides in breaking the glass ceiling surrounding women and policing.

Sources and Suggested Readings

DuPay, D. (2021, October 20). Will the real Penny please stand up? *Medium*. https://medium.com/@theresakennedydupay/penny-harrington-destroyed-more-than-the-blue-ceiling-at-portland-police-bureau-she-weakened-the-11ca4e56fd2f, date of retrieval January 22, 2024.

Forrest, J. (2021, September 17). Penny Harrington, Portland's first female police chief, dies at 79. *OregonLive*. https://www.oregonlive.com/pacific-northwest-news/2021/09/penny-harrington-portlands-first-female-police-chief-dies-at-79.html, date of retrieval January 23, 2024.

Harrington, P. (1999). *Triumph of spirit: An autobiography of Penny Harrington*. Brittany Publications.

Harrington, Penny. (2002, March 10). Telephone interview.

Jolin, Anja, & Jolin, Annette. (2022, December 30). Penny Ledyard Orazetti Harrington (1942–2021). *Oregon encyclopedia*, A Project of the Oregon Historical Society. https://www.oregonencyclopedia.org/articles/harrington-penny/, date of retrieval January 22, 2024.

Penny Harrington, Portland's first female police chief, dies [Video]. (2022). *KGW News*. YouTube. https://www.youtube.com/watch?v=4u73VOLPo_8, date of retrieval January 22, 2024.

Roman, I. (2018, September 5). A police pioneer on her unfinished business. *The Marshall Project*. https://www.themarshallproject.org/2018/09/05/a-police-pioneer-on-her-unfinished-business, date of retrieval January 22, 2024.

Seelye, Katharine Q. (2021, September 24). Penny Harrington, who broke a blue ceiling, dies at 79. *New York Times*. https://www.nytimes.com/2021/09/24/us/penny-harrington-dead.html, accessed August 5, 2024.

Thompson, Jeff. (2021, September 17). Penny Harrington, Portland's first female police chief, has died. *OPB*. https://www.opb.org/article/2021/09/17/penny-harrington-portlands-first-female-police-chief-has-died/, date of retrieval January 23, 2024.

Discussion Questions

1. How have conditions for women police officers changed since Penny Harrington started her law enforcement career?
2. In what ways does Penny Harrington's career demonstrate the importance of developing alliances with political leaders and leaders of rank-and-file groups?

Credit

CHAPTER 18

Greg MacAleese (1947-)

IMG 18.1

Under ancient Chinese law, a person that provided an anonymous tip to authorities about a crime would be executed, even if the accusation turned out to be true. The fear was that an anonymous accusation would make the accuser unaccountable for his or her actions. Today, American law enforcement and prosecutors rely on anonymous tips and community involvement for solving crimes. Contrary to the image often portrayed in film and on television, where crimes are solved by omniscient, all-seeing detectives, or by sophisticated technology and science, most crimes are solved through information provided to law enforcement. One great influence for this area of solving crime is Greg MacAleese, a former Albuquerque detective and the founder of Crime Stoppers. Crime Stoppers, started in 1976, is one of the most important innovations in law enforcement since the 1970s, not just in the United States, but around the world.

Early Life and Career

Greg MacAleese was born on January 23, 1947, in Picton, Ontario. The MacAleese family moved around Canada during Greg's childhood while his father served as an armaments officer in the Royal Canadian Air Force, but in 1961, when Greg was 14, his father moved the family to Albuquerque, New Mexico. Making his mark as an outstanding baseball pitcher in high school, Greg MacAleese attended the University of New Mexico on an athletic scholarship. However, an arm injury shortened his baseball career.

After graduating from college with a degree in journalism in 1969, he worked for the now-defunct *Albuquerque Tribune,* where he had interned as a sports columnist. After 1 year as a full-time employee with the *Tribune,* MacAleese went to work as the New Mexico state sports editor for the Associated Press. At age 25, Greg MacAleese was voted Sportswriter of the Year for New Mexico in 1972, but another health problem derailed his promising sports journalism career. MacAleese developed an ulcer and nearly bled to death. The ulcer was caused by the stress of his profession, the constant pressure to meet deadlines, and the long and irregular hours that his job demanded.

Law Enforcement Career

Acting on the advice of his physician to choose a profession with less stress, MacAleese quit journalism. Incredibly, he chose law enforcement as the answer to his problems, not because of a passion for public safety or crime detection, but because he thought that police work would be a good vehicle for authoring books. MacAleese had spent minimal time on crime stories, but in 1972, he worked as press release coordinator for the successful United States Senate campaign of Republican Pete Domenici, where he met law enforcement officers from all over New Mexico and developed a strong interest in police work.

Greg MacAleese began working with the Albuquerque Police Department in 1973, walking a beat before being promoted to violent crimes investigations in 1976. Like other Albuquerque police officers, MacAleese's job was far from boring. At the time, Albuquerque had one of the highest per capita crime rates in the United States. MacAleese found his niche in policing, especially detective work, but one of his greatest frustrations as a detective was not being able to solve cases, especially when he suspected that someone in the community had useful information but would not or did not know how to supply law enforcement with the information. Knowing that citizen cooperation is more essential to solving crimes than detective acumen or sophisticated technology, MacAleese tried to think of ways to get more public cooperation. He attributed lack of community involvement to apathy, fear of retaliation, and the police being disconnected from the community.

Crime Stoppers: The Genesis

In 1976, University of New Mexico student Michael Carmen was working in an Albuquerque gas station when he was robbed and shot at point-blank range with a 410 shotgun. He died 4 hours later in the hospital without being able to provide information about his assailants. Carmen was 2 weeks from marrying his high school sweetheart, and he was working an extra shift as a favor to a friend who needed the night off.

After 2 months of getting nowhere, MacAleese thought the crime would be solvable if he only had information pointing him in the direction of the killers. Based on the modus operandi of the killing, MacAleese suspected that the killers were responsible for a series of other armed robberies in the Albuquerque area. Knowing that everyone enjoys money—including potential criminal informants—and falling back on his experience as a journalist and his contacts in the Albuquerque television market, namely Max Sklower, the general manager of KOAT-TV, MacAleese devised a plan to elicit tips about the murder. Based on the information available, MacAleese decided to reenact the crime with KOAT filming the reenactment and then airing it on the local news broadcast. A tip line separate from the police department was set up so that people with information could phone in, having been clearly told that their identity would remain anonymous. The gas station offered a $1,000 reward for information leading to the killers' arrest.

MacAleese arranged to reenact the crime with as much accuracy as possible. He knew a 410 shotgun had been used, he had a description of the car, and he had been told that the suspects were two young African American men. MacAleese arranged for the service station that had been the scene of the murder to be used to stage the reenactment. He visited the local Job Corps and recruited two participants to play the role of the killers. MacAleese hired a University of New Mexico drama student to play the role of the victim. He visited car lots until he found a car exactly like the one seen leaving the scene, a black and yellow Chevrolet Charger. Everything was set for a perfect reenactment—except one detail. The crime occurred at night, but the television station would not pay its film crew to work overtime so the reenactment had to be conducted during the day.

On the day of the reenactment, everything went awry. The Chevrolet Charger had been sold the day before. The two youths from the Job Corps failed to show; in fact, they were arrested later that day in a barroom disturbance. MacAleese was forced to use his own unmarked car, and he and his lieutenant played the role of the killers. Prior to the "shooting," the drama student/victim asked what his motivation should be in the action. MacAleese responded "your motivation is that you are gonna die." As the two detectives acted out the shooting with the young drama student and fled, the student probably thought that motivation was coming to life. MacAleese did not realize that the shotgun casing they used to shoot blanks was so hot that it set the student's shirt afire. The young man was left to desperately shed his shirt and extinguish the fire as MacAleese drove away, all to the delight of dozens of nearby schoolchildren that had gathered to watch the reenactment in full view of the cameras. It was a comedy of errors.

Distressed by the amateurishness of the video, MacAleese was sure that nothing would come of it. It aired on September 8, 1976, with MacAleese performing the voice-over. After the reenactment KOAT's Neal Murray announced that detective MacAleese was standing by to receive phone calls. To MacAleese's surprise, not only was the Carmen murder solved, but another call led to solving an 18-month-old unrelated gang-rape case. The 13th caller had witnessed the Carmen shooting. Another caller knew the location of the car used in the robbery. MacAleese tracked the car and questioned the owner, who admitted to taking a share of the cut in exchange for the use of his car. He led MacAleese to the killers, and the case was solved. One of the arrestees was convicted and sentenced to life in prison. The other defendant was not convicted due to problems with the prosecution of his case.

KOAT management was delighted with the response they received to the reenactment. Other Albuquerque detectives wanted in on similar reenactments. Numerous reenactments were conducted with great success. Unfortunately, in time, this bred laziness on the part of detectives, who would sometimes wait for the reenactment rather than doing the legwork necessary to solve the case.

Crime Stoppers Is Established

Realizing that the nascent program was growing quickly, MacAleese approached his chief with an eye toward establishing a formal program. MacAleese knew that the program was getting too large to be strictly funded by the police department and that more public involvement was needed to sustain it. While the use of paid informants is hardly new—according to the New Testament, authorities paid one of Jesus's disciples 30 pieces of silver to betray him—MacAleese encountered opposition within law enforcement ranks to setting up such a program. In one meeting, an officer asked if it was right to pay citizens to merely perform their civic duty. MacAleese replied, "If people were doing their civic duty, we wouldn't be up to our ass in crime" (Ontario Association of Crime Stoppers, 2020, 0.50).

MacAleese also realized that since money was involved, the possibility of malfeasance existed. Taxpayer funds could not be used, as any taxpayer disbursement is subject to an audit trail, which would lead to the identity of the tipster. MacAleese knew that outside oversight was needed to prevent such abuse. With that in mind, Crime Stoppers was formally established with a board of directors comprised of non-law enforcement volunteers, procedures for operation, and fiscal accountability.

MacAleese also encountered resistance from within the legal system. Early in the history of Crime Stoppers, MacAleese and another detective nearly found themselves in jail for trying to protect the identity of a Crime Stopper informant. A shooting had occurred in an area of high drug activity in Albuquerque. An informant, a drug user who feared retaliation, took MacAleese by the place where the shooters were located. MacAleese arrested the suspects and found other corroborating witnesses. Once the case got to court, defense attorneys, who knew the case had been solved through a Crime Stoppers tip, demanded that MacAleese release the name of the original informant. MacAleese knew that doing so would ruin the program.

The judge agreed to take the matter under advisement, and MacAleese spent several days not knowing whether he would go to jail for contempt and whether Crime Stoppers would survive. As the case predated the hostility of media outlets toward police, the local media vociferously favored Crime Stoppers. The judge, thinking that the political fallout from ruining Crime Stoppers was greater than the legal issue involved, declined to hold the detectives in contempt.

Crime Stoppers Spreads

Because of his Crime Stoppers work, the Albuquerque Police Department nominated MacAleese for International Association of Chiefs of Police (IACP) officer of the year for 1977. The arrival of 12,000 police chiefs at the IACP meeting in Los Angeles was an enormous boon to Crime Stoppers. MacAleese had formally been nicknamed "Mac." His full new nickname was "Cecil B. DeMacAleese" (Robertson, 2016, para. 27), in mock homage to film director Cecil B. DeMille.

Crime Stoppers spread throughout the United States over the next several years. MacAleese eventually left the Albuquerque Police Department, and he maintained his affiliation with Crime Stoppers until 1983.

In 1984, MacAleese worked in Texas for the criminal justice division of Governor Mark White's office, where he helped establish a Crime Stoppers unit. In 1986, he went to work as the executive director for the greater Dallas Crime Commission, a position he held for 5 years. In that role, MacAleese sought support for police work from local businesses.

While in Dallas, MacAleese was also involved in Crime Stoppers and other crime-centered television productions. He was involved in a three-hour television show that profiled narcotics trafficking and its associated violence, with special focus on the recent influx of Jamaican drug dealers in Dallas. The show consisted of two hours of documentary and one hour of town hall meetings. The documentary offered reasons for drug use, pictures of known drug dealers, a profile of the Dallas drug market, and a help line for informants or those wanting treatment. Hundreds of phone calls came in, from those asking for help and those wanting to finger drug dealers. MacAleese grew frustrated with the Dallas Police Department, which was beset with bad morale, community relations problems, and poor training budgets.

Crime Stoppers Today

Crime Stoppers now numbers thousands of programs in more than 30 countries, with some chapters operating independently and some subscribing to national organizations and/or Crime Stoppers International. Crime Stoppers chapters have adapted to modern technology, accepting web-based and mobile phone tips. To keep the tips anonymous in the United States, tips are routed to collection centers in other states or countries so that they are not subject to discovery claims by defense attorneys, and tipsters are assigned a tip number, which is not traced to a person's identity.

Crime Stoppers claims to have cleared more than 1 million cases, led to more than 400,000 arrests, doled out more than $60 million in rewards, and recovered at least $1.3 billion in property and more than $4 billion in narcotics. Very few Crime Stoppers chapters have the resources or time to conduct sophisticated film reenactments of crimes, but chapters typically liaise with local media outlets to assist in their work. Perhaps even more significantly, Crime Stoppers reenactments spawned other crime-oriented reality shows, such as *Cops*, and *America's Most Wanted*, an idea that came to the show's creator while he was watching a Crime Stopper reenactment on a hotel room television.

Some criticize the cozy relationship that Crime Stoppers fosters between the media and police departments, fearing that it compromises the independence of both entities. MacAleese believes this is nonsense; organizations such as Crime Stoppers bring the police and the community closer together. Historically, many law enforcement agencies tried to distance themselves from the media, but Crime Stoppers does not. As a former police officer and former journalist, MacAleese provides an informed perspective on the proper role of both the police and the news media.

Retirement and Relocation

MacAleese returned to New Mexico in 1991, and from 1991 through 1995 he served as executive director of Crime Stoppers. Feeling burned out, MacAleese decided to try his hand at business. Several years ago, he moved to the Philippines to conduct Christian missionary work at hospitals, where he currently lives with his wife and their two sons. Greg MacAleese still promotes Crime Stoppers through speeches, podcasts, YouTube interviews, and other venues.

Sources and Suggested Readings

Carter-Landin, Eric. (2022). *Crime Stoppers founder Greg MacAleese* [Audio podcast]. True Consequences True Crime. YouTube. https://www.youtube.com/watch?v=qolAynT8nwI, accessed January 15, 2024.

Crime Stoppers International. (2024). *Crime Stoppers International is a global non-profit organization with 501(c)(3) charity status.* https://www.crimestoppersinternational.org/

Crime Stoppers of Puget Sound. (2024). *Welcome to Crime Stoppers of Puget Sound.* www.crimestoppers.com

Crime Stoppers USA. (2024). *Say it here.* https://www.crimestoppersusa.org/

CrimeStoppers1000. (2013). *Windsor & Essex County Crime Stoppers—Det Greg MacAleese 1976 reenactment* [Video]. YouTube. https://www.youtube.com/watch?v=QVEU9L8U5D0, accessed January 15, 2024.

KOAT. (2015). *APD detective, KOAT started Crime Stoppers* [Video]. YouTube. https://www.youtube.com/watch?v=Gt-2XphkUa8, accessed January 12, 2024.

KOAT. (2017). *Crimestoppers 40th anniversary* [Video]. YouTube. https://www.youtube.com/watch?v=XPhIDxHGpmE, accessed January 15, 2024.

MacAleese, G. (2002, January 18). Telephone interview.

MacAleese, G. (2023). Personal correspondence.

MacAleese, G., & Millar, C. (2016). *Crime Stoppers: The inside story.* CreateSpace Independent Publishing.

Millar, C. (2014). *What is Crime Stoppers?* CreateSpace Independent Publishing.

Ontario Association of Crime Stoppers. (2020). *News reporter footage for the news interview.* [Video]. YouTube. https://www.youtube.com/watch?v=qxQclsUb_bM, accessed January 15, 2024.

Robertson, I. (2016, July 30). The inside story on the birth of Crime Stoppers. *Toronto Sun.* https://torontosun.com/2016/07/30/crime-stoppers-legendary-beginning, accessed August 5, 2024.

StopCrimeHamilton. (2019). *The Crime Stoppers concept: An audience with Greg MacAleese* [Video]. YouTube. https://www.youtube.com/watch?v=uB5bFLra76A

StopCrimeHamilton. (2019). *Crime stoppers Greg MacAleese* [Video]. YouTube. https://www.youtube.com/watch?v=NEksR3wztVo

Discussion Questions

1. How did Greg MacAleese's background as a journalist contribute to his law enforcement accomplishments?
2. How has Greg MacAleese's career influenced other ventures between law enforcement and entertainment media?

SECTION III

LAW AND THE COURTS

This section contains short biographies of people that have made a significant contribution to the everyday practice of criminal justice, as well as some people who broke barriers in the legal profession, especially with the Supreme Court. This list is not a who's who of American jurisprudence, hence the omission of some people usually ranked as the greatest legal minds in U.S. history, like Oliver Wendell Holmes, Jr., Benjamin Cardozo, and Louis Brandeis. The following barrier-breaking criminal justice contributors are listed in chronological order based on their time periods of service:

- **Benjamin Lindsey** was a local judge in Colorado and a pioneer in establishing a system of justice for juveniles there, at a time when most states blended children with adults in courts and penal facilities.
- **Clarence Darrow** is a name that even the most casual observer of legal history knows. Often called the greatest courtroom orator of the 20th century, he is profiled here, with both his positive and negative attributes highlighted.
- **Earl Warren** served as chief justice of the United States from 1953–1969. He was the leader of the "due process" revolution, which settled the "incorporation debate" about whether the U.S. constitution should apply to the states. The Warren Court decisions, including

Mapp, Gideon, and *Miranda*, affected the everyday workings of police officers and local courts more than those of any other chief justice.

- **William Kunstler** was the radical lawyer admired by the far left and despised by conservative politicians and jurists. Never concerned with winning popularity contests, he nonetheless proved an able defense attorney and was adept at putting the legal system on trial—and he usually won.
- **Thurgood Marshall** was the first African American to serve on the U.S. Supreme Court. For that reason alone, he deserves recognition. He also deserves recognition for his work before joining the court, including his battles against segregation and advocacy for ethnic minorities he believed were being mistreated by the justice system.
- **Sandra Day O'Connor**, not Ruth Ginsburg, was the first woman to serve on the U.S. Supreme Court. She joined the legal profession at a time when there were few women lawyers, let alone female judges, and when it was considered practically impossible for a woman to join the U.S. Supreme Court. Even those who disagreed with her judicial philosophy and decisions admired her tenacity and the grace she exhibited as she broke the gender barrier on the Supreme Court.
- **Sonia Sotomayor** is the first Hispanic (thus the first Hispanic female) on the U.S. Supreme Court. Raised in lowly socioeconomic circumstances in a Bronx household where English was a second language, she overcame gender and racial barriers to become a successful prosecutor, corporate lawyer, and federal judge before being appointed to the Supreme Court.

Honorable Mentions

IMG III.1

John Marshall (1755–1835) was born in the Virginia colony 21 years before America declared its independence from Great Britain. John Marshall served as the fourth chief justice of the United States Supreme Court. He served from 1801–1835, the longest serving chief justice in American history. After serving in the Revolutionary War, Marshall earned his law degree from William and Mary College and entered private practice. President John Adams appointed him to a diplomatic post in France in 1797 and then to secretary of state, a position he held from 1800–1801.

The U.S. Constitution took effect in 1789. Article III, Section I of the Constitution states, "The judicial Power of the United States, shall be vested in one Supreme Court, and in such inferior Courts as the Congress may from time to time ordain and establish." Although the roles of three branches of government—executive, legislative and judicial—are well-established today, not many were sure what the role of the Supreme Court should be in the early days of the republic. The United States was trying to find its way with a system of government radically different from any that existed at the time, and trying to decide how much power should be placed in the hands of a central government.

Between 1789 and 1801, three men served as chief justice: John Jay, John Rutledge, and Oliver Ellsworth. In February 1801, as he was leaving office, President John Adams tagged John Marshall to serve as chief justice. One of the first, and undoubtedly most important, decisions of Marshall's long term as chief justice came in 1803. A complicated and bitter transition from the Adams presidency to that of his successor Thomas Jefferson resulted in incoming Secretary of State James Madison's refusal to deliver the commission of appointment to several judicial appointees, including William Marbury. Marbury and the other appointees sued for delivery of the commissions. The Marshall Court, using political and legal sleight of hand, declared that Madison's failure to deliver the commissions was illegal, but did not order him to deliver them because the law which authorized Marbury to bring his action to the Court, the Judiciary Act of 1789, was unconstitutional. The most significant ruling in Supreme Court history, *Marbury v. Madison* (5 U.S. [1 Cranch] 137, 1803) established the judiciary's right to rule on the constitutionality of legislation. Today, any legislator, governor, or president understands that any legislation is subject to review and nullification if the proper court declares it unconstitutional.

John Marshall's Supreme Court did not deal with many state and local criminal matters, as they were almost the exclusive province of state and local governments. But one case involving Marshall stands out, not because of his role as chief justice but in the role of presiding trial judge. In the Court's early days, Supreme Court justices would leave Washington D.C. to "ride circuit," i.e., sit as trial judges throughout the country when not in session. Marshall was called to preside over the 1807 trial of Aaron Burr. Burr had served as vice president during the first presidential term of Thomas Jefferson, from 1801–1805. Due to several misdeeds, the most prominent being Burr's killing of former Treasury Secretary Alexander Hamilton in a duel, for which he was not prosecuted, Burr made many enemies, including President Jefferson.

When word reached Jefferson that Burr was collaborating with the British to establish a separate nation in U.S. territory, the Jefferson administration had Burr tried for treason in Virginia, with Justice Marshall presiding. Burr was acquitted because the framers of the Constitution had set a high bar for treason convictions, knowing that such statues had been used to prosecute political dissidents in other countries. An outraged Thomas Jefferson called for Marshall's impeachment, to no avail. Marshall set the precedent for not weaponizing the justice process to pursue political opponents.

The phrase "criminal justice system" would be foreign to John Marshall, as the term did not come into everyday usage until 100 years after his death. Modern policing and institutional corrections would be foreign to him, as would the terms "probation" and "parole" as they are used today. But John Marshall's work in establishing the judiciary as a coequal branch of government with the legislative and executive branches is the reason even the most casual observer of the criminal justice system and lawmaking process should understand his importance.

For more on John Marshall, see below:

- Brookhiser, R. (2018). *John Marshall: The Man Who Made the Supreme Court.*
- Paul, J.R. (2019). *Without Precedent: Chief Justice John Marshall and His Times.*
- Strauss, R. (2021). *John Marshall: The Final Founder.*

IMG III.2

Roger Nash Baldwin (1884–1981) was born in Massachusetts and raised in affluence. Roger Nash Baldwin was the founder of the American Civil Liberties Union (ACLU). I grouped Baldwin with the courts and law group even though he never worked as a lawyer and did not have a law degree. The fact that he worked as a juvenile probation officer in St. Louis is irrelevant to his significance.

In 1917, as the United States was entering World War I, Baldwin joined the Civil Liberties Bureau which was established to support conscientious objectors. The group changed its name to the National Civil Liberties Bureau. When Baldwin refused to take his physical after being ordered to do so by the draft board, he was sentenced to 1 year in prison. After his release in 1919, Baldwin resumed his leadership of the NCLB, which changed its name to the American Civil Liberties Union.

A thorn in the side of federal and local governments, Baldwin thought the best arena for promoting his agenda was in the courts, not in the streets. The ACLU sought court cases they thought significant touchstones for civil liberties issues, often challenging local laws and ordinances they viewed as unconstitutional. The ACLU intervened in several high-profile cases, including the Scopes Monkey Trial, when a show trial was conducted challenging Tennessee's ban on teaching evolution, and the Scottsboro Boys case, where nine young African American men in Alabama were sentenced to death for the alleged rape of two White women.

The ACLU supported American involvement in World War II because of its hatred of far-right ideologies, but the group protected many who they believed were unfairly targeted for espionage charges. When the war ended in 1945, the ACLU turned its efforts to protecting free speech in the age of the Civil Rights Movement, the Cold War, and anti-communism, even though the ACLU had officially taken an anti-Communist stance in 1940.

After Baldwin was forced out as ACLU leader in the early 1950s, he remained vocal in support of civil liberties. Baldwin believed that the criminal justice system could be used to protect democracy, but that it could also be the means of its destruction. Unlike many on the political left who are perpetually pessimistic and hold a fundamental hatred of all things American, he loved the United States and believed in democracy, saying, "Democracy works. I have hope, but not optimism. But if you want to put a label on me, I'm an unhappy optimist."

For more on Roger Nash Baldwin, see below:

- Cotrell, R.C. (2000). *Roger Nash Baldwin and the American Civil Liberties Union.*
- Lamson, P. (1976). *Roger Baldwin: Founder of the American Civil Liberties Union.*
- Princetonacademics (2011). "Portrait of Roger Baldwin: 'Traveling Hopefully,' 1981. https://youtu.be/ND_uY_KXGgY?si=lMFdOsfigKHVL_Tl, retrieved January 30, 2025.

IMG III.3

F. Lee Bailey (1933–2021) was the most famous criminal defense attorney for the second half of the century. Born in Massachusetts, he attended Harvard University but left without graduating. Bailey became interested in law while serving in the Marines, and he eventually graduated from Boston University, working as a private detective while in law school.

The following are a few of his high-profile cases:

- **Sam Sheppard**, an Ohio physician, was convicted of killing his wife in 1954. Sheppard claimed that an intruder was the culprit and that pretrial publicity was to blame for his conviction. In 1961, Bailey undertook Sheppard's appeal with help from the ACLU. He convinced the Supreme Court to overturn Sheppard's conviction and order a new trial. Bailey represented Sheppard at trial, and Sheppard was acquitted. The case inspired the television series *The Fugitive.*

- **The "Boston Strangler,"** Albert DeSalvo, was accused of strangling 13 women in the Boston area between 1962 and 1964. Although DeSalvo was eventually convicted of burglary and other crimes and sentenced to prison (where he was murdered), Bailey saved DeSalvo from conviction on the murder charges.
- **The My Lai massacre** took place on March 16, 1968, at the height of the Vietnam War. U.S. Army troops under the command of Captain Ernest Medina killed more than 500 Vietnamese civilians. Bailey took on Medina's defense for a $79 fee. Bailey argued that Medina had not ordered the massacre, had no advance knowledge of it, and was not present at My Lai when it occurred. Bailey and military investigators shifted blame for the My Lai massacre to Lieutenant William Calley, one of Medina's platoon leaders, who was convicted of 22 of the My Lai murders. A military jury acquitted Medina.
- **Patricia Hearst**, a newspaper heiress in California, was kidnapped by members of a radical organization called the Symbionese Liberation Army in 1974. The sympathy for her turned to anger and confusion when she was caught on video camera participating in an armed robbery with the SLA. When Hearst was arrested, she claimed she had been brainwashed by the SLA. She was convicted and sentenced to prison, a case that Bailey lost.
- **O. J. Simpson**, an actor, and Pro Football Hall of Famer was accused of murdering his wife Nicole and an acquaintance, Ronald Goldman in Los Angeles in 1994. Represented by a "dream team" of wealthy defense attorneys, including Bailey, Simpson was acquitted by a jury despite overwhelming evidence pointing to his guilt. Carried in its entirety on television for several months, it was the most widely watched trial in American history. Simpson was eventually found liable in a separate civil trial.

Despite the enormous wealth he amassed, Bailey was often broke and was eventually disbarred in Florida for misconduct. F. Lee Bailey will go down not only as an amoral, grandstanding egocentric lawyer, and the "lawyer to turn to when you kill your wife" as some have called him, but he will also be remembered as one of the ablest criminal defense attorneys in American history.

For more on F. Lee Bailey, see below:

- Bailey, F.L. (1994). *To Be a Trial Lawyer.*
- Bailey, F.L. and H. Aronson (1971). *The Defense Never Rests.*
- Whitten, L. (1971). *F. Lee Bailey.*

G. Robert Blakey (1936–), born in North Carolina, is the principal author of the most influential criminal law of the second half of the 20th century, the federal Racketeer Influenced and Corrupt Organizations (RICO) Act, a law which has been replicated in most U.S. states. RICO, through its stiff criminal penalties and its civil asset forfeiture provisions, has devastated criminal enterprises ranging from multimillion-dollar Wall Street junk bond schemes to major mafia families to low-level drug dealers.

IMG III.4

Blakey earned his undergraduate and law degrees from the University of Notre Dame. A fervent labor advocate, Blakey's aim after graduation was to work for the National Labor Relations Board, but an offer from the Department of Justice came first. He started work with the DOJ in 1960, during the presidency of Dwight Eisenhower. He hoped to get on with the DOJ's labor rights unit, but he was assigned to the criminal division, an area about which he knew very little.

In 1961, John F. Kennedy succeeded Eisenhower as president and nominated his brother Robert Kennedy for the position of attorney general. Robert Kennedy was the first attorney general to declare all-out war on organized crime. Blakey was part of the team that assisted Attorney General Kennedy. On November 22, 1963, Blakey traveled to work as usual in Washington, D.C., to the U.S. Department of Justice. He spent the morning meeting with Attorney General Robert Kennedy, discussing plans for increasing organized crime prosecution efforts in Chicago. The meeting adjourned for lunch and was scheduled to resume that afternoon, but it never reconvened. During the lunch break, President Kennedy was assassinated while riding in a motorcade in Dallas, Texas.

A few months later, Blakey took a teaching position at his alma mater, Notre Dame. While at Notre Dame, he worked with the administration of President Lyndon Johnson on efforts to combat organized crime. The Omnibus Crime Control and Safe Streets Act of 1968 included a provision written by Blakey authorizing the expanded use of wiretaps to infiltrate criminal organizations. In 1970, Congress and President Richard Nixon enacted the Organized Crime Control Act of 1970 and the Organized Crime Control Act of 1970. Title IX of the act is called RICO, or Racketeer Influenced and Corrupt Organizations Act. For an offense to qualify as a RICO violation, prosecutors must prove a pattern of racketeering-type crimes—that is, two of the crimes listed under RICO within a 10-year period. Federal RICO violations carried penalties of up to 20 years in prison and a huge fine, plus the threat of forfeiting assets gained by the crimes.

RICO prosecutions were rare during the early 1970s, primarily because prosecutors did not know how to use the law. Prosecutions under the law accelerated in the 1980s and made dents in many powerful criminal organizations, including the five major crime families in New York. State RICO offenses, based largely on the original federal statute, have been used to confiscate houses, boats, and cars from drug dealers.

Blakey spent the remainder of the 1970s conducting research at the Cornell Institute on Organized Crime. In 1977, Blakey served as chief counsel for the U.S. House Select Committee on Assassinations, a specially convened committee assigned to reinvestigate the 1963 assassination of President Kennedy and the 1968 assassination of civil rights leader Martin Luther King, Jr. Blakey came away from the hearings convinced that organized crime played a role in the assassination of President Kennedy, contrary to the findings of the Warren Commission that concluded that Kennedy's assassin, Lee Harvey Oswald, acted alone. Blakey's view on the JFK murder has been discredited by most experts, including one of his top assistants, Ralph Salerno, who agreed with the Warren Commission findings. In 1980, Blakey returned to Notre Dame's law school to teach and write. He remained at Notre Dame until his retirement in 2012.

For more on Robert Blakey, see below:

- Rockwood, B. (2013). "Interview: G. Robert Blakey." https://www.pbs.org/wgbh/frontline/article/interview-g-robert-blakey/, retrieved January 30, 2025.
- University of Notre Dame The Law School (2025). "G. Robert Blakey." https://law.nd.edu/directory/g-blakey/, retrieved January 30, 2025.

Credits

IMG III.1: Henry Inman, https://commons.wikimedia.org/wiki/File:John_Marshall_by_Henry_Inman,_1832.jpg, 1832.

IMG III.2: Peggy Lamson, https://commons.wikimedia.org/wiki/File:Roger_Nash_Baldwin.jpg, 1917.

IMG III.3: Copyright © by www.celebrity-photos.com (CC BY-SA 2.5) at https://commons.wikimedia.org/wiki/File:F._Lee_Bailey-adjusted.jpg.

IMG III.4: Source: https://commons.wikimedia.org/wiki/File:Blakey.jpg.

CHAPTER 19

Clarence Darrow (1857-1938)

IMG 19.1

Clarence Darrow may have been the greatest courtroom lawyer of the 20th century; he was certainly the greatest courtroom orator. To his admirers, his name is synonymous with fighting for the right to think and speak freely, championing the rights of the underdog, and leading the charge against the death penalty. He was the quintessential American defense attorney or, as he has been called, the "attorney for the damned" (Farrell, 2012, title). To his detractors, he embodied several distasteful aspects of America's legal culture. Darrow was derided as a godless, amoral atheist, a cynical defender of cruel, remorseless criminals, and an overtly political partisan, rather than an emotionally detached advocate. No matter, no one ever accused Clarence Darrow of being dull, and no aspirant to the legal profession should be unaware of his career.

Early Life and Career

Clarence Seward Darrow was born on April 15, 1857, in Kinsman, Ohio, the fifth of eight children born to Emily Darrow and her husband Amirus, a village undertaker and coffin maker. In a foretelling of his opposition to the death penalty, young Clarence Darrow supposedly never visited his father's shop. The thought of seeing stacked coffins and corpses exacerbated his fear of death.

Darrow attended law school at the University of Michigan for 1 year before being admitted to the Ohio bar in 1878. He apprenticed in Youngstown for 1 year. He married Jessie Ohl, a farmer's daughter, in 1880. The marriage produced one child, Paul, who was born in 1883, 15 years before Clarence and Jessie divorced. Darrow remarried in 1903, this time to Ruby Hammerstrom, a woman 16 years younger than himself.

Darrow began his law practice in Ohio, first in Andover, then in Ashtabula, where he was also elected in 1885 to the part-time position of city solicitor (prosecutor). His first case as a defense attorney involved a boy accused of stealing a $15 harness, a case that he took to the Ohio Supreme Court and for which he was paid $5. Darrow practiced law in his home state until he moved to Chicago in 1887.

Darrow became famous for immersing himself in four social issues that made their way into an American courtroom: (a) organized labor, (b) freedom of speech, (c) civil rights, and (d) the death penalty.

Organized Labor and Socialism

Eugene Debs

In 1894, Darrow represented Eugene Debs, president of the American Railway Union and one of the most controversial labor leaders of his generation. This was the defining moment in Darrow's career. He had been associated with railroad management since moving to Chicago, and he could have been a success in the traditional manner of corporate attorneys of his time, but because Darrow admired the burgeoning labor movement in the railroad industry he quit the railroad to represent Debs. From that moment on, Darrow usually linked himself with defendants he perceived as "the underdogs."

Pullman Railroad employees had gone on strike in March 1894. The strike turned bloody, resulting in several deaths. The striking employees were ordered back to work, courtesy of a court injunction requested by Pullman management. When the workers refused, Debs was arrested and charged with criminal conspiracy and contempt of court for encouraging the workers to stay on strike. Darrow defended Debs passionately and eloquently, even telling jurors the case would "count much for liberty or against liberty" (lawjrank.org, n.d., para. 3). Debs was convicted and sentenced to 6 months in jail, but the notoriety from the case made Darrow famous.

Frank Steunenberg and the Western Federation of Miners

Former Idaho Governor Frank Steunenberg was killed by a bomb planted at the gate of his house in Wallace, Idaho, on December 30, 1905. Idaho investigators wasted little time in arresting Harry Orchard aka Albert Horsley for the murder. Idaho law enforcement, assisted by Pinkerton Agency detective James McParland, had little doubt that Orchard was acting on orders from the Western Federation of Miners (WFM), the most violent miners' unions in the western United States. Idaho authorities went to Denver, Colorado, and abducted three WFM bosses,

George Pettibone, Charles Moyer, and William "Big Bill" Haywood, the best known of the three.

Haywood's trial was the first scheduled, and he was represented by Clarence Darrow and Edmund Richardson. A team of special prosecutors was brought in with James Hawley and William Borah, two of the best-known litigators and political figures in the West. When Haywood's trial began in 1907, the national media had descended upon Boise, the site of his trial. The stage was set for the trial of the century: The victim was a former state governor, the defendant was one of the most well-known labor leaders in the country, the lawyers on both sides were equally well known, and Orchard had confessed to 18 murders, reportedly at the behest of the WFM.

Darrow attacked Orchard's credibility as a witness, arguing that he had acted alone and that he was merely trying to save himself by implicating WFM leadership after being badgered and coerced by McParland. Darrow argued that organized labor was on trial, not just the WFM. Haywood was acquitted. George Pettibone was tried next and also acquitted. Having lost two cases, the prosecution declined to put Charles Moyer on trial, and all three went free. Orchard was sentenced to death but had his sentence commuted to life in prison. The reason that Haywood and Pettibone were acquitted will never be known for sure. It could have been because the prosecution simply did not prove its case (Idaho law precluded conviction for a crime based solely on the testimony of one witness), or the jurors truly believed the unlikely explanation that the three leaders did not order the killing, or the jurors were intimidated by the WFM. But Darrow had succeeded, and his fame grew in organized labor circles as hatred toward him intensified among business leaders.

The *Los Angeles Times* Bombing

Darrow continued to represent organized labor until a 1911 case caused an irreparable break between Darrow and labor interests. Brothers James and John McNamara, two labor activists, were accused of bombing the *Los Angeles Times* building on October 1, 1910, a blast that resulted in 21 deaths. Their arrest came several months later, following an investigation headed by William Burns.

Delighted by another chance at the national spotlight, Darrow undertook the brothers' defense with his usual zeal. He accused Detective Bums of kidnapping the pair by illegally arresting them in Indiana. He argued that the McNamara brothers were the victims of a conspiracy against organized labor. With the help of other labor leaders, Darrow whipped the country into a frenzy. Newspapers around the country reported on the case, many siding with the defendants and Darrow. Darrow's defense and accusations of a conspiracy disintegrated when the brothers changed their plea to guilty in the middle of the trial. Darrow successfully argued for a life sentence instead of death, but his reputation with organized labor was ruined.

To make matters worse, Darrow was indicted on charges of jury tampering. He was eventually acquitted, though a great deal of evidence pointed to his guilt. It would take Darrow several years to repair the damage to his reputation, which he accomplished by publicly advocating the American war effort during World War I (1917-1918).

The Death Penalty: Leopold and Loeb

Darrow's most famous clash against the death penalty came with his defense of Nathan Leopold and Richard Loeb. Leopold and Loeb were teenaged friends (they may have been gay lovers, but the newspapers of the day only made subtle reference to that) who wanted to commit the perfect crime, purely for a thrill. They were wealthy, educated men with intelligence quotients at or above the genius level. Loeb, handsome and athletic, became a matinee idol, receiving marriage offers from female admirers. Richard Loeb had devised what he thought to be the perfect crime, and he needed Leopold's assistance in pulling it off. In the summer of 1924, Leopold and Loeb abducted Loeb's 14-year-old cousin, Bobby Franks, as he was leaving school. They bludgeoned him to death, used acid to disfigure his sexually mutilated body before dumping it into a creek, and telephoned Franks's father demanding a $10,000 ransom for his safe return.

The killers were cruel, cynical, and remorseless. They could not blame poverty or lack of education as an excuse for committing crime. It became known as the "thrill kill" (Baatz, 2008, title) case. Leopold and Loeb, it seemed, were poster children for the death penalty.

In a brilliant but unexpected move, Darrow had the two defendants plead guilty. He knew they stood no chance of acquittal before a local jury. He also knew that if the decision to sentence the pair were left to a jury, death would almost certainly be the outcome. With a guilty plea, Darrow figured his chances of sparing the two men's lives would be better if the sentencing hearing were conducted in front of a judge. His strategy worked in part because of his brilliant mercy plea and because the judge, John Caverly, also opposed the death penalty. Leopold and Loeb were sentenced to life in prison plus 99 years.

The Scopes Monkey Trial

Another high-profile case came in 1925 in Dayton, Tennessee. Several years prior, Tennessee had enacted a law banning the teaching of evolution in public schools. The law sat largely unnoticed and was not enforced. Government and business leaders in Dayton, eager for the money and attention that a celebrated trial would bring, secured the cooperation of a high school physics teacher named John Scopes to volunteer as a defendant charged with violating the law. Contrary to the image depicted in *Inherit the Wind*, a fictional play based on the trial, Scopes was a willing participant in the proceedings and never actually taught evolution. The recently founded American Civil Liberties Union (ACLU) relished the prospect of such a trial so that it could advance its reputation and agenda. The ACLU enlisted Darrow to aid in Scopes's defense. William Jennings Bryan, whose 1896 presidential bid Darrow had supported, was hired as a special prosecutor.

The stage was set (intentionally) for high drama, and the Scopes Trial lived up to its billing. It pitted Darrow—the greatest courtroom orator of the era—against Bryan—a three-time Democratic nominee for president, the voice of the common man, and the most eloquent political orator of the era. The case consisted mostly of emotional and theatrical speeches made by Bryan and Darrow. The highlight came when Darrow, stymied in his attempts to have academic experts testify on Scopes's behalf, questioned Bryan on the stand and poked holes in Bryan's arguments supporting a literal interpretation of the Bible. Darrow humiliated Bryan, leading him to make such nonsensical statements as, "I do not think about things that I do not think about," to which Darrow retorted, "Do you think about things that you do think about?" (Digital History, 2021, para. 65 and 66).

Wanting to avert an impassioned closing argument by Bryan, Darrow had Scopes plead guilty. His sentence was a $100 fine. Scopes's conviction was subsequently overturned by the state supreme court on procedural grounds, and Tennessee's law against teaching evolution was left intact. Although Darrow lost his battle in court, he won in the court of public opinion. The teaching of evolution flourished, while Bryan, suffering from bad health and despondent over his performance in the Scopes Trial, died shortly after the trial.

Civil Rights

Darrow became a celebrity among civil rights advocates for his defense of Ossian Sweet, an African American physician in Detroit. Sweet purchased a house in an all-white neighborhood, and in 1925, faced with protesters in front of his house, fired several gunshots from inside his house, killing one of the protesters. The first trial ended in a mistrial. Darrow defended Sweet during his second trial and won his acquittal, convincing an all-White jury that Sweet had acted in self-defense.

Another racially charged case, the last significant case of Darrow's career, took him to Hawaii. In 1932, he took on the defense of Navy Lieutenant Thomas Massie and three other men who were accused of killing a native Hawaiian. The deceased had, with other men, allegedly raped Lieutenant Massie's wife. Darrow managed to have the defendants exonerated, in exchange for Massie's wife agreeing to drop rape charges against the other Hawaiian defendants. In the eyes of some, Darrow had contributed to racial harmony in Hawaii, which had been forcefully annexed some 40 years earlier and was still an American territory at the time.

The FBI, the Public, and Attorney Tips

Darrow's notoriety and penchant for taking on left-wing causes caught the attention of the FBI, which conducted surveillance of suspected subversives during the 1930s. In May 1936, Darrow contributed an article to *Esquire* magazine called "Attorney for the Defense," in which he laid out some of his beliefs about the justice system and his courtroom tricks of the trade. An agent was assigned to read Darrow's article and relay his impressions about Darrow to FBI Associate Director Clyde Tolson.

During Darrow's lifetime, there were few, if any, expert jury consultants and researchers. Even the most prominent defense attorneys relied on their own past experiences and gut instincts in selecting a jury. Darrow's greatest talent was his persona and ability to play on a juror's emotions. Said Darrow, "The more a lawyer knows of life, human nature, psychology, and the reactions of the human emotions, the better he is equipped to select the twelve good men, good and true"(Darrow, 1936, p. 36). He thought it important that the attorney discover a potential juror's reading habits, type of friends, ethnicity, and religious beliefs, as Darrow was considered an almost fanatical atheist.

During the 1930s, prior to the age of political correctness, Darrow expressed his preferences and prejudices regarding certain ethnic groups and jury service in the *Esquire* article. Said Darrow, the "Irish are emotional, kindly and sympathetic, must have him … the German is not keen on individual rights, his ways are fixed by his race … the Scandinavians and Lutherans are quick to convict." Darrow avoided prohibitionists because they were "too solemn and holy." Darrow said that he avoided any "Presbyterian who rolls up his umbrella and calmly sits down." He reserved his greatest disdain for Baptists, saying, "The Baptists are more hopeless than the Presbyterians. They, too, are apt to think that the real home of all outsiders is Sheol and you do not want them on the jury, and the sooner they leave the better." (Darrow, 1936, pp. 37, 211). Not surprisingly. Darrow expressed a preference for agnostics. He also liked having Jews on his juries. As African Americans were almost totally excluded from jury service in many states, he formed no impressions concerning their jury service.

Darrow's greatest preference was for a man that laughs; his greatest prejudice was against wealthy men. He also expressed relief that his career was coming to an end as more and more women were starting to serve as jurors, because, in his words, women jurors "took their roles too seriously."

The *Esquire* article provided some insight into Darrow's worldview, which carried over into the types of cases he selected. One passage of the article, underlined by Clyde Tolson, best summarized Darrow's attitude toward the American justice system. It stated, "The litigants and their lawyers are supposed to want justice, but, in reality, there is no such thing as justice, either in or out of court. Most trials are contests between rich and poor."

Retirement and Death

The *Esquire* article was Darrow's last publication. He grew weak from heart problems, which eventually rendered him an invalid. The last year of Darrow's life was spent in semi-seclusion. He died on March 13, 1938, at the age of 80. A handwritten piece discovered after his death affirmed and summarized the worldview that drove his work. Darrow expressed admiration toward his father, a man who often found himself ostracized because of his unorthodox social and religious beliefs. Darrow's father passed on his unbending belief in the worth of the individual against a tyrannical majority. Darrow (1932, p. 369) wrote, "The fact that most of the community were on the other side made him so much surer of his cause."

Sources and Suggested Readings

Baatz, Simon. (2008). *For the thrill of it: Leopold, Loeb and the murder that shocked Chicago.* Harper.

Calabro, Martin. (1996). *Great courtroom lawyers: Fighting the cases that made history.* Facts on File.

Darrow, Clarence. (1932). *The story of my life.* Grosset and Dunlap.

Darrow, Clarence (1936). "Attorney for the Defense." *Esquire* May: 36,37, 211–213.

Digital History. (2021). *The Scopes Trial: Examination of William Jennings Bryan by Clarence Darrow.* https://www.digitalhistory.uh.edu/disp_textbook.cfm?smtID=3&psid=1160, accessed August 6, 2024.

Dubofsky, M. (1987). *"Big Bill" Haywood.* Manchester University Press.

Farrell, John A. (2012). *Clarence Darrow: Attorney for the damned.* Knopf Doubleday.

Geis, Gilbert, & Bienen, Leigh B. (1998). *Crimes of the century.* Northeastern University Press.

Law.jrank.org. (n.d.). *In Re: Debs: 1895.* https://law.jrank.org/pages/2717/In-Re-Debs-1895-Debs-Tried-Conspiracy.html, accessed August 6, 2024.

McWhirter, Darien A. (1998). *The legal 100: A ranking of the individuals who have most influenced the law.* Carol.

Orchard, Harry. (1907). The confessions and autobiography of Harry Orchard. *McClure's Magazine*, *30*(1), 113–129.

Orchard, Harry. (1948). *The autobiography of Harry Orchard written at the Idaho State Penitentiary, Boise.* Idaho State Archives.
Stone, Irving. (1941). *Clarence Darrow for the defense.* Doubleday and Company.
Tierney, Kevin. (2000). Darrow, Clarence (18 April 1857–13 March 1938), lawyer, orator, and author. *American national biography online.* Oxford University Press. www.anb.org, date of retrieval December 13, 2023.

Discussion Questions

1. What has been Clarence Darrow's impact on American society?
2. Which of Clarence Darrow's cases was the most significant?

Credit

IMG 19.1: Source: https://www.britannica.com/facts/Clarence-Darrow#/media/1/151820/85013.

CHAPTER 20

Benjamin Lindsey (1869–1943)

IMG 20.1

America's first juvenile court was founded in 1899 in Cook County, Illinois, but Illinois was not the only state that experimented with juvenile courts at the turn of the 20th century. While the idea of establishing separate courts for juveniles was gaining strides around the country during the Progressive Era (1890–1920), several pioneers were instrumental in shaping the modern juvenile justice system. One pioneer was Benjamin Lindsey, the "father of juvenile law" (Denver Public Library Special Collections and Archives, n.d., para. 1) an eccentric "kids' judge" (Molly Brown House Museum, n.d., para. 1) who presided over the founding of the juvenile court in Denver, Colorado.

Early Life and Career

Benjamin Barr Lindsey was born in Jackson, Tennessee, on November 25, 1869. His father was Landy Tunstall Lindsey, a former Confederate captain. His mother was Letitia Barr Lindsey, the daughter of a Tennessee plantation owner. Ben Lindsey's childhood was unstable, mostly because of his father, who was the likely source of his son's unconventional thinking. When Ben was 5 years old, Landy Lindsey converted his entire family from the Episcopal faith to Roman Catholicism, a highly unusual move in predominantly Protestant Tennessee.

Landy Lindsey's next unusual action was moving his family to Denver, Colorado, in 1880, in part to escape the dominance of his father-in-law. Benjamin's stay in Denver was short-lived. He was sent to preparatory school at the University of Notre Dame, where he would remain for 2 years until his father lost his job with the railroad, forcing Benjamin to return to Tennessee to live with his maternal grandfather. He stayed in Tennessee for 3 years, attending college prep at Southwestern Baptist University, no doubt an influential factor in Lindsey's subsequent decision to abandon the Roman Catholic faith, while retaining a strong Christian value system. Ben Lindsey was a gifted public speaker, winning medals in prep school and college. Benjamin Lindsey returned to Denver in 1887 because of his father's deteriorating health and financial problems. Landy Lindsey committed suicide while Ben was in his teens, leaving Ben, the oldest of four children, the head of his family.

As a struggling teen, Benjamin Lindsey served as a law clerk and office boy for the R. D. Thompson law firm in Denver. He developed a fascination with law, and he did not let the absence of a college degree keep him from pursuing a legal career. Like many lawyers in his day, Lindsey prepared for the legal profession by studying the law at work and in his spare time. While working at Thompson's law firm, Lindsey also helped make ends meet by delivering papers in the morning, cleaning a Denver office building at night, and working in a real estate office.

Lindsey struggled financially and emotionally as a young man. The burdens of heading his family, trying to advance his own life, and his despondency over his father's suicide at times were too much for him. He attempted suicide once by pointing a gun at his head and pulling the trigger. Fortunately, the gun jammed, and Lindsey had a change of heart. Despite the burdens placed on him, Lindsey passed the Colorado bar exam in 1893. In 1894, Lindsey represented his first criminal defendants. He served as court-appointed council for two young boys accused of burglary. From then on, Lindsey carried a passion for helping children get a fair shake in court.

Benjamin Lindsey started his own firm in 1896, in partnership with Fred Parks, a well-known Democrat in Denver. Parks's political connections, coupled with Lindsey's personal success in his new profession and his passion for Democratic Party principles, led to Lindsey's appointment as public guardian for Arapahoe County in 1899. His job involved planning for the care of abandoned or delinquent children. It laid the foundation for his future work as a juvenile court judge. In 1901, Lindsey was appointed to a judge's position, becoming the youngest judge in Colorado history at age 32.

The Kids' Judge

A seminal event occurred in the career of Judge Lindsey during the winter of 1901. A teenaged boy was brought before him charged with stealing several lumps of coal. The boy offered no defense and had been caught in the act by a railroad detective. Lindsey promptly sentenced the boy to reform school, which prompted a bloodcurdling scream from the boy's mother, who was seated in the courtroom. Badly shaken, Lindsey had the boy's sentence suspended, even though doing so was not legal under Colorado law at the time. That night Lindsey visited the boy's home, where he found the boy's father dying from lead poisoning. The family lived in cold, abject squalor. The boy had stolen coal to heat his family's home. Lindsey left, shamefully mindful of the way the justice system was perceived by the poor people of Denver. Shaken by this experience and remembering his childhood poverty, Lindsey resolved to make a difference in the lives of young people who came before his court.

Lindsey was as much a spokesperson for the newly emerging field of sociological jurisprudence as he was a judge. Unlike most judges of his day, he looked beyond the statute books in trying to reduce crime. He searched for crime's root causes, and much as sociologists in his day were doing, he looked beyond religious or moral explanations for crime. Like most of the juvenile justice pioneers and sociologists at the turn of the 20th century, Lindsey believed that juvenile crime was primarily the product of economic injustice, or as he wrote, "wholly one of environment and opportunity" (Lindsey, 1905, p. 167) and that treatment, rather than punishment, was the proper remedy. Lindsey took pity on many of the young offenders that came before his court. In cases of theft, he would investigate the reason the young person chose to steal. If he found that severe poverty or a dysfunctional home life was tied to the theft, he would often go easy on the youngster, sentencing the child to probation.

The Denver Juvenile Court

Lindsey cemented his place in history by promoting legislation to establish a juvenile court in Denver. He requested that all defendants under age 16 be sent to his court, where he would informally suspend their sentence and place them under supervision. He was elected to the post in 1900 and was continuously reelected until 1927, taking time along the way for an unsuccessful gubernatorial bid in 1906. In 1907, Colorado officially established a juvenile court.

While serving as juvenile court judge, he married Henrietta Brevoort, a former assistant probation officer from Detroit, in 1913. Unable to have children of their own, the Lindseys adopted a daughter.

Lindsey's colorful antics on the bench made good newspaper copy. Lindsey's tendency to view the world through a different lens than that used by most criminal justice officials also made for good reading. One example occurred when an 18-year-old boy, a frequent "visitor" to the Denver police station, appeared in Lindsey's court. Lindsey thought the boy amenable to rehabilitation. In this case as he had done for years, Judge Lindsey utilized the honor system he had created. Under his honor system, those sentenced to confinement were allowed to leave the court free from constraint, commitment papers in hand, with the promise that they report to the jail at the appointed time. This was done for two reasons: (a) to aid in the rehabilitation of the young offender by building character; and (b) to fight the graft in local jails stemming from the fees that jailers would charge indigent inmates. This particular 18-year-old was ordered to jail but was allowed to leave on his promise that he report to jail later that night. Since the boy had been in jail 13 times and had attempted to escape at least once, the jailer was surprised when the boy reported to jail as ordered. The next morning a police captain told the judge that he would fail if he took any more chances with the boy. Lindsey asked why he would fail, and the captain replied that the boy had been in jail 13 times. Lindsey responded to the captain, "Well, didn't it ever occur to you that the jail had failed thirteen times? You have failed with him. It's my turn now" (Larsen, 1972, pp. 88–89).

Lindsey passed on some of his ideas the role of adult offenders in juvenile crime. He pioneered legislation holding adults legally responsible for contributing to the delinquency of a minor. In 1903, Colorado enacted the Adult Delinquency Act, which put the idea into law. He tried to keep juvenile offenders from the glare of public scrutiny, a practice that continues to this day. It was one of many "Lindsey Bills" that the Colorado legislature would act on in the early part of the 20th century.

Lindsey, who detested institutions because he thought they were breeding grounds for crime, incarcerated offenders only as a last resort. He refused to charge anyone under age 16 with a crime, a radical step for the time. Unlike most judges who would (and still do) confine themselves to the courthouse, Lindsey visited juvenile offenders in jail and advocated cleaning up neighborhoods that he viewed as breeding grounds for crime.

Lindsey was a small man, only 5 feet tall and weighing 100 pounds. He was shy, unassuming, meek, and nonthreatening. However, his winning personality and easygoing facade belied a fierce sense of independence and nonconformity. Never one to take no for an answer, Lindsey, a pronounced nonconformist, often found himself on the receiving end of abuse from Denver's political power structure. In fact, one of Lindsey's weaknesses (or strengths) was his unwillingness to compromise and his tendency to view those who disagreed with him as enemies. Politicians were especially angry at Lindsey's attempt to generate support for his ideas by taking them public when political officials refused to support them. *The Beast,* published by Lindsey in 1910, chronicled his fight against corruption in Denver's government.

Beyond the Juvenile Courts

During the 1910s, Lindsey, while continuing his work as a juvenile court judge, stepped outside of this role to advocate for several controversial causes. He went to Europe in 1915 with automobile mogul Henry Ford to denounce World War I, which had begun in 1914 and which America would enter 2 years later.

Far more controversial were his stances on social issues. He joined a small but increasing fringe group of writers and academics who spoke frankly about sex, in a manner unheard of by most Americans prior to the 1920s. He stated that sex was a natural part of life. Unlike most adults who decried the "decadence" of 1920s youth, he expressed optimism over the exuberance and energy possessed by youth of the Jazz Age, which was replete with short-skirted, liberated, tobacco-smoking women and daring, carefree young men who flaunted Prohibition laws. During the 1920s, he advocated for birth control for young women (even for those who were not married) and sex education in public schools, both of which he thought would reduce illegitimate pregnancies and abortions. Both ideas were outlined in his book *The Revolt of Modern Youth*, published in 1935.

Lindsey's most controversial action was advocating for trial marriages. Contrary to the perceptions of his critics, his book *The Companionate Marriage*, coauthored with Wainwright Evans and published in 1929, did not criticize permanent, monogamous marriages. In fact, the beliefs Lindsey espoused in *The Companionate Marriage*, which he tried to apply in his own court, were harbingers of things to come in family law. He saw strict marriage and divorce laws as impediments to happiness. He advocated liberalizing divorce laws, criticized alimony payments for women who were young and childless, and argued against the idea that divorce was contrary to biblical precepts. He also argued in favor of people being married for companionship only, not necessarily for the sake of bearing children, which was an unorthodox idea at the time.

Scandal, Disbarment, and Relocation

Lindsey served as juvenile court judge in Denver until 1927. During the 1927 election his political enemies were finally able to harm him. Lindsey had clashed with the Ku Klux Klan (KKK), which enjoyed a national resurgence during the 1910s and the 1920s and operated openly. The chief targets of KKK anger in Colorado were Jews and Catholics, as the African American population in the state was very small. Lindsey, the partial product of Catholic upbringing, denounced the KKK, stating of dues-paying Klan members, "They had paid ten dollars each to hate somebody and they were determined to get their money's worth" (Larsen, 1972, p. 192). Throughout the 1920s, the Denver KKK targeted Lindsey for defeat.

Lindsey won his 1924 reelection bid against his KKK-backed opponent, Royal Graham, but the election was challenged. Graham and the KKK charged voter fraud. The case reached the Colorado Supreme Court in 1927, and the election was ruled invalid. In a move denounced by legal scholars around the country, Lindsey, the world's most famous juvenile court judge, was forced to resign on June 30, 1927. To make matters worse, Lindsey was accused of accepting payment for advice he offered in a New York case, something prohibited for judges in Colorado. The scandals forced his resignation from the bench and led to his disbarment in 1929, after he had left Colorado.

Lindsey moved to Los Angeles in 1928 and was promptly admitted to the state bar, California authorities believing the charges against him in Colorado were baseless. In California, Lindsey carried out reform efforts like those he had instituted in Colorado. He established California's first juvenile court.

In 1934, Lindsey was appointed labor compliance officer for the National Recovery Administration, one of the relief agencies created by President Franklin Roosevelt to provide employment during the Great Depression. He was elected superior court judge for Los Angeles County by an overwhelming margin in November of that same year. While serving as superior court judge, Lindsey lobbied for creation of a law entitled The Children's Court of Conciliation Law, which held that in any divorce case involving children, either spouse could petition the court to prevent a divorce before it was officially granted. It was believed to be the first law of its kind. While in Los Angeles, Lindsey continually lobbied for official appointment as juvenile court judge, but each year his request was denied.

Benjamin Lindsey served on several commissions, including the White House conference on child welfare. In addition to writing legislation in California and Colorado, Lindsey authored several books, articles, and pamphlets. Most of them reflected his beliefs about the way juveniles should be treated by the justice system. He wrote two stage plays and one screenplay, also reflective of his views on juvenile justice and delinquency.

In 1931, Lindsey published his autobiography, *The Dangerous Life*. By 1935, the KKK's influence in Colorado politics had waned, and Lindsey's petition for reinstatement to the state bar reached the Colorado Supreme Court. The Colorado Supreme Court reversed his disbarment. However, Lindsey chose to remain in Los Angeles rather than return to Colorado.

Death and Legacy

Benjamin Barr Lindsey died of heart failure on March 26, 1943, at the age of 73. True to his maverick spirit, Lindsey had requested that his body be cremated, that no conventional funeral service be held, and that his ashes be spread at the juvenile court in Denver. At his memorial service, Lindsey's widow read a letter from President Franklin Roosevelt, which said. "The memory of Ben Lindsey is best honored in the name of youth" (Larsen, 1972, p. 269).

Sources and Suggested Readings

Aley, Ginette T. (2003). Lindsey, Ben B. *American national biography online.* Oxford University. www.anb.org.

Denver Public Library Special Collections and Archives. (n.d.). Judge Benjamin Barr Lindsey (1869–1943). https://history.denverlibrary.org/colorado-biographies/judge-benjamin-barr-lindsey-1869-1943, date of retrieval January 20, 2024.

Hornbein, Marjorie. (1973). The story of Judge Ben Lindsey. *Southern California Quarterly, 55*(4), 469–482.

Larsen, Charles. (1972). *The good fight.* Quadrangle Books.

Lindsey, Benjamin B. (1905). The bad boy: How to save him. *Leslie's Month Magazine (1904–1905), 60*(2), 167–174.

Lindsey, Benjamin B. (1905). Eel Martin's record: The true story of the recovery of a bad boy judge of the juvenile court of Denver. *American Illustrated Magazine, 60*(6), 609–614.

Lindsey, Benjamin B. (1972, original publication date 1927). *The companionate marriage.* Ayer Publishing.

Lindsey, Benjamin B. (1931). *The dangerous life.* Horace Liveright.

Lindsey, Ben B., & O'Higgins. Harvey J. (2009; original publication, 1910). *The beast.* University Press of Colorado.

Lindsey, Benjamin B., & Wainwright, Evans. (1925). *The revolt of modern youth.* Garden City Publishing.

Molly Brown House Museum. (n.d.). Kid's judge: Benjamin Barr Lindsey. https://mollybrown.org/the-kids-judge-benjamin-barr-lindsey/, accessed August 6, 2024.

Slater, Peter Gregg. (1968). Ben Lindsey & the Denver juvenile court: A progressive looks at human nature. *American Quarterly, 20*(2), 211–223.

Weisberger, Bernard A. (1997). The kids judge. *American Heritage, 48*(1). https://web.p.ebscohost.com/ehost/detail/detail?vid=0&sid=0c684ee2-9811-4138-bbda-0977009903e6%40redis&bdata=JkF1dGhUeXBlPWlwLHNoaWImc2l0ZT1laG9zdC1saXZlJnNjb3BlPXNpdGU%3d#AN=9701292492&db=f5h. date of retrieval January 20, 2024.

White, James Terry. (Ed.). (1943). A biographical sketch of Benjamin Barr Lindsey, *The national cyclopaedia of American biography.* James T. White & Company.

Discussion Questions

1. What impact did Benjamin Lindsey's childhood and young adult life have on his career as a judge?
2. Which was more important, Lindsey's work as a judge or his influence with lawmakers?

Credit

IMG 20.1: Mary Griffin Webb and Edna Lenore Webb, https://commons.wikimedia.org/wiki/File:Famous_Living_Americans_-_Ben_B._Lindsey.jpg, 1914.

CHAPTER 21

Earl Warren (1891–1974)

IMG 21.1

Earl Warren served as chief justice of the United States from 1953–1969, one of the Supreme Court's most tumultuous periods. Warren led the "due process revolution," which significantly affected the way criminal justice officials, especially law enforcement officers, conduct their daily activities. Other Supreme Court justices have received higher accolades for their judicial intellect and talents, but in terms of the daily aspects of criminal justice administration, no chief justice has been as influential as Earl Warren. The Warren Court's influence on noncriminal matters was significant as well, as it fundamentally altered laws regarding race, birth control, prayer in schools, and voting rights. His efforts were criticized as social engineering by some, while being praised by others.

Early Life and Career

Earl Warren was born on March 19, 1891, in Los Angeles, the youngest of two children born to lower-middle-class immigrant parents. His father Methias, or Matt, was from Norway, and his mother Chrystal was from Sweden. Earl had no middle name because his father claimed the family was too poor to give him one.

Earl Warren spent much of his childhood in Bakersfield, California. At the turn of the 20th century, Bakersfield was a true frontier town with all the vices common to Wild West blue-collar areas. Matt Warren struggled to make a living as a railroad car repairman for Southern Pacific Railroad. Earl Warren also worked for Southern Pacific as a child. He developed an antipathy toward monopolistic power and political corruption during his time at Southern Pacific that would follow him into his adult life. Another activity he enjoyed as a child was riding his bicycle to the local courthouse to watch trials, which led him to study law.

Like most other towns in California prior to World War II, Bakersfield discriminated against the ethnic minority group that bore the brunt of much West Coast prejudice at that time, the Chinese. The plight of California's working class and the anti-Chinese discrimination Warren witnessed in Bakersfield remained an important influence on him throughout his career.

Legal Career

Warren attended the University of California at Berkeley where he majored in political science. Never an outstanding student, he nonetheless entered the Boalt Hall School of Law during his senior year and graduated from law school in 1914. His first job after graduation was with the legal wing of the Associated Oil Company, which he eventually left to join a local law firm, Robinson and Robinson.

Warren worked at Robinson and Robinson for about 18 months before trying to enlist in the army, as the United States was entering World War I, or The Great War. He was initially turned down by the army but landed a position training draftees in the Oakland, California area. He was transferred to Texas to serve as a bayonet instructor, attaining the rank of first lieutenant. His time there was brief as the war ended soon after his arrival.

After the War, Warren returned to California to work for Leon Gray, a Republican California Assemblyman, before joining the Alameda County (Oakland) District Attorney's Office as a deputy prosecutor. Warren's competence as a deputy prosecutor was equaled by his political acumen, so much so that he was appointed by California Governor Friend Richardson to complete the unexpired term of the incumbent district attorney in 1925. Shortly after assuming the office of district attorney, Warren married his wife Nina, a widow with one child and the daughter of Swedish immigrants. Their marriage would produce five more children.

Warren was elected to a term as district attorney in his own right in 1926, and he remained in office until 1938. Warren gained a reputation as a tough, effective prosecutor, bootleggers being a top prosecution target during the Prohibition years of the 1920s. During the 1930s, Warren, who would eventually be vilified by American law enforcement, was a celebrity in law enforcement circles, a frequent speaker and honored guest before Peace Officer Associations around the country. He befriended police chiefs throughout the country, including fellow Californians August Vollmer and O. W. Wilson.

Attorney General and Governor of California

Warren's prominence as a district attorney led to his election as California attorney general in 1938, a position that had been converted from an appointed to an elective office just 4 years earlier. His reputation as a tough law and order disciple grew, with special attention paid to vice crimes like prostitution and gambling.

In 1942, 1 year after America's entry into World War II, Warren was elected governor of California. He continued to build conservative credentials, emphasizing tax cuts and frugality with government spending. Warren signed legislation creating the California Department of Corrections, which centralized authority over all California prisons into one body.

As governor, Warren would make one of the most momentous decisions of his professional life and one that stains his name in the eyes of many Americans today. Warren, the great civil liberties hero of the 1950s and 1960s who loathed the anti-Chinese sentiment he witnessed as a child in Bakersfield, oversaw the evacuation of Japanese citizens to internment camps during World War II. Late in life, Warren acknowledged in his memoirs that the treatment of Japanese Californians had been unjust. This move by Warren, though reviled by many today, was a popular decision in 1940s California.

Warren was elected governor three times, though he did not finish his third term. Warren's popularity in California spread to the rest of the country. In 1948, he was chosen as Republican presidential candidate Thomas Dewey's running mate. Though Dewey and Warren lost the election to Harry Truman, Warren's name became better known than ever, partly because he was not as hyperpartisan as many politicians of his day.

Supreme Court Nomination

In 1952, Republican candidate and World War II hero Dwight Eisenhower was elected 35th president of the United States. Warren had worked to send California votes Eisenhower's way. In addition, he had done the party a favor by grudgingly turning down the vice-presidential nomination in deference to fellow Californian Richard Nixon. Both Eisenhower and Warren were moderate Republicans, and Eisenhower had promised Warren a nomination to the Supreme Court when a vacancy became available.

Chief Justice Fred Vinson passed away unexpectedly in September 1953, just 8 months into Eisenhower's term. As the Court was badly fractured, Eisenhower thought it would be a mistake to elevate one of the sitting associate justices to the chief justice position, thinking that instead a new face, an outsider and someone accustomed to the give-and-take of political dealings, would be a better choice. In Eisenhower's view, no one fit the bill better than Earl Warren. Warren was nominated by President Eisenhower to serve as Chief Justice of the United States Supreme Court and was confirmed by the Senate.

The End of the Incorporation Debate

Though the idea seems foreign to modern Americans, for the first 170 plus years of its history, the United States was torn over whether the U.S. Constitution, including the Bill of Rights, should apply to the states, and whether the federal government should have supremacy over state and local governments. The "incorporation debate" had become gradually more pronounced since the end of the Civil War in 1865.

The incorporation debate took a giant step toward being settled with the Warren Court's first landmark decision, *Brown v. Board of Education of Topeka, Kansas* (1954). Although it took many years to be fully implemented, *Brown* paved the way for school desegregation and signaled the beginning of the end not only of the incorporation debate but also the "separate but equal" doctrine on treatment of racial minorities that had been upheld in the 1896 case *Plessy v. Ferguson* (1896). What was also remarkable about *Brown* was that a Court that had been severely divided unanimously decided its outcome. Always regarded more for his political acumen than his giftedness as a legal scholar, Warren won accolades for building a consensus on the Court, as evidenced with *Brown*.

The Due Process Revolution

In the ensuing years, the Warren Court led the "due process revolution" in the United States. The Warren Court further settled the incorporation debate in 1961 with the *Mapp v. Ohio* ruling. In *Mapp*, the Court held that the exclusionary rule applied to the states—that illegally obtained evidence cannot be admissible in a criminal trial. This resulted in overturning common law enforcement practice as well as *Wolf v. Colorado* (1949), which had been decided only 12 years prior to *Mapp*.

Throughout the turbulent 1960s, many decisions handed down by the Warren Court were unpopular with police officers and political conservatives, but they coincided with many aspects of President Johnson's Great Society domestic agenda, which was characterized by increasing the involvement of the federal government in everyday lives and a progressive stance on civil rights. Despite the *Terry v. Ohio* (1968) decision, which affirmed the "stop and frisk" practices common in law enforcement and was a victory for police officers, Warren was accused of handcuffing police officers and the courts and unleashing a crime wave with the *Mapp v. Ohio, Miranda v. Arizona* (1966), and *Gideon v. Wainwright* (1963) decisions. He was accused of interfering with the electoral process in *Baker v. Carr* (1962), and of improper social engineering in *Griswold v. Connecticut* (1965), *Engel v. Vitale* (1962), and *Abington School District v. Schempp* (1963).

TABLE 21.1 Landmark Cases Decided By the Warren Court

Draper v. United States 358 U.S. 307 (1959)	Information from an informant may be probable cause for an arrest if it is corroborated by a police officer.
Mapp v. Ohio 367 U.S. 643 (1961)	Evidence obtained illegally is inadmissible; the "exclusionary rule" applies to the states.
Baker v. Carr 369 U.S. 186 (1962)	Federal courts can hear challenges to the Constitutionality of a state's drawing of electoral boundaries, making state legislatures accountable to federal courts when outlining electoral boundaries and thereby increasing the power of federal courts over state legislatures.
Engel v. Vitale 370 U.S. 421 (1962)	School-sponsored nondenominational prayer in public schools violates the Establishment Clause of the First Amendment.
Gideon v. Wainwright 372 U.S. 335 (1963)	The Sixth Amendment right to counsel in criminal cases extends to felony defendants in state courts. Anyone charged with a felony in state court is entitled to appointed legal counsel if they cannot afford an attorney.
Wong Sun v. United States 371 U.S. 471 (1963)	Evidence derived from an illegal police act, or "fruit of the poisonous tree," is inadmissible.
Argersinger v. Hamlin 407 U.S. 25 (1972)	The right to counsel for felony cases guaranteed in *Gideon v. Wainwright* applies to misdemeanants facing jail time.
Sherbert v. Verner 374 U.S. 398 (1963)	Denial of unemployment benefits to a South Carolina woman fired from her job because of her refusal to work on Saturday, the Sabbath day for Seventh-day Adventists, was unconstitutional.
Abingdon School District v. Schempp 374 U.S. 202 (1963)	Public schools cannot sponsor Bible readings and recitations of the Lord's Prayer under the First Amendment's Establishment Clause.
Escobedo v. Illinois 378 U.S. 478 (1964)	A person charged with a serious offense is entitled to counsel while in a police station.
Heart of Atlanta Motel, Inc v. US 379 U.S. 241 (1964)	Title II of the Civil Rights Act of 1964, which forbids racial discrimination in hotels, motels, restaurants, and other public accommodation, impacts interstate commerce and thus is subject to laws prohibiting racial discrimination in matters tied to interstate commerce.
Reynolds v. Sims 377 U.S. 533 (1964)	"Equal protection" under the Constitution requires that state legislative districts should be comprised of roughly equal populations if possible.
Griswold v. Connecticut 381 U.S. 479 (1965)	A Connecticut law banning the use of contraceptives for married couples constituted an invasion of privacy and was therefore unconstitutional.
Sheppard v. Maxwell 384 U.S. 333 (1966)	Reversed the conviction of Dr. Sam Sheppard ("The Fugitive" murder case) because of the judge's failure to protect the integrity of the proceeding from the effects of pretrial publicity.
Miranda v. Arizona 384 U.S. 436 (1966)	Information and confessions obtained from a suspect undergoing custodial interrogation is inadmissible unless the suspect understood that he/she had certain rights spelled out in the Miranda decision.
Harper v. Virginia Board of Elections 383 U.S. 663 (1966)	Poll taxes, fees required to vote in elections, are unconstitutional.
United States v. Wade 388 U.S. 218 (1967)	A criminal suspect has the right to the presence of an attorney during a lineup.
Katz v. United States 389 U.S. 347 (1967)	Electronic surveillance that is an invasion of privacy constitutes a search and is subject to the rules pertaining to illegal searches.
Loving v. Virginia 388 U.S. 1 (1967)	Laws that ban interracial marriage are unconstitutional.
Duncan v. Louisiana 391 U.S. 145 (1968)	A person is entitled to a jury trial if they are charged with a "serious" crime.
Terry v. Ohio 392 U.S. 1 (1968)	Police officers' "stop and frisk" is valid if it is based on reasonable suspicion.

Prior to his appointment as Supreme Court Chief Justice, Warren had been a lifelong Republican, albeit a moderate one compared to some of his contemporaries, such as Joseph McCarthy, Barry Goldwater, and Richard Nixon. Warren became very unpopular with fellow Republicans, including President Eisenhower, who reportedly said that Warren's Supreme Court nomination "was the biggest damn fool thing I ever did." Eisenhower said that he would like to shoot the person who first recommended Warren as chief justice. Warren's former running mate, Thomas Dewey, called Warren a "judicial wrecker."

The JFK Assassination

Earl Warren will be remembered for a role he reluctantly assumed at President Lyndon Johnson's request in 1963. President John F. Kennedy was assassinated in Dallas, Texas, on November 22, 1963. Texas Governor John Connally was wounded as well, and Dallas Police Officer J. D. Tippitt was murdered by the same man 45 minutes after the JFK murder. The accused assassin, Lee Harvey Oswald, who was arrested the day of the murder, was assassinated 2 days later on live television by Dallas nightclub owner Jack Ruby.

As there would be no trial in the JFK or Tippitt murders, Johnson asked Warren to head a bipartisan commission to investigate the assassination. Warren and several other distinguished politicians and statesmen, including future President Gerald Ford, issued a report on the assassination. The Warren Commission report has been subjected to intense scrutiny and criticism since its release in September 1964, although it is unlikely that many of its most strident critics have ever actually read it. Politicians, journalists, and conspiracy buffs, many of them defaming Warren in the process, have hotly debated the Warren Commission's findings, even though no one has successfully refuted the Warren Commission findings that both Lee Oswald and Jack Ruby acted alone and that there was no organized conspiracy to assassinate President Kennedy.

The Transformation of Earl Warren

Criminologist Samuel Walker stated that Earl Warren underwent a transformation from a tough law-and-order prosecutor, attorney general, and governor, to a champion of civil liberties as chief justice. Walker argues that Warren's transformation was in keeping with changing times. According to this view, Earl Warren, along with Supreme Court colleagues William Brennan (another Court nomination that President Eisenhower regretted) and Thurgood Marshall (the Court's first African-American Justice) embodied the transformation of the American conscience in matters of law and criminal justice and believed in protecting the rights of the "little guy" from all-powerful state and majority interests.

Warren biographer Ed Cray (1997) argues that Warren did not undergo a transformation. While Warren was always a disciple of law and order, he was also a strong proponent of procedural due process. Warren practiced what he preached in that regard long before he became chief justice. One case in point was his father's murder by an intruder in May 1938. The investigation led police to a San Quentin prison inmate serving time on other charges. When Bakersfield police officers suggested that a planted stool pigeon or eavesdropping device be used to catch the killer, Warren refused, stating he would not stoop to underhanded police methods even to catch his father's murderer. Matt Warren's murder was never solved.

Death and Legacy

Earl Warren died in 1974 at age 83, 5 years after retiring from the Supreme Court. In one of his most famous quotes, he said,

> I always turn to the sports pages first, which records people's accomplishments. The front page has nothing but man's failures.

Earl Warren's legacy is still debated, not just in judicial circles but by Americans who are still concerned about some of the issues dealt with by the Warren Court. Perhaps Earl Warren, like many others who spend so much time in Washington D.C. "drinking Potomac water," simply lost touch with his roots. Maybe he changed with the times, or maybe he never changed at all. Regardless of whether one thinks he was a great civil libertarian and jurist or the catalyst that provoked a "great American crime wave" amid the social unrest of the 1960s and banished prayer from schools, Earl Warren stands as one of the most important figures in the history of American criminal justice.

Sources and Suggested Readings

Brown v. Board of Education of Topeka, Kansas, 347 U.S. 483 (1954).

Cray, Ed. (1997). *Chief justice.* Simon & Schuster.

del Carmen, R., & Walker, J. T. (2019). *Briefs of leading cases in law enforcement* (10th ed.). Routledge.

Earl Warren. (n.d.). *Oyez.* https://www.oyez.org/justices/earl_warren

Griswold v. Connecticut. (n.d.). *Oyez.* https://www.oyez.org/cases/1964/496, date of retrieval January 22, 2024.

Justia. (2024). U.S. Supreme Court Center. https://supreme.justia.com/, date of retrieval January 22, 2024.

Legal Information Institute. (2024). *Baker v. Carr (1962).* Cornell Law School. https://www.law.cornell.edu/wex/baker_v_carr_(1962)#:~:text=Primary%20tabs-,Baker%20v.,

Fourteenth%20Amendment%20of%20the%20Constitution, date of retrieval January 22, 2024.

Moritz, Brian. (2024). "Earl Warren and the Sports Pages." https://sportsmediaguy.substack.com/p/earl-warren-and-the-sports-pages, date of retrieval January 16, 2025.

Newton, Jim. (2007). *Justice for all: Earl Warren & the nation he made.* Riverhead.

Plessy v. Ferguson, 163 U.S. 537 (1896).

Pollack, Jack H. (1979). *Earl Warren: The judge who changed America.* Prentice Hall.

Schwartz, Bernard. (1983). *Super chief: Earl Warren & his supreme court, a judicial biography.* New York University Press.

United States Courts. (2024). *Facts & case summary—Engel v. Vitale.* https://www.uscourts.gov/educational-resources/educational-activities/facts-and-case-summary-engel-v-vitale, date of retrieval January 21, 2024.

Walker, Samuel. (1997) *Popular justice: A history of American criminal justice* (2nd ed.). Oxford University Press.

Warren, Earl. (1977). *The memoirs of Chief Justice Earl Warren.* Doubleday & Company.

White, G. Edward. (1982). *Earl Warren: A public life.* Oxford University Press.

Wolf v. Colorado, 338 U.S. 25 (1949).

Discussion Questions

1. Of all the decisions handed down by the Warren Court, which one do you think is the most significant?
2. Throughout most of his career, Earl Warren was viewed as a friend to police officers, but by the time of his retirement, many police officers detested many of his decisions. Was this shift caused by a change in Warren or a change in the times?

Credit

IMG 21.1: Kamala Harris, https://commons.wikimedia.org/wiki/File:Earl_Warren_20th_Attorney_General_of_California.jpg.

CHAPTER 22

Thurgood Marshall (1908–1993)

IMG 22.1

As Thurgood Marshall biographer Juan Williams wrote, the three most important figures of the civil rights movement were Martin Luther King, Jr., Malcolm X (although he refused to be lumped in with civil rights leaders like King), and Thurgood Marshall. Thurgood Marshall had little use for King and his civil disobedience efforts, and Marshall abhorred the divisive, hateful, separatist rhetoric of Black militants like Malcolm X and the Black Panthers.

It is debatable which of the three was most impactful. In Marshall's view, the courts, not the streets, were the proper venue for civil rights battles. Legislatures were of little use since systematic Black voter disenfranchisement was rampant in Marshall's lifetime, and Black voices were not reflected in legislative elections. Thurgood Marshall bears the distinction of several firsts, the most significant being the first African American on the United States Supreme Court, but some argue that his greatest contributions came before his Supreme Court years.

Early Life

Thoroughgood Marshall was born July 2, 1908, in Baltimore, Maryland, the youngest of two sons. His mother Norma was a kindergarten teacher who could not work steadily during most of her sons' childhoods, and his father William, or Willie, worked as a railroad dining car waiter and later as a chief steward at a country club. The family relocated to New York City's Harlem area when Thoroughgood was 2 years old, but they returned to Baltimore when he was 6.

Fed up with the teasing from his first name, he started calling himself Thurgood and eventually convinced his mother to change the name on his birth certificate.

On days off, Willie would sometimes take Thurgood to observe local court proceedings and then debate the legal points with him. Unfortunately, Willie Marshall was an alcoholic, which had a negative effect on his family relationships and finances. His alcoholism forced Norma to work extra hard to see that their sons had a decent life.

Thurgood's older brother Aubrey, who eventually became a doctor, was more serious about life in general, had a more detached personality, and was a more dedicated student than his younger brother. Thurgood Marshall was friendly, gregarious, prone to pranking, and happy-go-lucky, i.e., the class clown. Thurgood was usually at best a B student at the sometimes overcrowded, underfunded segregated schools that he attended in Baltimore, and his clownish behavior frequently led to minor disciplinary problems. One of his punishments was being sent alone to the school basement and to read the U.S. Constitution. Thurgood Marshall later said that was how he first became interested in the Constitution.

His antics notwithstanding, Thurgood Marshall had talents that would serve him well as an adult. He was an excellent debater, and he had a knack for telling stories. His debating and oratory skills helped him as a lawyer. Among his acquaintances, he was known for humorous jokes and stories, which often contained a deeper message related to the law or a social issue.

The teenaged Thurgood Marshall was usually amiable and easygoing, and he got along well with people of all ethnic groups in the racially diverse Baltimore. But his father had always urged him to stand up for himself, and fight back if anyone bullied him. When Thurgood was 15, he ran errands for a Jewish clothing merchant named Schoen. Once while delivering some hats for Mr. Schoen, he attempted to board a streetcar, hats under his arms, and stepped in front of a White woman to board the car. The conductor scolded Marshall for stepping in front of a White woman, called him the "n" word, and removed him from the car. An infuriated Thurgood tossed the hats and fought back. Police arrived and arrested Thurgood. Only when Mr. Schoen came to vouch for him was he released. Thurgood apologized to Mr. Schoen, a man he and his family liked, for ruining the hats.

College and Law School

Although Thurgood Marshall was not a serious student, his grades were good enough to graduate with honors from Baltimore's Colored High and Training School in 1925, and he earned admission to Lincoln University. Located in Oxford, Pennsylvania, Lincoln is the oldest historically Black college/university

(HBCU) in the United States. Aubrey Marshall was already a student at Lincoln when Thurgood graduated from, high school. Thurgood's entrance into Lincoln was delayed 1 year as the family struggled to get enough money for both brothers to attend.

Consistent with his public school ways, Thurgood Marshall was a cutup. He was a typical fraternity party animal, once getting a 2-week suspension and nearly getting expelled for a fraternity hazing incident. In 1929, 1 year before he graduated from Lincoln, Marshall married Vivian "Buster" Burey, who lived with Thurgood's parents in Baltimore while he finished his final year at Lincoln. Realizing it was time to grow up, Thurgood Marshall became a dedicated student. Upon graduating with honors with a degree in American literature and philosophy, he decided to attend law school, but he would first have to work as a waiter in Baltimore to earn enough money.

Thurgood Marshall's first choice of law schools was the University of Maryland. But the UM Law School had only admitted two African American students in its history and was not accepting any Black students at the time Marshall applied. Distraught and bitter over being denied admission to Maryland, and knowing that he could not afford to attend any of the expensive law schools in the north that admitted African Americans, Thurgood Marshall reluctantly entered law school at Howard University, a private HBCU in Washington D.C. At the time of his admission, Howard was not accredited and was not prestigious. But thanks to the influx of new faculty and the skill of its new leader, Charles Houston, Howard was on the upswing during the time Marshall was there.

Private Practice and Civil Rights

Thurgood Marshall did not set his sights on being a civil rights trailblazer. Although he experienced racial discrimination while growing up in Maryland, his middle-class existence paled in comparison to the plight of poorer African Americans in other areas of the United States, especially some areas of the deep South. During his law school years, as his relationship with Charles Houston deepened, Houston—who was involved with the National Association for the Advancement of Colored People (NAACP)—took his young protégé with him on trips to the South, where Marshall saw poverty and discrimination on a scale he had not witnessed in Baltimore or Pennsylvania.

After graduating from Howard in 1934 and passing the bar exam on his first try (African Americans were excluded from the American Bar Association but not from the National Bar Association), Thurgood Marshall had a choice to make. Legal luminary Roscoe Pound, who had met Marshall while visiting Howard, offered him a scholarship to pursue an advanced law degree at Harvard in Massachusetts. Or he could try his hand at private practice. Although the

Harvard scholarship would have offered him stability, an important consideration during the Great Depression of the 1930s, Thurgood Marshall was tired of studying law and wanted to practice it; he was ready to leave the library and enter the courtroom, and he was ready to earn a living to support his wife.

Thurgood Marshall went into private practice in Baltimore. Paying clients were hard to come by for an African American lawyer in Baltimore, especially during the Great Depression. Most White clients and even some Black clients either had no confidence in a Black lawyer or preferred someone with experience. A disproportionate number of criminal defendants in Baltimore were African American, but as is usually the case with many criminal defendants, they could not afford a good lawyer. As local judges and other courthouse employees saw more of Thurgood Marshall, they began referring clients to him, but sometimes would tell the perspective client to go to Marshall because he was a "freebie" lawyer.

But his practice gradually picked up, oftentimes in indirect partnership with the NAACP. A significant case in the career of Thurgood Marshall, and a moment of satisfactory retribution came in 1935, when Donald Murray, an African American, was denied admission to the University of Maryland Law School. The University cited the *Plessy v. Ferguson* (1896) case where the U.S. Supreme Court affirmed the separate but equal doctrine regarding race and public institutions. Marshall teamed with his Howard mentor, Charles Houston, and noted civil rights lawyer Belford Lawson to challenge the University's decision. The local court ruled the University's policy unconstitutional, and the Maryland Court of Appeals affirmed the lower court decision.

In 1936, Thurgood Marshall went to work full time for the NAACP, which required a move to New York City. He eventually headed the NAACP Legal Defense and Education Fund. Many more cases between 1940 and 1950 would cement his reputation as the most potent civil rights legal voice in the United States. Five cases are highlighted here:

- *Chambers v. Florida*, 309 U.S. 227 (1940). Four African American men, all transients, were convicted and sentenced to death for the murder of an elderly White man. Teamed with other NAACP lawyers, *Chambers* was Thurgood Marshall's first victory in a U.S. Supreme Court case. Although Marshall did not argue the case before the Court, his team was successful in getting the convictions overturned, holding that the men's due process rights had been violated and that they were coerced during the investigation.
- *Smith v. Allright*, 321 U.S. 649 (1944). A 1923 Texas law allowed the state's political parties to exclude Blacks from participating in primary elections. Lonnie Smith, a Houston dentist, challenged the Democratic Party's exclusion based on race. Marshall and the NAACP represented Smith

before the U.S. Supreme Court. The U.S. Supreme Court struck down the Texas law, another Marshall victory.

- *Shelley v. Kraemer*, 334 U.S. 1 (1948). Marshall co-represented an African American family in St. Louis that had been denied a home purchase based on a neighborhood covenant that prevented the admission of "people of the Mongolian or Negro race." The Supreme Court ruled that the 14th Amendment precludes denial of housing rights based on race.
- *McLaurin v. Oklahoma State Regents*, 339 U.S. 637 (1950). A graduate student at the University of Oklahoma was admitted to the school but was provided separate facilities from the White students. In a unanimous decision, the Supreme Court ruled that a public education facility could not treat students differently based on their race.
- *Sweatt v. Painter*, 339 U.S. 629 (1950). Hemon Sweatt was denied admission to the University of Texas Law School because of his race. Marshall was successful in getting the U.S. Supreme Court to unanimously rule the school's action unconstitutional.

These cases and others laid the legal groundwork for the biggest case in Thurgood Marshall's career and one of the most famous court cases in U.S. history, the *Brown* case.

The End of Separate but Equal

Brown v. Board of Education of Topeka (1954) involved four cases from four different states: Kansas, South Carolina, Delaware, and Virginia. The central issue in the case was whether the "separate but equal" doctrine, handed down by the Supreme Court in 1896 in *Plessy v. Ferguson*, should still apply. Much had changed between 1896 and the early 1950s. The civil rights movement had gained traction, the United States military, which included thousands of African Americans, had fought a world war in the 1940s against Adolph Hitler's bigoted, racist Nazi regime, and Chief Justice Earl Warren—a former California governor and hard-nosed Republican prosecutor—had taken leadership of the Supreme Court.

Although the details varied with the students in the *Brown* case, in each instance, African Americans had been denied admission to all White public schools. In a unanimous decision, the Warren Court ruled school segregation unconstitutional, overturned the separate but equal doctrine, and ordered that state courts implement their ruling with "all deliberate speed," which in many states and counties took several decades. Thurgood Marshall was now a national celebrity. His picture graced the cover of *Time* magazine on September 19, 1955.

U.S. Court of Appeals and Solicitor General

Thurgood Marshall's notoriety grew in the 1950s, but tragedy struck as well. His wife "Buster" died from cancer in 1955. That same year, Thurgood Marshall married Cecilia "Cissy" Suyat, a NAACP secretary who would bear their two sons, John and Thurgood, Jr.

Dwight Eisenhower, who served as president from 1953–1961, was not passionate about civil rights, but the outrageous treatment of African Americans in some southern states forced his hand. The same could be said about Eisenhower's successor, Democrat John F. Kennedy, and his brother, Attorney General Robert Kennedy. Although President Kennedy had proclaimed civil rights a moral issue, Thurgood Marshall was wary of the Kennedy brothers, thinking they were more concerned with political calculus than the human rights of Black Americans. But President Kennedy made history in 1961 when he nominated Thurgood Marshall to serve on the Second Circuit U.S. Court of Appeals, based in New York City. While on the Court of Appeals, Marshall participated in 112 rulings, none of which were overturned by the Supreme Court.

Following President Kennedy's assassination on November 22, 1963, Lyndon Johnson, a loud, often crude, abrasive Texan, assumed the presidency. But Johnson, despite his frequent use of the "n" word and other unsavory racial epithets, would become the greatest advocate for civil rights of any president before him. In 1965, Johnson, having cemented Black support for the Democratic Party in 1964 with the Civil Rights Act, appointed Thurgood Marshall as Solicitor General of the United States. The Solicitor General's primary task is to represent the United States government, i.e., the presidency, before the Supreme Court. Marshall's oath of office for Solicitor General was administered by Supreme Court Justice Hugo Black, an Alabama native and former member of the Ku Klux Klan.

Supreme Court Confirmation

In 1967, Supreme Court Justice Tom Clark announced his departure from the Court. Eager to advance his civil rights agenda and thinking that doing so might bode well for his 1968 reelection bid (Johnson withdrew from the race in March 1968), President Johnson decided it was time to nominate an African American to the Court. While Marshall was one of the most respected figures in the civil rights movement, Johnson, who knew Marshall and had appointed him solicitor general, had reservations. He loudly stated to some of his aides, "That son of a bitch is lazy" and said he was not considering Marshall for the nomination. Those who knew Johnson didn't take his bluster too seriously, considering that he was adept at keeping people off guard and guessing as to his intentions. At a

July 13, 1967, press conference, President Johnson announced his nomination of Thurgood Marshall to become the first African American to serve on the U.S. Supreme Court.

Contrary to popular perception and constant misuse of the term, a president does not "appoint" anyone to the Supreme Court. The president only nominates. Appointment to the Supreme Court requires majority approval by the U.S. Senate. Some of the same senators that had opposed Marshall's appointment to the Court of Appeals opposed his appointment to the Court. Some, like Democrats Sam Ervin of North Carolina and Robert Byrd of West Virginia, the latter a former Ku Klux Klan chapter leader, said they opposed Marshall's nomination not because of race but because of his judicial activist philosophy. Marshall was opposed by other southern senators, including James Eastland of Mississippi, John McClellan of Arkansas, and the most strident segregationist of the U.S. Senate, Strom Thurmond of South Carolina, who peppered him with meaningless questions like "Tell us the names of the people on the committee that voted out the 14th Amendment" (Sherman, 2022, para. 14). Despite the opposition, Thurgood Marshall was confirmed on a 69–11 vote, and he took his seat on the Court in September 1967.

Legal Opinions

Thurgood Marshall spent 25 of the remaining 26 years of his life on the Supreme Court. Constructionist justices tend to apply Constitutional principles as they were intended by the Constitution's original authors. Other justices, including liberals like Marshall, see the Constitution as a "living document" (Marshall, 1987, p. 1342) that must be adapted to changing circumstances. Marshall's living document approach embodied the judicial activist philosophy that conservatives opposed.

Some Supreme Court historians rate Justice Marshall highly for his stances on civil rights, affirmative action, due process rights for criminal suspects, his advocacy for individual rights, freedom of speech, and his opposition to the death penalty. Generally, however, Marshall is typically rated somewhere in the middle compared to other Supreme Court Justices. He is remembered for his stances, but not for his written opinions. By his own admission, Marshall delegated much of his opinion writing to his clerks to a greater extent than his fellow justices.

Chronicling the written opinions of Thurgood Marshall requires at least one very large book on its own, but presented below are a few cases concerning criminal justice issues where Justice Marshall wrote the majority opinion:

- *Stanley v. Georgia*, 394 U.S. 557 (1969). A Georgia law criminalizing the possession of obscene materials in the privacy of a person's own home was unconstitutional.

- *Procunier v. Martinez*, 416 U.S. 396 (1974). The Constitution requires correctional facilities to give law students and legal paraprofessionals the full range of privileges accorded to attorneys in their meetings with prison inmates. (https://www.oyez.org/cases/1973/72-1465)
- *Steagald v. US*, 451 U.S. 204 (1981). The Fourth Amendment prevents police officers from searching for a suspect in the home of a third party without obtaining a warrant. (https://www.oyez.org/cases/1980/79-6777)
- *Berkemer v. McCarty*, 468 U.S. 420 (1984). An Ohio highway patrol officer erred in not advising a suspect of his Miranda rights before he made incriminating statements in a misdemeanor traffic case at the time of arrest.
- *Ford v. Wainwright*, 477 U.S. 399 (1986). Marshall, who categorically opposed the death penalty, wrote that execution of the insane was "savage and inhumane" and violated the Eighth Amendment ban on cruel and unusual punishment.

Isolation

From 1967 until the early 1990s, the White House was occupied by Democrats for only 6 years, the last 2 years of the Johnson Administration (1967–January 1969) and Jimmy Carter's years, 1977–1981. All the Supreme Court nominations came from conservative Republican presidents, Richard Nixon, Gerald Ford (although a Ford nominee, John Paul Stevens, became known as a leading Court liberal), Ronald Reagan, and George H. W. Bush. That era witnessed a transformation from the liberal policies of the Johnson years to the 1980s, when Ronald Reagan's brand of conservatism ruled supremely.

Marshall's liberal ally Earl Warren had been replaced as chief justice by Warren Burger, a Nixon nominee, in 1969, and then even more conservative William Rehnquist, who was nominated to the Court by President Nixon and elevated to chief justice by President Reagan in 1986. Consequently, Thurgood Marshall and William Brennan (an Eisenhower nominee), the Court's two leading liberals, were increasingly isolated from the other justices. While Thurgood Marshall, a large imposing man who could not walk into a room unnoticed, remained as outgoing and gregarious as ever—entertaining Justice Sandra Day O'Connor with stories and jokes that usually contained a valuable lesson—Marshall and Brennan were often alone in their opinions as the United States entered a get tough on crime era. Thurgood Marshall increasingly became a quaint anachronism to some (he still used the word "negro" (Sterling Rutherford, 2020, 1:31), rather than Black or African American) and an annoying relic to others.

Retirement

Compared to other justices, Thurgood Marshall kept a low public profile while on the Court, seldom making public appearances and rebuffing any attempts to write his biography. Thurgood Marshall vowed not to leave the Court while Ronald Reagan was in office, from 1981–1989. He did not want a conservative Reagan nominee to replace him. But President Reagan was succeeded by another conservative Republican, George H. W. Bush, Reagan's vice president. During the Bush presidency, Thurgood Marshall's health began to fail. When William Brennan left the Court in 1990, Marshall felt completely alone.

On June 27, 1991, Justice Marshall announced his retirement, which took effect on October 1. When asked at a press conference about his health, Marshall dryly replied, "I'm getting old and I'm coming apart" (Sterling Rutherford, 2020, 2:11). When asked what he planned to do when he retired, he replied, "Sit on my rear end" (Sterling Rutherford, 2020, 2:30). Marshall knew that President Bush would probably try to replace him with a conservative African American, a move he opposed, saying, "My Dad told me way back ... there's no difference between a *black snake* and a *white snake*, they'll both bite" (Tushnet, 1991, C-SPAN, 0.50). Marshall was replaced by the second African American to serve on the Court, Clarence Thomas, his polar opposite and a conservative hero.

Death and Legacy

Thurgood Marshall passed away at Bethesda Naval Hospital in Maryland on January 24, 1993, at age 84. He is buried at Arlington National Cemetery. Regardless of how one views Thurgood Marshall's performance on the Supreme Court, there is no question that he was a true pioneer in the justice system. Those who say that his greatest impact came before he assumed the position of associate justice may have a point. But Thurgood Marshall helped fundamentally remake American society, and for that reason he deserves to be remembered.

Sources and Suggested Readings

Brown v. Board of Education of Topeka, 347 U.S. 483 (1954).

Haygood, Will. (2015). *Showdown: Thurgood Marshall and the Supreme Court nomination that changed America*. Alfred A. Knopf.

Marshall, Thurgood. (1987). The Constitution's bicentennial: Commemorating the wrong document? *Vanderbilt Law Review*, *40*(6): 1337–1342.

NAACP. (n.d.). *Thurgood Marshall*. Civil Rights Leaders. https://naacp.org/find-resources/history-explained/civil-rights-leaders/thurgood-marshall, accessed July 1, 2024.

Office of the Solicitor General. (2023, September 18). *Solicitor General: Thurgood Marshall.* United States Department of Justice. https://www.justice.gov/osg/bio/thurgood-marshall, accessed July 4, 2024.

Plessy v. Ferguson, 163 U.S. 537 (1896).

Sherman, Mark. (2022, March 19). Marshall, 1st Black justice, faced down Senate critics. *The Associated Press.* https://apnews.com/article/ketanji-brown-jackson-race-and-ethnicity-racial-injustice-jackson-crime-e20eb531b5ff3d17544a79d7db33cafd, accessed July 3, 2024.

Starks, Glenn L., & Brooks, F. Erik. (2012). *Thurgood Marshall: A biography.* Greenwood.

Sterling Rutherford. (2020). *Thurgood Marshall speaks with the media about his retirement—June 28, 1991* [Video]. YouTube. https://www.youtube.com/watch?v=1iOxm0j-6WM, accessed July 5, 2024.

Thurgood Marshall. (n.d.). *Oyez.* Accessed July 5, 2024. https://www.oyez.org/justices/thurgood_marshall.

Tushnet, M. (1991, June 27). *Thurgood Marshall on his potential successor* [Video]. Clip 4935216. C-SPAN. Clip from *Retirement of Thurgood Marshall* [Video]. C-SPAN. https://www.c-span.org/video/?c4969799/user-clip-justice-thurgood-marshall-potential-successor; https://www.c-span.org/program/call-in/retirement-of-justice-marshall/13326

Tushnet, Mark V. (2001). *Thurgood Marshall: His speeches, writings, arguments, opinions, and reminiscences.* Lawrence Hill.

United States Courts. (n.d.). *Justice Thurgood Marshall profile—Brown v. Board of Education re-enactment.* https://www.uscourts.gov/educational-resources/educational-activities/justice-thurgood-marshall-profile-brown-v-board, accessed July 2, 2024.

Williams, Juan. (2000). *Thurgood Marshall: American revolutionary.* Crown.

Discussion Questions

1. What is the more important aspect of Thurgood Marshall's career, his work before he joined the Supreme Court or his service on the Court?
2. What lessons can be learned from the life of Thurgood Marshall?

Credit

IMG 22.1: Robert S. Oakes, https://commons.wikimedia.org/wiki/File:Thurgood-marshall-2.jpg, 1976.

CHAPTER 23

William Kunstler (1919–1995)

IMG 23.1

If anyone deserves the title of America's premier radical lawyer, it is William Kunstler. Kunstler biographer David Langum called him "the most hated lawyer in America" (Langum, 1999, title). He reveled in representing "unacceptable outcasts," particularly people on the political left. Kunstler viewed his job not only to defend his client, but to put the criminal justice system on trial. Citing the legal convictions and executions of innocents throughout history, from Socrates to Jesus, Kunstler stated that just because a person had been legally tried did not mean they were guilty, let alone wrong. He said:

> I suspect that better men than the world has known and more of them have gone to their deaths through a legal system then through all the illegalities in the history of man. (POV, 2010, 1:01)

Lack of confidence was never a problem for Kunstler. He sought the spotlight and usually found it. Kunstler's appearance was as unforgettable as his personality. His wily unkempt hair making him instantly recognizable, Kunstler seldom entered any room unnoticed. As a lawyer who traveled frequently, he saw little need to make good lasting impressions on those pitted against him.

Early Life and Career

William Moses Kunstler was born on July 7, 1919, in New York City, the oldest of three children born to Frances Mendelbaum Kunstler, a homemaker, and

Monroe Bradford Kunstler, a physician. William Kunstler grew up in a Jewish household near Central Park West. His identification with lawbreakers emanated from his own adolescent antics in New York. He belonged to a gang called the Red Devils, who specialized in petty theft and vandalism. Kunstler graduated at the top of his high school class in 1937 and entered Yale University. Even during his teenage years, he showed his proclivity toward being a daredevil. In 1935, while visiting Europe, the 16-year-old Kunstler drove an ambulance in the Spanish Civil War, but he came home at his mother's request.

At Yale, Kunstler embarked on a medical degree, assuming that he would follow in his father's footsteps, but he changed his major to French, graduating in 1941. Kunstler tried to enlist in the Navy in June 1941. He was rejected by the Navy and enlisted in the Army on September 5, 1941, 3 months before America's entry into World War II. Kunstler spent most of the War in New Guinea, rose to the rank of major, and received the Bronze Star Medal.

Law School and Early Legal Career

After the War, Kunstler enrolled in Yale Law School. While at Yale, Kunstler wrote book reviews for *The Atlantic Monthly*, the *New York Times*, and the *Chicago Tribune*. After graduating from law school, Kunstler practiced family law in New York City with his brother Michael but grew bored with the minutiae of family law. He taught part-time at New York University Law School and developed an interest in civil liberties law, an area he loved and where he would make his mark.

In Kunstler's view, the job of the defense attorney was not only to vigorously defend his client but to place the justice system on trial. He knew he was unpopular with much of the public and that his efforts would cost him friends; sometimes even his family criticized him. None of this deterred Kunstler because he believed that he was doing right and that his efforts represented an important step toward bringing true justice to all Americans and healing divisions within American society, whether based on racial, religious, or political differences.

Kunstler's list of clients reads like a who's who of the political and social left in the United States. He represented the following individuals and groups:

1. **Lenny Bruce** was a stand-up comic and political satirist who was convicted on obscenity charges during the 1960s. While Kunstler and other attorneys were appealing his convictions, Bruce died of a drug overdose in 1966. Bruce had provided drugs to Kunstler at least once.
2. **Stokely Carmichael** was a member of the radical Black Panthers indicted for sedition by the state of Georgia in the mid-1960s. Kunstler had the law invalidated.

3. **Hubert Geroid "Rap" Brown** was an African American 1960s radical that Kunstler called his best friend. Brown was charged with numerous crimes across the United States, some related to his advocacy of violence against "white oppression."
4. **Adam Clayton Powell** was an African American congressman and minister from New York City's Harlem community. Upon beginning his 11th term in 1967, Powell was denied a seat in Congress by his colleagues, who claimed that he was unfit to serve because of several fraudulent acts. Kunstler carried Powell's case to the United States Supreme Court, where he succeeded in having Powell reinstated.
5. **Kent State University students** who gathered on May 4, 1970, to protest American involvement in the Vietnam War. Four students were killed and nine were wounded when National Guardsmen opened fire against the group. Two of the dead were protesters and two were merely passersby. Also, 24 students and one faculty member were indicted for inciting a riot. Kunstler and several other attorneys worked to get one defendant acquitted and the remaining indictments dismissed.
6. **Attica Correctional Facility inmates** requested Kunstler's aid. On September 9, 1971, more than 1,200 inmates at the Attica Correctional Facility near Buffalo, New York, took over the prison, holding fellow inmates and staff members hostage and demanding better living conditions. The inmates requested that Kunstler and several others be called to mediate the dispute between the inmates and state authorities. While Kunstler and the other mediators were negotiating inmate demands with the state, New York Governor Nelson Rockefeller ordered that the prison be retaken by force. In a calamitous raid by state authorities, 39 people, including inmates and hostages, were killed, and dozens more were injured.
7. **Martin Luther King, Jr.** had several injunctions filed by Kunstler on his behalf. Kunstler also represented several of King's close associates. The attorney had agreed to file a federal lawsuit at King's request on behalf of striking Memphis sanitation workers, but the civil rights leader was assassinated in Memphis before he got a chance to review Kunstler's lawsuit.
8. **Freedom Riders** were civil rights activists that had ridden formerly segregated buses throughout the Deep South and been jailed for violating laws against segregation. In 1961, Kunstler went to Jackson, Mississippi, at the request of the American Civil Liberties Union to aid the Freedom Riders. He represented Nathan Schwerner, the father of Michael Schwerner, one of three civil rights workers murdered in Philadelphia, Mississippi, in 1964.

The American Indian Movement

The American Indian Movement (AIM) was founded in 1968. It was composed of Native Americans dissatisfied with the Bureau of Indian Affairs and the status of American Indians in general. Their early activities included occupying the abandoned federal prison complex on Alcatraz Island in California and a takeover of the Bureau of Indian Affairs building in Washington, D.C.

Kunstler became involved with AIM in 1972, when he defended members of the Iroquois Confederacy in Philadelphia on charges of resisting arrest and inciting a riot. In 1972, members of AIM, seeking to wrest power from reservation leaders and to commemorate the 1890 slaughter of 300 Miniconjou Lakota at the hands of American soldiers, began moving in large numbers to the federal reservation at Wounded Knee, South Dakota. AIM leaders took control of the reservation, refusing to let anyone, including federal authorities, on the reservation unless they were affiliated with AIM. Federal authorities sealed off Wounded Knee, refusing to allow the protesters to leave or to let others enter the reservation.

The federal government wanted to remove AIM from the reservation, but AIM issued several demands. Kunstler was one of those brought in to mediate the dispute. Kunstler was clearly on the side of AIM, and he sought to prolong the dispute in the hope that it would bring attention to the plight of Native Americans around the country. After 71 days, the Native Americans that had taken over Wounded Knee were allowed to leave, claiming that they had reached an accord with government negotiators. Kunstler claimed that the government reneged on every promise it made.

AIM leaders were indicted for several crimes, including illegally occupying Wounded Knee. Kunstler represented Russell Means, one of the leaders, in a 1974 trial in St. Paul, Minnesota. During the trial that lasted more than 8 months, Kunstler and his cocounsels argued that their defendants were political prisoners.

The defense strategy succeeded, but in an unusual way. One juror became ill during deliberations, and the prosecution refused to submit to an 11-member jury verdict. Furious over the prosecution's unwillingness to compromise, the presiding judge dismissed the charges and scolded the FBI in the process. Kunstler was elated over his victory but was soon dismayed when he realized the Wounded Knee saga did not improve the lot of Native Americans.

El Sayyid Nosair

Meir Kahane was the founder of Israel's anti-Arab Kach political party and the Jewish Defense League, a militant Zionist organization. Many Jews and practically all Arabs disliked Kahane, his incendiary anti-Arab rhetoric, and his assertion that most modern Jews had forsaken Judaism.

In late 1990, Kahane was assassinated in New York City. Kahane's death was not universally mourned to say the least, even in Israel. However, many Jews were nevertheless appalled when Kunstler, a fellow Jew, agreed to defend of El Sayyid Nosair, the accused killer who shot Kahane in front of a ballroom full of people. Jewish Defense League members picketed Kunstler's house, and his family expressed their displeasure.

Kunstler believed in the right for self-determination for Arabs just as strongly as he did for Native Americans, seeing some similarities in their status. He viewed Kahane and his ilk as impediments to Middle East peace. Kunstler believed that peace between Jews and Arabs was possible, and that although Arabs were responsible for many atrocities against Jews, some Jews were equally capable of barbaric and murderous acts against Arabs.

Kunstler's wanted Nosair to plead insanity, but Nosair wanted no part of an insanity defense. Kunstler's strategy was to fill the jury with non-Whites who bore a grudge against White society. Kunstler's strategy was partially successful. On December 21, 1991, a Manhattan jury found Nosair guilty of gun possession, assault, and coercion; but he was acquitted of murder. Kunstler and his fellow defense attorneys had successfully defended a client already found guilty in the court of public opinion.

The Chicago Eight

The year 1968 may have been the most turbulent year of the 20th century, at least in the United States. Opposition to the Vietnam War, racial tensions, the assassinations of Martin Luther King, Jr. and Robert Kennedy, and other social and political issues reached a boiling point that year. The place for that boiling point to explode was at the Democratic National Convention in Chicago.

Riots and demonstrations had become routine fare on the evening news by 1968. Given the political and social climate, most Americans fully expected some sort of demonstration at the convention. However, few anticipated the ferocity of what would occur.

During the month of August, approximately 10,000 young people descended on Chicago. The greatest object of the protesters' wrath did not even attend the convention. President Lyndon Johnson, the Democratic incumbent that had presided over the escalation of the Vietnam War, had chosen not to seek another term and did not attend. The Democrats had assembled to nominate Johnson's vice president, Hubert Humphrey, and the protesters feared that Humphrey would continue the Johnson policy in Southeast Asia.

Viewing any attempt to negotiate with the protesters in advance as weakness, Mayor Daley adamantly refused to recognize the protesters' right to demonstrate and ordered his police to use every means necessary to subdue protesters, hoping to show Democratic leaders and the rest of the world who really held power in Chicago. Some of the protesters were just as uncompromising and would not have agreed to cooperate with police officials anyway.

Daley's tactics backfired, horribly. Police officers beat and clubbed demonstrators in a full-scale battle between Chicago police and thousands of American citizens. Television cameras captured all the carnage, which was broadcast live. The riots disrupted proceedings in the hall, with Mayor Daley caught on camera screaming profanities at Senator Abraham Ribicoff, who compared Chicago police officers to the German Gestapo. Humphrey's nomination was overshadowed by the riots, and it fractured the party enough to hurt Humphrey in the November election, which he lost to Richard Nixon.

Some of the protesters saw the Chicago convention as the birthplace of another American Revolution. Many people faulted local authorities, specifically Chicago Mayor Richard Daley, for failing to anticipate and plan for the demonstrations.

After the convention, United States Attorney General Ramsey Clark brought indictments against eight police officers for interfering with the protesters' civil rights. Eight of the protesters were indicted under what was commonly called the Rap Brown Statute, which prohibited conspiring to travel across state lines to incite a riot, but none was ever convicted. The eight defendants represented a cross section of the 1960s counterculture. FBI director J. Edgar Hoover viewed the eight as quintessential hippies, college radicals, and militant Black leaders that needed to be dealt with forcibly as a deterrent to others. The eight defendants and their affiliations were:

- Rennie Davis and Tom Hayden (Students for a Democratic Society)
- Dave Dellinger (National Mobilization Committee to End the War in Vietnam)
- John Froines and Lee Weiner (teachers)
- Abbie Hoffman and Jerry Rubin (Youth International Party)
- Bobby Seale (Black Panther Party). Seale wanted no part of the other defendants and represented himself at trial.

The trial was pure theater. The defendants were deliberately incorrigible and showed no respect for U.S. District Court Judge Julius Hoffman. The trial lasted for 2 months. The defendants, along with Kunstler and his cocounsel Leonard Weinglass, reached unprecedented heights in audacious courtroom behavior. Bobby Seale's behavior so outraged Judge Hoffman that Hoffman ordered Seale bound to a chair and gagged during the trial, a move that played right into the hands of the defense's portrayal of the defendants as oppressed. Seale was bound and gagged for 3 days, until the presiding judge declared a mistrial in his case, making the Chicago Eight the Chicago Seven. On February 20, 1970, Davis, Hayden, Dellinger, Hoffman, and Rubin were found guilty. All seven defendants, plus Kunstler and Weinglass, had also been sentenced to prison for contempt. All convictions and most of the contempt citations were eventually overturned on appeal.

During the Chicago trial, Judge Hoffman told Kunstler that he was getting "awfully chummy" with his clients (UMKC, n.d.), due to his mirroring their abrasive behavior both in and out of the courtroom. The American Bar Association was also critical of the lawyer, as was conservative columnist William Buckley, who wrote that Kunstler should have been disbarred.

Lee Harvey Oswald and Jack Ruby

On November 22, 1963, President John F. Kennedy was assassinated while riding in an open car in a parade in downtown Dallas, Texas. Texas governor John Connally, who sat in the jump seat of the presidential limousine, was seriously wounded. Then, 45 minutes later, Dallas Police Officer J. D. Tippit was gunned down on a street a few blocks away. Lee Harvey Oswald, a disturbed loner and professed Marxist, was apprehended later that day and held as a suspect in the murder of President Kennedy, the shooting of Governor Connally, and the Tippit murder.

On learning that Oswald had been detained for more than 48 hours without legal representation, the American Civil Liberties Union contacted Kunstler and asked if he would fly to Dallas to represent Oswald. Believing that the trial of an accused presidential assassin would bring him enormous publicity, Kunstler accepted the offer. On November 24, Oswald was assassinated in front of a national television audience by Jack Ruby, a Dallas nightclub owner and small-time mobster.

Ruby was convicted and sentenced to death for Oswald's killing. While his conviction and sentence were being appealed, Kunstler joined the Ruby defense team, believing that Ruby was mentally unstable. In 1966, Kunstler and his fellow lawyers convinced the Texas Court of Criminal Appeals that a statement made by Ruby after the shooting ("I'm glad I got the son of a bitch.") should have been excluded from admission based on Miranda grounds. The court also ruled that Ruby's trial should have taken place outside of Dallas County. Even though the murder of Oswald was captured live on national television, Ruby's conviction was overturned on October 5, 1966, and a new trial was ordered. Jack Ruby died from cancer on January 3, 1967, before his second trial started, robbing Kunstler of his place in the limelight.

The 1993 World Trade Center Attack

On February 26, 1993, a bomb exploded in the parking deck of the World Trade Center in New York City, killing six people, and injuring more than 1,000 others. The bombers and their coconspirators, all with ties to Mideast terrorist groups, were eventually brought to trial. It would be difficult even for the most fervent or naive advocate of civil liberties and due process to grant credence to some of Kunstler's pleas on behalf of the 1993 World Trade Center bombers, like this one contained in his autobiography:

> I agree that bombing the World Trade Center was crazy, and I don't condone it. I can, however, understand why someone would want to bomb it for political reasons, for the building is a monument to American corporate structure and capitalism. I regret, as I suppose the bombers also regret, that people died in the process. (Kunstler and Isenberg, 1996)

The last statement by Kunstler is at best naive, and at worst despicable. Nonetheless, such was the essence of Kunstler. Kunstler wanted to defend the accused bombers but was denied permission by his peers with the Southern District of New York Criminal Justice Act Panel, who claimed Kunstler was not qualified to represent the defendants. El Sayyid Nosair, who Kunstler defended in the Meir Kahane killing, was convicted of participating in the WTC attack from behind bars, and he finally admitted to killing Kahane.

Colin Ferguson

Kunstler's last controversial case was that of Colin Ferguson, who murdered six commuters and wounded 19 others on the Long Island Railroad on December 7, 1993. Ferguson, who was by many accounts severely deranged, was allowed to represent himself at trial. Kunstler pursued Ferguson's case on appeal, angering many by raising the issue of Black rage as a form of insanity in Ferguson's defense.

Personal Life and Death

Kunstler's life away from the courtroom was not dull either. In 1992, he portrayed a judge who imprisons the title character in Spike Lee's *Malcolm X*, whose assassination investigation also involved Kunstler. He also played opposite Val Kilmer as Jim Morrison's lawyer in the 1991 movie *The Doors*.

Kunstler's first marriage ended in divorce in 1973. He attributed the marital breakup to his frequent travel and to his own marital infidelity. Kunstler lamely rationalized his sexual misadventures by claiming that young, attractive women aggressively pursued him because of his celebrity status. One was Margaret Ratner, an attorney who had worked with Kunstler on several cases. Kunstler and Ratner were married on October 6, 1975. Kunstler fathered four daughters.

Kunstler's fantasy death scenario was slumping down on a courtroom lectern after delivering an impassioned summation in a criminal trial, but that fantasy did not become reality. After experiencing declining health for several months, he suffered a heart attack and died on September 4, 1995. He was 76 years old.

Sources and Suggested Readings

Calabro, Martin. (1996). *Great courtroom lawyers: Fighting the cases that made history.* Facts on File.

CBS. (2010). *The life of William Kunstler* [Video]. YouTube. https://www.youtube.com/watch?v=BnMk0js5KPQ, date of retrieval January 19, 2024.

Democracy Now. (2009). *"William Kunstler: Disturbing the universe": New documentary examines life, legacy of famed radical attorney* [Video]. https://www.democracynow.org/2009/11/12/william_kunstler_disturbing_the_universe

Kunstler, W. M., & Isenberg. S. (1996). *My life as a radical lawyer.* Carol.

Langum, David. (1999). *William M. Kunstler: The most hated lawyer in America.* NYU Press.

McWhirter, Darien A. (1998). *The legal 100: A ranking of the individuals who have most influenced the law.* Carol.

Pearson, Richard. (1995, September 4). William Kunstler, fierce defender of radical causes, dies at age 76. *The Washington Post.* https://www.washingtonpost.com/archive/local/1995/09/05/william-kunstler-fierce-defender-of-radical-causes-dies-at-age-76/0d9105cd-e888-452e-aa36-0be25154465e/, date of retrieval January 19, 2024.

POV. (2010). The terrible myth—*William Kunstler: Disturbing the universe. POV on PBS* [Video]. YouTube. https://www.youtube.com/watch?v=Ft8UNDhV2Uc, accessed January 18, 2024.

SMU Jones Film. (2023). *William Kunstler discusses his experience with the Attica prison riots—September 23, 1971* [Video]. YouTube. https://www.youtube.com/watch?v=BhFJfBvm6qw, date of retrieval January 17, 2024.

UMKC School of Law. (n.d.). *William Kunstler.* Biographies, University of Missouri–Kansas City. http://law2.umkc.edu/faculty/projects/ftrials/Chicago7/KunstlerW.htm, accessed August 7, 2024.

YouTube Movies & TV. (2021). *William Kunstler: Disturbing the universe* [Video]. YouTube, https://www.youtube.com/watch?v=Nu26gAQeryE, date of retrieval January 18, 2024.

Discussion Questions

1. Despite his unpopularity, why does the American legal system need people like William Kunstler?
2. What will be William Kunstler's legacy in 50 years?

Credit

IMG 23.1: Copyright © by Los Angeles Times (CC BY 4.0) at https://commons.wikimedia.org/wiki/File:William_M._Kunstler_at_Los_Angeles_protest_rally,_1970.jpg.

CHAPTER 24

Sandra Day O'Connor (1930–2023)

IMG 24.1

The three most prominent institutions in the federal government are the presidency, the Congress and the United States Supreme Court. Presidential cabinets have included very few females since Frances Perkins served as Secretary of Labor under President Franklin Roosevelt in the 1930s. In 1917, Jeannette Rankin of Montana became the first woman elected to the United States Congress, and she was succeeded by many other women in subsequent decades, though the number serving is still not in proportion to the female population in the United States. But the United States Supreme Court remained a male institution from the year of its founding, 1789, until 1981, when Sandra Day O'Connor became the first female justice to serve on the Court. While her legacy and reputation as a justice is mixed and she will go down in history as the "swing vote" on the Court (Supreme Court of the United States, n.d., para 2)—a label she disliked—her life as a pioneer for women was exceptional.

Early Life

Sandra Day was born March 26, 1930, in El Paso, Texas, the oldest child of Ada and her husband Harry, an Arizona rancher. Another daughter, Ann, and a son, Alan, would follow, but they were so much younger than Sandra that she essentially grew up as an only child. Unlike many other Supreme Court Justices, she was a product of the West. Sandra grew up on the family ranch, the Lazy B, in Duncan, a small town in southeastern Arizona. In Sandra's words, the Lazy B was "no place for sissies" (Supreme Court of the United States, n.d., para 1). Sandra's childhood consisted of hunting, ranching, and shooting wild animals. She was always more comfortable in fishing gear than in formal wear, and outdoor activities were her lifelong interest.

Her parents were traditionalists and politically conservative, but they encouraged their daughter to be confident and independent. Sandra grew up during the Great Depression and World War II. In 1945, she witnessed the first detonation of an atomic bomb from 180 miles away—during the presidency of Franklin Roosevelt, who radically altered the significance of the federal government in the lives of everyday Americans through his New Deal domestic agenda. Harry Day's federalist mentality—the belief that government power should be shared equally between the federal and state governments—was passed on to his daughter. It characterized the conservatism that became associated with the Republican Party of the 1960s and 1970s and its ideological leader, Senator Barry Goldwater of Arizona, and the man who would carry the mantle of Goldwater conservatism into the White House, Ronald Reagan.

Stanford

Knowing that quality educational opportunities were lacking in rural southern Arizona, the Days sent their daughter to live with her grandmother in El Paso, where she attended private schools for most of her childhood. After graduating from high school at age 16, Sandra Day enrolled at Stanford University in Palo Alto, California, more than 900 miles west of her Arizona hometown. While Stanford was one of the most elite universities on the West Coast with President Herbert Hoover among its first graduates, it was only emerging as the academic powerhouse that it would later became, especially after the male student population had been devastated by World War II. Though younger than most of her classmates, Sandra Day was popular, social, and a good student. She graduated in 1950 with a degree in economics.

While getting any college degree from a coeducational institution was slightly unusual for most American females in the early 1950s, going to law school was almost unheard of. Traditional female domains included nursing, education, or home economics. But Sandra Day entered Stanford Law School in 1950. There were 150 students in her class at Stanford. Compared to subsequent decades, admission standards for Stanford Law School were low in the early 1950s. Stanford only established its law review in 1948. While she was outnumbered by men as an undergraduate, Sandra was vastly outnumbered as a female law student. Growing up on a ranch and being mentored by a tough, domineering but encouraging father had prepared her for the difficulties she faced as a female law student.

A popular, articulate, and social young woman described as more serious than most students her age, Sandra Day had several relationships with male students at Stanford. One of those students was William Rehnquist, the future chief justice of the U.S. Supreme Court. In fact, Rehnquist proposed to her. Although the engagement broke off, "Bill" Rehnquist and "Sandy" Day enjoyed a special friendship until his death in 2005.

Marriage and Early Career

In 1952, Sandra Day graduated from Stanford Law School and married John O'Connor, another Stanford Law School student who became a successful attorney and a strong supporter of his wife's career. Initially the young married couple stayed in California, with Sandra working as a deputy attorney for San Mateo County, 30 miles south of San Francisco. While searching for a job as a lawyer, Sandra Day O'Connor (SDO) was usually questioned about her typing and clerical skills, as that was all most women were assumed capable of doing. She was frequently asked if she could balance the demands of a job with running a household, a question typically not posed to men.

In 1953, John O'Connor entered the military. For much of his army tenure he was stationed in Frankfurt, West Germany, where he served as a lawyer. Sandra accompanied him and worked at the Quartermaster Corps, dabbling in legal matters occasionally. Upon completion of John's military obligations, the couple returned to Arizona. Sandra worked in private practice in the Phoenix suburb of Maryvale. The marriage would bear three sons, Scott, Brian, and Jay, all born between 1957 and 1962.

Political Career

Some Supreme Court justices rise to the nation's top Court via the academic route, or they establish a reputation for their intellectual prowess and academic mastery of the law, often getting appointments to federal judicial appointments. For other justices, like Earl Warren, elective office was a springboard to the Court. That was the route SDO would take, although there is little indication that joining the Court was on her radar as a young lawyer. In the 1960s, SDO became involved in Republican Party affairs in Arizona. Unlike most women, who stayed in the background or functioned as silent supporters of their husbands' political activities, Sandra was visibly involved. Dwight Eisenhower, a moderate Republican, occupied the White House throughout most of the 1950s, and SDO was an Eisenhower Republican, holding to the idea that states should be wary of federal government overreach and that a strong military was a necessity. She held a cautionary attitude, though not outwardly bigoted, on social matters such as civil rights. Although she leaned to the right on some social issues, Eisenhower Republicans like SDO were not attached to the Christian religious element that would dominate the Republican Party in the 1980s.

In 1965, SDO began working as assistant attorney general for Arizona. Her star rose in Arizona Republican Party circles. She and John became known as one Arizona's most popular power couples—both attractive, smart, politically active, and successful lawyers. SDO continued her involvement in the Republican Party, and in 1969, was appointed to fill the unexpired state senate term of Isabel Burges. SDO was elected to a term in her own right in 1970. In 1972, SDO's senate colleagues elected her senate majority leader, a noteworthy feat for a young senator with only 3 years' experience and a particularly extraordinary accomplishment for a female, especially in the macho western state of Arizona. SDO was the first female state senate majority leader in U.S. history. In 1972, she headed the Arizona chapter for President Richard Nixon's successful reelection campaign. Meanwhile, earlier that year, her former Stanford boyfriend William Rehnquist took a seat as associate justice on the U.S. Supreme Court, after being nominated by President Nixon.

SDO left the State Senate in 1975 to become superior court judge in Maricopa County (Phoenix). Many Supreme Court justices never preside over a jury trial or deal with lawyers, criminal defendants, police officers, and crime victims before sitting on the Court. SDO experienced justice in the everyday working world of the criminal justice system, which contributed to her pragmatic approach to decision-making while on the Court. After serving as a local trial judge for 4 years, SDO was sworn in as a judge on the Arizona Court of Appeals. By 1979 she was one of the most esteemed women in Arizona political circles and had attracted the attention of Republicans outside Arizona.

Supreme Court Justice

When former California Governor Ronald Reagan launched his second presidential bid in 1980, he knew he needed a strong showing among females if he wanted to defeat incumbent Democratic President Jimmy Carter. The Republican Party was perceived as the party of White men, and Ronald Reagan's macho image reinforced the idea in some voters' minds that he was insensitive to women. Reagan promised to nominate a woman to the Supreme Court when the first seat became vacant. Jimmy Carter was enormously unpopular, and voters elected Reagan in a landslide. Ronald Reagan assumed the presidency in January 1981.

It was not long before President Reagan had a chance to make good on his campaign pledge. When Potter Stewart retired in the summer of 1981, Reagan nominated O'Connor to the Court, encouraged in part by William Rehnquist and other Arizona Republicans. While her Senate confirmation would not be as bruising as some that would follow, the principal issue that she faced was her stand on right to privacy as it applied to abortion, more specifically whether she would vote to overturn *Roe v. Wade* (1973), the ruling that legalized abortion nationwide. While stating that she personally opposed abortion, she was fuzzy on whether she had endorsed legislation in Arizona that made it legal (she had), but she stated that she believed in a woman's right to choose. This stance would be echoed in several Court decisions during her tenure. Some Senate Republicans, encouraged by the Christian right, expressed doubts about her nomination. Nevertheless, SDO was confirmed in a 99-0 vote, and on September 25, 1981, she became the first female associate justice of the Supreme Court.

Life for any new Supreme Court justice in the "Marble Palace" can be rocky, but the public attention on Sandra Day O'Connor was multiplied geometrically as the Court's first female justice. Some East Coast Court observers saw her as an affirmative action appointment not only because of her sex, but because of her non-Ivy League background. She was already acquainted with some of the justices, including William Rehnquist and Chief Justice Warren Burger, a man described as often condescending and long winded but basically a decent person. While her experience in politics and in the everyday world of criminal and civil law were assets that some justices did not have, she was remedial in other areas and, like most other justices, depended heavily on her clerks to increase her knowledge.

In his SDO biography *First*, Evan Thomas (2019) includes information gathered from many of the people who worked closest with her—her law clerks. A clerkship with a Supreme Court justice is a plum first job for law clerks, and the Court attracts the most elite recent law school graduates in the country. Clerks typically work for the Court for one year, often working 80 hours per week. While SDO valued a good educational pedigree, she valued life experience just as much. She intentionally hired both Democrats and Republicans because she did not want to merely have more people in her personal echo chamber who always agreed with her. SDO, who jokingly characterized herself as "bossy" (knowing the term was offensive to modern feminists for whom she cared little), could be stern and abrupt. Though she was sometimes curt, she was not intentionally abusive, as other justices were toward their clerks. But she was usually serious and demanded obedience, even requiring all female clerks to exercise with her every morning in the Court gym. Always a dutiful host at her home, she seldom delegated cooking duties to others, instead personally preparing meals and hosting her clerks at her home.

One of the most traumatic moments in SDO's career came in 1988, when she was diagnosed with breast cancer. She underwent a mastectomy and chemotherapy treatment for 1 year. But during her year of treatment, she seldom missed work, except when confined to a hospital bed.

Legal Opinions

During her 24-year tenure on the Court, SDO wrote 645 opinions, with a roughly equal balance of majority, concurring, and dissenting opinions, more balanced than most of her ideologically driven colleagues. She sometimes sided with more conservative colleagues, including William Rehnquist (who was elevated to chief justice by President Reagan) and later Antonin Scalia and Clarence Thomas, the conservative icons of the Supreme Court. But she often sided with the more liberal members of the Court including William Brennan, Thurgood Marshall, and John Paul Stevens. O'Connor came to be labeled the swing vote on the Court, alternately praised and criticized by liberals and conservatives alike for being wishy-washy, but also praised for her political and judicial pragmatism and forthrightness, both in her demeanor on the Court, with colleagues and clerks, and in her written opinions.

The following were some of the significant cases in which SDO provided the deciding vote or authored the majority opinion:

- *Mississippi University for Women v. Hogan,* 485 U.S. 718 (1982). In her first term on the Court, one of SDO's first major opinions dealt with affirmative action, an issue which would come before the Court several times during her tenure. Joe Hogan, a registered nurse, was denied admission to the all-female university's nursing program based on his sex. Writing for the Court, SDO wrote that Mississippi's statute prohibiting male admittees to the university violated the Equal Protection Clause of the 14th Amendment.
- *Strickland v. Washington,* 466 U.S. 668 (1984). In this capital punishment case, SDO, writing for the Court, established the standard that defendants sentenced to death must meet when alleging inadequate counsel during trial: (a) counsel's performance must be deficient; and (b) the deficient performance must have prejudiced the defense to deprive the defendant of a fair trial.
- *City of Richmond v. J.A. Croson Company,* 488 U.S. 469 (1989). In another affirmative action case, SDO wrote that Richmond's requirement that 30% of city contracts be awarded to minority-owned businesses was unconstitutional, that such a rigid quota system undermined the Constitution.
- *Hudson v. McMillian,* 503 U.S. 1 (1992). Keith Hudson, a Louisiana prison inmate, was beaten by two correctional officers, but the lower court held that he was not entitled to damages because it was not proven that he suffered "significant injury," and therefore the cruel and unusual clause of the Eighth Amendment was not violated. Writing for the Court, SDO ruled in Hudson's favor, that he was entitled to damages.

- *Harris v. Forklift Systems,* 510 U.S. 17 (1993). Teresa Harris alleged that she was sexually harassed at work but was denied damages because it was determined that the "abusive work environment" had not inflicted "concrete psychological harm." In a rare unanimous decision, SDO wrote for the Court that the conduct itself was the issue, not the psychological impact, and that Harris was entitled to damages.
- *Davis v. U.S.,* 512 U.S. 452 (1994). Robert Davis had been imprisoned for murder but claimed that his conviction should have been overturned because during questioning, he made an ambiguous request about talking to a lawyer. In another unanimous decision, the Court, led by SDO, ruled against Davis, a victory for police officers interviewing suspects.
- *Bush v. Gore,* 531 U.S. 98 (2000). The 2000 Presidential election pitting Republican Texas Governor George W. Bush against Democratic Vice President Al Gore was very close, with the deciding factor in the Electoral College vote coming down to the results in Florida, especially several counties in south Florida. While Gore demanded a recount of the votes in several Florida counties, Bush objected, wanting the official results to stand. The drama over the political back and forth was heightened by the fact that Bush's brother Jeb happened to be the Governor of Florida, and Katherine Harris, the Florida Secretary of State charged with certifying the election results, served as Bush's co-campaign chair for Florida.

  After a fierce back and forth in the media and in Florida courts, the matter went to the Supreme Court in December 2000, just over one month before President Bill Clinton was to leave office. In a *per curiam* decision, the Court ruled in Bush's favor. The vote ran along party and ideological affiliation, 5–4, with O'Connor and four other conservatives on the Court ruling for Bush, and the four liberals siding with Gore. The Court's reputation as politically nonpartisan suffered because of *Bush v. Gore.* It was one case that SDO avoided discussing. She stated later that the Supreme Court should have let Florida courts deal with the matter.
- *Hamdi v. Rumsfeld,* 542 U.S. 507 (2004). Following the al-Qaeda-led terrorist attacks against the United States on September 11, 2001, the United States led an invasion of Afghanistan. Yaser Hamdi, an American citizen, was captured there and detained as an enemy combatant. The Bush administration and the Department of Defense argued that as an enemy combatant, Hamdi was not entitled to challenge the legality of his indefinite confinement. SDO and the Court ruled in Hamdi's favor in part, stating that Hamdi enjoyed the right of *habeas corpus* that applied to other U.S. citizens.

Retirement, Accolades, and Death

By 2005, SDO was at a crossroads. John O'Connor's Alzheimer's disease had progressed to the point where he needed full-time care. Her old friend and Chief Justice William Rehnquist was dealing with cancer, but he did not reveal the extent of his condition to SDO. SDO and the Chief Justice discussed retirement, namely who should retire first. In July 2005, SDO sent her letter of resignation to President George W. Bush, stating that she would remain on the Court until a successor (Samuel Alito) was named. In September of 2005, while SDO was serving as a "lame duck" on the Court pending confirmation of her successor, Bill Rehnquist passed away. A weeping SDO was filmed on the steps of the Supreme Court as her old friend's casket was carried. John Roberts succeeded Rehnquist as chief justice.

SDO stepped down on January 31, 2006. It was a decision she would soon regret. She continued hearing circuit court cases, kept her office at the Supreme Court, assumed a 7-year tenure in the ceremonial role of chancellor of the College of William and Mary in Williamsburg, Virginia, but she officially moved back to Arizona to care for her husband. However, John's condition deteriorated to the point where he had to be placed in assisted living and eventually to the point where he did not recognize his family members, including SDO. John O'Connor passed away November 11, 2009, three months after President Barack Obama awarded SDO the Presidential Medal of Freedom, the nation's highest civilian honor.

SDO continued to be active socially and professionally even after turning 80 in 2010. But by around 2012–2013, those around SDO noticed that she was becoming forgetful and irritable, once at a public forum at the New York Public Library with former Secretary of State Madeleine Albright alongside. Not long after, SDO was diagnosed with dementia. In 2015, she gave up her office at the Supreme Court and most other activities. She did not totally retire from public life, establishing Camp O'Connor, a civics program for seventh and eighth graders. On October 23, 2018, Sandra Day O'Connor announced her retirement from public life.

A 2015 forum hosted by the Newseum in Washington D.C. featured the four women who, up to that point, had served as justices on the U.S. Supreme Court. SDO was flanked by the three women who followed her, Ruth Bader Ginsburg, Sonia Sotomayor, and Elena Kagan. The other three were nominated by Democratic presidents and differed with SDO on many political and legal matters. But all three expressed their admiration for SDO. Most people who knew SDO knew her as a strong woman, but not ostentatious or abrasive. When asked repeatedly whether family or career should come first, she always answered unhesitatingly, family. Justice Elena Kagan, who first met SDO while clerking for Thurgood Marshall, said of her, "No one could have done it better." Sandra Day O'Connor passed away on December 1, 2023, in Phoenix, Arizona, at age 93.

Sources and Suggested Readings

Murgai, P., & Cohen, D. (2023, December 1). Sandra Day O'Connor, first woman Supreme Court justice, dies at 93. *Politico*. https://www.politico.com/news/2023/12/01/sandra-day-oconnor-female-supreme-court-justice-034753, accessed December 1, 2023.

National Archives Online. (2021, March 19). First Congresswoman Jeanette Rankin. https://museum.archives.gov/featured-document-display-first-congresswoman-jeannette-rankin#:~:text=Four%20years%20before%20ratification%20of,House%20of%20Representatives%20in%201941, accessed December 1, 2023.

O'Connor, Sandra Day, & Day, H. Alan. (2003). *Lazy B: Growing Up on a cattle ranch in the American Southwest*. Random House.

Roe v. Wade, 410 U.S. 113 (1973).

Sandra Day O'Connor. (n.d.). *Oyez*. https://www.oyez.org/justices/sandra_day_oconnor

Sandra Day O'Connor College of Law. (2023). Sandra Day O'Connor: Her life and legacy: Biographical timeline. Arizona State University. https://libguides.law.asu.edu/sandradayoconnor/biography, accessed November 29, 2019.

Sandra Day O'Connor College of Law. (2023). Sandra Day O'Connor: Her life and legacy: Opinions. Arizona State University. https://libguides.law.asu.edu/sandradayoconnor/federalopinions#:~:text=During%20her%2024%20years%20on,O'Connor%20wrote%20645%20opinions, accessed November 28, 2023.

Supreme Court of the United States. (n.d.). *Sandra Day O'Connor: First woman on the Supreme Court*. Visiting the Court. https://www.supremecourt.gov/visiting/exhibitions/SOCExhibit/Section1.aspx, accessed August 7, 2024.

Thomas, Evan. (2019). *First: Sandra Day O'Connor*. Random House.

Toobin, Jeffrey. (2008). *The nine: Inside the secret world of the Supreme Court*. Anchor.

Discussion Questions

1. Sandra Day O'Connor did not like being labeled the "swing vote" on the Supreme Court. Do you think that label is unfair, or should she be praised because of her judicial pragmatism?
2. Sandra Day O'Connor rose through the political ranks to get to the Supreme Court. What do you think of her route to the Court?

Credit

IMG 24.1: Steve Petteway, https://commons.wikimedia.org/wiki/File:Sandra_Day_O%-27Connor.jpg, 2011.

CHAPTER 25

Sonia Sotomayor (1954-)

IMG 25.1

Like other pioneers profiled in this book, Sonia Sotomayor represents several "firsts" or innovations, the most notable being the first Hispanic female to serve on the United States Supreme Court. Her ascendance from the South Bronx to one of the nation's most prestigious judicial appointments was not an easy one, but it is one that in many respects is the fulfillment of the American dream.

Early Life

Sonia Sotomayor was born June 25, 1954, in New York City's South Bronx, one of two children born to Juan and Celina Sotomayor, who had moved to New York City from Puerto Rico in 1944. New York City had been one of the most popular areas for Puerto Ricans since 1917, when citizens of the Caribbean Island were allowed to move to and from the United States without a passport. Puerto Rico was seized by force by the United States after the American victory over Spain in the Spanish-American War of 1898. Relations between Puerto Rico, a place with its own distinct culture and language, and mainland United States were problematic from the moment Puerto Rico became a U.S. territory. Attitudes of distrust, resentment, and racial prejudice characterized Puerto Rico–U.S. relations, especially in the first half of the 20th century when the United States imposed its political will on Puerto Rico and forced students and teachers to speak English in schools. American business interests were also exploiting Puerto Rican labor and resources, especially with the island's main cash crop, sugar.

Sonia, whose name means "wisdom," and her younger brother Juan, or "Junior," grew up during a time when Puerto Ricans were considered second-class citizens by many Americans and when cultural and language barriers impeded their attempts to succeed in the English-dominated education system. Her father Juan was a factory worker with a third-grade education who never mastered English. Assimilation was not easy, and the thought of being looked up to as a female coming from her macho, paternalistic culture and raised in public housing seemed fanciful in the 1950s and 1960s.

As if language, cultural, and ethnic barriers did not present enough obstacles, Sonia Sotomayor was diagnosed with juvenile diabetes at age 7. But in an indicator of the tenacity that would serve her during her adult years, she learned to inject herself with insulin at that young age. In 2019, Sotomayor published a children's book, *Just Ask!*, where she challenged children not to be defined by adverse health conditions or other impediments.

Another complicating factor in Sonia's childhood was Juan Sotomayor's alcoholism, which embarrassed his family and created a tumultuous homelife for Sonia and Junior. Celina worked at a hospital, often putting in long hours so that she could send her children to a private Catholic school, and Juan's alcoholism rendered him emotionally absent from his children. Although the Sotomayor's enjoyed a good relationship with extended family, Sonia and Junior were often on their own at night. When her mother was queried as to why her children were allowed to study while watching television, she responded that if their grades were good, nothing else mattered. Sonia Sotomayor wrote in her autobiography that television was her window to a world outside her Bronx neighborhood. Books, especially a set of *Encyclopedia Britannica*, were her refuge.

Few people in post-baby boom generations are familiar with the popular television show *Perry Mason* that ran from 1957–1966, but anyone who grew up watching television in the 1950s and 1960s and for many years in reruns, knew *Perry Mason* well. Based on a series of novels by Erle Stanley Gardner, *Perry Mason* was a series about a crafty, almost omniscient Los Angeles criminal defense attorney, portrayed by Raymond Burr. The lawyer always got his clients acquitted of murder and also fingered the actual culprit, usually in open court in dramatic fashion. Like other *Perry Mason* viewers, Sonia Sotomayor developed a fascination with the law and was inspired to attend law school by watching Raymond Burr's fictional character, even though the show bore little resemblance to real life.

Princeton and Yale

Her less-than-ideal childhood circumstances notwithstanding, Sonia Sotomayor was an excellent student. She graduated from Cardinal Spellman High School, a Roman Catholic school in the Bronx, in 1972, earning valedictorian honors. Due to her stellar academic performance, her economic need, and the desire for universities to increase the presence of ethnic minorities on their campuses, Princeton University granted her a full undergraduate scholarship. Even though she was an outstanding student at her Catholic high school, her mastery of English was lacking when she got to Princeton. Sonia had to take additional English classes to get up to speed with her colleagues.

While Sonia Sotomayor was never involved with the militant or violent elements of Puerto Rican nationalism, she was concerned about the plight of Puerto Ricans in the United States and the lack of Latino representation at Princeton. Never one given to loud protest or carrying signs, Sonia Sotomayor saw formal, legal action as the better way to achieve her goals. She joined and eventually cochaired Acción Puertorriqueña, a Puerto Rican student activist group at Princeton, and lodged formal complaints against Princeton for lack of minority hiring.

A history major, Sonia's senior thesis was devoted to Luis Munoz Marin, the first popularly elected governor of Puerto Rico. When Sonia was notified that she would receive Princeton's Moses Taylor Pyne Honor Prize, an award given to Princeton's best undergraduate performing student, she had to be told what the award was given for. After graduating from Princeton, Sonia married Kevin Noonan, her high school sweetheart from New York City, who was attending college in New York.

Sonia Sotomayor continued her quest to become a lawyer, entering Yale Law School in 1976. She excelled at Yale, serving as editor of the *Yale Law Journal*, a duty reserved for top students. It was a job previously held by Samuel Alito, who would one day serve on the U.S. Supreme Court with Justice Sotomayor. Sotomayor admitted that she found Yale intimidating, but that she always found people who would help her through rough times.

New York Assistant District Attorney

Sonia Sotomayor graduated from Yale Law School in 1979 and returned to New York, where she passed the bar in 1980 and, at age 25, took a position as a prosecutor under Manhattan District Attorney Robert Morganthau. While working as an assistant district attorney, she prosecuted every imaginable criminal case and developed considerable trial experience in the day-to-day workings of an American criminal courtroom, especially dealing with urban street crime—qualifications that many Supreme Court justices do not have. Robert Morganthau described the young Sotomayor as a "fearless and effective prosecutor" (The White House, 2009, para 7). One of Sotomayor's most notable cases was the "Tarzan Murderer Case." In the Tarzan case, Richard Maddicks, a burglar and career criminal, would swing into apartment buildings from rooftops, shooting anyone who got in his way. Thanks to Sotomayor's efforts, Maddicks was convicted and sentenced to 137 years in prison. Sonia Sotomayor said that of all the cases she prosecuted, the Tarzan case had the greatest impact on her and sensitized her to the traumatic effects of violent crime on victims.

In 1980, while beginning her career as a prosecutor, Sonia Sotomayor found the time to engage in *pro bono* work, serving on the board of directors for the Puerto Rican Legal Defense and Education Fund, which was started in the early 1970s by several Puerto Rican lawyers. Her experience with the PRLDEF was brief but also a bonus for her credentials in later years when she was undergoing scrutiny for judicial nominations. She and Kevin Noonan divorced in 1983.

Private Practice

Sotomayor worked as an assistant district attorney for 5 years before going to work with Pavia and Harcourt, a Madison Avenue business law firm, in 1984. By 1988, she became a partner, at age 34. One of her most notable clients was the Italian luxury goods retailer Fendi, who employed her to fight manufacturers of knockoff handbags bearing its logo. Sotomayor developed an expertise in intellectual property litigation. Despite her lack of civil litigation experience prior to joining Pavia and Harcourt, Sotomayor was a fast learner and an effective civil litigator. She also accompanied police raids on fake handbags shops in New York, gaining more firsthand experience working alongside law enforcement officers.

From 1987–1992, Sotomayor served on the board of the State of New York Mortgage Agency (SONYMA). SONYMA's mission was to seek ways for low-income families to obtain mortgages. While SONYMA's mission may have been noble, and many applauded their work, the Agency and Sotomayor came under fire after the housing and mortgage collapse of 2008, which ushered in a severe recession. Critics charged that naïve or careless agencies and mortgage companies like SONYMA provided loans to those who could not afford them, causing the collapse of 2008 and the recession that followed. She also served on the New York City Campaign Finance Board, where, in a harbinger of her future Court rulings, she favored strict regulations on campaign finance contributions, seeing large campaign contributions as a way of buying political influence—in contrast to her opponents who claimed that such limits interfere with First Amendment freedom of speech rights.

District Court Judge

In November, 1991, President George H. W. Bush nominated Sonia Sotomayor to serve as Federal District Court judge for the Southern District of New York. As was the custom with such nominations, her name was given to the president by a U.S. senator from that state, even if the senator and the president belonged to different political parties. In her case, the senator was longtime Democratic stalwart Daniel P. Moynihan, a giant of the U.S. Senate. Sonia Sotomayor was unanimously confirmed the following year by the U.S. Senate. She became the first Hispanic judge in a federal court in New York and the first female Puerto Rican judge in any federal court. She was also the youngest federal district court judge at the time.

As the Southern District of New York encompasses Manhattan, any federal district court judge there is likely to be thrown into the spotlight. In her 6 years as district court judge, Sotomayor heard many cases, many with life-or-death implications, but the case that propelled her into the public spotlight more than any other came in 1995. Since August 12, 1994, Major League Baseball (MLB) players had been on strike. The 232-day work stoppage was not only the longest player strike in the game's history, but it had forced the cancellation of the 1994 World Series, an unfortunate first.

MLB owners were trying to force the hand of the Major League Baseball Players Association by hiring replacement players. In March 1995, the National Labor Relations Board sided with the players' union in their complaint that the attempt to hire replacement players constituted an unfair labor practice. On March 31, Judge Sotomayor sided with the players and issued a preliminary injunction against the owners. The strike ended on April 2, the season started a few days late, and an appellate court upheld Judge Sotomayor's ruling.

U.S. Court of Appeals

In June 1997, President Bill Clinton nominated Judge Sotomayor to serve on the United States Court of Appeals for the Second Circuit. Her confirmation hearings before the Senate Judiciary Committee came in September, but the Committee did not approve her recommendation for a full Senate vote until March 1998. In 1998, Congress was in the throes of impeachment proceedings against President Clinton, and many agenda items were held in abeyance during the impeachment hearings and the Senate trial. (Clinton, who was accused of lying under oath in a civil lawsuit stemming from his alleged sexual misconduct, was impeached by the House of Representatives but was not convicted by the Senate.) Sotomayor's confirmation to the Court of Appeals finally came in October 1998. Judge Sotomayor would serve on the Court of Appeals for 10 years, authoring more than 400 opinions.

Supreme Court Justice

In 2009, soon after he took office, President Barack Obama nominated Sonia Sotomayor to replace the retiring David Souter on the United States Supreme Court. She was confirmed by the U.S. Senate in a 68–31 vote, the opposition coming from conservative Republicans. She became the first Hispanic, the first female Hispanic, and the third woman (after Sandra Day O'Connor and Ruth Bader Ginsburg) to be seated on the United States Supreme Court. At 54, she was young compared to many Supreme Court justices, but she had more than 17 years of experience as a judge, including experience as a trial judge, and 5 years of experience as a prosecutor, considerably more in either area than some of her senior colleagues.

Consistent with her appointment by a progressive Democrat, Justice Sotomayor has generally leaned left on her decisions and is part of the Court's liberal wing. She has differed in opinion from her fellow Catholics on the Court at the time of her appointment, including Chief Justice John Roberts, and Associate Justices Clarence Thomas, Samuel Alito, Anthony Kennedy, and Antonin Scalia. Since she joined the Court in 2009, the Court has been dominated by a conservative majority, often leaving Justice Sotomayor in the minority, sometimes writing dissenting opinions, many of them blunt and scathing. Her positions and some of her opinions and dissents are presented here:

- *Berghuis v. Thompkins*, 560 U.S. 370 (2010). In this case, a majority of the Court ruled that a suspect who had made a voluntary statement to police during questioning had waived his right to remain silent after hearing and understanding his Miranda rights. Justice Sotomayor, a former prosecutor, dissented, signaling her inclination to side with defendants rather than law enforcement in matters concerning procedural due process.
- *J. D. B. v. North Carolina*, 564 U.S. 261 (2011). In an opinion authored by Justice Sotomayor, the Court held that police violated the rights of a 13-year-old by questioning him for 30 minutes about a series of robberies without informing him of his Miranda rights or allowing him to contact his guardian or telling him he was free to leave the room. It signaled an expansion of Miranda rights for juveniles, again consistent with Sotomayor's progressive leanings.
- *Missouri v. McNeely*, 569 U.S. 141 (2013). In an opinion authored by Justice Sotomayor, the Court ruled that police must obtain a warrant before obtaining an involuntary blood sample from a drunken driving suspect. In this case, most of the conservative justices, at least in part, sided with Justice Sotomayor.

- *Collins v. Virginia*, 584 U.S. ___ (2018). Justice Sotomayor authored the majority opinion for the Court in ruling that a warrantless search of a vehicle within the curtilage of a home is unconstitutional, unlike the automobile exception to a warrantless search that may apply when the vehicle is on the road.

Sotomayor has written dissents in several cases where the Court's majority favored law enforcement, including *Navarette v. California* (2014), *Mullenix v. Luna* (2015), and *Utah v. Strieff* (2016). Justice Sotomayor has consistently sided with criminal defendants or civil litigants and against police officers in matters involving procedural due process or civil liability. Despite her Catholic background, Justice Sotomayor has favored abortion rights. In 2021, she bluntly stated "this is not justice," sharply criticizing the Court's majority ruling that a federal execution be allowed to happen and signaling her opposition to capital punishment.

Conclusion

As of this writing, Sonia Sotomayor's legacy as a Supreme Court Justice is still being written. She has been regarded and ranked as one of the most liberal members of the Court since the beginning of the 21st century. To her admirers, she is "the conscience of the Supreme Court," "the truth teller of the Supreme Court," and "the real liberal queen of the Supreme Court," (Hassan, 2024) the last accolade also being the chief reason why so many conservatives oppose her opinions. Irrespective of one's assessment of her performance as a justice or her political ideology, Sonia Sotomayor stands as a true trailblazer and pioneer.

Sources and Suggested Readings

ALM Law.com. (2009, May 28). *Sotomayor's civil practice was with a small, but specialized, firm.* https://www.law.com/almID/1202431039295/, accessed June 21, 2024.

Carney, John. (2009, June 22). Sonia Sotomayor's mortgage policy wrecked America. *Business Insider.* https://www.businessinsider.com/sonia-sotomayors-mortgage-policy-problem-2009-6, accessed June 20, 2024.

de Vogue, A. (2021, July 26). Celina Sotomayor, mother of Supreme Court justice, dies at 94. *CNN Politics.* https://www.cnn.com/2021/07/26/politics/celina-sotomayor/index.html, accessed June 2, 2024.

Hassan, M. (2024, April 1). For the sake of all of us, Sonia Sotomayor needs to retire from the US Supreme Court. *The Guardian.* https://www.theguardian.com/commentisfree/2024/apr/01/for-the-sake-of-all-of-us-sonia-sotomayor-needs-to-retire-from-the-us-supreme-court, accessed June 21, 2024.

Justia. (n.d.). *Justice Sonia Sotomayor.* US Supreme Court. https://supreme.justia.com/justices/sonia-sotomayor/, accessed June 2, 2024.

Lamb, B., Swain, S., & Farkas, M. (Eds.). (2010). *The Supreme Court: A C-SPAN book featuring the justices in their own words.* C-SPAN Books. Public Affairs.

Latino Justice PRLDEF. (n.d.). *Our bold history.* https://www.latinojustice.org/en/history, accessed June 21, 2024.

Legal Information Institute. (n.d.). *Writings by Justice Sotomayor.* Cornell Law School. https://www.law.cornell.edu/supct/justices/sotomayor.dec.html, accessed June 1, 2024.

Mullenix v. Luna, 577 U.S. 7 (2015).

Navarette v. California, 572 U.S. 393 (2014).

PGO. (2009). *Confirmation hearing on the nomination of Hon. Sonia Sotomayor, to be an associate justice of the Supreme Court of the United States.* https://www.govinfo.gov/content/pkg/CHRG-111shrg56940/pdf/CHRG-111shrg56940.pdf, accessed June 21, 2024.

Princeton University Alumni. (2019, June 11). Princeton University establishes Sonia Sotomayor 1976 scholarship fund. https://alumni.princeton.edu/stories/princeton-university-establishes-sonia-sotomayor-1976-scholarship-fund, accessed June 1, 2024.

Reyes, Raul A. (2021, January 17). 'This is not justice': Justice Sonia Sotomayor offers fierce dissent in death penalty case. *NBC News.* https://www.nbcnews.com/news/latino/not-justice-justice-sonia-sotomayor-offers-fierce-dissent-death-penalty-n1254554, accessed June 20, 2024.

Savage, Charlie. (2009, May 29). A long record on campaign finance, often in support of regulations. *New York Times.* https://www.nytimes.com/2009/05/30/us/politics/30judge.html, accessed June 20, 2024.

Sonia Sotomayor. (n.d.). *Oyez.* https://www.oyez.org/justices/sonia_sotomayor, accessed June 3, 2024.

Sotomayor, Sonia. (2013). *My beloved world.* Alfred A. Knopf.

Sotomayor, Sonia. (2019). *Just ask!: Be different, be brave, be you.* Philomel.

Supreme Court Historical Society. (n.d.). *The current court: Justice Sonia Sotomayor.* https://supremecourthistory.org/supreme-court-justices/associate-justice-sonia-sotomayor/, accessed June 21, 2024.

United States Senate Committee on the Judiciary. (n.d.). *Testimony of District Attorney Robert M. Morganthau before the Committee on the Judiciary of the United States Senate.* https://www.judiciary.senate.gov/imo/media/doc/07-16-09MorganthauTestimony.pdf, accessed June 21, 2024.

Utah v. Strieff, 579 U.S. ___ (2016).

The White House. (2009, May 26). *Background on Judge Sonia Sotomayor.* https://obamawhitehouse.archives.gov/the-press-office/background-judge-sonia-sotomayor, accessed June 8, 2024.

Zirin, J. D., Roosevelt, K., & Roosevelt, K. III. (2016). *Supremely partisan: How raw politics tips the scales in the United States Supreme Court.* Rowman and Littlefield.

Discussion Questions

1. What lessons or messages can be learned from the life of Sonia Sotomayor from people who immigrate to the United States, especially those whose first language is not English?
2. Provide your thoughts on Justice Sotomayor's background and qualifications before joining the Supreme Court.

Credit

IMG 25.1: Steve Petteway, https://commons.wikimedia.org/wiki/File:Sonia_Sotomayor_in_SCOTUS_robe.jpg, 2009.

SECTION IV

CORRECTIONS

It is difficult to become famous working in the corrections profession. The bars and barriers that separate prison inmates from the public also isolate those who work behind those barriers. The public knows little about what goes on behind prison or jail walls—and often cares little. Probation and parole are also misunderstood and underappreciated practices as well. But knowing what happens after conviction is part and parcel to understanding criminal justice. I have devised three rough, imperfect categories for corrections groups: the innovators, the managers, and community corrections pioneers. We will consider those who have served in each category.

The Innovators

- **John Haviland** was the architect who designed Eastern State Penitentiary in Philadelphia. Pennsylvania was the birthplace of the American penitentiary. Haviland, an English immigrant, also designed prisons and jails for other states.
- **Dorothea Dix** is remembered for her efforts to assist the mentally ill. Dix was instrumental in reforming existing "insane asylums" and trying to free the mentally ill from jails.

The Managers

- **Zebulon Brockway** was both a manager and an innovator. Brockway's advocacy for the indeterminate sentence, a necessary element in early release from prison and the parole supervision that follows, make him a significant figure in the history of penology.
- **Thomas Mott Osborne** is remembered for colorful and controversial attempts to make inmate self-governance part of prison life. His personal story of advocating for better lives for prisoners includes serving time in disguise with inmates and employing his theatrical skills.
- **Miriam Van Waters** worked to improve the lot of female prisoners in Massachusetts. Her attempts to make female prisons more like home environments were consistent with gender roles at that time and still have relevance today, although like the experience of most penal reformers, her efforts were met with some degree of disappointment, widespread disapproval, and scandalous accusations.
- **Joseph Ragen** is remembered as one of the most skilled prison managers of the 20th century. His no-nonsense approach to cleaning up the mess that was Stateville Correctional Center in Illinois, one of the toughest prisons of its era, makes him a case study for other prison leaders.
- **Clinton Duffy**, one of a few almost destined from birth to be a prison warden, managed one of the most notorious prisons in the United States, San Quentin in California. Duffy was an innovator and effective manager who introduced Alcoholics Anonymous and other programs designed to rehabilitate inmates at San Quentin.
- **Kathleen Hawk Sawyer** (1950–) served as the first female director of the Federal Bureau of Prisons (BOP). She presided over the BOP at the height of the retributive era of the 1990s and during the reintroduction of federal government executions. She graciously provided most of the information in her chapter through a series of emails and telephone conversations with me, for which I am grateful. I am also indebted to Arthur Beeler, a retired BOP warden, East Carolina University alum, and good friend, for introducing me to Dr. Sawyer.

Community Corrections Pioneers

- **John Augustus** is credited with the founding of probation in the United States. A Boston shoe cobbler, Augustus's volunteer work in the 19th century with Boston's lower class paved the way for the establishment of probation systems in the federal government and in the states.

- **Jane Addams**, a founding mother of social work, is profiled here for her work with women and girls in Chicago at the turn of the 20th century. Her work at Hull House, a refuge for disadvantaged women and children, many of whom had served short sentence for minor crimes, is part of correctional history. Addams was a social worker before the term required specific educational credentials, and she integrated the fields of social work and penology.

Honorable Mentions

IMG IV.1

Thomas Eddy (1758–1827) was born in Philadelphia 18 years before America declared its independence from Great Britain. Eddy is often compared to England's John Howard, the world's most renowned prison reformer of the 18th century. The founding of the American penitentiary is due as much to the work of philanthropists like Thomas Eddy as to government officials.

A New York City merchant during the Revolutionary War, Eddy was imprisoned in New Jersey by the British on suspected spying charges, even though he was nominally a loyalist who opposed American independence. He was locked in a dungeon for 10 days in filthy crowded conditions before being released in a prisoner exchange.

After the war, Eddy established a successful insurance business and engaged in philanthropic work. Remembering his own hellish prison experience and sickened by the public punishments, corporal punishments, and executions prevalent at the time, Eddy was one of the prime movers in establishing a penitentiary in New York. He successfully lobbied the New York legislature to build a prison in Auburn. Like all other advocates of the early penitentiary, Eddy believed that religious and moral instruction was fundamental to the penitentiary, i.e., a place to make penitence.

Like many penal reformers, Eddy realized that the lofty goals of the penitentiary did not measure up to their outcome. Logistical realities and human imperfections got in the way of attaining the penitentiary's aims. But Eddy continued in his efforts to establish humane facilities for prisoners, especially young prisoners, long before separate juvenile justice systems came into existence. His advocacy extended to other states and countries, but not the American South. Expending such effort on governments that allowed slavery was a waste of time. His life symbolizes the history of correctional reform as a series of successes and setbacks.

For more on Thomas Eddy, see below:

- Eddy, T. (1801). *An Account of the State Prison or Penitentiary House in the City of New York.*
- Ekirch, A.A (1943). "Thomas Eddy and the Beginnings of Prison Reform in New York." *New York History* 24 (3): 376–391.
- Knapp, S. L. (1834). *The Life of Thomas Eddy.*
- Philanthropy Roundtable (n.d). "Thomas Eddy." https://www.philanthropyroundtable.org/hall-of-fame/thomas-eddy/, retrieved January 30, 2025.

IMG IV.2

Katharine Bement Davis (1860–1935) was New York City's first female commissioner of corrections, a position she attained at the age 53 after a career as a corrections pioneer, social reformer, social hygienist, and accomplished academic in New York, Pennsylvania, Illinois, and Europe. Born in Buffalo and raised in a lower-middle-class family, Davis worked her way through college teaching nutrition and was sent to Chicago's World Columbian Exposition (World's Fair) in 1893. Her job was to demonstrate how a family of five could live a healthy lifestyle in a two-story home on a $500 monthly income. While in Chicago, Davis became attracted to the idea of imparting her home economics expertise to the lower classes, and she relocated to Philadelphia to work with the city's poor African American community. Establishing a healthy home with an emphasis on good diet, healthy lifestyle, and literacy were her priorities.

In 1897, Davis began working on a doctorate degree at the University of Chicago, a pioneering ambition for a turn-of-the-20th-century female. She also assumed leadership of the Bedford Hills Reformatory for Women in New York, making her formal entrée into the corrections field. Given her background in home economics, it was natural that Davis tried to model the reformatory along the lines of the ideal middle-class home. Davis emphasized homemaking duties, but she prepared her charges for employment in the community as well, offering vocational classes and educating the women about health and medical issues.

John D. Rockefeller, Jr., the premier philanthropist and robber baron in New York, took notice of Davis's work. He invited her to establish the Laboratory of

Social Hygiene, a combination research and social work venture designed to aid New York's female underclass and prostitutes. In 1914, Davis was named New York City's first female commissioner of corrections, at a time when women were not allowed to vote in some states, including New York. She also served as parole board chair. The fact that Davis supervised over 600 employees and thousands of prison inmates of both sexes gave her a bully pulpit to advocate another passion, universal women suffrage, which came to New York in 1917 and to all American women in 1920.

Davis resumed her research on health and sexuality at New York's Bureau of Social Hygiene, taking the radical step of examining the most intimate details of the sex lives of both straight and lesbian females. Unfortunately, Davis joined the bandwagon of Americans (and people in other countries) who advocated eugenics, i.e., breeding of a superior race through sterilization. Katharine Bement Davis retired in 1932 and moved to California, where she died in 1935.

For more on Katharine B. Davis, see below:

- Davis, K.B. (1916). "Probation and Parole" (Report of the Committee of the American Prison Association). *Journal of the American Institute of Criminal Law and Criminology* 7 (2): 165–172.
- Deegan, M.J. (2003). "Katharine Bement Davis (1860-1935)." *Women and Criminal Justice* 14 (2/3): 15–40.
- Eichel, M.J. (1928). "Katharine Bement Davis." *Woman's Journal* 13 (4): 20–21, 41.
- Marshall, E. (1914). "New York's First Woman Commissioner of Corrections." *New York Times* January 11.
- Petrash, A. (2018). *New York's Remarkable Women: Daughters, Wives, Sisters and Mothers Who Shaped History.*

IMG IV.3

Maud Ballington Booth (1865–1948) was the daughter of an Anglican minister in England who, along with her mother, ministered to the poor and destitute in London as a young person. Much to the dismay of her traditionalist Anglican father, Maud became involved with the Salvation Army as a teen. Founded in 1865 in London, the upstart, evangelical Salvation Army was unpopular among established religious leaders in London and throughout Europe.

Maud Charlesworth became inextricably linked to the Salvation Army when she married Ballington Booth, the son of the

Army's founder General William Booth. Maud assumed her husband's first and last name.

The couple was ordered to move to New York City to reorganize the Army chapter there. While living in nearby Montclair, New Jersey, the Booths carried out Salvation Army functions, which included working with at-risk female runaways and prostitutes in the New York slums. Their work brought publicity and much-needed respect for the Army.

When the Booths were reassigned to positions outside the United States, the couple refused and resigned from the Army to establish God's American Volunteers. It was with God's American Volunteers that Maud Booth began working with imprisoned and released inmates. Her primary message was evangelical, spreading her Christian beliefs, encouraging prayer, following the Golden Rule, and obeying the law and prison regulations.

After visiting New York's Sing Sing prison, she established the Volunteer Prison League (VPL) in 1896. The VPL opened Hope Hall in Flushing, New York, a halfway house for released inmates. Hope Halls sprang up in other locales. Maud Booth became more formally involved with correctional organizations, including the American Prison Organization, the Committee on Probation and Parole, and the National Prisoner's Aid Association, all the while spreading her Christian message.

Booth spent much of World War I ministering to soldiers in the United States and Europe, working with the Young Men's Christian Association (YMCA) and United Service Organizations (USO). Maud resettled in the United States after the War and continued her prison assistance work, but health problems slowed her work in the early 1930s. She remained active after her husband's death in 1940. Maud Ballington Booth died in New York in 1948.

For more on Maud Ballington Booth, see below:

- Booth, M.B. (1903). *After Prison, What?*
- Virginia Commonwealth University (n.d.). Maud Ballington Booth. https://socialwelfare.library.vcu.edu/people/booth-maud-ballington/, retrieved January 30, 2025.

George Beto (1916–1991), born in Montana, was a Lutheran minister and "accidental penologist" who presided over the rise of a world-renowned prison system in Texas—only to watch it systematically dismantled by social change and judicial mandate. Beto was as renowned in the academic arena as he was in penological circles.

IMG IV4

George Beto spent most of his childhood in Illinois where his father worked as a Lutheran minister. Following in his father's footsteps, Beto was educated at Concordia Seminary in St. Louis. He moved to Austin, Texas, to teach at Concordia Lutheran College from 1939-1949 and to serve as president until 1959. He earned a master's degree in medieval history, and a doctorate degree in educational administration from the University of Texas at Austin.

While in Austin, Beto became immersed in state politics and the Texas penal system. In 1953, he began work on the Texas prison board. In 1959, Beto became president of Concordia Theological Seminary in Springfield, Illinois. He was appointed to the parole board, a part-time position. While there, he was mentored by Stateville Warden Joseph Ragen.

Beto assumed directorship of the Texas Department of Corrections (TDC) on March 1, 1962, also serving as chief chaplain. Beto believed that prisons served three purposes: (a) to deter crime, (b) to serve as punishment for those who had forfeited the right to live in free society, and (c) to rehabilitate the inmates. Beto acquired the nickname "Walking George" because of his penchant for showing up at TDC units unannounced and walking about prison yards and hallways to talk with whomever he met, both inmates and staff.

Beto set out to run the Texas prison system as an efficient business in agriculture and industry. George Beto did what few prison bosses have done; he made his prison system an international showcase. In 1963, Beto persuaded Governor John Connally to enact a state's use law that required state agencies to buy goods made by prisons. TDC's manufacturing output increased from $600,000 in 1964 to $6 million per year in 1972. Another hallmark of Beto's prison was the building tender (BT) system, something he inherited from previous TDC administrations. The system utilized tough veteran inmates, called *building tenders*, to maintain order and discipline in Texas prisons. The BT system would eventually become a lightning rod for criticism of the TDC.

Beto retired from the TDC in 1972 to become professor at Sam Houston State University in Huntsville, a small east Texas town that is home to several prison units and a location where TDC staff had long been trained. Then he watched as the TDC system disintegrate with inmate lawsuits and prison gangs becoming a new dominant force in TDC prisons. Inmate lawsuits and judicial mandates brought about a TDC that differed radically from the system built and maintained by Beto.

While at Sam Houston State, Beto taught corrections courses. He served as dean of the College of Criminal Justice on two occasions. He did not allow food or drink in his class, and any tardy student would find himself on the receiving end of Beto's piercing glare and sharp wit. Yet he enjoyed informal lunches, banter, and debate with students, having a particular affinity for Asian students.

He visited graduate students, including the author of this book, in the center's basement or "dungeon" just to chat.

In 1991, Beto retired from Sam Houston State and moved to Austin to serve as chief of chaplaincy for the Texas Youth Commission. On November 9, Beto gave his last formal address at Valparaiso University and, citing a lament common among penologists, said, "As I reflect on forty years involvement in the criminal justice system in one capacity or another, I cannot escape the conclusion that the system is no better than it was almost one-half century ago." Beto died of a heart attack on December 9, 1991.

For more on George Beto, see below:

- Crouch, B. and J.W. Marquart (1989). *An Appeal to Justice: Litigated Reform of Texas Prisons.*
- Horton, D.M and G.R. Nielsen (2005). *Walking George: The Life of George John Beto and the Rise of the Modern Texas Prison System.*

IMG IV.5

Leon E. DeKalb (1907–1994) is among those whose life I expect was intriguing, especially because of my bias for probation officers as a former probation officer myself. Leon DeKalb was the first African American to work as a probation officer for the United States Administrative Office of the Courts, i.e., U.S. probation. Was DeKalb the first African American probation officer in the United States? Probably not, but whether a state or municipality hired someone of color prior to DeKalb's appointment cannot be known. What is known is that Leon Dekalb worked for New York City's probation office before joining U.S. probation in the Southern District of New York (Manhattan). He likely had some African American colleagues there.

Born and raised in New York City, DeKalb obtained his bachelor's degree from Lincoln University in Pennsylvania, where he was mentored by fellow Alpha Phi Alpha fraternity brother and future Supreme Court Justice Thurgood Marshall. DeKalb earned his master's degree from Columbia University. Before his probation career, DeKalb worked as a schoolteacher and welfare overseer in Virginia and North Carolina. DeKalb was appointed to the U.S. probation system on December 1, 1941, less than 1 week before the United States entered World War II. He served in the Army for 2 years and attained the rank of second lieutenant.

DeKalb's approach to probation supervision might best be described as "synthetic," a blend of treatment and enforcement. DeKalb was especially interested in helping offenders with alcohol and drug problems at a time when addiction was viewed as more of a moral failing than a disease. Not limited to supervising a caseload, DeKalb conducted workshops for federal judicial officials on the workings of probation and served on the National Council on Crime and Delinquency, an exceptional honor for any probation officer. In 1972, DeKalb achieved another first, becoming the first African American Deputy Chief U.S. Probation Officer. He retired in 1974 after 33 years of service. By that time, 10% of the U.S. probation officers in his district, the Southern District of New York, were African Americans.

DeKalb claimed that he never experienced problems because of his race, saying that his supervisor told all officers that they had a territory to cover and a job to do and that was it. He told Yvonne Samuels, a fellow officer that he mentored, "'Don't give up. Keep trying,' whenever things got tough for one of us in the office. We worked hard to build trust with the individuals we worked with. It was, and still is, important for them to feel comfortable confiding in us, so that we can better help them stay on the right path" (United States Courts, 2021).

The following sources provide more information about Leon DeKalb:

- United States Courts. (2021, February 25). *Leon DeKalb: U.S. probation's first Black officer.*
- https://www.uscourts.gov/news/2021/02/25/leon-dekalb-us-probations-first-black-officer
- file:///C:/Users/jonesg/Downloads/ProQuestDocuments-2024-07-11.pdf
- Boyd, Michael Leon, grandson of Leon E. Dekalb. Telephone and email conversions.
- Correspondence with Noah Joseph and Joshua Sparks, U.S. Probation Southern District New York.

Credits

IMG IV.1: Source: https://nyprisonoriginscom.wordpress.com/julia/quakers-prisons-and-thomas-eddys-newgate-policy/.

IMG IV.2: George Grantham Bain, https://commons.wikimedia.org/wiki/File:Katharine_Bement_Davis.png, 1914.

IMG IV.3: Gertrude Käsebier, https://commons.wikimedia.org/wiki/File:Maud_Ballington_Booth.jpg, 1902.

IMG IV.4: Copyright © by Concordia University Texas. Reprinted with permission.

IMG IV.5: Copyright © by Southern District of New York Probation Office. Reprinted with permission.

CHAPTER 26

John Augustus (1784-1859)

IMG 26.1

John Augustus did not invent probation. In fact, according to the modern definition of probation, John Augustus was not even a probation officer; he performed pretrial supervision, not probation supervision. Unlike most modern probation and pretrial supervision officers, he worked as a volunteer and never received compensation for his work. Despite the differences between Augustus's work and that of modern probation officers, he is rightly credited as the patriarch of modern American probation. Although Augustus's contributions to the genesis of American probation are very significant, he did not live to see how far his innovations would go, even in his hometown.

Some American courts had already begun using prison alternatives before John Augustus began his work. During the 1830s, Massachusetts Judge Peter Oxenbridge Thatcher, after finding a defendant guilty, suspended sentence and allowed her to be free on her own recognizance "for her appearance ... whenever she should be called for, to go at large" (Grinnell, 1941, p. 22). During the 1830s, Massachusetts (illegally) used recognizance as a way of allowing first offenders to escape a criminal conviction.

Unlike many other community corrections pioneers, John Augustus worked with adults. Most correctional innovators, including the founders of the penitentiary, the indeterminate sentence, and the juvenile justice system, directed their efforts toward young offenders, believing that adults over the ages of 25 to 30 were practically beyond help. Augustus did not subscribe to this idea.

Few if any historians have found serious blemishes on Augustus's character or his sincerity. Even criminal justice historian Samuel Walker, author of one of the most cynical works on criminal justice history ever published, said that Augustus had a "genuine sense of compassion for the downtrodden" (Walker, 1997). The worst that can be said about Augustus is that he was puritanical, naive, and generous to a fault, and that his outspokenness alienated those around him. These characteristics were part of his personality and were also his greatest attributes.

Early Life

John Augustus was born in 1784 in Woburn, Massachusetts. Little is known about his childhood or family background. Most of what is known about Augustus is contained in his own account of his work, called *A Report of the Labors of John Augustus*, which also contains some very sketchy biographical and supplementary material contributed by the American Probation and Parole Association (1984). At age 21 Augustus moved to Lexington, Massachusetts, and became a shoemaker. The Jonathan Harrington house, now a Lexington landmark, was Augustus's base from 1811–1827. A successful businessman and landowner, Augustus always possessed a philanthropic mentality as evidenced by his donation of several acres of land to the local Lexington Academy in 1819.

Around 1813, he married Sally, who bore him one daughter named Harriet. Both Sally and Harriet died when Harriet was about 1 year old. Years later, Augustus married Harriet Stearns, who bore one daughter that died at about age 10. Harriet Augustus also gave birth to two sons.

Augustus moved to Boston in 1827 and continued his shoemaking business. He was successful enough to have several assistants work for him, which would eventually free enough time for him to engage in the philanthropy that would make him part of America's correctional history.

The Genesis: Wanderers from Virtue

While operating his shoemaking business, Augustus viewed Boston street life. He witnessed firsthand the activities and sorry states of many drunkards, prostitutes, and petty thieves. He observed the revolving door justice system in Boston, with the same people repeatedly arrested, disappearing for a while, and then reappearing on the streets, only to be arrested again and again.

Augustus was an active member in several temperance societies in the Boston area during the 19th century. Anti-alcohol organizations were a powerful force in 19th century America. Their members viewed alcohol as a social evil that destroyed lives, homes, careers, and the very moral and economic fiber of the entire country. Augustus wanted to rid Boston of the evil of alcohol, an ideal that seems naive by contemporary standards but one that enjoyed considerable popularity among mainstream Protestant America at that time. More importantly, Augustus decided to intervene in the lives of those who suffered the ill effects of alcohol, namely repeated arrests for petty crimes.

Probation Begins

Augustus made his first trip to a local Boston court in 1841. One day, Augustus watched a man who could not pay his fine be arraigned on a charge of drunkenness. Augustus "requested that the man be allowed a short probation period and be placed in his care." From then on, Augustus was a frequent presence in Boston's police and municipal courts. His primary targets at first were male drunkards, but he eventually offered his services to women as well. Augustus would look over the defendants as they were brought into courts and interview them to determine whether they were receptive to his assistance.

In 1856, a Boston journalist named Ball Fenner profiled Augustus for a work called *Raising the Veil*. In *A Report on the Labors of John Augustus*, the American Probation and Parole Association quote Fenner extensively. Fenner provides one of the few external glimpses into Augustus's personality and homelife. Fenner wrote that Augustus's home resembled a harem, except that the women were not attractive and they were not there to indulge his sexual desires. The women in his home were those he tried to assist. There is no indication that Augustus ever tried to take advantage of the women he helped. Likewise, he never exploited the men he helped by requiring them to supply free labor for his business interests.

By Fenner's account, Augustus would fit the modern profile of a type A personality. Fenner described him as a "fidgety old fellow" (American Probation and Parole Association, 1984, p. xxii). He lived in a constant state of excitement and agitation. One passage from *Raising the Veil* reads, "John can talk very rapidly. He will reel off more lines from the end of his tongue in fifteen minutes than any ordinary man could accomplish in four times that space" (American Probation and Parole Association, 1984, p. xxiii). Criminologist Sheldon Glueck called Augustus a "dynamic synthesis of Paul Revere, John Howard (an English penological pioneer), and Florence Nightingale" (American Probation and Parole Association, 1984, p. xxv).

Whether Augustus was aggressive about promoting his religious or political beliefs is not clear. Ball Fenner wrote that Augustus would not share his religious or political ideas with anyone unless asked. But Augustus was fanatical about his work. He was also very brash. He never hesitated to argue with judges, even in open court. One such encounter, recounted by Augustus in his memoir, provides an example of this brazenness (American Probation and Parole Association, 1984, pp. 9–10):

> Mr. John Augustus, who was present, and standing near the prisoner, mildly observed, "she said, your Honor, that she had been in the House of Correction *once*."
>
> *Justice*. She did not say so,—I heard what the woman said, that *she never was in the House of Correction in her life.*

> *Police Officer.* That is true, your Honor, she said so.
>
> *John Augustus*—(warmly), But I said she did not say so! I heard the words she used, and I appeal to the spectators.
>
> Considerable excitement began to manifest itself among the few spectators of this highly dignified dispute, and several voices exclaimed, "She did not say so,—Augustus is right!" In fact there were not three persons present but heard Bridget distinctly admit that she had been in the House of Correction once.
>
> *Officer.* Silence in the court!
>
> *Justice*—(with temper), Mr. Augustus, hold your tongue, sir! Sit down, or I'll direct an officer to take you out of the room!
>
> *Augustus.* I *will* say what I heard.
>
> *Justice.* (Rising with a *show* of dignity), you can't say any thing! Take a seat, instantly sir! (The incorrigible philanthropist seated himself, and the justice readjusted his spectacle.) Sir, you intrude upon the patience of the court; you contradict me, and appeal to the spectators, as though I did not know what was said as well as they. (Augustus rising) Keep your seat and be silent, or I'll have you taken out of the room. What right have you to interfere in a question of veracity between a highly respectable officer, so far as I know, and this woman?
>
> *Augustus.* But I wish to explain the—
>
> *Justice.* Not another word, sir!

Augustus was particular about who he assisted. He would target those who "were indicted for their first offence, and whose hearts were not wholly depraved, but gave promise of better things" (American Probation and Parole Association, 1984, p. 19). Unlike today's community corrections and pretrial service officers, who use scientifically validated assessment instruments to gauge an offender's needs and risks, Augustus had to rely on his own intuition. But he tried to use a measuring stick of the offender's amenability to assistance based on his own experience. Augustus would determine depravity and promise by interviewing defendants as they arrived in court. He would consider his estimation of a person's background and character and likely influences in the individual's future. Although his methods were not scientific by modern standards, and Augustus admitted that he did not rigidly adhere to these criteria, his practice of targeting first offenders and those who seemed amenable to change set the standard by which probation operated for many decades and is still largely used today. In fact, although Augustus was not scientific in his assessment of offenders fit for probation supervision, he probably exerted more effort in this area than most courts do today, as most offenders are placed on probation for the court's administrative convenience or because of plea negotiations or sentencing guidelines.

Augustus also set the standard for probation work by not defending his charges when they would not cooperate with his efforts at assistance. His offer of help was not unconditional. When bailing an offender, his announcement to the court would often follow this line: "I'll bail that young woman for thirty days, your honor. If I can't reform her, I'll bring her into court at the expiration of that time, to be disposed of as you will" (American Probation and Parole Association, 1984, p. xxii).

Augustus was conscious of what would later be called "labeling theory" and both formal and informal collateral consequences of an arrest or conviction. According to Augustus, a person that was punished throughout their life, subject to "the finger of scorn," (American Probation and Parole Association, 1984, p. 49) took on poor self-esteem. Augustus called female offenders, many of whom were very young, "wanderers from virtue" often due to being the victim of "heartless seducers." They also suffered the label and thus could only be associated "with those who would plunge her soul deeper in the pit of error."

At the time Augustus was conducting his work in the 1840s and 1850s, there were no distinctions between adult and juvenile courts. Juvenile courts would not exist for another 5 or 6 decades. Juveniles went through the same judicial process as adults. Augustus assisted children as young as 6 or 7 years. Augustus often targeted teenagers for assistance. In his memoirs, he recalled one rather touching account of his efforts to assist a group of teenaged boys. It demonstrates his selfless dedication to his volunteer work. It also is one of the few occasions in which Augustus referred to his work as "probation" supervision. The following is excerpted from his written account (American Probation and Parole Association, 1984, p. 34):

> In 1847, I bailed nineteen boys, from seven to fifteen years of age, and in bailing them it was understood, and agreed by the court, that their cases should be continued from term to term for several months, as a season of probation; thus each month at the calling of the docket, I would appear in court, make my

> report, and thus the cases would pass on for five or six months. At the expiration of this term, twelve of the boys were brought into court at one time, and the scene formed a striking and highly pleasing contrast with their appearance when first arraigned. Seven of the number were too poor to pay a fine, although the court fixed the amount at ten cents each, and of course I paid it for them; the parents of the other boys were able to pay the cost ... this class of boys could be saved from crime and punishment, by the plan which I had marked out, and this was admitted by the judges in both courts.

Peter Funk Philanthropist

Naturally, Augustus had his detractors, especially among the police ranks. In a scenario that would seem incredible today, police officers were paid a small bonus if their courtroom testimony resulted in a conviction and they received an additional fee if the conviction led to incarceration. If court officers knew a case was coming in which Augustus might bail the defendant, they would wait for him to leave and then ask the case to be called.

Some called him a "mock philanthropist." He was accused of encouraging criminal behavior through his "mollycoddling" of offenders. Once, when he became openly indignant because court officers had not saved a seat for him in court, he had a physical altercation with a constable that tried to remove him. Some charged that Augustus sought to profit from his intervention. One newspaper report was especially vicious, calling Augustus a "Peter Funk" (shill bidder or swindler) philanthropist who took advantage of defendants, especially females, and needed to be taught some "decency" (American Probation and Parole Association, 1984, p. 34). August replied that bailing prisoners "drains my pockets instead of enriching me," (American Probation and Parole Association, 1984, p. 103) that profiting from bailing poor people out of jail was impossible, and that he had to work nights at his shoe shop to make up for time lost in court.

Although many police officers and judges disliked Augustus, several local judges appreciated his work, most notably Peter Oxenbridge Thatcher and some in the local news media. Word of his efforts spread around Boston, and some contributed to help him out. He received no financial assistance from 1841-1842, during which he spent his own money. In 1843, he received $758 in contributions. He received $1,213 per year from 1844-1846. He was sued four times for the bail money owed when a defendant absconded, but most of the people he served fared well. He received approximately $1,776 each year from 1847-1852, the year he penned his personal memoirs.

Decline, Death, and Legacy

Augustus kept meticulous records of the number of people he bailed and assisted, including the amounts he paid for bail. From the time he started in 1841 until the time he was forced to stop in 1858, Augustus had supervised 1,152 men and 794 women. Augustus's generosity ruined his business. He received financial support from several well-known philanthropists, such as Horace Mann, Theodore Parker, and Wendell Phillips. But that did not rescue Augustus from financial peril. Augustus eventually went broke and gave up his shoemaking business before his death in 1859 at the age of 75.

Augustus did not live to see probation become an integral part of the criminal justice system. That task would fall to his successors, most of whom supported Augustus during his lifetime. Augustus did not even live to see Massachusetts appoint America's first paid probation officer—Edward Savage, a Boston police captain, in 1878, 19 years after Augustus's death. Although it is likely that someone else would have eventually started probation had Augustus not performed his work, it is no coincidence that the first paid probation officer worked in Boston and that other pioneering probation and pretrial service work originated in the Northeast, especially in Massachusetts.

As Augustus's labors lacked the flash and salaciousness of so many other criminal justice pioneers, relatively little has been written about him, and Hollywood has never produced a major work about his efforts. A made-for-television movie was aired in 1955, titled *John Augustus: Sentence Deferred*. It starred Edgar Buchanan as Augustus and was promoted by film legend Barbara Stanwyck. The film paints an overly rosy picture of Augustus's demise, but it also portrays some of the obstacles and successes that he encountered.

Augustus's idealism is seldom found in American courthouses today, and his unswerving devotion to rehabilitation is not as common in probation supervision as it once was. Augustus would frown on the law enforcement focus that overtook probation in the 21st century, and, if he were alive today, he would care little for research reports suggesting that rehabilitation does not work. Augustus believed that human beings could be redeemed. He believed that substance abuse was the great evil of his time, and he believed that as a "probation officer," he was performing God's work by assisting petty criminals. Augustus did not care how many failures he experienced with his charges, if there was one success. His philosophy is best summed up in an adaptation from the New Testament letter of James, chapter 5 verse 20, which he related to Ball Fenner: "I don-no what proportion (of his clientele are reformed), but suppose one out of ten was reclaimed, would not that be well worth the time, labor and money that is expended on the whole? Do we not read that he who turns one sinner from the error of his ways, shall save a soul from death, and hide a multitude of sins?" Apparently John Augustus thought so, which is the reason that his name lives on as the father of probation.

Sources and Suggested Readings

American Probation and Parole Association. (1955). *John Augustus: Sentence deferred* [Video].

American Probation and Parole Association. (1984; original publication date 1852). *A report of the labours of John Augustus—Bicentennial Edition.*

Anonymous. (1858). *Letter concerning the labors of Mr. John Augustus, the well-known philanthropist, from one who knows him.*

Grinnell, Frank W. (1941). The common law history of probation—An illustration of the equitable growth of criminal law. *Journal of Criminal Law and Criminology, 32*(1), 15–34.

Lindner, Charles. (2006). John Augustus, father of probation & the anonymous letter. *Federal Probation, 70*(1), 77–78.

Lindner, Charles. (2007). Thacher, Augustus, & Hill—The path to statutory probation in the United States & England. *Federal Probation, 71*(3), 36–41.

Panzarella, Robert. (2002). Theory and practice of probation in the report of John Augustus, *Federal Probation, 66*(3), 38-42.

Walker, Samuel. (1997). *Popular justice: A history of American criminal justice* (2nd ed.). Oxford University Press.

Discussion Questions

1. How is John Augustus's work similar and different from that of modern probation officers?
2. Was John Augustus's religious devotion a positive or negative legacy for American community corrections?

Credit

IMG 26.1: Curtis, https://www.nps.gov/people/john-augustus.htm, 1848.

CHAPTER 27

John Haviland (1792–1852)

IMG 27.1

The Commonwealth of Pennsylvania provided the blueprint for the American penitentiary concept. The concept of solitary confinement and hard labor was the conceptual brainchild of Pennsylvania penologists. One of the first prisons in America was the Walnut Street city jail in Philadelphia, which had been alternately used as a military prison, temporary detention facility, and as a long-term facility throughout the 18th and early 19th centuries. But the Walnut Street jail could not accommodate the Pennsylvania concept. Although others devised the concept of solitary confinement and hard labor that defined the Pennsylvania system, it took the talent and efforts of English-born architect John Haviland to put the Pennsylvania system into operation.

During the early years of the American penitentiary, two systems competed for preeminence on the national and world stage of penology. New York's Auburn system, or the Congregate system, emphasized group work. The Pennsylvania system placed a premium on solitary confinement, thus providing the inmate an opportunity to make penitence, hence the word "penitentiary." In theory, solitary confinement would isolate the inmate from unhealthy or sinful influences that were partially responsible for the inmate's incarceration. This idea presented a considerable challenge to any architect.

The concept of the Pennsylvania system originated in 1787 with a group of reformers called the Philadelphia Society for Alleviating the Miseries of Public Prisons. The group's name was later changed to the Pennsylvania Prison Society. Several driving forces were behind the establishment of the penitentiary. One was the thought that penitentiaries would serve as a humane alternative to corporal and shaming punishments administered in public. Another was that offenders would seek penitence if left alone to reflect on their actions.

Early Life and Career

John Haviland was born on December 12, 1792, near Taunton, England, the son of Anne Cobley Haviland and James Haviland, a prominent Anglican minister. Haviland, at 15, was assigned to work with James Elmes, a successful London-based architect and writer. After acquiring the needed skills to set out on his own, Haviland left England for St. Petersburg, Russia, around 1815.

Haviland stayed in Russia for 1 year before immigrating to the United States. He met several people in Russia that significantly influenced his career and life. He met John Quincy Adams, the American minister (ambassador) to Russia and future United States president. Adams wrote papers of introduction on Haviland's behalf to U.S. President James Monroe. Another Russian that had a strong influence on Haviland was Count Nikolai Semenovich Mordvinov, a naval minister and the husband of Haviland's aunt. Mordvinov was a good friend of Englishman John Howard, the world-renowned penal reformer that passed away in 1790 while touring Russian prisons. Haviland's interactions with his Russian uncle spurred his interest in prison architecture. Haviland also met George von Sonntagg, an American-born admiral in the Russian navy. It was von Sonntagg who encouraged Haviland to immigrate to the United States, advising him that prospects for a successful architectural career were better in the United States than in Russia.

Haviland arrived in Philadelphia in September 1816, one of the few skilled architects in the young nation. Shortly after his arrival, he married Mary von Sonntagg Wells, a widow with two children and the sister of George von Sonntagg. The couple would have two more children, one of whom, Edward, would also become an architect.

American architecture had been dormant for several years because of the War of 1812, and Haviland found Philadelphia ripe with opportunities. Not only was Haviland sought out for his penchant for creative designs in architecture, but Americans were interested in his ideas on how to install central plumbing and heating systems. One of his first jobs that received the attention of American government leaders and builders was a series of volumes he wrote called *The Builder's Assistant*, a pioneering work for American builders and carpenters with little exposure to European architects trained in classic Greek and Roman orders of architecture. Haviland's first major project in Philadelphia was the design of the First Presbyterian Church, which was constructed in 1820.

Eastern Penitentiary and Beyond

The design of Eastern State Penitentiary would garner worldwide fame for Haviland and solidify his place in the history of American criminal justice. At that time, Pennsylvania was at the forefront of the penitentiary movement in the 1820s, largely due to Quaker influence. The penitentiary as a place to isolate offenders and allow them to reflect on their misdeeds and make penitence for them was an emerging concept in American penology—an idea without practical implementation. Haviland's design made that concept a reality.

Haviland's design for Eastern was adopted, but actual construction of the facility originally fell to a rival architect named William Strickland. Soon after construction began, Strickland was fired and replaced by Haviland. Construction on the prison began in 1821 and was finished sometime between 1823 and 1825. The genius of Haviland's design made him and Eastern the object of attention around the world.

At the time Eastern was constructed, it occupied 11 acres just outside Philadelphia. It opened its doors to prisoners on October 23, 1829, and was regarded by some as western civilization's first modern penitentiary. Although Western Penitentiary, a less impressive structure, had already been constructed near Pittsburgh, Eastern immediately generated attention. Two visitors to Eastern were Frenchmen Gustave de Beaumont and Alexis de Tocqueville, whose 1831 observations about America are classics in the study of American history, penology, and political science. They praised the prison, but Charles Dickens, the famed English novelist, did not, calling it in his 1842 visit "cruel and wrong" (Brewer, 2017, title).

The first thing one noticed at Eastern was the foreboding austerity and enormity of the prison. By design, Eastern, with its Gothic facade, resembles a combination giant fortress and castle, designed to intimidate its residents. Haviland designed the cells large enough to accommodate only one prisoner, as solitary confinement was the most essential aspect of the penitentiary idea. Haviland also faced the challenge of making the cells large enough to allow inmates to work in them; each cell was used as a one-man workshop. The cells had high-walled exercise pens outside so that prisoners could exercise outdoors and remain in solitude at the same time.

Security was also a concern with which Haviland had to contend. He adopted an idea from English philosopher and penologist Jeremy Bentham. Haviland's design was a radial plan in which a centrally located hub or station provided staff the ability to look down several corridors almost simultaneously. To fully implement the Pennsylvania concept of total isolation, inmates were disallowed from speaking with each other. Enforcing this ideal was laid at Haviland's feet as well. To accomplish this aim, Haviland designed the prison's corridors and the pipes that ran along the corridors to be airy enough to detect the slightest sound, which would carry down the corridor to the guard station located in the middle of the building.

A challenge that faced all institutional facilities in the 19th century was sanitation, especially waste disposal. Flush toilets, septic tanks, and sophisticated municipal sewage systems were practically nonexistent in the 19th century, and prisons and jails were always unspeakably filthy, smelly, and disease-ridden. Through Haviland's design, Eastern State Penitentiary became the first large-scale building in the United States to have indoor flush toilets. Each cell had its own water tap and heating system, something found in only the most affluent American households at the time.

National and International Influence

Other states and countries adopted the Pennsylvania concept, and with it, Haviland's design. Haviland's services were much in demand after the construction of Eastern. In 1830, the Pennsylvania legislature authorized the revamping of Western Penitentiary in Pittsburgh, with the conditions that it be designed to implement the Pennsylvania system of solitary confinement and that John Haviland be hired as the architect. Haviland was paid $2,000 per year and, because he began to split his time between Pittsburgh and Philadelphia, was given $300 in traveling expenses.

On February 10, 1834, the Western Penitentiary designed by Haviland opened with 108 cells to wide critical acclaim. One observer described the cells as "well ventilated, with sufficient light, and an admirable apparatus for observing cleanliness. The cells themselves are built of freestone, in a manner which reflects great credit on the skill and judgment of the architect and workmen" (DePuy, 1954, p. 133).

In addition to the penitentiaries in Philadelphia and Pittsburgh, Haviland designed prisons in Rhode Island and New Jersey. The New Jersey prison followed an Egyptian design, as did a prison Haviland designed in New York, called the Halls of Justice, which was nicknamed "The Tombs." The Gothic style at Eastern was evident in his designs of the Pennsylvania Fire Insurance Company and the Pennsylvania Institute for the Deaf and Dumb. Haviland designed penitentiaries for Missouri and Arkansas, and he designed county prisons in Harrisburg, Reading, and Lancaster counties in Pennsylvania. He also designed the Harrisburg State Hospital (originally The Pennsylvania State Lunatic Hospital).

Setbacks and Advances

Haviland's architectural skills did not save the Pennsylvania concept. The prison system in Pennsylvania fell victim to its popularity with the public and with judges by becoming overcrowded. Inmates had to double up in cells. Isolation, an extremely flawed idea to begin with, went away for practical reasons. The system of silence, also a flawed concept, gradually became impossible to enforce. The Pennsylvania system of isolation and silence was founded on Quaker religious ideals rather than any scientific hypothesis. Being quiet and sitting in contemplative meditation may have made for meaningful worship experiences, but as a way of institutional life, it was fundamentally flawed. The system was officially abandoned in 1913, though it had gradually broken down several decades prior.

Haviland's career as an architect thrived throughout the 1830s and 1840s, thanks to his work with Eastern and other Philadelphia landmarks, including several churches and theaters. He opened a drawing academy and taught at the Franklin Institute (later sold and renamed the Atwater Kent Museum), a building he designed. In 1833, he revised a classic 1805 work titled *Young Carpenter's Assistant*, which was originally written by Owen Biddle. In 1836, Haviland cofounded the Institute of American Architects, a forerunner to the American Institute of Architects.

Haviland's most severe professional setback came about because of his work on Philadelphia's Labyrinth Garden in 1828. He invested his own money in its construction and operation, and the venture turned sour, compounding problems brought about by other ill-fated real estate speculations. At the time that his debts were mounting, Haviland was under contract with the federal government to design the U.S. Norfolk Naval Hospital in Virginia. To avoid bankruptcy, Haviland diverted government funds for the Norfolk project to cover his debts. His misdeeds were discovered, and although he was not criminally prosecuted, the result was the termination of federal government contracts and a permanent stain on his reputation.

Death and Legacy

In 1958, the city of Philadelphia officially designated Eastern as historic property. It was designated as a historic landmark by the federal government in 1965. Its historical notoriety was boosted by housing famous criminals, including "Slick Willie" Sutton, a notorious Depression-era bank robber who escaped from Eastern in 1945 (only to be recaptured shortly), and Al "Scarface" Capone, the Prohibition-era bootlegger and crime kingpin of Chicago.

With the facility in general disrepair and becoming increasingly unsafe, Eastern State Penitentiary closed its doors in January 1970. Efforts to demolish the deteriorating facility were floated throughout the 1970s and 1980s, but a group of concerned architects, penologists, and other citizens lobbied Philadelphia Mayor Wilson Goode to prevent commercial interests from taking over Eastern. Their efforts were successful, and Eastern opened for limited tours in 1988. Thanks to a grant from the Pew Charitable Trust, the facility was restored well enough to open its doors for daily tours in 1994. Today the prison and its museum attract more than 65,000 visitors each year. Its eerie atmosphere, even in the daytime, has made it one of Philadelphia's favorite party spots every Halloween, a tradition that started (illegally) during the 1970s while the facility was abandoned. Hard hats are required for anyone who enters the prison because of the danger of falling objects.

One also notices that Eastern has two parts, one from the original construction and another section constructed long after Haviland's death. Against expectations, the newer portions are not in better condition than the much older portions designed and built by John Haviland. This is a credit to the quality of Haviland's work and an indication of how concern over quality of prison construction declined in the late 19th and 20th centuries.

John Haviland died of a stroke on March 28, 1852, in his Philadelphia home at the age of 59. More than 150 years after Haviland's death, the place of the penitentiary in American history remains undecided. Is the penitentiary good, bad, or a necessary evil? That is a question beyond the scope of this writing, but however one chooses to assess the place of the prison in American history, the name John Haviland is inextricably linked to that history.

Sources and Suggested Readings

Ashmead, Isaac. (1852). *Obituary notice of John Haviland, esq.,* [Pamphlet].

Benson, Bronwyn Mroz. (2015, August 10). John Haviland and radial prisons. https://whatsomeonewrotedown.wordpress.com/2015/08/10/john-haviland-and-radial-prisons/ date of retrieval January 11, 2024.

Brewer, Kirstie. (2017, September 29). Over a century ago, Dickens said it was cruel, wrong and "tampered with the brain." So why is solitary confinement still allowed? *Prospect.* https://www.prospectmagazine.co.uk/politics/45096/over-a-century-ago-dickens-said-it-was-cruel-wrong-and-tampered-with-the-brain.-so-why-is-solitary-confinement-still-allowed#:~:text=Charles%20Dickens%20was%20in%20America,the%20mysteries%20of%20the%20brain.%E2%80%9D, accessed August 8, 2024.

Cohen, Jeffrey A. (2002). Haviland, John (1792–1852), architect. *American national biography online.* Oxford University Press. https://www.anb.org/search?q=john+haviland&searchBtn=Search&isQuickSearch=true

DePuy, LeRoy B. (1954). The triumph of the "Pennsylvania system" at the state's penitentiaries. *Pennsylvania History: A Journal of Mid-Atlantic Studies, 21*(2), 128–144.

Independence Hall Association. (n.d.). John Haviland. *U.S. History.org.* https://www.ushistory.org/people/arch_haviland.htm

Johnston, Norman B. (1955). John Haviland. *The Journal of Criminal Law, Criminology & Police Science, 45*(5), 509–519.

Johnston, N. B., Finkel, K., & Cohen, J. A. (1994). *Eastern State Penitentiary: Crucible of good intentions.* Philadelphia Museum of Art for the Eastern State Penitentiary Task Force of the Preservation Coalition of Greater Philadelphia.

Mannheim, Herman. (1955, February). John Haviland, *The Journal of Criminal Law, Criminology and Police Science*, *45*, 5.

Discussion Questions

1. What would the state of American penitentiaries be were it not for architects like John Haviland?
2. What does John Haviland's work say about the need for penologists to appreciate other academic disciplines, including architecture?

Credit

IMG 27.1: John Neagle, https://commons.wikimedia.org/wiki/File:John_Haviland_MET_DT243863.jpg, 1828.

CHAPTER 28

Dorothea Dix (1802–1887)

IMG 28.1

One of the greatest challenges facing American society is proper treatment of its mentally ill. The American criminal justice system has been on the front lines of this challenge for more than 2 centuries. Courts and lawmakers wrestle with definitions of insanity and other mental health issues brought up by defense attorneys seeking to mitigate the crimes committed by their clients. Even more vexing is the problem of the chronically mentally ill that continually populate American jails and prisons—many of which are ill-equipped to treat these inmates. Although this problem remains, Dorothea Dix made positive contributions to the state of America's mentally ill population. She was one of the most passionate social reformers of the 19th century.

Early Life

Dorothea Lynde Dix was born on April 4, 1802, in Hampden, Maine, one of three children born to Joseph and Mary Bigelow Dix. As a descendant of Boston's elite social and economic class, Dorothea Dix, nicknamed "Dolly" by her parents (Logan, 2017, para. 1), lived a life of privilege, attending the finest schools in New England. Despite being financially comfortable, her childhood was not a happy one. Her parents were alcoholics, and Joseph was abusive.

The Dix's climb up the Boston social ladder was halted when Dorothea Dix's paternal grandfather died in 1809. Joseph Dix, a minister and wealthy landowner thanks to his deceased father, moved the family to Barnard, Vermont, in 1812, just as war with the British erupted. In Vermont, Joseph Dix opened a business selling tracts and sermons written and delivered by John Wesley, the Methodist faith pioneer. To the consternation of her Methodist parents, Dorothea Dix found her religious home in Unitarianism.

Unhappy with her home situation, Dix ran away to her grandmother's house at age 12 but returned shortly thereafter. She left for good in 1816 at the age of 14 to live with Sarah Fiske, a wealthy relative in Worcester, Massachusetts. She eventually settled in Boston, taking custody of her 9-year-old brother Charles after their father's death in 1821. Dix biographer Thomas Brown (1998) states that her childhood and early adulthood were marked by a frustrating search for happiness and a sense of purpose. She opened a school, but was unpopular with her students because of her sternness, which led to the closing of the school. She prized her sense of independence and dated frequently but never married, which led to frequent bouts of depression. Health problems dogged Dix throughout her young life, including a bout with tuberculosis in 1827 and a collapsed lung in 1836.

Dix found a niche in writing, publishing five children's textbooks and storybooks in the late 1820s. Thanks to the help of wealthy New England friends, Dix toured extensively throughout New England and other parts of the world. She traveled to the Caribbean in 1830, spending most of her time in the Danish West Indies (now the U.S. Virgin Islands).

There she had her first encounter with slavery, an extinct institution in New England by that time. Dix held an attitude toward slavery that was inconsistent with her otherwise compassionate attitude toward the downtrodden. While slavery was tearing America apart in the first half of the 19th century, Dix could not understand the uproar over an institution whose cruelty seemed to escape her attention. She made scant mention of slavery in her writings from the West Indies, and in later years, Dix would decry both militant proponents and opponents of slavery. During a visit to Raleigh, North Carolina, in 1848, Dix remarked, "The negros [sic] are gay, obliging, and anything but miserable," and "thoughtless and irresponsible" (Brown, 1998, p. 158).

Dix's disregard for the evils of slavery would serve her subsequent crusade for the mentally ill in a roundabout way. Had she been a staunch abolitionist she would have been unable to gain access to southern mental hospitals and jails, let alone legislatures in southern states, as the southern and northern states grew increasingly alienated from one another. Southern slave owners and northern "moderates" blamed "radical" abolitionists for tearing the country apart. Dix was like many northern politicians who were ambivalent about slavery but did not think it their place to tell southerners what to do. These northern "moderates" included three U.S. presidents, Millard Fillmore of New York, Franklin Pierce of New Hampshire, and James Buchanan of Pennsylvania, the presidents of the 1850s typically ranked among the worst in U.S. history.

Dix's interest in education and spreading Christianity led her to helping prisoners and eventually the mentally ill. The major turning point in Dix's life, which gave her the mission she had always sought, came in 1841. She visited the Middlesex (Massachusetts) County jail where she taught Bible study to the inmates and invited local ministers to preach sermons. She generated enough local support to start a prison library and construct a prison chapel.

Dix and the Mentally Ill

Dix experienced another seminal life event as she read a pamphlet written by a Boston physician named Edward Jarvis. The pamphlet, titled *Insanity and Insane Asylums*, discussed an emerging strategy for the treatment of the mentally ill. The strategies for treating the mentally ill had long been characterized by primitive, aggressive measures such as bleeding, and it was assumed by many in the religious community that most mentally ill people were under the control of malevolent spirits and therefore needed to be avoided. Jarvis advocated "moral treatment" (Northampton State Hospital, n.d., para. 4), attempting to instill a sense of self-control through gentle persuasion. Dix saw memorization of Bible scripture as key ingredient to this approach.

Dix began visiting prisons, jails, almshouses, and insane asylums throughout Massachusetts in 1842. She was appalled at the living conditions of the mentally ill, but she would attribute them more to pervasive and malign neglect than outright abuse, although some mentally ill inmates were abused by their captors and other violent prisoners. As she was led into separate facilities for mentally ill inmates, she was met by screams and moans from people living in unfathomably barbaric conditions, even by the standards of that era. In some facilities, mentally ill prisoners lived in worse conditions than people in the general prison population. In one Massachusetts facility, mentally ill inmates were not even allowed to have heat from a fire because authorities believed their charges would set themselves and the facility on fire. She found this to be the case in most other facilities in other states as well. Adopting the moral treatment approach to address the mentally ill, Dix used religious instruction and literature as her primary treatment tools.

Lobbying for Change

Dix was not content to work for prison reform within the prisons. She wanted to effect change at a higher level. Dix analyzed Massachusetts's laws on the treatment of the insane and was determined to change those aspects that she viewed as unfair to the mentally ill. Dix wrote *Memorial to the Legislature of Massachusetts, 1843.* Claiming to have relied solely on firsthand observations,

Dix wrote, according to Thomas Brown (1998), "I tell what I have seen!" (Dix, 2006, p. 622). She claims to have seen the mentally ill in "cages, closets, cellars, stalls, pens … chained, naked, beaten with rods, and lashed into obedience" (Dix, 2006, p. 622). Although *Memorial* was widely renowned by its readers, it did not persuade the Massachusetts legislature to enact any significant change.

Despite this setback, Dix knew she had found her calling. Dix traveled to other states seeking similar reforms. She traveled tirelessly, to Vermont, New Hampshire, Rhode Island, and into Canada, usually by stagecoach at night so she could visit facilities during the day. She was successful in Rhode Island, persuading private donors to establish an insane asylum for the poor near Providence.

In 1843, Dix went to New York, visiting 60 county jails in 10 weeks, an arduous task given the primitive modes of transport available at that time. She presented a report to the New York legislature in 1843, evaluating each jail and almshouse she visited, noting that abuse and neglect were common. She reported seeing insane paupers confined to dark cellars, chained to beds, and scarred from beatings. Dix advocated a new facility for insane paupers, but only succeeded in having wings added to an existing mental health facility in Utica.

Dix kept up her hectic pace, visiting Pennsylvania, New Jersey, Ohio, Maryland, and Virginia. Dix gradually endeared herself to the medical establishment in the states she visited. No longer a lone pioneer, she sought to enrich the moral approach to treating the mentally ill. Unlike many other "experts" of her day, she thought that mental illness was attributable to brain lesions or defects rather than spiritual flaws. In addition to writing, Dix found that she had a penchant for personal lobbying. Reluctant legislators would often come around to Dix's point of view after meeting with her in person. By 1845, Dix had traveled 10,000 miles over a 3-year period, visited more than 300 almshouses, 300 county jails, 18 state prisons, and numerous hospitals and insane asylums.

In 1845, Dix weighed in on one of the great penological debates of the 19th century. The debate was whether the congregate system in New York prisons was superior to the solitary system in Pennsylvania, especially the Eastern State Penitentiary near Philadelphia. Dix decided that the Eastern system was better because perpetual isolation was more conducive to spiritual growth and rehabilitation than having prisoners work in groups. She was oblivious to the now well-known deleterious effects of isolation. She also advocated corporal punishment for some unruly inmates, not unlike even the most fervent penal reformers of her day. According to criminal justice historian Samuel Walker, Dix stated that whipping might be the only way "by which an insurrectionary spirit can be conquered" (Walker, 1998, p. 89). She also advocated the "prudent and careful use" (Walker, 1998, p. 89) of shower baths. Dix taught Sunday school at Eastern and recruited ministers to deliver sermons, her reputation well-established enough to attract the best-known clergy. Her 1845 publication

Remarks on Prisons and Prison Discipline in the United States made her one of the most admired women in American public life during the 1840s.

Dix began earnest reform efforts in southern states, something that many New England reformers would never have attempted, given that the aversion to slavery would have precluded serious efforts to work with southern politicians. She successfully advocated for building an insane asylum for poor prisoners in Kentucky. She was successful in other southern states as well, ignoring the plight of slaves but tirelessly advocating for mentally ill prisoners.

Throughout the 1850s, the increasingly rancorous debates over slavery and secession annoyed Dix, who could not understand why such a seemingly innocuous institution could threaten the very existence of the United States as a nation. Dix even supported the infamous *Dred Scott v. John F. A. Sandford* (1857) decision of the United States Supreme Court, which essentially placed an official government imprimatur on the institution of slavery, declaring that slaves, as noncitizens, had no rights in U.S. courts. She was a frequent visitor to the presidential mansion (the term "White House" was not yet commonly used) during the 1850-1853 administration of Millard Fillmore. Had Fillmore alone been the deciding voice, Dix would have been successful in having enormous federal funds set aside for institutions for mentally ill paupers, but Fillmore, one of the weakest presidents in American history, could not persuade Congress to accede to Dix's request. Fillmore's successor, Franklin Pierce, an even more feckless president and a slavery appeaser, was not enthusiastic about Dix or her efforts.

Efforts in Europe

During the 1850s, Dix traveled to Europe and Russia to engage in similar reform efforts. In 1854 and 1855, she worked in England and Scotland, which resulted in Queen Victoria's appointment of a royal commission to investigate the plight of England's mentally ill. Parliament passed laws mandating better treatment for the mentally ill throughout Great Britain. Although her reform efforts in Europe were partially successful, she was frustrated with the inertia of European governments and wrote that Americans should be grateful for what they had.

Another reason for Dix visiting Europe was Florence Nightingale. Nightingale, a British-born nurse, had become an internationally renowned figure for her efforts to aid wounded soldiers in the Crimean War, a military quagmire that pitted Russia against Great Britain, France, and Turkey. Dix viewed Nightingale, now acknowledged as the matriarch of modern nursing, as her role model. Although Dix never met Nightingale, she met other European dignitaries, including Pope Pius IX.

Dix and the Civil War

Although Dix's indifference to slavery made her anathema to northern abolitionists, she was viewed positively in the South, where many saw her as a unifying and intersectional healing force. Despite such hopes, America erupted in civil war in 1861. The outbreak of war saddened Dix, but she viewed the war as a necessary evil to heal America of its divisions. Although her efforts to aid mentally ill prisoners slowed because of the war, Dix set out to become the Florence Nightingale of America. She treated war prisoners on both sides, seeing all of America's war casualties as victims of the American penchant for giving in to uncontrolled passions, as Thomas Brown states (1998). She thought that the Civil War was much ado about very little, and that she should act as a divinely inspired healer in the bloody rift between the two sides.

Dix met President Abraham Lincoln at the White House in April 1861. She petitioned President Lincoln and Secretary of War Simon Cameron to oversee administration of military hospitals. Although military hospitals are commonplace today, they were not in 1861. Only Florence Nightingale had undertaken such an effort before. Dix had many obstacles to overcome, one of which was military doctors' opposition to having women serve as nurses in a military setting. Medical qualifications for nurses were minimal, so Dix, who had no formal medical training of her own, made moral and spiritual qualifications the most important factor in deciding who should serve.

Characteristically, Dix plunged into her new job with all the energy she could muster. But as the Civil War dragged on and became much bloodier than the Union had predicted, it took its toll on Dix. She lost weight and suffered another bout of extreme depression. Her vision of the war acting as a form of spiritual cleansing faded. Dix's public reputation took a pounding as well, with many people, especially disgruntled job seekers, critical of her administration of the military nursing department.

Dix survived the Civil War, receiving two national flags for her efforts to aid Union soldiers, and she resumed her advocacy on behalf of the mentally ill in prisons, jails, and hospitals in the United States and other countries. She even convinced the Japanese Special Chargé d'Affaires, who was paying a visit to Washington, to have an insane asylum built in Kyoto. However, she did not pursue reform on behalf of the mentally ill with the same vigor as she had before the Civil War, partly because she was well into her 60s by this time.

Retirement, Death, and Legacy

In October 1881, she visited the New Jersey State Lunatic Asylum in Trenton—a building that existed as one of the crowning achievements of her career as a reformer. While there she collapsed, complaining of chills and pain in her lungs. When it became evident that Dix needed constant care, arrangements were made for her to live in the asylum permanently, alongside the residents for whom she had so tirelessly advocated years before. Although her medical attendants predicted that Dix would not live for long after her admission, her condition stabilized and she was able to live a somewhat normal existence within the asylum, reading constantly and entertaining guests as best as her health would allow. Gradually, Dix's eyesight and hearing failed. She died on July 18, 1887, at the age of 85.

The plight of the mentally ill is still a blight on the social conscience of the United States and other countries. Mental illness still carries a negative stigma that is a holdover from the days when practically nothing was known about such conditions. In the eyes of many criminal justice professionals, the idea of mental illness conjures images of slick defense attorneys inventing syndromes so that defendants escape responsibility. Others view the mentally ill as a burden on courts and local jails and/or a source of perverse amusement.

Dorothea Dix only made a dent in the problems facing America's mentally ill, but she succeeded in raising the consciousness of the nation. America and its criminal justice system still have much progress to make in this area, but despite her glaring flaws surrounding slavery and race relations, much of the progress that has been made can be credited to Dorothea Dix. She summarized her life best when she said, "In a world where there is so much to be done, I felt strongly impressed that there must be something for me to do" (Unitarian Universalist Association, n.d., para. 1).

Sources and Suggested Readings

Brown, Thomas J. (1998). *Dorothea Dix: New England reformer.* Harvard University Press.

Dix, Dorothea. (2006). 'I tell what I have seen'—The reports of asylum reformer Dorothea Dix. *American Journal of Public Health, 94*(1), 622–625.

Dred Scott v. John F. A. Sandford, 60 U.S. 393 (1857).

Northampton State Hospital. (n.d.). *The History of Northampton State Hospital.* https://www.smith.edu/nsh/narrative.html, accessed August 8, 2024.

Lightner, David L. (1999). *Asylum, prison & poorhouse: The writings & reform work of Dorothea Dix in Illinois.* Southern Illinois University Press.

Logan, Shawn. (2017, July 26). *Dorothea Dix: Crusader for the Insane.* Eastern State Hospital, Educational. Kentucky Historic Institutions. https://kyhi.org/2017/07/26/dorothea-dix-crusader-for-the-insane/, accessed August 8, 2024.

Norwood, Arlisha R. (2017). *Dorothea Dix.* National Women's History Museum. https://www.womenshistory.org/education-resources/biographies/dorothea-dix, date of retrieval January 16, 2024.

Unitarian Universalist Association. (n.d.). *Session 13: Peaceful choices.* https://www.uua.org/re/tapestry/children/lovesurrounds/session13, accessed August 8, 2024.

Walker, Samuel. (1998). *Popular justice: A history of American criminal justice* (2nd ed.). Oxford University Press.

Wilson, Dorothy Clarke. (1975). *Stranger and traveler: The story of Dorothea Dix, American reformer.* Little Brown.

Wood, Arthur. (2000, February). Dix, Dorothea Lynde. *American national biography online.* Oxford University Press. www.anb.org/articles/15/15-00181.html, August 19, 2002.

Discussion Questions

1. How far has the state of mentally ill prisoners come since Dix's lifetime? Which changes still need to be made?
2. What are your reactions to Dix's ambivalent attitude toward slavery considering her compassionate attitude toward the mentally ill?

Credit

IMG 28.1: Source: https://commons.wikimedia.org/wiki/File:Dix-Dorothea-LOC.jpg.

CHAPTER 29

Zebulon Brockway (1827–1920)

Parole has its genesis in the prison. Parole, or its close counterpart, post-release supervision, was founded with high ideals and with a firm reliance on the indeterminate sentence, under which the amount of time inmates serve depends on their behavior while incarcerated. One of the most instrumental figures in implementing the indeterminate sentence was Zebulon Brockway, the "grand old man" of American wardens who served as superintendent of New York's Elmira Reformatory from 1876 to 1900.

IMG 29.1

Early Life and Career

Zebulon Reed Brockway was born on April 28, 1827, in Lyme, Connecticut, one of seven children born to Caroline and Zebulon Brockway, the latter a wealthy businessman, politician, state prison commissioner, and philanthropist. The younger Brockway attended good schools and had a steady dose of Christian teaching. Why Brockway developed a keen interest in prison work is not revealed in his autobiography. With his family wealth he could have had a successful business career, but perhaps guided by a sense of *noblesse oblige*, he chose prison work.

His first prison job was as an officer (or a guard as they were called at the time) at the Connecticut state prison in Wethersfield. The Wethersfield facility had been strongly influenced by a family of prison wardens named the Pilsburys, who had turned the prison into a giant and profitable industrial facility. Although the Pilsburys no longer worked at Wethersfield during Brockway's tenure as officer and later as a clerk, their influence remained. While at Wethersfield, Brockway became enamored not only with management's ability to use prison labor for industrial purposes, but also in using Bible study as a rehabilitative influence, which was an interest of most early prison pioneers.

In 1851, Brockway accepted a position as deputy superintendent at the Albany (New York) County Penitentiary, in part because he wanted the opportunity to work directly under Amos Pilsbury, whom he had come to admire. Brockway called his time at Albany "a period of severe but serviceable training" (Brockway, 1912, 50). The county penitentiary, which had initially been little more than a county jail, became a profitable enterprise under their leadership.

Pilsbury recommended Brockway for the warden's position at Rhode Island Penitentiary, but instead, Brockway accepted a job as superintendent of the Albany Municipal and County Almshouse in 1853. The Almshouse, which catered to the "diseased, defective, and dependent denizens who furnish the perennial supply of misdemeanant offenders who people the jails and short-term prisons," (Brockway, 1912, p. 51) was located less than a mile from the Albany penitentiary. While there, Brockway oversaw construction and presided over America's first county hospital for the insane. Also in 1853, Brockway married Jane Woodhouse, who would bear two daughters.

In 1854, Brockway became superintendent of the Monroe County (Rochester) New York Penitentiary, where he remained until 1861. He maintained his allegiance to prison industry, stating, "Public expenditure for prisons should be limited to the cost of providing the plant" (Brockway, 1912, p. 59). He established Bible study classes at Monroe County, in large measure due to a religious revival that swept Rochester, referred to as the "City of Revivals" at the time. Unlike most other wardens at the time, Brockway utilized academic education as a means of rehabilitation in addition to vocational and religious instruction. Although not a bleeding heart as later accusations indicated, Brockway was much more humane than many of his contemporaries.

Brockway's real passion was working with young offenders, who he believed were more amenable to rehabilitation than offenders over age 30. With that in mind, he accepted a position as director of the newly built Detroit House of Correction in 1861. Under a law just enacted by the Michigan legislature, felons between the ages of 16 and 21 were no longer sent to the state prison at Jackson, but to Detroit instead. The House of Correction accepted its first inmates on August 1, 1861.

As he had before, Brockway made industrial output and vocational education one of the basic and successful ingredients of the Detroit House of Correction, which was quite a remarkable achievement given that most inmates served sentences of less than 100 days, thus allowing for little training time. Brockway instituted regular school sessions, getting teachers, professors, and college students to teach classes that usually met two nights per week. Lecture topics included the nobility of work, how to do business, ancient architecture, flowers, humorous poetry, chemical combinations of bread, money management, banking, and the emerging field of psychology.

While at Detroit, Brockway's beliefs about the causes of crime crystallized. He began to discount the idea that free will was the sole determinant of criminal behavior. Nor did he buy into the long-held idea that crime was equated with sin. Like many other penitentiary pioneers, he believed that factors in an offender's social environment were correlated with criminal behavior. In addition, Brockway joined a growing number of penologists in the United States and Europe who believed that physical and medical factors were associated with criminal behavior. In his autobiography, he wrote that the dismissal of free will and sin "cleared the field of our endeavor and opened wide to science that which had been dominated by sentiment alone" (Brockway, 1912). Brockway did not abandon religious instruction of inmates, but he began to see that religious instruction alone would not rehabilitate inmates.

In 1869, Brockway wrote a bill for the Michigan legislature called the "three years law," (Brockway, 1912, p. 108) which allowed prison administrators discretion in releasing inmates, and which allowed prison authorities to arrest recently released inmates and re-incarcerate them. Thus, the indeterminate sentence and parole supervision were born. The law applied only to women offenders in Wayne County (Detroit) and it soon became useless, dependent largely on judicial interpretations of how the statute was to be applied. Nevertheless, Brockway was encouraged by the results of the experiment and received public praise from many notable citizens, including Dwight L. Moody, the most renowned Christian evangelist of the 19th century.

The Cincinnati Congress

Brockway's place in American penological history was solidified with his presentation in 1870 of a paper titled *The Ideal of a True Prison System for a State* at the National Prison Congress in Cincinnati. The meeting gave birth to the National Prison Association, later renamed the American Correctional Association. Brockway's address set the stage for penology for the next several decades. The central thesis in Brockway's speech is summarized in this quote from the paper:

> The prison system of a state should partake of the "same spirit" of the other parts. Legalized degradation of any criminal inflicts injury upon the whole social organism, while efforts for the highest and best welfare of any person promote the general good. (Brockway, 1995)

Brockway viewed the job of prisons to either cure the inmate of his wrongdoing ways or restrain him from harming society if he would not or could not be cured. He called for graduated freedoms among inmates, culminating in a planned program of release into the community, and community supervision conducted by local law enforcement. He also called for specialized institutions for young offenders, for elderly offenders, and for women. Brockway also called for creation of "reception center" facilities, much like classification centers today, to assess a newly sentenced inmate's "ancestral history, their constitutional tendences, their early social condition, and its probable influence in forming their character ... upon which basis a plan of treatment may be outlined." The crux of his plan was the indeterminate sentence and parole supervision, an idea that had already been implemented in Ireland and Australia by British authorities.

Despite his exalted status within the field of penology, Brockway's tenure at Detroit came to an end shortly after the Cincinnati Congress due to public accusations of serving unsuitable food and disciplining harshly, the latter accusation being one that would recur many years later. Although he was exonerated of any wrongdoing, his reputation was tarnished.

The Elmira Reformatory

In December 1872, Brockway went to work for the Michigan (Railroad) Car Company in Detroit. He remained there until May 1876 when he was offered the chance to put his prison administration principles into operation at the New York State Reformatory at Elmira. The invitation to accept the position came from Louis Pilsbury, the son of Amos Pilsbury, whom Brockway had worked under in the 1850s.

Although the Reformatory had a board of managers, which included Louis Pilsbury, Brockway had a free hand in running the facility. Brockway drafted an indeterminate sentence law in 1877, which was enacted by the New York legislature. Borrowing an idea introduced by Englishman Walter Crofton's prison governorship in Ireland, Brockway instituted a marks system under which prisoners earned or lost marks depending on their behavior and progress toward rehabilitation as perceived by prison staff. The more marks prisoners earned, the more privileges they were given, and the sooner their release date. Brockway's marks program functioned as the first formal parole program in the United States. Volunteers in the community supervised those who were released on parole for 6 months. Parole, translated from the French term *parole d'honneur* (word of honor) and historically applied to released war prisoners, was becoming a significant component of the criminal justice system.

Although Brockway held firm to his Christian beliefs and continued to believe that reforming prisoners was the essence of Christian principles, he lost faith in evangelism as a rehabilitation tool. Instead, he believed that intellectual education, or at least basic literacy, vocational training, and coercion were the best instruments of rehabilitation. Elmira suffered a blow in 1888 when the New York legislature, under pressure from organized labor and business groups, banned inmate labor that competed with similar labor in the private sector. Although he initially fought to preserve such labor, Brockway was relieved when the ban came to pass because he no longer had to worry about turning a profit with the reformatory. He was free to concentrate on reforming the prisoners. He concentrated on instilling military-style discipline among the inmates by bringing in a former West Point instructor to train the inmates in drill and caring for their cells. The reformatory had a state-of-the-art gymnasium both for recreation and for testing inmates' mental and physical agility. The gymnasium contained gymnastics and exercise equipment (basketball had not been invented). Brockway wrote about the purpose of the gymnasium:

> The intention was to invigorate by means of physical culture the entire prison population and, particularly through specific scientific physical renovation, to improve defectives and dullards in their mental and moral habitudes. (Brockway, 1995)

According to Brockway, identifying and treating crime had become a scientific process, an idea that was emerging but not part of mainstream thinking. Brockway became immersed in the now-discredited pseudoscience of phrenology, identifying a criminal based on physical characteristics. He advocated sterilization of inmates who came from criminal backgrounds or were judged as degenerates (sex offenders). Brockway also experimented with changing the caloric intake of inmates, but the results of these experiments were inconclusive.

One of Brockway's greatest innovations was his system of classifying inmates. His system was based on intellectual capacity and physical abilities. Although his system seems rather crude by modern standards, it was innovative for its time. Inmates were placed in one of the following seven categories (Brockway, 1912, pp. 360–361):

1. Five grade divisions based on the character as it is determined during the imprisonment
2. Three school grades and 28 school classes governed by the ascertained intellectual quality and proficiency alone
3. Thirty-six trade divisions looking to industrial efficiency and economical engagement on or after the release
4. Four battalions and 16 military companies, which embraced all the able-bodied prisoners
5. Five religious divisions according to the denominational affiliation

6. Three general divisions and 75 subdivisions, interchangeable, of the manual training class
7. Six designated groups of the very defective prisoners arranged based on the physician's opinion of requirements

Brockway became renowned the world over for his work at Elmira, especially for his use of the indeterminate sentence and parole, but also for his bold experiments in prison management and rehabilitation. However, as with the case in Detroit, he encountered serious opposition close to home. Allegations of brutality surfaced again. Rather than deny the accusations, Brockway admitted that he and other prison officials utilized the "paddle" to administer corporal discipline to inmates Brockway thought could be reached no other way. Corporal punishment, which the penitentiary was designed to stop, had fallen out of favor with most New York penal reformers.

In addition, Elmira, like many prisons during the 1890s, was beset by crowding and fiscal problems. The problem at Elmira was aggravated by the massive immigration from Europe to New York shores during the 1880s and 1890s. Inmates unaccustomed to American cultural norms and/or who could not speak or read English created new challenges for Brockway and his staff at Elmira.

Life and Death After Elmira

In 1900, New York Governor Theodore Roosevelt, who would assume the offices of both vice president and president of the United States the following year, appointed a commission to study ways to improve New York prisons. According to the commission, one way was to ask Brockway to resign. Brockway did resign in July 1900, the official explanation being "disability due to old age" (Opdycke, 2002).

The Brockways stayed in Elmira with their widowed daughter. In 1905, he was elected mayor of Elmira on the short-lived Fusion ticket. He served a 2-year term and was defeated in his reelection bid. Before and after his term as Elmira mayor, Brockway spent much of his time delivering speeches and consulting on prison administration throughout the United States and Europe.

Jane Woodhouse Brockway died on February 8, 1911. Brockway wrote these concluding words in his 1912 autobiography, titled *Fifty Years of Prison Service*:

> At this writing, March 13, 1912, the eighty-fifth anniversary of the birth of my lifelong companion, I am indeed bereft and sorrowfully tarrying to meet my own last summons.

Although he remained active, Zebulon Brockway lived his remaining years lonely and heartbroken. He died on October 21, 1920, in Elmira, New York, at the age of 93.

Sources and Suggested Readings

Brockway, Zebulon Reed. (1912). *Fifty years of prison service: An autobiography.* Charities Publication Committee.

Brockway, Zebulon Reed. (1995). The ideal of a true prison system for a state. *Journal of Correctional Education*, *46*(2), 68–74.

Eggleston, Carolyn Rebecca. (1989). *Zebulon Brockway & Elmira Reformatory: A study of correctional/special education.* University Microfilms International.

Opdycke, Sandra. (2002). Brockway, Zebulon Reed. *American national biography online.* www.anb.org/articles, date of retrieval August 19, 2002.

Study of prison reform. (1912, July 20). *New York Tribune.* https://www.proquest.com/docview/574940018?accountid=10639)&parentSessionId=28LdzWCRNRA1SG4i7Iba2LHIwaRRVPzlbyAGg5NI%2FKs%3D&sourcetype=Historical%20Newspapers, date of retrieval January 11, 2024.

Walker, Samuel. (1997). *Popular justice: A history of American criminal justice* (2nd ed.). Oxford University Press.

Discussion Questions

1. After reading about Zebulon Brockway, how do you think idealism collides with reality in penal reform?
2. What legacy did Zebulon Brockway leave for American parole?

Credit

IMG 29.1: Source: https://commons.wikimedia.org/wiki/File:Zebulon_Reed_Brockway.png.

CHAPTER 30

Thomas Mott Osborne (1859–1926)

IMG 30.1

It takes a strong and unorthodox personality to innovate in the corrections fields and withstand the criticism that comes with innovating. Thomas Mott Osborne's unorthodox personality was his greatest asset as a penal reformer, and it would also work to his detriment. His attempts at implementing inmate self-governance are his legacy, one that is still debated.

Early Life and Career

Thomas Mott Osborne was born on September 23, 1859, in Auburn, New York, the city attached to one of the major schools of correctional thought in the 19th century and home to New York's first penitentiary. Osborne was the third of four children born to Eliza Wright Osborne and David Munson Osborne. A sense of social conscience ran through Osborne's family. His great aunt was Lucretia Mott, one of the great philanthropists of American history and a passionate antislavery advocate. Another aunt was married to William Lloyd Garrison, the most prominent abolitionist of the 19th century.

David Osborne was a wealthy farm implement manufacturer. Thomas Osborne was a self-described "momma's boy" who enjoyed sewing and other traditionally feminine activities as a child. He attended public schools through grade school, even though his father could have afforded private schools. He attended a private prep school and was admitted to Harvard in 1880. Like most young men at Harvard, Osborne assumed he was destined to enter business with his father after graduation. The idea of following in his father's footsteps did not appeal to Osborne, whose passions were playing football, dancing, playing the piano, and, above all, acting.

Throughout his adult life, Osborne was active in the Unitarian Church and has been described by his biographers as spiritual but devoted to a specific religious denomination. Osborne spent much of his time with other social liberals, like his uncle William Lloyd Garrison, who described Osborne as a natural leader but cool and aloof. Osborne developed many other friendships at Harvard, but he also made some important enemies that would haunt him, including William Randolph Hearst, the future newspaper magnate that would persecute him in the press, and Theodore Roosevelt, the future New York Governor and United States president.

After graduating from Harvard in 1884, Osborne returned to Auburn and reluctantly took over his father's business. In 1886, he married Agnes Devens, a young Bostonian. The marriage would produce four sons before Agnes's death in 1896. Osborne never married again, saying that to do so would be polygamous. Soon after his father's death, Osborne gladly sold the business to International Harvester, which freed him to do the things he loved most, including his three intertwined interests, theater, politics, and philanthropy.

Politics and Philanthropy

Osborne's foray into public service came in 1885 when he was elected to the local board of education, a position he held until 1894. Though he came from a Republican family, Osborne served as a delegate to the Democratic National Convention in 1892. He made an unsuccessful bid for lieutenant governor on the Citizens Union ticket in 1894. He was elected mayor of Auburn that same year.

Given Osborne's personality, it was strange that he succeeded at politics. Politics is about slyness, conformity, and compromise, none of which was part of Osborne's personality. He was forthright and abrupt rather than sly; he seldom conformed to anyone's norms other than his own; and he was uncompromising when he believed he was right, a trait that made him many enemies. Osborne detested the Tammany machine that dominated New York City and the New York state legislature, and he did not get along with the most prominent New York politician of the era, Theodore Roosevelt. Roosevelt called Osborne part of the "lunatic fringe" in New York politics, a phrase Roosevelt made famous. Rudolph Chamberlain, author of Osborne's biography, wrote "Few men have ever been so unerring in their choice of the losing side" (Chamberlain, 1936).

Nevertheless, Osborne was reelected mayor of Auburn. He decided to discover firsthand some of the problems confronting Auburn residents on the streets, but he felt that he could not do it adequately if citizens recognized him. He embarked on what became his trademark, going about town incognito. He relied on his intuitive theatrical ability to alter his appearance and his personality, visiting Auburn streets and saloons in disguise, using the alias Harun-al-Rashid.

Osborne also developed an interest in reforming the state penitentiary in Auburn. As a child he had visited the penitentiary but stayed away because the experience traumatized him. He became more interested in effecting positive change as he grew older. The turning point came in 1912 after he read Donald Lowrie's *My Life in Prison*, which crystallized his belief that prisons were a failure. Osborne stated that trying to study criminals in prison was like studying "polar bears from one bear in a zoological garden" (Chamberlain, 1936, p. 237). He saw courts and prisons as impediments to reforming criminals. In a 1906 speech before the Congress of the National Prison Association at Albany, Osborne said that prisoners must have as much freedom as possible as only liberty can prepare a man for liberty.

The answer, said Osborne, was inmate self-governance, an idea he acquired from another penal reformer and prison warden named William George, who while serving as warden at a New York juvenile reformatory, created a system known as George Junior Republic. It consisted of an inmate self-governance structure, a governance manual, and prison recreation programs. From the moment he began believing that inmate self-governance was the key to penal reform, Osborne never wavered; once he reached a conclusion on any issue, no reasoning could move him.

Thomas Brown: Inmate

Osborne once remarked that he had put himself "on trial in the court of conscience and a verdict has been rendered of 'guilty'—guilty of having lived for many years of my life indifferent to and ignorant of what was going on behind these walls" (New York Correction History Society, n.d., para. 15). In September 1913, Osborne put his words into action. Osborne went into the warden's office at Auburn prison at 10 a.m. He emerged as Thomas Brown, inmate #33,333x. Osborne, a former Auburn mayor and one of New York's leading citizens, had with the warden's permission assumed the identity of an inmate to spend 1 week in prison at hard labor. Osborne had contemplated going in without the warden's knowledge, but he feared that the inmates would discover his identity and view him as a spy. So instead, he went in under an assumed name with the warden, staff, and inmates all aware of his identity.

Osborne's experience with drama served him well in his participant observer research. He completely immersed himself in the role of inmate Tom Brown. While he was working in the inmate factory, a tour group including Osborne's nephew and some friends came through the prison. Osborne's transformation into Tom Brown was so complete that he was not even recognized by his friends and his nephew. Osborne wrote in his diary, *Within Prison Walls*, that he objected to having to sleep in his underwear without pajamas, to sleeping in a bed without linens, to throwing slop buckets with human waste into the river, and most of all to constantly being told what to do and where to go. Prison, said Osborne, was "admirably suited for performing the operation of breaking a man's spirit" (Osborne, 1914).

Osborne quickly adopted the inmate attitude toward the prison officers, all of whom were aware of his identity. Osborne thought some officers were simply brutal people but that most were decent men working in a brutal system. In his diary he wrote that "in prison, as elsewhere, when men are dominated by fear, brutality is the inevitable result" (Osborne, 1914).

Osborne observed that men placed in solitary confinement entered sane but came out raving mad, so he faked a work stoppage to get himself placed in solitary. After 3 hours in solitary, an officer opened Osborne's cell door and told him he could leave, but Osborne, by now completely immersed in his Tom Brown role, refused out of pure hatred and resentment toward the man that opened the door. How dare he, thought Osborne, presume to deprive him of his freedom and then restore it to him in just as authoritative a manner. He stayed an additional 11 hours. He emerged from solitary and later that week from prison, convinced that he had seen the light and that he would be God's instrument in making a difference in penal reform. Word of Osborne's experience spread to newspapers across the United States, with some criticizing his efforts and others applauding it. The *New York Times* called it "well intended yet ill advised" (Tannenbaum, 1933, p. 69).

The Mutual Welfare League

In December 1913, with the warden's permission, Osborne started an inmate governance organization called the Tom Brown League. The general committee included 49 inmates, with Osborne elected as chair, even though he was no longer an inmate. The league drafted a set of bylaws and an organizational structure. The league would include 49 delegates elected every 6 months, with a nine-member executive board. A grievance committee, sworn in by the warden, vowed to promote fair dealing between inmates and staff.

The league changed its name to the Mutual Welfare League (MWL), and its membership stood at 1,350, each of whom wore a small green and white shield on his coat. All their initial actions were radical and, in many cases, unprecedented in American prison history. Their first action was to ask for the right to listen to music. They were successful in abolishing the rule of silence, which disallowed inmates from openly speaking with each other. They abolished "Blue Sunday," which required inmates to rest all day in their cells, a maddening monotony that often led to fights on Mondays. The MWL established an inmate athletic program that allowed recreation facilities in the yard. Staff feared that the yard would be a location for settling scores, but instead the first day was more akin to a family reunion as inmates finally openly communicated with each other after months and years of having to communicate in silence.

Although the MWL succeeded in many respects, it suffered from some unsolvable problems. Contrary to league dictates, inmates refused to report other inmate violations, still fearing the snitch label. Another problem was the way violations were handled. Many officers still used physical punishment, much to the consternation of the league. Political infighting within the league became a problem as inmates jockeyed for power. The novelty of privileges wore off, and inmates began to take them for granted. Inmates whined more than before, which Osborne detested. The only thing he hated more than brutality was pampering.

Up the River

Despite its shortcomings, word of the MWL spread around the country. On December 1, 1914, Osborne was appointed warden of New York's infamous Sing Sing Correctional Facility in Ossining. Sing Sing was one of the country's most notorious prisons. Its location 40 miles up the Hudson River from New York City made the phrase "up the river" a euphemism for going to prison. Osborne was given a mandate to establish a MWL there, and Sing Sing inmates called their organization The Golden Rule of Brotherhood. The inmates requested weekend visitation, the right to purchase stamps and write to people not on a preapproved list, movies to be shown on Sunday, better facilities for crippled and sick prisoners, and no more doubling of prisoners in small cells.

Scandal accusations surfaced about Sing Sing. One was that regular inmates had been allowed access to talks with death row inmates about their cases. One such instance especially irked Governor Charles Whitman because he had been the prosecutor in that case. Osborne made no secret of the fact that he would stay up all night talking with death row inmates just prior to their execution. He publicly stated that watching an electrocution sickened him, although he was not categorically opposed to capital punishment.

Scandal

The biggest blow to Osborne came from allegations made by an inmate named James Harvey, nicknamed "Jack the Dropper" because of his frequent participation in homosexual activity. Harvey claimed that he had "given himself" for sex to 21 inmates and that Osborne knew about it. Osborne did know about it, and he claimed that he punished the inmates involved, but his critics accused him of behaviors ranging from not punishing the misdeeds enough to actual participation in prison sex.

On December 28, 1915, Osborne was indicted by a Westchester County Grand Jury on charges of perjury, neglect of duty, and engaging in "various unlawful and unnatural acts with inmates of Sing Sing prison, over whom he had supervision and control" (Chamberlain, 1936, p. 329). The legal proceedings were widely reported in the press, with numerous character witnesses lining up behind Osborne, including some he had known 30 years earlier at Harvard. Many former inmates and well-known penologists also lined up behind Osborne, as did many New York newspapers. Osborne was successful in painting prosecution witnesses as unreliable. Most of them were former prison inmates; some were former staff members. The charges were dismissed before the case came to trial.

Resignation and Continued Advocacy

Osborne returned to Sing Sing in July 1916 to a hero's welcome, but the damage to his reputation was irreparable, and he resigned in October. He continued his prison reform efforts, resuming his Tom Brown persona to investigate the naval prison at Portsmouth, New Hampshire, in January 1917. On August 1, 1917, he took over as warden at Portsmouth, even though he had never been in the military, and he implemented inmate self-governance there as well. One program was tied to his lifelong passion, an inmate drama club.

On March 17, 1920, Osborne resigned from Portsmouth and returned to Auburn. He was sad to discover that conditions at Sing Sing had returned much to the way they were prior to his working there. The new warden had practically dismantled the MWL, making it a puppet organization for prison administrators.

Osborne toured the country, serving as consultant to state prison systems. He also gave speeches and consulted on prison matters throughout Europe. He advocated two courts, one of condemnation, to ascertain whether one committed a criminal act, and a second, a court of release, consisting of experts who should decide when to release a person from prison. Osborne did not believe that judges should be expected to decide both guilt and punishment in one proceeding.

Death and Legacy

Thomas Mott Osborne died on October 20, 1926, at the age of 67. He died on an Auburn street while walking home. Former Auburn inmates served as pallbearers at his funeral.

The question of what rights prison inmates should have is still a thorny one for prison managers. In a 1977 article, Peter Scharf and Joseph Hickey called prison democracy a "hopeless enterprise" (Scharf and Hickey, 1977, p. 3), as evidenced by the fact that so many inmate government organizations have been abandoned. But others, both on the political right and left, see it as a chance for inmates to learn by doing, rather than being robotically controlled to the point where they cannot do anything without explicit instructions, or as a way of pacifying or channeling inmate discontent, as Scharf and Hickey note.

Although much of Osborne's dream of prison reform went unfulfilled, many of his changes and reforms were not forgotten, and some are still in effect today. Osborne's work predated the era of inmate litigation that forced reform and forced correctional officials to grant inmate demands. His approach to reform may seem naive to some today just as it did then, but Osborne was caught in the same dilemma that faces modern American society—he detested prisons but saw no acceptable alternative.

Sources and Suggested Readings

Chamberlain, Rudolph Wilson. (1936). *There is no truce: A life of Thomas Mott Osborne, prison reformer.* Routledge.

Chapman, John Jay. (1927). Thomas Mott Osborne: Osborne's place in historic criminology. *Harvard Graduates' Magazine.*

Gortier, Shai. (2022). Participatory panopticon: Thomas Mott Osborne's prison democracy. *Constellations, 29,* 343–358.

Janitz, John. (1971). The Osborne family papers: Spotlight on Thomas Mott Osborne. *The Courier, 8*(2), 11–18.

New York Correction History Society. (n.d.). Thomas Mott Osborne's *Within prison walls.* https://www.correctionhistory.org/auburn&osborne/tombrown/html/wpw_ch02.html#:~:text=I%20have%20put%20myself%20on,was%20going%20behind%20these%20walls, accessed August 9, 2024.

Osborne, Thomas Mott. (1914). *Within prison walls: Being a narrative of personal experience during a week of voluntary confinement in the state prison at Auburn, New York.* D. Appleton & Company.

Osborne, Thomas Mott. (1917). Health conditions in prisons. *American Journal of Nursing, 17*(10), 881–888.

Osborne, Thomas Mott. (1918). Common sense in prison management. *Journal of the American Institute of Criminal Law & Criminology, 8*(6): 806–822.

Osborne, Thomas Mott. (1924). *Prisons and common sense.* J.B Lippincott.

Scharf, P., & Hickey, J. (1977). Thomas Mott Osborne and the limits of democratic prison reform. *The Prison Journal, 57*(2), 3–15. https://doi.org/10.1177/003288557705700202

Tannenbaum, Frank. (1933). *Osborne of Sing Sing.* University of North Carolina Press.

Yeager, Matthew. (2018). *Reforming American prisons: A memoir of my time at Sing Sing Prison by Warden Thomas Mott Osborne.* Edwin Mellen Press.

Discussion Questions

1. Should more correctional officials do as Thomas Osborne did, living in a prison for a short period of time to get a firsthand idea of what prison life is like?
2. What do you think of Osborne's ideas about inmate self-governance?

Credit

IMG 30.1: Bain News Service, https://commons.wikimedia.org/wiki/File:Thomas_Mott_Osborne_circa_1910_at_his_desk_(cropped).jpg, 1910.

CHAPTER 31

Jane Addams (1860–1935)

IMG 31.1

Many of the subjects in this book possess (or possessed) a strong social conscience that enabled them to work toward detecting and reacting to crime in extraordinary ways. It takes a strong social conscience to work toward the prevention of crime, especially when it involves working hand in hand with the lowest echelon of society. Jane Addams possessed the rare gift of being as comfortable with Chicago's poorest turn-of-the-century immigrants as she was with the highest political and business leaders of her day in Europe and the United States. With these talents, this controversial author and social reformer, now often called the "mother of social work" (FSU College of Social Work, 2022, para. 4), made a name for herself that lives on to this day. The phrase "Hull House" has been indelibly etched in the annals of literary and criminal justice history.

Early Life and Career

Laura Jane Addams was born on September 6, 1860, in Cedarville, Illinois. Jennie, as her family called her, was the eighth of nine children born to John Huy Addams and Sarah Weber Addams. John Addams was a Hicksite Quaker, a group of Quakers who split with mainstream Quakerism and adopted a more liberal, less literal view of the Bible. John was the greatest influence on Jane Addams's career and life. John Addams stressed the importance of helping those less fortunate than he, and he instilled a sense of social responsibility in his daughter. He owned a grain mill, served as a bank president, owned interests in railroad and insurance companies, and was one of the founding members of the Republican Party. A slavery opponent, John Addams served in the Illinois State Senate and was a close friend of Abraham Lincoln, another pioneering Illinois Republican. Sarah Addams died in 1863, leaving Jane's rearing to her older siblings until her father remarried in 1868 to Anna Haldeman.

Jane Addams enrolled in the Rockford Female Seminary in 1877, one of the few institutions of higher learning for women in the United States. Addams served as class president for 4 years. In 1881, she was the school's first graduate and its first valedictorian. The same year she enrolled at Women's Medical College in Philadelphia. Her career there was cut short by health problems, but she recovered well enough to visit Europe from 1883 to 1885.

Throughout most of her life, Addams was a strong Christian, spending her adult life in the Presbyterian Church following a Quaker childhood. But Addams criticized modern religion for being long on dogma and short on love and self-sacrifice. She saw Jesus more as a moral hero than as the son of God. Frustrated by a desire to effect social change and the limitations placed on most women in her day, Addams expressed her distress through writing, a medium that suited her well. She began writing in earnest for college publications while at Rockford and continued writing from the time she was in her late 30s until her death.

Addams was not content to write about life; she was determined to bring about social change. While in Europe, Addams visited Toynbee Hall in London, a settlement house for London's poor, especially its destitute women, both those who ran away from home and mothers without any other means of support.

Hull House

As the Industrial Revolution and increased urbanization swept the United States, Addams was appalled at the living conditions of Chicago's poor. Like Dorothea Dix, Addams was frustrated, in part because of her own experience, at the paucity of opportunities for women in American society who wanted to work outside the home. A firm believer in the idea of *noblesse oblige*, Addams established Hull House in 1889, a settlement house in Chicago along the lines of London's Toynbee Hall. The name came from the previous owner of the house, Charles Hull, who had the mansion built in the 1850s. Addams and Hull House became the topic of great interest throughout the United States. Poor immigrants, widows, single mothers, and other women without a place to go came to Hull House and received nurturing, care, and a chance for self-improvement.

Addams's original intention was to make Hull House a place where women intellectuals could discuss literature and poetry with poor, uneducated women. Hull House offered practical services such as day care, basic literacy, medical care, and legal services. It was also a center of cultural education and activity. Art exhibitions, small theater productions, music classes, and recitals were a part of Hull House. A coffeehouse and gymnasium were added in 1893. For several decades, thousands of men, women, and children participated in Hull House activities. Most were part of Chicago's lower class; many were poor immigrants who stood little chance of anything but a life of abject poverty had it not been for Hull House.

Although she was aloof, one of the most remarkable aspects of Addams's personality was her ability to interact not only with street people and poor immigrants, but also with Chicago intelligentsia. This was one of the keys to the success of Hull House. Addams succeeded in bringing in some of Chicago's leading political theorists, musicians, artists, writers, and poets to share their ideas with Hull House residents.

Not content to let Hull House be her sole endeavor, and in sync with the Progressive Era thinking that characterized America during the 1890s, Addams plunged headlong into an effort to improve living conditions for Chicago's poor. One of her concerns was garbage collection, which was atrociously inadequate and resulted in breeding disease in Chicago's slums. In Addams's view, the problem was the politicization of the city's sanitation department. She worked for civil service reform to reduce the role of politics in that department. Addams was appointed garbage inspector for Chicago's 19th ward in 1895.

While Hull House was a remarkable achievement as the forerunner of the modern halfway house, Addams can lay claim to even greater achievement in juvenile justice. The state of Chicago's justice system was a passion of Addams. There was no separate court or correctional facility for children. Addams was one of the prime movers in the establishment of America's first juvenile court system in 1899 in Chicago.

Addams spread the word about Hull House through prestigious publications, including *The Atlantic Monthly*, *The Christian Century*, and *North American Review*. In 1902, she published her first book, *Democracy and Social Ethics*. Addams wrote that humanity was moving toward a higher social morality, and that members of a democracy are bound to move together. Addams wrote *Newer Ideals of Peace* in 1907, *The Spirit of Youth and the City Streets* in 1909, and her crowning literary achievement, *Twenty Years at Hull House*, in 1910.

Dedicated to her father's memory, *Twenty Years at Hull House* describes the formative influences in her life, her father and Abraham Lincoln, the latter whom she credits with giving America its title to democracy. Addams exhibited her emotional side in describing the heart-wrenching lives of many people who sought care at Hull House. Between 1910, when it was first published, and 1935, the year of Addams's death, *Twenty Years at Hull House* sold 80,000 copies. Called by at least one critic "an indispensable classic of American intellectual and social history," the book reflects Addams's gift for blending social thought and action. She viewed Hull House as true democracy in action, exemplifying the best undertakings in philanthropy and civic and educational action, and as an attempt to socialize democracy.

Between 1890 and 1910, Addams directed most of her energy to improving life in Chicago, serving on the city's school board from 1905 to 1909. After the release of *Twenty Years at Hull House*, Addams continued her work at Hull House but focused less energy there and spent more time on other issues and causes. She worked for women's suffrage, convinced that voting women could undo many of the world's problems. Addams traveled to Budapest, Hungary, in 1913 and was the keynote speaker in a women's suffrage meeting. In 1912, she attacked prostitution, another social evil visited on women, in *A New Conscience and An Ancient Evil.*

World War I and Pacifism

As the 1910s wore on, Addams became involved in efforts to promote world peace, against a rising tide of warmongering sweeping Europe and culminating in the outbreak of World War I in 1914. Addams, who had met Leo Tolstoy (the author of *War and Peace)* during a visit to Russia in 1896, was impressed with his belief that war only begat misery, and said, "We cannot do without patriotism, but we must cease founding that patriotism on war" (Elshtain, 2002, p. 219).

She campaigned for peace throughout the United States but encountered opposition for her outspoken objection to America's 1917 entry into the Great War. Her opponents included many former friends from America's progressive sector. While she was not alone in her opposition to American involvement in the War, Addams's pacifist attitude during World War I cost her both popularity and her alliance with former President Theodore Roosevelt, a perennial war hawk. Addams viewed war as a pathetic means of resolving human differences and as antithetical to the positive evolution of humanity.

Post-War Activities

After the war, Addams formed the Women's International League for Peace and Freedom and supported the creation of the League of Nations, the ill-fated brainchild of President Woodrow Wilson that the United States never joined. Although she was the most admired woman in America prior to World War I, second only to Thomas Edison among all Americans, her reputation never fully rebounded because of her pacifism and attachment to leftist causes, especially anarchism, an ideology ostensibly opposed to all of forms of central government and a close cousin of the emerging doctrine of communism in Europe, which was viewed with suspicion in the United States.

In 1919, the New York legislature blacklisted Addams for her defense of anarchists, radicals, and communists. As far back as 1901, she defended Abraham Isaak, an anarchist who was arrested but never charged, for alleged involvement in the 1901 assassination of President William McKinley. Like most American assassins, McKinley's assassin, Leon Czolgosz, was too much of misfit to partner with anyone. Despite no evidence that Czolgosz acted in concert with anyone else, hundreds of raids and assaults against suspected anarchists and their institutions took place after the McKinley assassination, in part because some anarchists, while not involved with the assassination, applauded Czolgosz.

Hull House was raided by angry protesters as well, as were many other leftist institutions in Chicago, a hotbed of anarchism. Hull House, which was populated by many Russian Jewish immigrants (a group often accused of including a disproportionate number of political radicals), had long been attacked as a haven for radical political and social thought, but the accusations grew more intense during World War I. Addams was viewed by military hawks as a dangerous radical and as a traitor, a reputation enhanced by her support for labor leader Eugene Debbs's unsuccessful presidential bid in 1920.

Nevertheless, Addams continued to assist future President Herbert Hoover in his famine relief efforts for Europe. Hoover was elected to the presidency in 1928, less than 1 year before the stock market crash of 1929, which signaled America's spiral into the Great Depression of the 1930s. In 1932, Democrat Franklin Roosevelt challenged him for the presidency. While Hoover was abandoned and vilified by millions who had supported him 4 years earlier, Addams did not abandon her old friend, publicly advocating Hoover's reelection.

Addams's energies in the 1920s were focused on promoting peace and speaking at conferences dominated by women's groups aimed at avoiding future wars. But history demonstrated that her efforts were futile. After only a brief respite from war during the 1920s, World War II erupted in Europe, North Africa, and Asia in the 1930s. Addams repaired the damage to her reputation from World War I. Her determined peace efforts were rewarded in 1931 when she shared the Nobel Peace Prize with Columbia University's Nicholas Murray Butler for her European famine relief efforts.

Personal Life, Death, and Legacy

Addams never married. Her close relationship with Mary Rozet Smith (1868–1934) has given rise to speculation that Addams was gay, a damning accusation during her time. Although Addams and Smith were very close, spending summers together and alone at Smith's home in Maine, it is unlikely that their relationship was sexual. As with many single women of America's 19th and early 20th centuries, the more likely scenario is that the two women were lovers, but in a nonsexual context; at that time sexual relations between women were seldom seriously contemplated in private, let alone acknowledged or discussed in public.

Addams was diagnosed with a tumor in 1931 and underwent surgery to have it removed. The initial diagnosis was promising, but the surgery was not successful. Addams lived for several years before dying of intestinal cancer on May 21, 1935, at the age of 74.

Addams might scoff at being labeled a criminal justice pioneer; her thinking went beyond administering a system of criminal justice. Hull House and other settlement houses of that era were the forerunners of the modern halfway house. Her most important contribution to the administration of criminal justice may be her role in the creation of the Illinois juvenile justice system. While many who work in criminal justice can take issue with Addams's political philosophy, all will agree that Jane Addams is synonymous with many of the reforms and changes of America's Progressive Era, including the founding of its juvenile justice system, and that she deserves the moniker, the mother of social work.

Sources and Suggested Readings

Addams, Jane. (1912). My experiences as a progressive delegate. *McClure's Magazine, 60*(1), 12–14.

Addams, Jane. (1990, original publication date 1910). *Twenty years at Hull House.* University of Illinois Press.

Berson, Robin K. (2004). *Jane Addams: A biography.* Greenwood Press.

Brown, Victoria Bissell. (2000, February). Addams, Jane (06 September 1860–21 May 1935), social reformer and peace activist. *American national biography online.* Oxford University Press.

Elshtain, Jean Bethke. (2001). Jane Addams & the social claim. *Public Interest, 145*, 82–92.

Elshtain, Jean Bethke. (2002). *Jane Addams and the dream of American democracy.* Basic Books.

Farrell, John. (2019, original publication date, 1967). *Beloved lady: A history of Jane Addams's ideas on reform & peace.* Johns Hopkins University Press.

FSU College of Social Work. (2022, March 15). *Famous social workers in history: The mother of social work Jane Addams (1860–1935).* Florida State University. https://onlinemsw.fsu.edu/blog/famous-social-workers-in-history#:~:text=The%20Mother%20of%20Social%20Work%3A%20Jane%20Addams%20(1860%20%E2%80%93%201935)&text=By%20the%20age%20of%2021,founded%20Hull%20House%20in%20Chicago, accessed August 8, 2024.

Jane Addams Hull-House Museum. (2024). About Jane Addams and Hull-House Settlement. https://www.hullhousemuseum.org/about-jane-addams
Knight, Louise W. (2010). *Jane Addams: Spirit in action*. W. W. Norton.

Discussion Questions

1. How has the juvenile justice system changed since Jane Addams's time? Would she approve of the contemporary juvenile justice system?
2. In what ways did Jane Addams embody social work ideals?

Credit

IMG 31.1: Moffett, https://commons.wikimedia.org/wiki/File:Jane_Addams_profile.jpg, 1914.

CHAPTER 32

Miriam Van Waters (1887–1974)

IMG 32.1

No correctional pioneer encountered more controversy than Miriam Van Waters, a turn-of-the-20th-century scholar who spent her life trying to improve the lot of female offenders in the community and behind prison walls by applying the principle of maternal justice. Her private life is shrouded in mystery and intrigue as well, and it has made her the object of fascination to those who are interested in corrections and female sexuality.

Early Life and Career

Miriam Van Waters was born on October 4, 1887, in Greensburg, Pennsylvania, the daughter of George B. Van Waters, an Episcopalian minister, and Maud Van Waters. Miriam was the second of six children, but her older sister died at age two, before she was born. The Van Waters family moved to Portland, Oregon, in 1891, where George Van Waters served as rector of St. David's Episcopal Church for 17 years. Due to her mother's physical and emotional problems that often kept her away from home, Miriam assumed many of the maternal duties for her younger siblings.

George Van Waters embodied the social gospel movement of the early 20th century, which merged Christian ideals with a liberal/progressive social agenda in the belief that the two could rectify social inequalities. Between her father instilling in her a sense of social justice and her quasi-maternal role in her family, Miriam's future as a matronly social reformer seemed preordained from childhood.

Never one to accept the subservient positions of many women of her era, Van Waters took the unusual step of earning a bachelor's and a master's degree in philosophy from the University of Oregon between 1905 and 1910. Unlike most women of her era, she never married. Instead she embarked on a career, thinking that womanhood and public service were perfectly compatible, but she did not engage in "radical" behaviors like smoking and wearing makeup.

Van Waters enrolled at Clark University in Massachusetts in 1910, where she earned a doctorate degree in anthropology. Although her degree was in anthropology, Van Waters was at heart a devoted social worker. Social work degrees were rare in the 1910s, even though the field was growing rapidly. One of her greatest influences was Jane Addams. Van Waters adhered to Addams's belief that modern civilization lacked the appropriate channels for youthful impulses. Van Waters believed that recreation, education, and labor were proper treatments for criminal behavior and that most criminal behavior was traceable to environmental factors, especially a dysfunctional homelife, as opposed to the psychological and mental explanations that were in vogue at the time.

While at Clark, she passed the Massachusetts bar exam, but she never practiced law. Van Waters also studied medicine and interned at a mental hospital, but she was not a physician. Although she did not agree that biological or Freudian factors caused crime, she believed that the scientific method could be applied to correctional intervention. She spent a year as a social worker in the Boston Children's Aid Society and worked as a probation officer in a juvenile court.

In 1914, Van Waters returned to Portland and started work as superintendent at the Frazer Detention Home, a juvenile facility. She put her maternal justice ideas into practice by eliminating corporal punishment, improving the diet for juveniles, and enhancing sanitation and medical facilities. Far from being a strictly bureaucratic warden, she would take the children to her father's rectory for religious instruction and also take them on outdoor excursions to her family's summer camp. Van Waters worked herself into a state of exhaustion by 1915, though more than likely she had contracted tuberculosis. Like so many penal reformers, her efforts were short-lived. After she left, the home reverted to the jail facility it had been before.

Van Waters moved to Pasadena, California, to seek medical treatment. In 1917, she was well enough to take a civil service job at the Los Angeles County Juvenile Hall working with young delinquents. Los Angeles was experiencing greater growth than any other county in the United States because of western migration, which brought increased delinquency. She worked as a juvenile court counselor until 1920 when she was appointed juvenile court referee, a quasi-judicial position. While in Los Angeles, Van Waters earned a national reputation for implementing her maternal justice ideals, seeing young delinquents as children that needed a mother figure.

Van Waters gave keynote addresses before major gatherings of correctional and juvenile professionals and taught part time at UCLA. She served on the

1926 Harvard Crime Survey at the request of future Supreme Court Justice Felix Frankfurter. Van Waters headed the juvenile section of the Wickersham Commission, a first-of-its-kind task force established by President Herbert Hoover that studied the administration of justice in the United States and made the term "criminal justice system" part of the American vocabulary.

At the juvenile hall, Van Waters hired medical and psychiatric staff, and she sought to improve morale among children by emphasizing the "redeeming power of recreation" (Freedman, 1996, p. 80). Van Waters was praised by the *Los Angeles Times* and *Good Housekeeping* for her "unfailing courtesy, and chivalry" (Freedman, 1996, p. 81). Although her administration was popular with the press and with most offenders, she was not popular with staff, even surviving one poisoning attempt from a disgruntled staff member.

In her widely acclaimed 1925 book *Youth in Conflict*, Van Waters presented her views on the causes and remedies for juvenile delinquency, especially females. She blamed social disorganization in large cities, popular entertainment that promoted sexual promiscuity, and impoverished environments. She maintained that all children were innately good and that delinquents could trace most of their problems to bad parenting. Because of its sense of vision, its straightforwardness and its emphasis on compassion, *Youth in Conflict* became required reading in the United States and the United Kingdom for many who studied delinquency. Van Waters's *Parents on Probation*, published in 1928, was not as critically acclaimed as *Youth in Conflict*, but it sold well.

Personal Life and Continued Work

Van Waters never married, nor did she bear any children, but in June 1929 she adopted a 7-year-old girl that she met in court. She changed the girl's name to Sara Ann Van Waters. Around that same time, she met Geraldine Thompson, a native New Yorker 15 years her senior. The two women became lifelong friends and pen pals. Their letters have become the object of fascination to gay studies students and Internet surfers today. Very few American women would publicly admit having a lesbian relationship during the 1930s, especially a woman like Van Waters who was in the public eye and worked with delinquent children. Whether the two had a sexual relationship is unknown, but allegations of lesbianism would haunt her in later years, at a time when such an allegation was damning.

Van Waters was appointed superintendent of the Massachusetts Reformatory for Women in Framingham in March 1932. An outspoken critic of the 55-year-old reformatory, Van Waters was determined to make social service, not punishment, the prime focus of the institution. She faced an uphill battle. The 1930s was the era of the Great Depression, and few people who were struggling to survive cared about reforming female prisoners. At the same time, creating a homey environment was also paramount to Van Waters, who stated that the goal of the "modern institution must be to have institutional life approximate outside normal life as nearly as it can" (Freedman, 1996, p. 188).

Van Waters tried to run the reformatory like a school, even referring to the inmates as students. Good behavior led to increased privileges, including access to letters and better meals. The "school" had a library, an unusual feature for prisons of the 1930s. Van Waters actively solicited community involvement in the reformatory. She encouraged local women's groups to volunteer in the facility. In another groundbreaking move, Van Waters initiated an internship program for recent college graduates.

Despite the public shift toward social conservatism, Van Waters continued the social gospel tradition of blending Christian ideals with secular correctional intervention. She adhered to what she called the social gospel truth: Every child is a child of God and is capable of redemption. She championed "Christian penology," stating that she tried "to dwell within the Law of the Kingdom of God on earth—and laws of health, medicine, psychology and social work" (Freedman, 1996, p. xiv). She defied a purely clinical approach, choosing to blend spiritual and psychological approaches to rehabilitation.

Ever possessive of the scientific mindset, Van Waters viewed her reformatory job as a research experiment and as a model of progressive education. She believed that the students could learn from doing. She had them work 8-hour days making flags and clothing, staging theater productions, and organizing a Glee Club. Long before the study of Black history was in vogue, she encouraged the African American inmates to study Black history, and she encouraged volunteer work from the National Association for the Advancement of Colored People (NAACP), a radical idea for its time. Van Waters invited an editor from *The Atlantic Monthly* to teach a poetry class. She initiated a program for mothers and babies, allowing mothers frequent contact with their children, even those who bore their children out of wedlock, at a time when doing so stigmatized both mother and child. The reformatory had a nursery with lessons in health care and maternal education. She organized a weekly mothers' club so inmates could gather and share concerns. In 1945, First Lady Eleanor Roosevelt visited Framingham to observe Van Waters's work, saying that Framingham "shows in the most conclusive way what the soul and spirit of an individual can mean in an institution" (Roosevelt, 1945, para. 3).

The prevailing thought in community corrections circles, both past and present, is to discourage offenders from having contact with one another. Prison and parole authorities usually disallow or discourage inmates from having contact with each other once they leave the facility. But Van Waters encouraged some women to continue friendships after release, and she encouraged them to maintain contact with the reformatory as well. Van Waters established a transition program for those whose release dates were approaching and set up domestic cleaning jobs for them in the community (very few other employment opportunities were available). Some inmates even got jobs working at the prison after they were released.

Van Waters criticized prison sentences for women convicted of alcohol offenses and prostitution, calling such behaviors social rather than criminal problems. She was outraged at women being sent to prison for lewd conduct when their offense was publicly admitting to bearing a child out of wedlock and then pursuing their former lovers for child support.

Van Waters never embraced the role of a typical warden; she never approved the use of force as a punishment. She dreaded visits from the parole board because they tended to pay more attention to past failures than recent inmate progress. She stuck unfailingly to her liberal convictions; her only compromise was that she appointed a few political cronies to appease some of her superiors.

Controversy

Despite her resolute outward appearance, Van Waters was full of self-doubt as indicated in some of her diary entries. She was frustrated by not being able to create a kingdom of heaven on earth and being unable to change lives or the social system that produced female criminals. Her attempts to make a kingdom on earth collided squarely with real-world opposition in 1948 in a very public and embarrassing way.

Deputy Commissioner Frank Dwyer charged that a former reformatory inmate had been beaten to death because of homosexual jealousies—the death had initially been ruled a suicide. The incident opened the reformatory to other charges, such as the misuse of inmate labor, employment of former inmates in the facility, and the allegation that Van Waters was condoning and perhaps participating in homosexual relations among inmates. William Randolph Hearst, her former Harvard classmate and nemesis and by then the San Francisco-based muckraking king of "yellow journalism" (Office of the Historian, n.d., para. 2) joined the bandwagon, saying that Van Waters had been chased from California to Massachusetts for homosexual scandals.

The incident became a public battle to preserve Framingham, with many women's rights advocates lining up behind Van Waters and others lining up against her. America was swept up in anti-Communist hysteria, and anything that smacked of perversion also smacked of Communism and things that were deemed to be un-American. Some also charged that Van Waters associated with Communists in Framingham.

Van Waters was fired from the reformatory on January 7, 1949. In firing her, Governor Paul Dever charged her, in addition to the charges just mentioned, with being too liberal with the inmates by allowing them to attend movies, eat in restaurants, and the like, but the greatest focus was on sex within the prison. Van Waters remained warden pending appeal. Between January 13 and March 11, 1949, the hearings became a cause celebre for women's libbers around the country. A woman known only to penologists and social workers suddenly became a household name due to the press coverage.

Dismissal, Demise, Heartbreak

Van Waters won her appeal, but her life was never the same. One positive outcome from the hearings was the founding of the Friends of Framingham, a group of Van Waters's supporters who successfully lobbied for legislation that legalized inmate apprenticeship. Still, the accusations of rampant homosexual behavior persisted. A Smith College student entered the prison posing as an inmate for 10 days, and she emerged with stories of vicious homosexual behavior among the women in addition to narcotics smuggling.

Van Waters was further hurt by the death of her adopted daughter in an auto crash in 1953. Van Waters began an intimate relationship with former inmate Helen Bryan in 1953, but Bryan left when the affair was made public and she was suspected of Communist sympathies.

Van Waters's behavior, namely her overfamiliarity with her charges, would not be allowed today. But Van Waters simply could not deal with the increasing bureaucratization of prison administration. She did not understand the need for keeping her personal and professional lives separate. She had always viewed the reformatory as a sort of home for women who had been rejected by mainstream society, and she was sincere in her attempts to nurture and rehabilitate them in a homelike atmosphere. By the 1950s, she was dealing with a different and often more manipulative and dangerous class of inmate than the ones she had worked with in the 1930s. Although most crimes, especially violent crimes, were committed by men, women had made unfortunate "strides" in committing crime as well. Escapes became more frequent, as did racial conflicts between inmates.

Miriam Van Waters retired from the Framingham Reformatory in October 1957. She lived with two former Framingham inmates for several years, and she continued to support inmates and their children. She collaborated with Burton Rowles in a sanitized, journalistic autobiography titled *The Lady at Box 99*, which was published in 1962. In 1972, Van Waters suffered a stroke that left her in poor health until her death on January 17, 1974, in Framingham at the age of 86.

Sources and Suggested Readings

Chlup, Dominique T. (2006). The legacy of Miriam Van Waters: The warden who would be their teacher first. *Journal of Correctional Education*, *57*(2), 158–187.

Eliot, Thomas H. (1954). *The Van Waters case: Inter-University case program #22.* Bobbs-Merrill.

Freedman, Estelle B. (1998). *Maternal justice: Miriam Van Waters and the female reform tradition.* University of Chicago Press.

Freedman, Estelle B. (2004). Miriam Van Waters. *Encyclopedia of lesbian, gay, bisexual & transgender history in America* (M. Stein, Ed.). Charles Scribner's Sons. https://go.gale.com/ps/retrieve.do?tabID=T003&resultListType=RESULT_LIST&searchResultsType=SingleTab&retrievalId=e105b9c0-0d3f-47c4-9f09-7c43451c424c&hitCount=3&searchType=AdvancedSearchForm&currentPosition=1&docId=GALE%7CCX3403600520&docType=Biography&sort=Relevance&contentSegment=&prodId=GVRL&pageNum=1&contentSet=GALE%7CCX3403600520&searchId=R1&userGroupName=ncliveecu&inPS=true, date of retrieval January 8, 2024.

Mennel, Robert M. (2000, February). Van Waters, Miriam. *American national biography online.* Oxford University Press. https://www.anb.org/display/10.1093/anb/9780198606697.001.0001/anb-9780198606697-e-1400658, date of retrieval January 2, 2024.

Miriam Van Waters Papers, 1861–1971. (n.d.). Item description, dates. A-71, folder #. Schlesinger Library, Radcliffe Institute, Harvard University. https://researchworks.oclc.org/archivegrid/collection/data/122583318

Office of the Historian. (n.d.). *U.S. diplomacy and yellow journalism, 1895–1898.* United States Department of State. https://history.state.gov/milestones/1866-1898/yellow-journalism, accessed August 9, 2024.

Roosevelt, E. (1945, November 2). My day. *The Eleanor Roosevelt Papers Digital Edition* (2017). https://www2.gwu.edu/~erpapers/myday/displaydoc.cfm?_y=1945&_f=md000172, accessed August 9, 2024.

Rowles, Burton J. (1962). *The lady at box 99: The story of Miriam Van Waters.* Seabury Press.

Van Waters, Miriam. (1926). *Youth in conflict.* Republic Publishing.

Van Waters, Miriam. (1927). *Parents on probation.* New Republic.

Discussion Questions

1. What would modern correctional officials think of Van Waters's conduct, especially her fraternizing with former inmates under her control?
2. Van Waters's sexuality was a beneath-the-surface issue throughout her career. Should the sexuality of a correctional official be a factor now as it was during Van Waters's lifetime?

Credit

IMG 32.1: Source: https://commons.wikimedia.org/wiki/File:Miriam_Van_Waters_in_1928.jpg.

CHAPTER 33

Joseph Ragen (1897–1971)

IMG 33.1

The history of American prison reform is strewn with good intentions gone awry. Well-intended reformers like Thomas Mott Osborne and Miriam Van Waters have been frustrated in their attempts to make prisons democratic centers of humanity, both because of inmates that abused the privileges and because of outsiders who distrust people that are kind to convicted criminals. Many prison officials have gone in the opposite direction, preferring brutality to anything smacking of kindness and humaneness. Others have sought a balance, preferring a professional, impersonal, bureaucratic approach devoid of brutality or affection. This was the approach of Joseph Ragen, the warden of the Illinois Penitentiary at Stateville from 1936–1961.

Early Life and Career

Joseph Edward Ragen was born on November 22, 1897, in Trenton, Illinois. He grew up in an area of southern Illinois called "Little Egypt" (O'Brien, 2018, title) replete with dirt roads, miners, and farmers. Ragen's father, William, was the exception, spending most of his working life on the public payroll, just as his son would. William Ragen served as sheriff of Clinton County for 3 terms and as judge for 1 term.

Joseph Ragen, 20 years old when the United States entered World War I, served in the Navy during and immediately following the war. In 1922, he began working for his father as a deputy sheriff, a position he held until 1926, when he was elected sheriff of Clinton County. Shortly before he was elected sheriff, Ragen married Loretta Heyer, who would bear two children. Like many small-town sheriffs of the 1930s, the Ragens lived in a small apartment on a floor above the county jail. Ragen served as sheriff until 1930.

Ragen's biggest challenge, like many Prohibition-era law enforcers, was bootleggers. Most of the bootlegging Ragen faced originated in East St. Louis, Illinois, a haven for bootleggers. Ragen left law enforcement in 1930, preferring the office of Clinton County treasurer, also an elected position and one he held until 1933. Ragen made political contacts in Illinois that would serve him well in years to come. He also learned the art and science of politics. In 1933, he received a gubernatorial appointment as warden of Menard Correctional Center in Chester, Illinois, a town 60 miles southwest of Clinton County. Despite his youth, in his early 30s when he took over as warden, Ragen impressed his superiors, including Governor Henry Horner, who in 1935 appointed him to the most lucrative, but daunting, task in Illinois corrections—running the penitentiary at Stateville. As Chicago was home to some of the nation's most notorious criminals during the Prohibition era and the Great Depression, Ragen was assuming control of one of the most infamous prisons in the United States.

Stateville

On making his initial visit to Stateville, Ragen realized the gravity of the task. When Stateville opened in the 1920s, it was hailed as a penological marvel, containing amenities not common to many Americans, let alone prison inmates (or convicts as they were typically called), including hot water baths. It featured a rarely employed panopticon design originally created by English philosopher Jeremy Bentham, with a control center standing in the middle of a building surrounded by cell blocks, enabling officers a panoramic view of the cells.

But conditions at Stateville had deteriorated. One of Ragen's first observations was the smell. The odor of pet smells was noticeable, as was the smell of marijuana, which was smoked openly and grown on prison grounds. Blanket permissiveness and a complete lack of discipline pervaded Stateville among both the staff and inmates. Inmates could come and go at will, even in places where they did not belong. Many inmates spent most of their time sitting in the prison yard. Organized gambling operations operated openly. Liquor was sold openly. Prison gangs ran the institution. Shanties with posted signs reading "officers not wanted" served as gang headquarters. Unauthorized conjugal visits took place with the consent of officers. Bribery was rampant, part of which Ragen attributed to the fact that guards/officers made only $112 per month. Neither inmates nor officers were properly attired.

Upon arriving to work the first day, the 36-year-old Ragen was told by his embittered predecessor, "Hello, warden. There's an execution tonight. It's your job now" (Erickson, 1957, p. 36). Ragen's first task was to not only supervise an execution, something he detested because he did not believe in capital punishment, but to mobilize officers to control a near riot among those wanting to view the execution.

Ragen took immediate and strict control of Stateville, vowing to change the attitudes and behaviors of the staff and the inmates. Many of his measures are part and parcel of prison administration today but were uncommon in the 1930s. He announced the following 10-point plan for running Stateville:

1. *Eliminate politics from the hiring of prison personnel.* Although Ragen's ability to practice politics in his own right and for the good of the facility was one of his strengths, he knew that many bad hires came from political connections. Ragen had the strong backing of the governor in taking this first step. His strength was picking loyal middle managers. As is the case at many prisons, Ragen instilled an almost God-like loyalry among staff. In his Officer's Rule Book, he wrote, "If you work for a man, in Heaven's name, work for him ... speak well of him, and stand by him, and stand by the institution he represents" (Ragen, 1962, p. 648). Civil service reforms that were under way in state government helped as well.
2. *Build an efficient officer force through careful selection and set up training facilities for new officers.* In one of Ragen's first announcements as warden, he said, "As of now, the first guard to appear on friendly terms with an inmate will be fired" (Erickson, 1957, p. 53). Far from viewing this as brutal, Ragen saw this as a way of preventing favoritism and corruption among staff. Only selected officers were allowed to use force, and only in cases where an officer had been struck. Ragen forbad staff from associating with inmates, former inmates, or the families of inmates. One officer was reprimanded for letting a recently released inmate buy lunch for him. Ragen issued a staff handbook that contained 89 general rules and 1,222 specific rules. He fired officers that were not physically fit. The off-duty lives of officers came under Ragen's control as well. They were not allowed to loiter or gather in places of ill repute such as gambling houses.
3. *Keep the inmates working.* Ragen, who saw Stateville as a potentially self-supporting enterprise, allowed no idle gangs where trouble developed. Inmates were required to work either on farms, in coal mines, or in one of the industries in the prison. He believed that idle hands are the devil's playground and that many inmates had never learned good work habits.
4. *Closely regulate all prisoner movements.* Regimentation became the rule at Stateville. All inmate motions were subject to control. Ragen had to control 3,500 inmates in one-tenth of a square mile. He lobbied for an increase in the number of staff. He reached his goal of having 300 officers and 100 clerks and foremen, a ratio of roughly 12 inmates per staff member.
5. *Enforce tight restrictions on inmate possessions.* Ragen allowed no money in the prison yard at any time, for any reason. Liquor and gambling businesses were shut down. Officers tightened contraband enforcement.

6. *Give every prisoner equal treatment.* Stateville housed Illinois's most notorious criminals. Some, like Chicago mob boss and bootlegger Roger Toughy, had acquired hero status within the inmate population and in the free world. Officers and inmates alike had placed inmates in a hierarchy, which Ragen banned. Whether this was a good move is debatable. Even Ragen's protégé, future Texas prison boss George Beto, believed that prison bosses must recognize and choose inmate leadership so as not to allow inmates to pick leaders themselves.
7. *Place first emphasis on security, secondary emphasis on rehabilitation.* Ragen believed that before the latter could be accomplished, the former must be present. A strong work ethic and educational opportunities were the prime ingredients in Ragen's rehabilitation scheme.
8. *Permit no prison bargaining groups or other intercessory.* Each prisoner was allowed to approach the warden directly with requests and complaints. At no time were inmates allowed any organizations of any kind. In a model diametrically opposed to that espoused by reformers like Thomas Osborne, Ragen abolished all inmate organizations unless he officially approved them. This made all inmates equal and placed total control in the hands of prison administration.
9. *Anticipate trouble and, when possible, deal with it beforehand.* If trouble occurs, deal with it in quick, direct measures without show of weakness. At no time, even during a time of trouble, were inmates allowed a voice in the operation of the prison. Ragen's mere presence cowed some abrasive inmates and officers. He walked around the prison unaccompanied and without a weapon, seeing it as a show of strength and authority.
10. *Operate the prison with a maximum of cleanliness and neatness, both as a matter of health and as an essential part of security.* Pets were removed from the prison. Inmates and staff alike were required to make cleanliness and neatness an absolute priority.

Departure and Return

Ragen was widely hailed for his reforms at Stateville, but a new governor in 1940 threatened his employment. He resigned in March 1941, and, with the Department of Justice worried about sabotage and espionage as American involvement in World War II seemed inevitable (the United States entered the War in December 1941) Ragen got a job setting up internment camps for illegal immigrants. He also worked briefly as superintendent of security at a car company.

Ragen was rehired at Stateville in October 1942, thanks to a mass escape led by Chicago mob boss Roger Touhy, which cost the warden his job. When Ragen returned, Touhy told him, "Well, Warden, I got your job back for you" (Erickson, 1957, p. 172). For the next 20 years, Ragen, who gradually assumed celebrity status within the field of penology, ran Stateville, making it a model prison for observers from around the world. Texas prison boss George Beto modeled his system after Ragen's. Celebrities, including actor Jimmy Stewart and boxer Rocky Marciano, visited Stateville, which expanded to include several prison units, 5,000 inmates, and almost 500 staff.

Stateville's prison industry included the largest farm in Illinois. Each year it produced 300,000 gallons in its cannery, 4 million pounds of soap, 1 million yards of fabric, plus mattresses and shoes. The prison had a bookbinding center, a stone quarry, a sheet metal factory, and a barber college. Ragen still ruled inmates and staff with an iron hand, exercising more authority over his nonunionized staff than most wardens would be able to do today.

Ragen was a sought-after speaker, sharing his views on prison administration and crime causation to audiences around the country. His views on the causes of crime reflected Midwestern conservative ideals. A religious man, Ragen advocated church attendance as a method of preventing crime. He saw the dissolution of the traditional family structure as an important factor in delinquency. He once said (Erickson, 1957, p. 243),

> "The best way to lower prison populations is to stop delinquency at its inception … The first line of defense in this matter are the parents and guardians. There are more delinquent parents than there are delinquent children. Discipline is important in the home and in the school. But juvenile delinquency is every citizen's business. This is true because of the high tax money that each delinquent causes the state … (and) every citizen is a potential victim of each new criminal."

Compared to many other prison administrators in the United States who still ran brutal chain gangs, Ragen was relatively liberal. He advocated the use of the indeterminate sentence, even for murderers. He spoke out against the death penalty, believing it did not deter crime. In short, Ragen stopped being a disciplinarian and became a penologist. In her biography of Joseph Ragen, Gladys Erickson asked several inmates their assessment of Ragen. Not surprisingly, some of the inmates had little good to say. But one infamous inmate sang his praises. Nathan Leopold was one of two men, Richard Loeb being the other, who were convicted of the 1924 murder of a boy named Bobby Franks. The Leopold and Loeb case was one of the most infamous murders of the 20th Century, due to many factors, the primary ones being the intelligence of the two murderers, who were both wealthy and highly educated, the second being the motive; they simply wanted to commit the perfect crime. Loeb was murdered in prison in 1936. Leopold lived long enough to work with some of the preeminent academic criminologists of the day, and was eventually paroled. Leopold said of Ragen, "I have no hesitation in saying without reservation that today I like, admire, and respect Warden Ragen enormously. I believe he is making a permanent mark on American penal history" (Erickson, 1957, p. 195).

Retirement, Death, and Legacy

By the 1960s, the Ragen era in Illinois had faded. Inmates and staff alike gained more rights through unionization and litigation. As ethnic minorities were overrepresented in Illinois prisons, prisons became focal points for civil rights advocates. Some labor and business interests complained that inmate labor constituted unfair competition. Although he was still well known in Illinois political circles, a new political era had dawned. Ragen stepped down as warden at Stateville in 1960 and assumed directorship of the Illinois Department of Public Safety. He was asked to resign in 1965 at age 68. Ragen continued consulting and public speaking after his retirement, and he served as vice president for marketing at the Louis Joliet Bank.

Joseph Ragen died on September 22, 1971, in Joliet, Illinois, at the age of 74. There was nothing fancy or stylish about Joseph Ragen. Throughout his life, Ragen was very down-to-earth, so down-to-earth that he did not fly on airplanes because he literally wanted to keep his feet on the ground. He cared little for international travel, save Canada, because he thought America had everything that one needed. He did not try to win popularity contests, either with prison inmates or with the people that worked for him. Some called him the J. Edgar Hoover of prisons. Like Hoover, he inspired great loyalty from many of the people who worked for him, many of whom went on to assume positions of leadership in prisons around the country.

Although no prison warden should aspire to be popular with inmates, Ragen, despite his no-nonsense bureaucratic style of prison administration, had admirers among that group as well. One inmate wrote a poem about Ragen that read (Erickson, 1957, p. 76):

> There's a Man in charge at Stateville;
>
> Who has changed things all around;
>
> From a madhouse to a prison,
>
> Wherein Hope and Cheer abound.

Sources and Suggested Readings

Chasing Crime. (2023). *Inside Stateville: Illinois' violent maximum security prison* [Video]. YouTube. https://www.youtube.com/watch?v=xPJCzHJ-9Sc&t=423s, date of retrieval January 4, 2024.

Clemmer, Donald. (1940). *The prison community.* Christopher.

Erickson, Gladys A. (1957). *Warden Ragen of Joliet.* Dutton.

Jacobs, James. (1977). *Stateville: The penitentiary in mass society.* University of Chicago Press.

Joseph Ragen dies, Illinois penologist. (1971, September 27). *Washington Post Times Herald.* https://www.proquest.com/docview/148080784/fulltextPDF/4770D194D-B454EEBPQ/1?accountid=10639&sourcetype=Historical%20Newspapers, date of retrieval January 4, 2024.

Kantrowitz, Nathan. (1996). *Close control: Managing a maximum security prison.* Harrow and Heston.

O'Brien, Darcy. (2018). *Murder in little Egypt.* Porchlight.

Ragen, Joseph E., & Finston, Charles. (1962). *Inside the world's toughest prison.* Charles C. Thomas.

Discussion Questions

1. Ragen was not a well-traveled man and was in many respects the prototypical dry bureaucrat. Was that a help or a detriment to his work as a prison official?
2. What do you think of Ragen's assessment of the American family and its impact on crime?

Credit

IMG 33.1: Source: https://www.chroniclingillinois.org/items/show/28724.

CHAPTER 34

Clinton Duffy (1898–1982)

IMG 34.1

Clinton Duffy, who served as warden at California's San Quentin prison from 1940–1952, was destined for a career in prison work practically from birth. The same can be said for many who work in corrections, but Duffy's commitment to kind treatment of inmates in a prison long associated with nothing but the darkest side of human nature makes him a notable figure in the history of American corrections.

Early Life and Career

Clinton Truman Duffy was born on August 4, 1898, in San Quentin, California, in the town's prison village. He was the son of William Duffy, a farmer turned prison guard (now called correctional officer) who had a 35-year career at San Quentin. Clinton Duffy grew up in the San Quentin prison village, or "prison town" as it was often called, living in a prison environment and associating mostly with the families of other prison employees. He attended San Quentin Grammar School, which was primarily populated by children of other prison employees. Rather than playing cops and robbers or cowboys and Indians, Duffy and his friends would play guards and prisoners, with most children emulating the inmates because they knew and liked them.

One of his childhood friends was Gladys Carpenter, the daughter of a correctional officer. The two childhood sweethearts were so immersed in prison culture that their imaginative play included climbing the warden's terrace and pretending to be "Mr. and Mrs. Warden," a childhood dream understood only by those who grew up in a self-contained prison village like San Quentin. However, Duffy thought being a warden was a pipe dream as likely as "winning the Chinese lottery."

One of Duffy's vivid childhood memories was walking the streets of the San Quentin village and hearing prisoners cry in pain from hours spent in a straitjacket. Duffy had vivid memories of prisoners being punished for reading newspapers, being forced to wear straitjackets from their neck to their ankles, being forced to swallow laxatives, and wearing a straitjacket for a week, which sometimes resulted in the inmate being permanently crippled.

Convinced that the son of a prison guard/officer could not rise to prominence in San Quentin circles, Duffy enlisted in the Marines after graduating from high school. He served during World War I. After the war ended in 1918, Duffy returned to the California Bay Area and took a job in Sausalito with the Northwestern Pacific Railroad. He married Gladys Carpenter, by then an elementary schoolteacher in San Quentin, on December 31, 1921. Their son, Jack, was born in November 1922.

San Quentin

Duffy continued working for the railroad and then for a construction company until 1929, when he visited San Quentin's prison to notarize a document. While there, he was offered a job as secretary/assistant to the warden. Duffy began his duties on November 1, 1929. During this time, Duffy's correctional philosophy took shape, but he could do little to put it into practice. The original prison at San Quentin was a floating hulk that settled at Point San Quentin during the San Francisco gold rush of the 1850s. It had been a political football for California politicians since its inception and was often staffed by incompetent political hacks that knew or cared nothing for humane and secure administration of penal facilities, prisons being in their infancy in the nineteenth century. Corporal punishment and filthy living conditions were the hallmarks of San Quentin from its beginning to Duffy's arrival in 1929.

One of the most unpleasant aspects of Duffy's position as assistant was attending executions, which he was required to do because his warden boss refused to witness them alone. Although he grew up in San Quentin, Duffy was unfamiliar with certain of the prison's darker sides. In 1930, Duffy went to San Quentin's dungeon for the first time. What Duffy found shocked him, despite his lifetime of living practically within the confines of the prison. Inmates lived in deplorable conditions with no light or ventilation; officers poured buckets of lye on inmates as punishment; and length of time that an inmate stayed in the dungeon was a matter of officer discretion.

One of Duffy's duties as assistant was notifying inmate families of bad news, such as an inmate death. Duffy developed strong sympathies for the wives and mothers of inmates, realizing that incarceration inflicted punishment on people other than the inmates themselves. In addition to developing an anti-corporal punishment stance, Duffy opposed the death penalty. Asked when he changed his mind about capital punishment, he replied that he had never changed his mind; he had been opposed to it even as a child growing up in San Quentin, in part because of the prospect of wrongfully convicted inmates being executed. Once, on hearing that new evidence had been found that pointed to an inmate's innocence, the governor's office telephoned Duffy and instructed him to halt a scheduled execution. Frantically, Duffy phoned the execution chamber only to find that the inmate had already been hung. After informing the governor's representative that the execution had already taken place, Duffy was told to forget about the phone call—should word leak out of the call, the governor's office would deny it happened. On another occasion, an inmate hung himself in his cell shortly before Duffy found a letter on the warden's desk from an appellate court stating that his conviction had been reversed.

Scandals plagued San Quentin throughout the 1930s. In 1935, four inmates shot, beat, and robbed the warden at his official residence and escaped with his car. The local district attorney killed one escapee; two more were convicted and hung; another was given a life sentence. That same year the Secret Service busted a major counterfeiting ring operated by San Quentin inmates. A new warden brought his assistant with him, which resulted in Duffy's reassignment to the position of historian to the Board of Prison Directors. He also served as a secretary to the Board of Prison Terms and Paroles. Although the warden was replaced, little changed. Inmate crime continued to flourish, as did abusive behavior by staff, and the infamous dungeon was still in full operation.

Warden Duffy

As scandal, inmate unrest, and reports of brutality continued to filter from San Quentin to the governor's office in Sacramento, Governor Culbert Olson tired of dealing with San Quentin headaches and fired the prison board for which Duffy worked. Someone suggested that Duffy serve as temporary warden at San Quentin. Even though appointing a career San Quentin employee and resident seemed to be the least likely way to change the mindset at San Quentin, Duffy was appointed for a 30-day period starting July 13, 1940, while state officials took time to look for a permanent replacement. At the time of his appointment, San Quentin housed 5,500 inmates.

Those who thought that Duffy would continue business as usual were surprised. Duffy was a quiet, nonthreatening, staid person without swagger or a macho facade. His meek demeanor belied a fierce sense of integrity and liberal idealism that was put into action at San Quentin. His first act was to abolish the dungeon. He fired six guards/officers for brutality. He banned the use of whips, rubber hoses, and all forms of corporal punishment, which had long been a staple of San Quentin discipline, and which was common in American prisons at the time. Duffy abolished head shaving for inmates, a holdover from California's

Spanish colonial period. He got rid of numbers on inmates' shirts, thinking it was dehumanizing to refer to humans as numbers.

Duffy's changes were acclaimed by some, but not by all—particularly those who were old enough to remember him as a child and viewed him as a young meddler. He galled and amazed veteran guards by walking through the recreation yard alone, something totally unheard of at San Quentin, especially after the near death of one of Duffy's predecessors only 5 years earlier. Duffy improved the quality of food for inmates, and he insisted that all inmate clothes be ironed. The actions of the young Duffy (at age 42) impressed state government officials so much that he received a 4-year appointment in September 1940. Duffy and his wife, Gladys, took up residence at the official warden's mansion. His childhood pipe dream had come true.

Duffy still opposed capital punishment on moral grounds, thinking it was not a deterrent and a punishment that fell heavily on the poor and was unfairly apportioned, with a lengthy appellate process and the chance of wrongful conviction. He also simply believed it was wrong to kill, no matter the crime of the person being executed. His opposition to capital punishment notwithstanding, Duffy took steps to at least make the death penalty more humane in its application. He authorized the expenditure of $15,000 to install a gas chamber and abandoned the gallows. Duffy detested presiding over executions, calling hangings in particular a "brutal spectacle." He allowed condemned inmates a few last minutes of exercise (one last breath of fresh air) and a chance to write a last letter. In 1962, Duffy published a book titled *88 Men and Two Women*, an account of his experience overseeing executions.

As warden, Duffy housed some of the most infamous inmates in California penal history. One was Caryl Chessman, a celebrity death row inmate who became a bestselling author while fighting his rape conviction and death sentence in courts for 12 years, an extraordinarily long length of time for that period. Chessman was executed in 1962, 8 years after Duffy resigned as warden.

Duffy attracted attention for his opposition to capital punishment and his unswerving devotion to rehabilitation. Prior to Duffy's time, rehabilitation often meant trying convert inmates to Christianity. While a professing Christian, who believed that inmates could benefit from religious instruction, Duffy did not believe in force-feeding religion. He relied mostly on secular intervention.

A hallmark of Duffy's leadership included giving the inmate a sense of self-worth through constructive activities and medical treatment. His efforts were buttressed by the 1942 election of Earl Warren as governor. Warren, a former Alameda (Oakland) County district attorney, former state attorney general, and future chief justice of the United States, endorsed Duffy's attempts to rehabilitate inmates. Duffy's innovations included the following:

- Making available corrective surgery for inmates with obvious physical deformities when possible.

- Establishing an inmate debating society—Caryl Chessman was one of its best debaters.
- Starting an inmate newspaper, the *San Quentin News*. It was California's first prison newspaper sold to the public. For $1 per year subscription, the public could get a look at "Mr. Average Inmate," which was entirely appropriate according to Duffy since "Mr. Average Citizen" was footing the bill for prisons. The paper was free to inmates.
- Contributing to a column in the paper, usually to quiet false rumors spreading throughout the prison.
- Allowing inmates to have radio headsets and listen to radio programs from 6 to 9 p.m. each evening, including some programs that originated within the prison.
- Launching the San Quentin prison radio show titled "San Quentin on the Air" on KFRC in San Francisco on January 12, 1942. Within weeks it spread to more than 200 radio stations across the United States, thanks to the Mutual Broadcast Network, one of the major radio news networks in the United States. The program featured songs written and performed by San Quentin inmates.

A bedrock of Duffy's penal philosophy was instilling a good work ethic for the inmates. He believed that most inmates lacked good habits and thus found crime the easiest way to get what they wanted. One key to good work habits was an education. Duffy implemented literacy classes, thinking that an inmate's morale increased when he learned to read. Early in his administration, he recruited schoolteachers from the local high school. He established grammar school and high school diploma programs at San Quentin through San Rafael High School. Duffy established college preparatory programs through the University of California at nearby Berkeley, which prepared some inmates to enter the university after their release. Duffy worked for the increased use of parole, to protect the community and to help guide the parolee.

Alcoholics Anonymous

One of Duffy's most notable contributions came about as a result of an inmate survey he directed. He found that 65% of newly admitted San Quentin inmates claimed either that they were alcoholics or that alcohol played a part in the commission of their crime. Duffy conceded that alcohol does not make anyone do anything, but he said, "A few drinks and the brakes are released." All prison employees, not just counselors and psychologists, received substance abuse training, an unusual measure for the time.

Duffy took the radical step of inviting representatives from Alcoholics Anonymous (AA) to visit San Quentin once each month, eventually establishing an AA chapter within the prison. Having been founded in 1935 in Ohio, AA was still in its infancy when Duffy brought it to one of America's most notorious prisons. Prison wardens across the country criticized Duffy for bringing drunks in to talk with other drunks, which is now commonplace in American prisons. Duffy's AA experiment gained him notoriety around the country, and he often spoke to AA groups outside the confines of San Quentin, where he sometimes met former inmates who thanked him for starting an AA chapter at San Quentin.

Duffy's Fame Spreads

Duffy lobbied the California legislature for a bill that allowed inmates to make their own hobby goods and sell them to other inmates. The result was the San Quentin Hobby Association, which produced belts, wallets, picture frames, and other goods, the proceeds of which often went to inmate's families. Duffy's efforts attracted the attention of gossip columnist Walter Winchell, first lady Eleanor Roosevelt, and blonde bombshell actress Mae West, whose visit to San Quentin created considerable excitement among the inmates. Other celebrities, including actors William Powell, Glenn Ford, Edward G. Robinson, Cesar Romero, and baseball manager Leo Durocher visited San Quentin. Duffy's reputation also brought a visit from Harry Houdini, the 20th century's greatest escape artist.

Doubleday and Company invited Duffy to write his story for publication, which he did (with Dean Jennings) in *The San Quentin Story*, which was released in 1950. In 1954, he was contacted about an hour-long television pilot based on his life and career. As the idea developed, an additional 18 minutes were added. The result was a motion picture titled *Duffy of San Quentin*. Actor Paul Kelly, who had served time at San Quentin for manslaughter in the 1920s, portrayed Duffy. A sequel, also starring Kelly, titled *The Steel Cage*, was released later. In 1959, Gladys Duffy wrote her account of life at San Quentin titled *Warden's Wife*.

Retirement, Legacy, and Death

Duffy retired in 1952, after serving 12 years as warden at San Quentin. In subsequent public speeches and books, Duffy advocated as he always had for prison systems to be in the business of making better neighbors, always making people mindful of the prospect that anyone could have an ex-convict as their next-door neighbor. In his later years Duffy savored the tales of inmates he encountered. One inmate, a former prizefighter who fought under the name Kid McCoy, was serving time for the accidental killing of his girlfriend. According to California folklore, McCoy once got into a bar fight with a man who did not believe he was the real Kid McCoy. After McCoy floored the man in the bar, the man admitted, in a line that was repeated in the local press, that his assailant was "the real McCoy" (Cronin, 2012, para. 7), and the term *real McCoy* became a part of everyday language.*

Duffy filled his books and speeches with colorful stories that could be told by many people who work at large prisons like San Quentin. What set Duffy apart from the others is his allegiance to rehabilitation and his able administration as a warden of one of the country's most notorious prisons. His allegiance to the rehabilitative ideal may seem quaint or even contemptible by today's standards, but Duffy was ahead of his time. For those who think that such a philosophy could not work, it should be noted that during Duffy's 12-year tenure as warden, San Quentin did not experience a single major riot or disturbance. Duffy, who made a habit of dining with inmates at least 3 nights each week while he was warden, was not a naive do-gooder; he was a competent and no-nonsense prison manager. After working for penal reform and as an advocate for AA for many years, Duffy died in 1982 at the age of 82.

Sources and Suggested Readings

Cronin, Brian. (2012, October 4). Did the phrase 'the real McCoy' derive from boxer Kid McCoy? *Los Angeles Times.* https://www.latimes.com/sports/la-xpm-2012-oct-04-la-sp-sn-real-mccoy-kid-mccoy-20121004-story.html, accessed August 10, 2024.

Duffy, Clinton. (1962). *88 men and two women.* Victor Gollancz.

Duffy, Clinton T. (1963, July 8). *Prisons, prisoners and parole.* Pacifica Radio Archives, BB0384. KPFA.

Duffy, Clinton. (1965). *Sex and crime.* Pocket Books.

Duffy, Clinton, & Jennings, Dean. (1950). *The San Quentin story.* Doubleday.

Duffy, Gladys Carpenter, & Lane, B. W. (1959). *Warden's wife.* Gollancz.

Semper Eye. (2021). *Interview: San Quentin State Prison warden Clinton T. Duffy (WFAU Radio—Augusta, ME, May 26, 1967* [Video]. YouTube. https://www.youtube.com/watch?v=j2obJo-pd7A, accessed December 12, 2023.

https://gugogs.org/2024/06/18/i-didnt-want-to-want-to-grapevine-article-june-1960-by-warden-clinton-duffy/accessed January 9, 2025. Note insertion of this citation.

Discussion Questions

1. Could Clinton Duffy thrive as a warden in today's correctional environment? Why or why not?
2. If you had your choice, who would you hire as warden—Clinton Duffy, Joseph Ragen, or Thomas Osborne? Why?

Credit

IMG 34.1: Ann Rosener, https://www.loc.gov/item/2017867419/, 1943.

* Other explanations have been offered as to the saying's origins.

CHAPTER 35

Kathleen Hawk Sawyer (1950-)

IMG 35.1

Historically, women interested in a career in institutional corrections were relegated to working with female prisoners or juveniles. Working with adult men in prisons and jails and holding the same authority as male employees is probably the last frontier for women who aspire to a career in criminal justice. In 1992, Kathleen Hawk Sawyer became the first female director of the Federal Bureau of Prisons (BOP), laying the groundwork for other females who aspire to positions of leadership within the field. But her rise to such an important position was not an easy one.

Early Life and Education

Kathleen Hawk was born in 1950 in rural West Virginia, the daughter of a steelworker and a homemaker. No one in her family had worked in the criminal justice field and few people growing up in rural West Virginia in the 1950s attended college, let alone graduate school. Upon her father's death when she was just 10 years old, Kathy Hawk had to grow up faster than most children her age. Her father's death forced her to be more serious and more focused than most of the children around her. At an early age, she developed empathy for others who, like her, had experienced childhood traumas. As an eighth grader, Kathy Hawk decided to become a psychiatrist. But the idea of getting a medical degree did not appeal to her, so Kathy turned to psychology, with a special interest in mental illness.

Kathy Hawk entered Wheeling College (now Wheeling University), a small Jesuit college in West Virginia, where she majored in psychology. Kathy Hawk appreciated the Jesuit approach to higher education, which encourages critical thinking more than just acquiring knowledge. As a Roman Catholic, Kathy felt at home at Wheeling, but she lived at home to support herself while attending college.

Kathy Hawk continued her educational pursuits at West Virginia University (WVU) in Morgantown, earning her master's degree in counseling psychology. She still had not worked in a correctional facility or in a criminal justice setting. But that changed after she obtained her master's degree; Kathy worked with juvenile justice offenders and in community mental health. She continued this task while attending WVU to work on her doctoral degree in counseling psychology.

Corrections Career

Kathy Hawk's entrance into the Federal Bureau of Prisons came with a paid internship at the Federal Correctional Institution (FCI) in Morgantown, West Virginia. She worked as a psychology intern while pursuing her PhD. After finishing her doctoral studies, Kathy stayed on as a psychologist, officially starting in 1976. She was promoted to chief psychologist in 1983. According to Kathy Hawk Sawyer, there are few places better than a prison to witness and apply what one learns in the academic study of psychology. Moving up in the BOP ranks, she served as associate warden at the Federal Medical Center Fort Worth, Texas, and as warden at the Federal Correctional Complex at Butner, North Carolina.

After serving at FCI for 7 years, Kathy Hawk was sent to the Federal Law Enforcement Training Centers (FLETC) in Glynco, Georgia, and trained as a supervisory instructor. She was eventually promoted to associate warden at FCI, then to director of training for the entire BOP, then warden at FCI. In 1989, Kathy Hawk was appointed assistant director of the Program Review Division of the BOP, where she implemented a system of internal controls for all BOP facilities.

BOP Directorship

In December of 1992, during the final weeks of the presidency of George H. W. Bush, Kathy Hawk was appointed BOP director by Attorney General William Barr, becoming the first woman to hold the position. The hallmarks of Hawk's tenure as director included an emphasis on secondary education—with opportunities at every BOP facility—substance abuse treatment, and employment opportunities for released inmates. In our 2023 telephone interview, Dr. Sawyer mentioned two issues that stand out in her memory: the increase in the inmate population and the reintroduction of capital punishment. These issues are addressed in the next sections.

Prison Population Boom

The first issue was the increase in the BOP inmate population. It started with the Sentencing Reform Act of 1984, which eliminated parole for federal crimes committed after November 1, 1987. The Act also authorized the creation of the United States Sentencing Commission, an independent body within the Judiciary Branch to promulgate sentencing guidelines for individuals convicted of federal crimes. These moves came during a retributive movement sweeping the country, which included a "war on drugs" led by the Ronald Reagan administration and other conservative state governments, along with an increased number of crimes subject to federal prosecution.

According to Dr. Sawyer, the increased penalties for federal crimes that accompanied this movement witnessed a form of gamesmanship in local law enforcement. In instances where an offense violated both state and federal statutes, local and federal law enforcement agency would decide where to have a case prosecuted based on which jurisdiction carried the stiffest penalty. Consequently, many law enforcement cases that heretofore would have been prosecuted locally were prosecuted in federal courts. The result was a tremendous increase in the BOP inmate population during Dr. Sawyer's tenure as director. When she assumed directorship, the BOP population stood at around 88,000; by the time she exited the population had increased to over 172,000, an increase of over 95% in 10 years.

The retributive period also led to a construction boom for the BOP, with the number of institutions almost doubling, from 65 to over 100. Congress was generous with funding for federal prison construction, but the challenge facing Sawyer and the BOP was that inmate populations and constructions were increasing at a faster pace than the time it took to adequately hire and train staff.

Capital Punishment Redux

The second issue that stands out in Dr. Sawyer's mind is the reintroduction of capital punishment by the federal government. Prior to her assumption as director in 1993, the federal government had not carried out a nonmilitary execution since 1963. On April 19, 1995, a truck bomb exploded outside the Alfred P. Murrah Federal Building in Oklahoma City, killing 168 people and injuring over 600 others, including 19 children, some of whom were at a day care center in the building. It was the deadliest terrorist attack in the United States before 2001. Authorities prosecuted three Army veterans for the murders: Timothy McVeigh, Terry Nichols and Michael Fortier. The cases were tried in federal court. In 1997, McVeigh was found guilty of the murders of the eight federal law enforcement officers in the building. The murders of the other victims were not tried in state courts. McVeigh was sentenced to death. Nichols was sentenced to life in prison. Fortier, who assisted with the preparation for the bombing and had advance knowledge of the attack but did not actively participate, pleaded guilty and was sentenced to 12 years in prison in exchange for his testimony against McVeigh and Nichols.

After McVeigh exhausted his appeals, his execution was set for June 2001. As director, the duty fell to Kathleen Sawyer to oversee the first BOP execution in 38 years. All executions undergo some scrutiny, but in the case of Timothy McVeigh, practically the entire world was watching. Preparation for the McVeigh execution presented enormous complications for BOP staff throughout the country, not just at the Federal Correctional Institution in Terre Haute, Indiana where the execution was set to be administered. The federal government had agreed to live stream the execution to the victims and families of victims in Oklahoma City. BOP officials had to take the necessary steps to prevent hackers from intercepting the live stream.

Even more complicated than the technical issues was the toll the execution took on BOP staff and leadership. In Kathy Sawyer's (2023) words, "No one joins the BOP to kill somebody." Dr. Sawyer told me that the people who constantly clamor for capital punishment never think of the people who must carry it out. Selecting BOP staff from around the country meant picking people who understood the magnitude of their task. Sawyer did not call for volunteers, but she also did not order anyone to take part who wished not to. Staff from outside Terre Haute was brought in to administer McVeigh's execution.

After the McVeigh execution on June 11, 2001, Sawyer oversaw three more executions. Dr. Sawyer felt special sympathy for the warden at Terre Haute who had to oversee the executions firsthand. That warden had some interaction with Timothy McVeigh prior to his execution and with the families of two other inmates awaiting executions. The experience was very difficult for the warden. Eventually, a warden from outside Terre Haute was brought in to oversee executions. According to Sawyer, executions took something from the soul of those who took part, and she felt enormous sympathy for those who must carry them out.

Low points of Sawyer's career came with the deaths of two BOP staff at the hands of inmates. Her greatest highlight as director was visiting the institutions and interacting with BOP staff. She stated that dedicated staff made her job easy. Dr. Sawyer said she encountered no serious obstacles because of her sex; if the negative attitudes toward her were there, she did not take the time to notice them. Many doors had already been opened toward accepting females as full partners in the traditionally male-dominated BOP.

However, she spoke of the paternalism among some BOP male staff and leadership. On one occasion, while visiting a BOP facility, the warden ordered his staff to constantly escort Dr. Sawyer as she walked around. Although she did not want to embarrass the well-intentioned warden, Sawyer eventually asked him if he would insist on the same type of escort if the director were a man. Walking through the facility constantly accompanied by "bodyguards" projected an image of weakness, something that Sawyer, who spent her entire career inside penal facilities, could not abide. Kathy Sawyer, a petite 5′4″ female, insists that one does not have to be big and bad to earn respect as a prison official.

Retirement and Return

Kathleen Hawk Sawyer left her position as BOP Director in 2003, but not before receiving accolades from officials of both political parties (and marrying Jack Sawyer, a Methodist minister with one son, in 1998):

- Attorney General's Award for Excellence in Management (under President George H. W. Bush) in 1992;
- Presidential Rank Award for Meritorious Service, an honor she received in 1994 and 2000 (under President Bill Clinton);
- Presidential Distinguished Executive Award, the highest government award for professionals in her line of work, in 1997;
- Surgeon General's Medallion in 1997;
- Association of State Correctional Administrators' Michael Francke Award in 1998;
- Edmund Randolph Award for outstanding service in the Department of Justice in 2001 (under President George W. Bush).

Much changed between 2003 and 2019; namely, the Department of Justice shifted its focus from conventional crime to terrorism as a result of the September 11, 2001, terrorist attacks. The BOP suffered as a result, with prisons opening but severely understaffed and underfunded. Sawyer states that her successors had a more difficult task than she did because of this shift. The inmates kept coming, but the funding did not match the increasing populations. The repercussions of underfunding carried over into the 2020s.

In 2019, 16 years after her departure, the BOP was under the interim directorship of Mark Inch, who was appointed by Attorney General Jeff Sessions. Inch, a retired Army major general with experience in military prisons but not with the BOP, struggled as director, and he left the director's position during

Jeff Sessions's tenure as attorney general. A significant blemish on Inch's record was the highly publicized suicide of Jeffrey Epstein. Epstein, a multimillionaire investor and convicted sex offender with legions of connections to celebrities and politicians around the world, was found dead in his cell at the Metropolitan Correctional Center, a federal detention facility in New York City. Epstein's suicide stemmed from negligence on the part of detention center officials. Kathleen Sawyer (2023) firmly asserts that Epstein's death was a suicide, not joining the conspiracy theorists who believe that he was murdered.

In 2019, Sessions was replaced by William Barr, the same attorney general who hired Kathleen Hawk in 1992. Reluctant to return to the directorship after 16 years away, Barr coaxed her out of retirement. In 2019, Sawyer, testifying before the U.S. Senate Judiciary Committee, stated that the long-term lack of permanent leadership, the lack of funding, and dramatically increased prison populations had led to a "less than stellar performance" (Sawyer, 2023). Prison staffing, never a daunting problem for the BOP before, had become a challenge, especially for prisons in rural areas.

The advent of cell phones and drones, things she did not have to contend with in the 1990s, had created enormous challenges for prison staff, as did the aging infrastructure of some BOP units. As for cell phones and the internet, the challenge was not only preventing unauthorized use by inmates but controlling staff usage as well. Limiting staff times on phones and making computers usable only for business purposes were steps she took when reassuming directorship.

Corrections in Higher Education

Dr. Kathleen Sawyer left the BOP in February 2020. I asked for her thoughts on attracting people to the corrections profession. Acknowledging that very few people grow up aspiring to work in a prison, she said that it is incumbent on those in the field to inspire young people to consider prison work, a fascinating career that never gets monotonous, and the perfect environment to attempt lasting change in the minds and lives of those incarcerated.

Kathy Sawyer decries the dearth of corrections professionals in higher education. Sawyer, who holds a doctorate degree, minced no words about academic "experts" without professional experience in corrections:

> For educators in corrections to project themselves as 'experts' in a field which they have personally never spent any significant time, and for many never want to spend any time, makes their claim as expert a falsehood. To believe you can truly prepare someone for work in corrections simply by presenting research findings or reading a text is sorely lacking. The best education combines a good

> mixture of practitioners, researchers, and pure academics, coupled with on-site opportunities to experience correctional settings firsthand to eliminate myths and misperceptions and provide real life experience. (Sawyer, 2023)

As a person with an advanced degree and a true pioneer in the corrections field, Kathy Sawyer's words carry a lot of weight.

Sources and Suggested Readings

Andress, Jamal. (2019, November 19). Bureau of Prisons director answers to Congress for Epstein's death. *Scripps News*. https://scrippsnews.com/stories/bop-director-speaks-to-congress-on-jeffrey-epstein-s-death/, date of retrieval December 5, 2023.

Barr, Luke. (2020, January 14). Bureau of Prisons director cutting internet access, technology usage for staff to 'limit distractions.' *CBS News*. https://abcnews.go.com/Politics/bureau-prisons-director-cutting-internet-access-technology-usage/story?id=68278126, date of retrieval December 5, 2023.

Congress.gov. (2019). *Kathleen Hawk Sawyer, director Federal Bureau of Prisons*. https://www.congress.gov/116/meeting/house/110089/witnesses/HHRG-116-JU08-Bio-SawyerK-20191017.pdf, date of retrieval December 5, 2023.

Every CRSReport.com. (2023). *Federal sentencing guidelines: Background, legal analysis, & policy options*. https://www.everycrsreport.com/reports/RL32766.html#_Toc225069433, date of retrieval October 1, 2023.

Lucas, Ryan. (2019, August 22). What's changed since Kathleen Hawk Sawyer last headed prison bureau? *NPR*. https://www.npr.org/2019/08/22/753337544/whats-changed-since-kathleen-hawk-sawyer-last-headed-prison-bureau, date of retrieval December 5, 2023.

Munley-Norris, Tricia. (2001, October). Commission salutes corrections' finest. *Corrections Today, 29*.

Sawyer, Kathleen Hawk. (2023, September 14). Phone interview and email correspondence.

United States Department of Justice. (2019, August 19). *Attorney General William P. Barr appoints new leadership team at the Bureau of Prisons*. Office of Public Affairs. https://www.justice.gov/opa/pr/attorney-general-william-p-barr-appoints-new-leadership-team-bureau-prisons, date of retrieval December 5, 2023.

United States Department of Justice. (2019, November 19). *Statement of Kathleen Hawk Sawyer director Federal Bureau of Prisons before the Committee on the Judiciary United States Senate*. https://www.judiciary.senate.gov/imo/media/doc/Hawk%20Sawyer%20Testimony.pdf, date of retrieval December 5, 2023.

United States Department of Justice. (2023). United States Parole Commission. https://www.justice.gov/doj/organization-mission-and-functions-manual-united-states-parole-commission#:~:text=The%20Sentencing%20Reform%20Act%20of,under%20the%20witness%20protection%20program, date of retrieval September 30, 2023.

Discussion Questions

1. What are your thoughts regarding Dr. Sawyer's statements on the death penalty?
2. What are your thoughts regarding Dr. Sawyer's statements about corrections experts in academe who have never worked in or spent substantial time in a correctional setting?

Credit

IMG 35.1: Source: https://commons.wikimedia.org/wiki/File:Kathleen_Hawk_Sawyer.jpg.

Index

Y

Z

About the Author

Mark Jones is professor emeritus, Department of Criminal Justice and Criminology at East Carolina University. His research interests include community corrections and criminal justice history. He is the author of *A History of the United States through High-Profile Assassinations*, published by Cognella. Dr. Jones holds a Ph.D. in Criminal Justice from Sam Houston State University and an M.S. in criminal justice from Georgia State University.

www.ingramcontent.com/pod-product-compliance
Ingram Content Group UK Ltd.
Pitfield, Milton Keynes, MK11 3LW, UK
UKHW052003041026
15590UKWH00008B/2120

9 781793 58960